# WIDOWHOOD

# IN AN AMERICAN CITY

# WIDOWHOOD

# IN AN AMERICAN CITY

Helena Znaniecki Lopata

**SCHENKMAN PUBLISHING COMPANY, INC.**
Cambridge, Massachusetts
*Distributed by General Learning Press*

Schenkman books are distributed by
General Learning Press
250 James Street
Morristown, New Jersey

# Contents

List of Tables     vi

Preface     x

Introduction     1

1   Widowhood in America: An Overview     15

2   Widowhood as the Last Stage
in The Role of Wife     39

3   Widowed Mothers     95

4   Social Roles in Kin Groups     151

5   Friendship in Widowhood     177

6   Involvement in the Community     219

7   Summary, Conclusions, and Implications     263

Appendix A: The Interview Schedule     278

Appendix B: Background Characteristics of Chicago
Area Older Widows     303

Appendix C: Significant Relations Between Background
Characteristics and Role Involvements
or Attitudes of Chicago Area Older Widows     323

References     347

Index     357

# LIST OF TABLES

Table 1: Marital Status by Color of American Women Aged 50 and Over, 1960                                          22

Table 2: Percetage of American Women Who Are Widowed, 1890–1950, by Color                                         23

Table 3: The Median Age of American Women Who Are Fourteen Years Old or Over in Different Marital Situations by Race and Urban-Rural Residence                                          24

Table 4: Living Arrangements of Widows in the United States, March 1961                                          25

Table 5: Median Number of Years of Schooling Completed by Persons Aged 65+, by Color and Residence, March 1966           28

Table 6: Household Income of Owner and Renter Occupied Dwellings Containing One Person Only, Aged 65 or Over in the City of Chicago, 1960                                          31

Table 7: Age Distribution of Chicago Area Respondents            32

Table 8: Age at Widowhood of Chicago Area Respondents            33

Table 9: Interviewer's Judgment of the Respondent's Appearance in Terms of Neatness and Quality of Clothing and That of Her Home in Terms of Neatness and Cleanliness                  34

Table 10: Educational Achievement of the Respondent and of Her Last Husband                                          35

Table 11: Occupational Distributions of Respondent's Father, Husband's Father, Husband, Self in Best Job and Self in Last or Present Job                                          36

Table 12: Highest and Current Family Income                       37

Table 13: Length of Time the Respondent Cared for Her Husband at Home During His Last Illness                           48

Table 14: Length of Time of Grief After the Death of the Husband   51

Table 15: Proportion of Chicago Widows Receiving Designated Levels of Help from In-Laws in Selected Areas of Life           57

Table 16: Sources of Financial Help Obtained by the Widow Right After the Death of Her Husband                          58

Table 17: Agreement with the Statement "My Husband Was an Unusually Good Man," by Expressed Wish to Remarry             62

Table 18: Distributions of Agreement with the Statement "My Marriage Was Above Average and No Second Marriage Could Match It" by the Expressed Wish to Remarry                       63

Table 19: Agreement with the Statement "My Sexual Relations with My Husband Were Very Good Until His Last Illness," by Wish to Remarry   66

Table 20: Forms of Loneliness Listed as a Problem of Widowhood   71

Table 21: The Rank Order of the Role of Wife As One of the Six Roles Most Important to Women, by the Race of the Respondent 81

Table 22: Age at Major Life Events of Black Widows   82

Table 23: Sex of Child Giving Most and/or Least Amount of Help in Selected Areas, to Widowed Mothers of More Than One Child   101

Table 24: The Number of Children Living with a Widow by Her Age in Decades   110

Table 25: Agreement with the Statement: "I Like Living Alone" by the Number of People in the Household, Including the Widow   113

Table 26: Percentages of Widows Who Have Designated Numbers of Children Living in the Same Dwelling, in the Same Building, in the Same Block, Somewhere Else in the Neighborhood, One Hour or Less, Over One Hour, or Over One Day Away, by Number of Living Children   126

Table 27: Percentages of Widows Who Have the Designated Number of Children Residing Outside of Their Home, Whom They See Daily, Weekly, Monthly, a Few Times a Year or Less, by Number of Living Children   130

Table 28: Scores in the Role of Mother Scale by Frequency of Contact Scale   140

Table 29: Average Frequency with Which Respondents Interact with Their Siblings, by Age Decade   161

Table 30: Percentages of Respondents Finding True the Statement "My Brothers and Sisters Became Much More Important to Me After I Became a Widow," by Other Attitudes, with Gamma Associations   162

Table 31: Percentages of Widows Who Find True the Statement: "My Brothers and Sisters Became Much More Important to Me After I Became a Widow," by Scores in the Different Scales   164

Table 32: Scores in the Role of Sibling Scale by Age of the Respondent in Decades   165

Table 33: Percent Distributions and Tests of Association of the Score on the Sibling Scale and Agreement with Items on the Relations-Restrictive Attitude Scale   168

Table 34: Percentages of Widows Who Have a Feeling of Closeness to Some of Their Grandchildren and Great-Grandchildren   170

Table 35: Reasons Given by Respondents for Feeling Closer to Some Grandchildren and Great-Grandchildren   171

Table 36: Relatives Living in Respondent's Neighborhood   174

Table 37: The Percent of Friends of Respondents Who Are of the Same Religion and Nationality as the Respondent   185

Table 38: Changes in Quality and Quantity of Social Life with Widowhood   187

Table 39: Reasons for Changes in Social Life Since Widowhood   189

Table 40: Relation between the Collapsed Scores of the Role of Friend Scale and Reported Financial Conditions   211

Table 41: Significant Associations between the Role of Friend Score and Some Items of the Relations Restrictive Attitude Scale   213

Table 42: Relation between the Collapsed Scores of the Role of Friend Scale and the Relations-Restrictive Scale   214

Table 43: Ratings by Interviewer of Respondent's Residence, in Selected Traits   224

Table 44: Percentages of Widows Who Engage in Specified Frequencies of Interaction in the Seven Forms of Neighboring   233

Table 45: Percentages and Numbers of Respondents Reporting Frequent and Total Absence of Interaction in Specified Forms of Neighboring, by Race   238

Table 46: High, Medium, and Low Scores on the Role of Neighbor Scale by Agreement with Selected Relations-Restrictive Attitudes   242

Table 47: Association between the Neighboring Scale and the Frequency of Contact Scale (Both Collapsed)   244

Table 48: The Number of Associations the Respondents Belonged to Prior to Widowhood and the Ones in Which They Are Now Active, by Their Age in Five Year Intervals   249

Table 49: The Number of Organizations of Which Respondent Was a Member Before Becoming a Widow, by Education of Respondent   249

Table 50: Occupational Distributions of Respondent in Best Job and in Last or Present Job   254

Table 51: Average Number of Years of Black and White Widows in Their Best and in Their Latest Job and the Percentages of Women in Each Community Who Have Such a Work History   257

Table 52: Percentages of Negro and White Widows Using Selected Means of Obtaining Funds for Self-Maintenance After the Husband's Death   258

Table 53: Percentages of Women Assigning the Role of Worker to One of Six Positions in a Rank Order of Importance by the Proportion of Time They Worked During Marriage 259

Table 54: High, Medium, and Low Scores on the Relations-Restrictive Attitude Scale by the Same Levels of the Social Isolation Scale 267

Table 55: Significant Relations and Associations between the Social Isolation Scale and Other Scales and Specific Attitudes 267

Table 56: Significant Relations and Associations between the Frequency of Contact Scale and Other Scales and Specific Attitudes 268

Table 57: High, Medium, and Low Scores on the Social Isolation Scale by Education of Respondent 269

# Preface

This study resulted from my realization that I knew nothing about what happens to families, particularly to wives, after the death of the husband, in spite of the fact that I had been studying American urban women for more than twelve years. I soon learned that most literature dealing with family relations does not contain adequate data about widows. Demographic analyses of populations simply show that the average woman in America is widowed at fifty-six years of age, that she lives alone or with unmarried children rather than in three-generation households, and that she is apt to have a low annual income. These facts do not provide complete pictures of the forms and styles of involvement of widows in social relations, the more complex social roles, social groups and societies, nor of the factors which affect such engagement. Not surprisingly, my father, Florian Znaniecki, influenced me into believing that these are the four major areas of social life which sociologists must study. My work on this book has filled a gap in my knowledge and forced me to re-examine some of my assumptions about social relations, social roles, social groups and societies. If it accomplishes the same for its readers, it will have served well the progress of this ever-changing science.

The Administration on Aging, a division of the Department of Health, Education and Welfare, facilitated this project with a research grant while Roosevelt University, with which I was identified in many ways at its beginning, cooperated fully. Additional encouragement came early in the form of a conference on "Death, Grief and Bereavement," held at the University of Minnesota under the leadership of Professor Robert Fulton. I learned then of several psychiatrically based research projects dealing with grief, particularly the very productive one at the Harvard Medical School, and talked with Dr. Eric Lindemann, who pioneered this work. He convinced me that widows need to talk about their feelings and problems and that the interviews which I had planned with them would be beneficial rather than harmful. Dr. Lindemann believes strongly that modern urban societies deprive the griever of many opportunities to do "grief work," a process which requires talking about personal reactions to death, about the deceased, about the whole series of events leading to death, and about the life changes that follow it. Thus, the interview could have a therapeutic effect on the widow, as well as provide information which could benefit other women in the same situation.

In spite of the reassurance of psychiatrists who help grieving people and confidence in my own scientific training, I found myself hesitant about actually going into the field. I realized that I was spending excessive time reading peripheral subjects rather than going out and talking with widows. I had not, until then, been aware of how deeply my attitudes were entrenched in the American culture which shuns the subjects of death and bereavement. It took almost a whole year of exploratory work, of taping many hours of free-flowing interviews, of immersing myself in the world of widows of different social classes and life circumstances, before the feelings of hesitation and avoidance vanished sufficiently to facilitate a completely "normal" or comfortable interview. I thus became convinced that only highly trained members of a research group, preferably of an age relatively close to the sample I wanted to obtain, should undertake the interviews in the main study. Because I wanted professionals to handle the situation, I turned to the National Opinion Research Center to conduct the interviews. Even though some of their interviewers were hesitant in asking some questions, their results were excellent, and I would like to thank the entire NORC staff which worked on the study.

Many other people helped me in this work. I would first like to thank Ethel Shanas, Bernice Neugarten and Robert Winch, who served as my consultants. Of continued help have been all the members of the Midwest Council of Social Research on Aging, among whom I first thought of the project and tested many of the intermediary ideas. This of course includes Warren Peterson and Jack Sigler, whose Institute for Community Studies has provided many opportunities for intellectual exchanges. I have discussed the study with Douglas Marshall, Robert McNamara, Tery Pihlblad, Howard Rosencranz, Rodney Coe, Vivian Wood, Gordon Bultana, Charles Horn, Jean Tomich, Jon Doerflinger, David Janovy, Eva Kahana, Arnold and Caroline Rose, Alan Booth, Harold Orbach, George Peters and Robert Habenstein. Our students in the inter-university training program were also of help in idea development, particularly David Adams, David Oliver and David Maines (who are all from the University of Missouri) and Sister Constance Ludwig. Loyola's Bill Bates and Kathy Norr went over some of my manuscripts and made important suggestions, and Paul Zelus, Daryl Chubin and Frank Steinhart contributed additional statistical analyses.

My husband Dick, daughter Teddy, and son Stef helped me through all the stages of pleasure and pain that this study involved, as they had with my earlier book *Occupation: Housewife*. I think they will admit that I was easier to live with this time around. Wanda Jefferson, Phillis Knights and Pamela Rose valiantly made tables, hunted down references and helped in the many ways research assistants make work easier. My mother, Eileen Markley Znaniecki, has returned to her voluntary job of editing manuscripts and with deft hand corrected and clarified various statements (at the age of 85!). Sheila Segal and Patti Wallace of Schenkman Publishing Company continued the process, working the bulky manuscript down to reasonable size, and Mary Sherwood typed many versions of this book and related papers.

I remain forever grateful to my late father for teaching me the excitement of being a sociologist. His role theory forms an excellent foundation for this work, as it did for prior research.

Helena Znaniecki Lopata

# Introduction

The studies furnishing the basis for this book were focused upon the role involvements and role clusters of widows aged fifty and over, living in a major metropolitan center of the United States. There are several cogent reasons for studying this particular segment of the population. In the first place, widowhood is likely to be experienced in increasing frequency by older women the world over; as medical science expands the life span of the feminine segment of society, modern urban life prevents a commensurable reduction of the death rate of men. In the second place, this large aggregate of older widows lives in urban centers, as a result of the migration patterns of the whole population. In the third place, an understanding of the life styles of American urban widows may enable us to predict worldwide trends in increasingly urbanized societies. As Winch and Blumberg (1968), Goode (1963), and others (e.g. Nimkoff and Middleton, 1960) have observed, the "world revolution" currently taking place is one of combined urbanization, industrialization, and increased societal complexity, with consequent alterations in family roles and structures. The effects of family modifications in urban societies throughout the world have been felt most strongly by women, who have been traditionally bound to the family roles that are now changing so rapidly. Thus an analysis of the life styles of American widows in a metropolitan center may bring insight into the future forms of widowhood in all changing societies. The experiences of our respondents can be interpreted as indexes to the life changes of an increasing segment of people the world over.

## BASIC CONCEPTS

The theoretical framework for this set of studies is dependent upon the Znaniecki (1965) concept of social role. According to that formulation, a social role is a set of functionally interdependent, patterned *relations* between a *social person* and the participants in his *social circle,* consisting of his *duties* and the *personal rights* that they grant him in order that he

be able to carry out his part. A social circle thus consists of all those with
whom the person interacts in a certain role. As Merton (1957) pointed
out, these individuals may not necessarily form an organized social group,
as in the case of a doctor's patients. The concept of social person is an
interactional one, expressing a sociological awareness that the *total* human
being does not enter any one social role; only some of his wealth of characteristics and actions are engaged in any one role, while other "packages"
of characteristics and actions form interactional complexes in other roles.
Changes in personality and in the manner of handling the self and others
are visible whenever an individual shifts from one social role to another
as in the shift from wife to mother.

A social person enters a social role when he and at least two other
persons enter relations which are in some way mutually interdependent
and which are directed toward one or more goals or functions. A role
title summarizes the function in the minds of participants and often serves
as a guide for behavior and for a set of expectations, *but the role itself
is a set of relations.* Sociologists are able to generalize about social roles
(as, for that matter, societal members do) which bear the same title
because they tend to involve similar relational features in a particular
society. At the same time, each role is unique in that its historical development creates aspects of the relations which differ from those of other
roles bearing the same title. The day by day performance of a particular
role is influenced by a number of social and socio-psychological factors,
and not all the behaviors which could be part of any set of relations are
activated by all social circles at any one time. Most of the roles include
large complexes of permissible actions and interactions, forming a pool
out of which only particular sets are selected by a team in any situation.
Roles vary in the degree to which they are definite and specific in the
duties and rights that they demand, and many female roles have a very
indeterminate form (see Mack, 1956).

Each member of a society carries on a number of social roles with the
cooperation of a variety of social circles, at various stages of the life cycle.
At any time the individual may be initiating interaction leading to new
social roles, phasing out old ones, expanding or contracting social circles
or modifying the content, thus altering the duties or rights of any set of
interdependent relations. Certain events in the life cycle of an individual,
such as the death of a role partner, inevitably produce changes in one or
more social roles and in the manner in which these are related to each
other.

Human beings differ in the composition of their role cluster in three
major ways (Lopata, 1966, 1969a). The first basic difference is in the

number of social roles in which they are engaged during the course of the life span or at a particular time. In addition, roles are organized both *hierarchically and institutionally*. *Hierarchical organization* refers to the more or less conscious rank order of importance or preference that each person assigns to the roles within his cluster. This order is most often realized by the individual when role conflict occurs—when various roles compete for time, space, energy, or sentiment. *Institutional organization* of social roles in the role cluster of any person exists because each role is basically grounded in some cultural institution.[1] Roles based on the same institution, such as the family, tend to be more similar to each other than roles focused on different institutions. People differ in the degree to which the various roles they perform are grounded in a single institution or in a multi-dimensional range of institutions. The concept of *social life space* used by many sociologists can thus be modified to include a recognition of the dimensionality or institutional complexity of their extension in societal life.[2] Some roles, of course, contribute more than others to the multi-dimensionality of the social life space by having a "bridging" content. (For example, the role of teacher in a parochial school bridges religious and educational institutions, which have been consciously separated in American society.) As we shall see in the case of urban widows, the complexity of the prior social life space becomes a very important influence upon a person's adjustment to crises and to the complexity of societal life.

In the same way as individuals organize their social roles into hierarchies of values, so do societies. Hierarchical systems are in fact developed for many sets of social objects. Traditional societies build complex patterns of norms to insure crystallization of the status or position of objects into different hierarchical systems around each person. A major means for such crystallization is the *status role*, whose only function is to guarantee the maintenance of status relations.[3] Societies for whom status roles formed the nucleus of life styles insured that they be preserved by organizing other social objects into appropriate hierarchies and assigning them to the same steps of the pyramid. (India's caste system is probably the most complicated of these.) Other social roles which were specialized, not universal, were divided into those appropriate for people in each status role position. Women obviously formed part of the status hierarchies, and widowhood either created for them a separate status role or restricted them to appropriate styles of life.

One of the major changes in modern urbanized, industrialized, and complex societies has been the pushing of status roles into the background, as sets of relations with other functions increased in value. Attempts to match positions in various status systems for each person began to break down, resulting in the status de-crystallization observed by Lenski (1954). This trend is bound to effect the life of widows.

## METHODOLOGY

The study of widowhood in an urban center (using Chicago as the example) took several different forms. The first was purely exploratory and involved attendance at meetings of NAIM (a Catholic organization for the widowed); observation of the activities of older people in public housing buildings, in the YMCA, and in groups for senior citizens; group discussions; taped interviews with the friends and relatives of widows; collections of diaries; in-depth interviews with widows living in a variety of life circumstances; and the perusal of all literature related to the subject. The background data were assembled from sex and marital statistics of those aged fifty and over, from descriptions of family life in many societies, from items contained in the Human Relations Area Files,[4] from the theoretical content and formulations of social gerontology and the sociology of the family, and from literary works delving into the everyday life of different kinds of families (see Lopata, 1971b). Detailed descriptions of widowhood in small towns of Missouri were found in the works of Pihlblad and Rosencranz (1968) and Adams (1969). Professor Felix Berardo (1967, 1968) has also been studying widowhood as experienced by both men and women in urban and rural areas of Washington, and his publications make a direct contribution to understanding the manner in which widows in Chicago resemble, or are divergent from, those in other parts of the country. Peter Marris's (1958) analysis of the reactions of women newly widowed, whose husbands had died before reaching their fiftieth birthday, provides insights into the problems of grief, as does the work of Eric Lindemann (1944) and others at the Harvard Medical School, including C. Murray Parkes (1964a and b, 1965), David Maddison (1968), and Robert S. Weiss (1969).

The second year of research on the Chicago area widows consisted of the preparation, testing, administration, and analysis of interviews with a modified area probability sample of 301 women living in sixty neighborhoods of this metropolis selected by the National Opinion Research Center. These have been analyzed with the help of their computer facilities.

The widows who provided the information upon which this book is based were asked a number of questions about their life prior to their husband's death. The purpose of these inquiries was not so much to pinpoint accurately the facts as to obtain the woman's present interpretation of the past. Concerning some facts, such as residence prior to widowhood, we can expect relatively little distortion in memory; in others, such as judgment of the quality of the marriage, we not only expect a great deal of it, but we use the distortion itself as a datum of the study. One aspect of living as a widow, as of any situation or social role, is the interpretation given to it by the individual. Because an interview obtained at any period of a person's life gives his picture of the world from the vantage point of that period, we must consider both the content of the picture and the factors which contributed to its formation. Human beings have the unique ability to explain, sometimes to rationalize, but always to define, the situation in which they are acting in terms of past, present, and future. The source of their explanation can be any appropriate knowledge that they have internalized or that they find in the world around them, and the sources can differ according to factors such as economic class or ethnic affiliation. For example, the black woman in a ghetto is not likely to have a doctor or psychiatrist handy as a frequent source of knowledge. Nor is she likely to assimilate the information given her by the middle-class physician, if she does come into contact with one. Three hundred and one answers to the same set of questions can thus provide 301 interpretations of marriage and life in the past, the present, and the future. When these are compared, grouped according to selected items of content, and analyzed according to background facts, such as education, various patterns of similarity and of difference emerge and provide insights into the symbolic world of the speakers.

One of the problems of interpreting answers to open-ended questions or to pre-coded queries where the respondent must choose between stated alternatives is the need to separate the factors which contribute to life definitions. For example, all social gerontologists who are concerned with interpreting an attitudinal or behavioral pattern as a consequence of age must caution themselves to keep separate the factor of historical career. People of different ages also differ in experience, depending on whether their generation went through a war, a depression, prosperity, etc. This is the case in this study: i.e., careful analyses of the actual answers of several people indicated that loneliness means different things to different classes of widows and that hostility toward men has a different basis in the white community than in the black culture. The widow's memory of the amount of help given by her different children during their father's illness and funeral is related to the conditions and societal problems in which it occurred, as well as to her expectations. Thus, her own circumstances, the structure of society, and her generational history influence how she interprets her current situation and her past life.

The responses of the Chicago area widows to the questions in the interview schedule were not only analyzed singly and in cross-tabulations, but combined into several scales. In the first place, all references to each of the major roles were combined into a *role scale,* such as "the role of mother," and "the role of neighbor." Items which were used to build up each scale included the rank given this role in relation to other roles, references to the role partner as a helper or close associate, attitudes toward the relation, and the amount of actual interaction. The "role of mother" score combined the number of living children, their distance from the mother, and frequency with which a child, rather than a sibling or friend, was named as providing help or companionship, etc. Women without children were not considered in statistical computations measuring association between the mother score and other characteristics of respondents. The scores were often collapsed into high, medium, and low levels for ease of presentation.

A second major type of summary statistic, called the *social isolation scale,* was utilized in this study of widows. This scale combined selected answers to a set of forty-five questions which measure the extent to which a widow lacks the kinds of personal and community contacts normally available to widowed women. A highly isolated woman, then, would be one who lives alone and either has no children, grandchildren, great-grandchildren, or siblings or only sees these close relations less than a few times a year. She might also lack memberships in voluntary associations, a car for transportation, hobbies involving others, courses taken with various groups, friends, daily phone calls, monthly letters, familiarity and interaction with neighbors, and activities during the day, evening or weekend which involved other people. The highly isolated widow often claims not to have been helped by in-laws since her husband's death, not to have been helped in several areas of life by her children, if she has any, and not to have had overnight visitors, taken trips, or visited anyone overnight during the past year. The highest score on this scale could be eighty points, indicating an extremely high degree of isolation. These scores were also collapsed into high, medium, and low levels for easier presentation.

A third type of scale is a contrast to the isolation scale and has been named the *frequency of contact scale.* The two are not the opposites of each other, since the former records only a lack of interaction, not the frequency of contact. The latter scale combines, for example, the number of phone calls, the number of letters, and the number of nights spent with others, rather than just keeping track of whether such events occurred or not.

The final scale is called the *relations-restrictive attitude scale,* which consists of thirty-six items that measure the degree of agreement of each widow with statements referring to various types of social relations. The first of these statements are more general than personal, such as: "Relatives are your only true friends" or "People take advantage of you when they find out you are a widow." The second set consists of directly personal statements, such as: "My husband was an unusually good man," or "My married friends were not much help to me in my period of grief." This scale is very interesting, both in the clustering of items and in their relations to other scales and background characteristics.

Because of the wealth of data, only tables deemed immediately relevant or necessary for understanding the discussion are included in the body of this book. Additional tables are contained in Appendix B, which should be checked when references are made throughout the book. Each set of tables, those integrated into the body of the presentation and those in the Appendix, is listed separately.

## WIDOWHOOD IN URBAN SOCIETIES: A CROSS-CULTURAL APPROACH

### The Disorganization of Life with the Death of the Husband

The social roles which widows enter after reaching this position and their life styles in the cluster of these roles vary greatly from society to society, and even within a single social group. The cross-cultural survey of situations of widowed throws some light on alternative life styles and provides a list of factors which contribute to the ascription or choice of any one of these by different widows (Lopata, 1970b, 1971d).

A woman who has been established in a set of social roles usually experiences a disorganization of this pattern immediately after her husband's death. Subsequent to this disorganization, certain changes take place, changes that depend upon the opportunities available for new involvement and life styles. The degree of change between her life before and after widowhood can be located on a continuum, made up of the actual situations of women all over the world. At one end of such an analysis continuum we can locate a woman whose life does not become highly disorganized when her husband dies; at the other end, one for whom all roles and relations must be modified. Historical and current data of world societies indicates that the two extremes of the continuum would be *suttee* (Ward, 1963; Thomas, 1964) and either *widow inheritance* (Schapera, 1941) or *levirate* (Bohannan, 1963). *Suttee,* the self-immolation of a widow on the funeral pyre of her husband, can be judged as the most disorganizing, for every one of her sets of relations experiences total disruption and no re-engagement takes place (see Cumming and Henry, 1961, for the disengagement theory). The least disorganizing situation is *widow inheritance,* the rapid replacement of the husband by another man of the same kin group. A widow who is "inherited" by a close agnate of her deceased husband continues in the same relations with the rest of his kin, particularly if she is assigned the same position in his home as she held in that of the deceased. A similar situation exists in the case of *levirate,* since the late husband remains the social father of her children, while the man who "raises up his seed" often carries out many other duties of a husband. However, the situation of the widow may still be less firm than in remarriage, as she has fewer official rights over the *levir* than over a husband. The degree of life change in re-engagement may be especially low, if the widow is allowed to remain in her own home and to carry on her roles of mother and housewife in a style similar to the one she experienced prior to the death of her husband.

Between the two extremes, but very close to *suttee,* is the *status role* of widow, which was enforced in traditional India, but is currently decreasing (Felton, 1966; Sarasvati, 1888).[5] In this social context a widow, particularly if she was a child bride, had to relate to everyone in such a manner as to maintain the constant status distinctions which cut her off from the normal flow of life. The status role of widow had as its main function the isolation of the woman, reinforced by physical characteristics, such as a shaven head and special clothing guaranteeing distinctive and unattractive appearance.

Most societies with extended family systems have incorporated their widows into the social structure with few problems, either by allowing them to return to (or to remain within) the family of orientation or by finding a new place for them in the late husband's family.[6] In such family structures, widows with grown children usually remain with married sons or daughters, depending on the lineage orientation of the society and the assumption of basic links. The older Chinese or Indian widow with a grown son who inherited the male headship of the family was often able to retain a flow of life similar to that before the death of her husband because she stayed in her own house. In urban areas of America and even India, widows who break up their housekeeping and move into the homes of married offspring lose many role functions and some social status (Ross, 1961). In patriarchal and partilineal families, widows are considered outsiders, and their lives become disorganized when the deceased husband's kin insist that the children of that marriage remain with them, while the widow is encouraged to leave. Returning to the family of orientation disrupts not only the in-law relations but also the role of mother.

The kind of life which is available to, or selected by, a widow is determined by many factors, including: the alternative styles developed by her society, her location in the social structure, and her personal characteristics. A major influence is what Paul J. Bohannan (1963) calls the set of rights the man and his family gains over the wife through the marriage contract. In its strongest form, the contract gives the husband the right to live with the wife in a domicile judged his, with a division of labor required to maintain the family unit; the right to any property she possesses or obtains during marriage; sexual rights; and *in genetricem* rights, which require her to bear the children who become filiated to his family. Such an arrangement usually ties the woman to her husband's kin even after his death, since she cannot take her children away, and it often means that the kin group inherits many, if not all, of the above listed rights. Thus *widow inheritance, levirate,* or at least *male guardianship* may restrict the widow's choice of social roles in societies institutionalizing extensive rights over women by their husbands and in-laws.

## Functions Assigned to Widows

The type and content of the social roles available to a widow in any society are dependent upon the hierarchy of functions that she is expected or able to fulfill by her actions or her presence in the group  Various patterns of interaction have been built around these functions by the societies of the world as "solutions" to widowhood. Most of them are dependent upon the fact that women have traditionally been placed, whether by choice or by predetermined division of labor, into the roles of wife and mother. The removal of one of these basic roles is often assumed to free the woman for other tasks or to make other contributions to the group. This is particularly true if she has not yet entered the role of mother or if that set of relations has receded in importance because of the decreasing needs of her offspring.

One of the basic contributions a widow can make to a social group is to continue the role of wife. Two forms of such continuity have been developed: one insists that certain duties of the wife continue to be performed after the death of her husband. In various societies these duties may require the maintainance of his social existence in this life or afterlife. For example, widows of the Kganda of Africa are specifically required to "tend the grave" of their dead husband, while remaining socially married to him (Schapera, 1941). The second means by which a widow can maintain the role of wife is by remarriage, either to a man selected for her because of his relation to the deceased or to someone of her own choice. American society tends to encourage the remarriage of young widows, while not being equally concerned with insuring the remarriage of older women who have already spent years in the role of wife.

A function which has often been assigned to widows in linearly-oriented societies of either line of descent is that of reproduction. Many groups are very concerned with having their women continue to reproduce as long as biologically possible, and several techniques have been devised for meeting these needs, including the already mentioned *levirate* and *widow inheritance*. More often than not the biological father is expected to be the social father, due to assumptions of line "purity," although some groups allow the widow full partner choice. Others insist on combining the role of wife with those of mother and of kin member by insuring that all young widows marry again or at least provide new offspring by selected procedures.

Some social groups define the function of social motherhood as the most important one for a widow to perform. The procedures for insuring such a role depend on several aspects of the relation of the mother to a child and of the offspring to other members of the community. The social functions of mothering usually involve physical, affective, and socialization care of the new member. Most societies, such as that of the United States, assign this function primarily to the biological mother, minimizing obligations of line continuity and placing most responsibility for child-rearing on this woman. In order to do this, she is given the right of control over the means for the child's rearing, such as inherited financial objects, societal support, and the right to make decisions regarding the child's welfare. Special circumstances may limit the rights of women assigned the function of social motherhood. Trusts, guardianship, restriction of facilities and similar circumstances may severely hamper widows from carrying out the duties of the role. Many European countries allow the biological mother of upper-class children to rear them in the absence of the father, but only under the supervision of a male guardian. The function of child-rearing may be connected with the duty of filiation, of guaranteeing that the young grow up as present or future members of the kin line. Whether matrilineal or patrilineal, the system demands that the widow who is allowed to rear her young must insure their identification with the proper group. She is often directly assisted in this process, in a more controlling manner than guardianship, by a male of the line, her brother in the case of a matriarchal group, or her husband's brother in case of a patriarchy.

Another function often assigned to widows is contributing to a work group. Societies with an institutionalized high "bride price" may demand that even an aged woman remain after the death of her husband with the group which had pooled its resources to obtain her. Such a pattern was prevalent in South and Southeastern China, as well as in other societies in which each member of a family is regarded as indispensable to its economic welfare (Freedman, 1965). After a woman is widowed she may be required to continue managing a household work-group, to perform economic tasks outside of the home, or to change her schedule to such peripheral tasks as baby-sitting, geese-walking, or cow-tending (Buck, 1934, 1946). Her main contribution may be to free other family members to perform more effectively their economically productive social roles than they could without her help or than she could do. Widows may also be assigned to non-economic roles outside of the family institution. They may become religious functionaries, tending temples or insuring the proper sequence of necessary ceremonials; they may be educators of the young, contributing to recreational activities; or they may even be politically regulative officials (Simmons, 1945).

Finally, widows may simply be assigned only the responsibility for self-maintenance, with the primary object of saving others the task of caring for them. Part of this function may involve the obligation of serving as models of selected forms of behavior. Older widows may serve as models of aging, reinforcing the concept of human dignity, while young widows may prove the virtue of celibacy, much as a priest does (Ward, 1963; Goode, 1963).

Whatever the functions generally assigned to or made available for widows, each social group must develop more than one style, because it has more than one sub-group of widows. Older women cannot be assigned the reproductive function, and the whole class structure may prevent upper-class widows from behaving in a manner inappropriate to the current or the traditional status role to which their fathers and husbands have bound them.

In general, the greatest control over the life of a widow is maintained in patriarchal, patrilocal, and patrilineal extended-family systems where there is a bride price and a strong concern with line continuity. The least control exists in societies with neolocal family groups, self-selective partner choice, relatively high status of women in the nuclear unit, weak kin connections, and strong rights of property inheritance on the part of the wife. The latter configuration is typical of American society, in which the husband and wife select each other, set up their own housekeeping, build up an economic unit which is relatively self-sufficient, and develop companionate relations. However, this type of family structure, which tends to emerge in urban areas, usually reduces the woman to the relatively functionless position of self-maintenance, once the role of mother is diminished through the independence existence of children and the role of wife is diminished through the death of her husband. There are, of course, many other roles available to the American adult reaching into all but the physically decapacitated years, and these could be used to build flexible life-careers and relational cycles.

## NOTES

1. I am sorry that modern sociology has been neglecting the field of social institutions in its emphasis upon social organization. Joyce Hertzler's *Social Institutions,* Boston: Allyn and Bacon, Inc., 1961 is out of print and David Street formerly of the University of Chicago is one of the very few focusing on this subject.

2. The concept of "social life space" has been developed with the help of several scientists. As far as I can tell, Kurt Lewin used "life space" first, as a major psychological field concept (see a summary of the theory in Morton Deutsch's "Field Theory in Social Psychology" in Volume One of Gardner Lindsey, ed., *Handbook of Social Psychology,* Cambridge, Massachusetts: Addison-Wesley Publishing Company, Inc., 1954). Richard H. Williams and Martin Loeb seem to have been the first to use the concept of "social life space" in a paper delivered at an American Gerontological Association meeting and the first author used it in "Changing Status, Roles and Relationships," in Clark Tibbits, ed., *Handbook of Social Gerontology,* Chicago: University of Chicago Press, 1960. It has since then become a major concept of various members of the Committee on Human Development of the University of Chicago, generally in references of the person's extension into social roles and social relations. The content analyses of open-ended interviews with Chicago housewives suggested to me the fact that this social life space is institutionally organized. That is, the roles and relations are not randomly located within the person's life but often form subclusters because they are located in the same social institution. Thus a multidimensional social life space is one which contains several social roles in different institutions, while a single-dimensional life is one in which all social relations are focused upon one institution, such as the family.

3. A typology of social roles can be developed, Znaniecki suggests, on the basis of their major functions. In this case, the concept of *status role,* whose only function is to maintain the hierarchical position of the person *vis-a-vis* other persons, can be used to assist the understanding of societal organization. Societies differ in the importance they assign status roles and in the degree to which they build whole relational and cultural complexes around them. (See Helena Znaniecki Lopata, "A Restatement of the Relation between Role and Status," *Sociology and Social Research,* 49 (October, 1964): 58–68.)

4. The Human Relations Area Files proved to be very difficult because data on widowhood is scarce and references casually thrown into discussions on other subjects. Each source is incomplete since the subject is cut off at the end of the page. It became necessary to go back to the original sources. A major factor contributing to the scarcity is that widowhood is not a basic concept of anthropological research or classification. The HRAF was useful in locating basic sources.

5. Pundita Ramatai Sarasvati quotes the code of Manu regarding the widow: "At her pleasure let her emaciate her body by living on pure flowers, roots and fruit; but she must never even mention the name of another man after her husband has died." (*The High-Caste Hindu Woman*, Philadelphia: The James B. Rodgers Printing Company, 1888, p. 40.)

6. The young women may be allowed to return home, if the bride price is returned, as among the Kganda of Africa (see I. Schapera, *Married Life in an African Tribe, op. cit.*), or she may be required to remain and continue bearing children for the family through a levirate relation.

# 1

## Widowhood in America: An Overview

### FACTORS AFFECTING WIDOWHOOD

As American society becomes more urbanized and industrialized, its major institutions and their numerous sub-institutions continue to become more complex and more segregated from each other. They are operated by large complicated organizations, participation in which requires voluntary entrance, with specified qualifications and through bureaucratic procedures. Only the family, the local parish, and the informal peer group of neighbors still offer relatively automatic entrance to individuals. Such small and stable social groups in which people have traditionally been able to immerse their activities and identities are insufficient for maintaining urban life. They are being supplemented, and sometimes replaced, by formal groups whose formally educated members have the ability to enter and withdraw from a variety of social relations. Although the growing urban centers may make difficult the maintenance of life around a secure small group, the city and its environs can provide its residents with a great range of activities and encounters, developing and utilizing their potentials. Urbanites can have a multi-dimensional and institutionally-rich social life space, involving a number of different roles entirely absent in a village or small town. They can carry on diverse activities and relate to a great diversity of people in primary and intimate, or in secondary and even fleeting interaction.

The changes in rapidly urbanizing and industrializing societies such as America are not, however, experienced evenly by their members. Many people lead very restricted or isolated lives even within the wealth of opportunities technically available to them. The social life space of each person is dependent upon his or her location in the social system and his ability to utilize the resources offered by the society. This ability includes understanding of the social system and knowledge of how to mobilize the environment to meet needs. In our heterogeneous society, many members are restricted in the life styles available to them. This is particularly true of older widows, socialized into traditional roles, encouraged into passive stances *vis-à-vis* the world and with limited skills because of age and sex.

The factors constricting the choices of life styles available to older widows include their ethnic group affiliation. Ethnic cultures, based upon past heritage and present conditions in the adopted land, stipulate the proper living arrangements for widows, as well as for the other members of the group. Those in marginal positions may build combined patterns, with the help of varying degrees of cooperation from the two groups between which they are located, but the gradual dissolution of the ethnic community has left many of them socially isolated and restricted.

The location of the widow in the social class system also affects her life style. The older woman is apt to have obtained no, or minimal, training in roles providing a source of livelihood in an urban setting. She is likely to have depended upon her husband as the main breadwinner of the family. His income was generally not high enough for them to save much money, nor did he invest heavily in insurance, so they did not build an estate sufficient to maintain the widow above the poverty line once he died. At the same time the traditional attitude of rejecting financial help from the society and even from families prevents the older woman from increasing her income this way. She holds dilemma-producing attitudes, not wanting to take "charity" from the government, yet being unwilling to become dependent on married offspring by moving in with them or even exchanging services. Traditional means of self-support are becoming less available for the elderly in modern society, due to their movement off the land, their consumption-oriented spending habits, and the inflation which drastically reduces the purchasing power of past savings. Many are home owners, particularly in the latter part of life, but the sale of these structures does not bring enough to cover rent for more than a very limited time. Income from lodgers has decreased as an easily available source of livelihood for older women, since immigration laws and the high American marital rate make boarders a rarity. Technological change makes past skills out-dated and new ones hard to learn. Job placement is becoming more and more formally organized, with intermediary agencies not known to older people who have been trained for a more direct system. Thus, for the older widow especially, the increasing openness of the economic sphere of life has simply increased the gap between the opportunities to live a desired life at any social level and the ability of the woman to take advantage of them.

The decline of the community and the extended family as protective systems insuring that financially uneducated women would not be cheated by non-altruistically inclined petty and major criminals has resulted in a loss of millions of dollars by widows who suddenly acquired even a small inheritance or life insurance payment. Many widows are not so old as to desire disengagement from society at the time of their husband's death. Women are living much longer than in traditional America, while men have not expanded their life expectancy in equal proportion.

Since women marry men older then themselves, they have a very high probability of becoming widows, their average age when that event occurs being 56 years. Despite this statistical fact, life styles for American widows are generally built upon the assumption either that they are young and can soon remarry or that they are very old and removed from the realm of active involvement. The trouble is that most widows are neither, but the society has not taken sufficient cognizance of this fact to modify the facilities and roles available to them. As a result, their potential for action is lost to the community, leaving many widows idly to perform tasks in functionally insignificant social roles. There are three widows to every widower aged sixty-five and over in America. The widowers have a wider range of choice for a second wife, especially since they can go out of their age group in a relatively open way, which the older widows cannot do (Leslie: 1967, 632–636; Metropolitan Life Insurance Company: 1945, 1–3). Although widowers have less of a problem with remarriage, they, too, usually lack appropriate living facilities, as Felix Berardo (1967, 1968), Pihlblad and Rosencranz (1968), and Adams (1969) have recognized.

The status of the widow tends to be peripheral in other aspects of society's life. In general, her status is not as high as that of wife, since women have traditionally derived most of their social position from that of their husband. Only in cases where the husband had been an outstanding public figure may the wife retain special status after his death. Some women have professions or are involved in respected volunteer work to the extent that their status undergoes no change in the transition from wife to widow, but they are rare. Because American society is increasingly leisure-oriented, the prestige of the non-working woman may become higher than it has been in the past. But the advantages brought about by a decrease in the puritanical work-orientation may not always be enjoyed by a widow if her single status excludes her from much of the leisure activity in a couple-companionate environment.

Even the religious institution has changed sufficiently to make strong involvement in its groups difficult for the widow. The value system has become increasingly secular and, as Geoffrey Gorer (1965) concluded, even the rituals, such as those of mourning and bereavement, have become de-institutionalized in the Western world. Religion is tending to become bureaucratically rational, making older people uncomfortable in the changing churches. Many of the activities are directed toward young families and those who are older feel left out of the social life.

One of the most difficult changes in the lives of older widows has been their decreasing functionality in the family institution. Particularly in the wide belt of its middle classes, the American society is developing a neolocal, bilateral, and egalitarian family. Each family unit is small, increasingly independent and isolated from the others. In spite of the occasional service interchange observed by Sussman, Litwak, and Shanas and Streib (contained in Shanas and Streib, 1965), each unit of husband, wife, and small children is based separately, often in relatively far time-distance locations from kin members. This means that the daily life of each family has become the sole responsibility of the adults managing each household, making it less likely that the widow can fill her life with interaction from her own household. Within each homestead of even married children, let alone siblings, there is no central role available to her. The widow herself does not wish to relinquish her own independent position for the periphery of someone else's life. Most older people in America, as in the European countries of England and Denmark, do not wish to live with their married children; they define the ideal situation as what is called in Austria, "Intimacy at a distance" (Rosenmyar and Kockeis, 1963). Other assessments of the ideal situation are not so rosy. Reports of contacts are not necessarily reports of intimacy, as Irving Rosow (1967) has pointed out. The American family system involves interaction from separate households, which is not guaranteed to provide intimacy.

Mate selection in this society is based increasingly on "love" developed during a dating and courtship period of the teen years. Self-selection of the mate and the fundamental isolation of the married unit have placed a heavy burden of affective, economic, and child-rearing functions upon the couple. In the middle classes, and on up from there, the wife is expected to be a companion and major assistant to her husband. The burden has produced a variety of "solutions," as reflected by the whole range of marital relational styles, from divorce and desertion to close companionate ties. Widowhood affects women differently, depending on the location of their marriage along the continuum of closeness.

The marriage contract varies from state to state as to inheritance rights, but in general, the American widow may inherit all or a sizable segment of the estate. If no formal will is registered, she is apt simply to take over the management of the property after her husband's death. She is usually the guardian or at least one of the guardians of goods held in

trust for the children. No system of levirate or widow inheritance operates in this society, although cases of voluntary marriage by the deceased
husband's brother are occasionally reported. The *in genetricem* rights of
the male kin group are no longer viable in any but the upper class, and,
as we shall see later, most widows do not continue a close relation with
that group once the connecting link is gone. Even the children's obligation to retain the family name of their late father is regarded more as a
duty to him than to his kin. Small children may even take the last name
of the mother's new husband, if she remarries, for the responsibility of
making them feel part of the new unit may outweigh loyalty to the former
husband.

The life styles of American widows vary so greatly that it is impossible
to define "the American widow" beyond the simple statement that she
is a woman whose husband has died. Her style varies not only by her
location in the social system, be it an upper-class suburb, the slum or the
"gold coast" of a city, an ethnic community, a small town, or a farm, but
by her own combination of characteristics. Patterns emerge when such
factors as the educational achievement of the woman is compared to her
social life space so that we find that the more training she has, the more
social roles and social relations she is able to enter and maintain. At the
other side of the picture, we find widows immersed in kin relations wh⌐
infrequently see anyone else. Old neighborhoods still exist in urban
centers, where the elderly continue to live near people they have known
all their lives. Public housing high-rises bring together people in similar
circumstances, creating opportunities for the new friendships found by
Rosow (1967) to be facilitated by high density situations in Cleveland.
Small towns in Missouri (Pihlblad and Rosencranz, 1968), Wisconsin
(Bultena and Marshall, 1969), and other Middle West states attract the
widows of farmers from nearby areas and often have as much as a 150
percent proportion of the "normal" number of aged. Specially developed
"leisure world" (*Practical Builder,* 1966) communities of same age peers
guarantee care-free and non-lonely living (Bultena and Wood, 1969).
Other towns have become focal points of seasonal migration for the "snow
birds" who live in age-segregated environments for only part of the year.
Widows with sufficient money travel a good deal and often comprise a
major segment of the passengers on tours or cruises.

Younger widows face problems of child-rearing, returning to work, and
re-establishing themselves as eligibles in the marriage market. Older
widows may also hold jobs, full- or part-time, and join voluntary associations. Some combine these with an active family interaction, others with
a clique activity with women in the same circumstances. Some widows
remarry. Since the years of widowhood are often long, involvement in

one set of roles can shift into another as life circumstances change. The degree of flexibility in life styles varies considerably. Some women become "perpetual widows"; others move from work roles to an increased involvement in the lives of their grandchildren.

## Demographic Facts

At the time this book went to print the detailed characteristics of the American population of 1970 had not become publicly available, and it will be another year or so before more complicated calculations concerning any category of member are worked out. The figures which are now available show that 12.5 percent of all women aged 14 and over were widows in 1970, 22.1 percent being single, 58.4 percent being married with the spouse present, 3.5 percent being married with the spouse absent and 3.5 being divorced. Forty-three percent of the households headed by women are minus a male head because of death. The latter figure is a drop from 50.9 percent of female heads of households who were widows in 1960, due to an increase in the proportion of divorced and married women with spouse absent from the home. (U.S. Bureau of the Census: 1971:29).

The detailed demographic characteristics of widows in America have been most effectively summarized as of 1960 by the Statistical Bulletin of the Metropolitan Life Insurance Company:

*During the past two decades the number of widows in the United States has been growing by more than 100,000 a year, compared with an annual increase of about 80,000 in the 1920's and of about 50,000 at the turn of the century. In March 1961, there were approximately 8¼ million widows in the country, and it is expected that their total will continue to rise rapidly.*

*Widows in the population have been outnumbering widowers by a steadily widening margin—a consequence of the higher mortality among men than women, and also of the higher remarriage rate among widowers. Currently the ratio of widows to widowers is 4 to 1; about 50 years ago, it was little more than 2 to 1.*

*In 1961, almost three-fifths of the widows in the United States were 65 years of age or older. One in every 4 widows was in the age group 55–64 years, and only 1 in every 17 was under age 45.*

*It should be noted, however, that a large number of newly widowed women are still in their middle years. Of the 550,000 women widowed in 1961, about 90,000 were under age 45; somewhat over half of the total were under 60 years of age.*

*At all but the oldest ages, widows constitute a smaller proportion of the women residing in farm areas than those living in our cities and small towns. At ages 75 and over, the percentage widowed is practically the same in both groups.*

*Three-fourths of the women who become widows at age 45 can expect to
live an additional 25 years. The same number of years remain to 9 out of
every 10 women widowed at ages 35 or earlier. Of the widows bereft of their
spouse at age 65, somewhat more than half can expect to live 15 years longer
and about a third still have 20 years of life before them.* (Metropolitan Life
Insurance Company, 1962: 1–4).

The greater the age gap between husband and wife (with the husband
being the older, as is traditional in America), the greater the probability
that the woman will become a widow. For a woman aged fifty-five or
younger the odds are approximately fifty-four out of a hundred that she
will be left a widow if she is married to a man five years her junior; sixty-
four out of a hundred if he is five years her senior; and eighty out of 100
if he is ten years older. (Metropolitan Life Insurance Company, 1969:
10–11).

The United States is not the only country facing an increase of the
proportion of widows over widowers. An American government report
on "Changes in Mortality Trends in England and Wales, 1931–1961"
concludes that "One feature of the mortality rates throughout the whole
period 1931–1961 is the widening gap between the sexes. This has occurred at every age from one to eighty-four, and for almost every disease
which has been considered; evidently there are some factors in modern
society which are inimical to the survival of the male but are beneficial
to the female." (National Center for Health Statistics, 1965:35). This
trend is most obvious among older people. "For elderly persons, sixty-five
to eighty-four years of age, the male death rate in 1931 was about thirty-
one percent higher than the female rate, whereas in 1961 it was sixty
percent higher." (National Center for Health Statistics, 1965:36).

By percentage of total and by race, the detailed distribution in the
United States of females aged fifty and over indicates a slight increase,
parallel with age increase, of the proportion who never married (see
Table 1). A simultaneous decrease in the proportion of older women who
have been divorced is indicative of the national trends, for it is only in
recent years that marital dissolution has increased in popularity. The
figures do not indicate who among the currently married had been in the
divorce category in prior years. The proportions in the single and divorced columns are relatively small however, and have not changed as
dramatically as those for the married and widowed American females.
With each decade of life the proportion of women who are married decreases as the proportion of widows increases so that in fact three-fourths
of the women in their early eighties are widowed. The table also indicates
the inequality of widowhood rates between white and non-white members
of our society. In all age decades, the non-white woman has a much

TABLE 1: MARITAL STATUS BY COLOR OF AMERICAN WOMEN AGED 50 AND OVER*, 1960

| Age | Single | | | Married | | | Widowed | | | Divorced | | |
|---|---|---|---|---|---|---|---|---|---|---|---|---|
| | % of Total | White | Non-W. | % of Total | White | Non-W. | % of Total | White | Non-W. | % of Total | White | Non-W. |
| 50–54 | 7.6 | 7.8 | 6.1 | 77.0 | 77.9 | 68.9 | 11.1 | 10.2 | 19.8 | 4.2 | 4.1 | 5.2 |
| 55–59 | 8.2 | 8.4 | 6.9 | 69.9 | 70.9 | 60.7 | 17.9 | 16.8 | 28.2 | 3.9 | 3.9 | 5.2 |
| 60–64 | 7.7 | 7.9 | 4.7 | 61.4 | 62.3 | 52.0 | 27.6 | 26.5 | 39.9 | 3.3 | 3.3 | 3.3 |
| 65–69 | 7.9 | 8.2 | 4.3 | 51.6 | 52.4 | 42.5 | 37.9 | 36.7 | 50.6 | 2.7 | 2.7 | 2.5 |
| 70–74 | 8.4 | 8.7 | 4.4 | 39.1 | 39.6 | 32.4 | 50.4 | 49.6 | 61.2 | 2.1 | 2.1 | 2.0 |
| 75–79 | 8.8 | 9.1 | 4.4 | 27.4 | 27.8 | 22.9 | 62.2 | 61.6 | 71.3 | 1.5 | 1.5 | 1.4 |
| 80–84 | 9.5 | 9.9 | 4.5 | 16.2 | 16.3 | 14.8 | 73.1 | 72.7 | 79.6 | 1.1 | 1.1 | 1.1 |
| 85 and over | 9.6 | 10.0 | 4.3 | 8.2 | 8.1 | 9.3 | 81.4 | 81.0 | 85.4 | 0.8 | 0.8 | 1.0 |

* Source: The United States Census of Population, 1960 U.S. Summary, Detailed Characteristics, segments of Table 176, pp. 1–427–435.

smaller chance of remaining married and a much greater chance of being widowed than the white woman. The largest gap between whites and non-whites, one of fourteen percent, is in the age group of the sixties. The difference in the proportion of white to non-white widows decreases in the very latest decades of life, but at no time is the non-white rate lower than that of the whites.

The distribution of the widowed in the population of American females has changed since 1890, the year for which we have the first set of even partial census statistics.

TABLE 2: PERCENTAGE OF AMERICAN WOMEN WHO ARE WIDOWED, 1890–1950, BY COLOR*

| Age Decade | 1950 Total | 1950 White | 1950 Negro | 1940 Total | 1940 White | 1940 Negro | 1930 Total |
|---|---|---|---|---|---|---|---|
| 45–49 | 8.6 | 7.4 | 19.1 | 10.7 | 9.4 | 24.0 | 11.6 |
| 50–54 | 13.9 | 12.6 | 27.4 | 15.9 | 14.6 | 31.5 | 16.9 |
| 55–59 | 20.5 | 19.3 | 35.1 | 22.4 | 21.3 | 37.9 | 23.4 |
| 60–64 | 29.7 | 28.6 | 44.9 | 31.3 | 30.3 | 46.8 | 33.1 |
| 65–69 | 41.1 | 39.7 | 56.7 | 43.1 | 41.8 | 58.8 | 44.1 |
| 70–74 | 53.3 | 52.3 | 68.0 | 55.5 | 54.5 | 70.0 | 55.9 |
| 75–79 | 65.1 | 64.6 | 74.6 | 67.3 | 66.8 | 76.9 | 73.9 (75 and |
| 80–84 | 75.9 | 75.5 | 82.9 | 77.1 | 76.7 | 84.2 | over) |
| 85 and over | 82.9 | 82.9 | 83.4 | 85.1 | 84.7 | 89.1 | |

| Age Decade | 1920 Total | 1910 Total | 1900 Total | 1890 Total |
|---|---|---|---|---|
| 45–54 | 15.3 | 15.7 | 17.6 | 18.4 |
| 55–64 | 29.5 | 30.0 | 32.3 | 33.3 |
| 65 and over | 58.4 | 58.1 | 59.3 | 58.6 |
| Age not reported | 14.6 | 16.5 | 15.7 | 17.3 |

* United States Census of Population, 1960 United States Summary, Detailed Characteristics, PC (I)-1D Table 177, pp. 146–148.

A comparison of Table 1 and Table 2 shows that in the years between 1950 and 1960 there is a decrease in the proportion of widows to the total number of American women in every age decade of life. The same tendency can be observed for 1930 and for 1940, which is the last year for which we have the same statistical categories. In other words, the proportion of women who are widows has decreased since at least 1930 and probably since 1890 (it definitely has decreased, if comparisons are made between 1890 and 1930, but the figures for the years of 1920 and 1910 are harder to categorize). However, the percentage of widows in the American population has increased, with one exception, from a low of 10.3 in 1910 to 10.8 in 1920 and in 1930, 11.8 in 1940, 11.0 in 1950, and 12.2 in 1960.

The discrepancy between the rates of widowhood of whites and Blacks is a continuous one with a long history (see Table 2). Black women have also experienced a drop in the proportion who are widowed at about the same rate as white women. Unfortunately, before 1940 the data was not broken down by color. A more detailed comparison between the two groups in the decades contained in the two tables shows that the gap between rates of widowhood has decreased steadily in all but the eldest group. The amount of decrease is less as the widows grow older, leaving minute figures of change, particularly in the 1940–1950 period, for women who are over sixty years of age. Even within this group, the black rates dropped between 1950 and 1960. Black women aged fifty to fifty-four had a 16.9 percent higher rate of widowhood than white women in 1940, a 14.8 percent higher rate in 1950, and a 9.6 percent higher rate in 1960. This indicates a higher death rate on their part, a lower death frequency on the part of the male, or marriage to younger men.

Facts concerning the women fourteen years of age or older who were analyzed in the 1960 Census Summary indicate some factors that contribute to marital differences in this country. The median age of the American woman above the childhood years (up to fourteen) is 40.8; that of the man is 40.0 (see Table 3).

TABLE 3: THE MEDIAN AGE OF AMERICAN WOMEN WHO ARE FOURTEEN YEARS OLD OR OVER IN DIFFERENT MARITAL SITUATIONS BY RACE AND URBAN-RURAL RESIDENCE *

| Category of Women | Total | Single | Median Age by Marital Status | | |
| --- | --- | --- | --- | --- | --- |
| | | | Married | Widowed | Divorced |
| Total | 40.8 | 19.0 | 40.7 | 67.8 | 44.9 |
| White | 41.3 | 19.0 | 41.0 | 68.4 | 45. |
| Non-White | 37.2 | 18.9 | 38.1 | 62.2 | 41.5 |
| Urban | 41.0 | 19.8 | 40.5 | 67.4 | 44.9 |
| Rural, Non-farm | 39.6 | 17.7 | 39.8 | 68.7 | 44.9 |
| Rural farm | 42.9 | 17.8 | 45.1 | 69.7 | 44.6 |

* United States Census of Population, 1960 United States Summary, Detailed Characteristics, PC (I) -iD, Table 176, pp. 1–427–435.

The rural farm and the rural non-farm girls get married and fall out of the single category at the earliest ages. Next come the non-whites. The urban women are the slowest to marry. The youngest divorced group is composed of non-white females, who are also the youngest to be widowed. The rural women on or off the farm are the oldest widows, which indicates mobility of the younger women from rural areas to cities, or a longer life span of males. Younger widows seem to gravitate to urban areas, which means that the older women who remain form a disproportionate part of the rural population.

The highest proportion of American widows lives alone or with unmarried children. The older the woman (up until the last stages of life when physical health problems make maintenance of self and house impossible), the more likely she is not to have anyone else in the household (see Table 4). This table also indicates the widow's dependence upon unmarried offspring or other young people.

TABLE 4: LIVING ARRANGEMENTS OF WIDOWS IN THE
UNITED STATES, MARCH 1961
(NUMBERS IN THOUSANDS)

| Living Arrangement | Total | Urban and Rural Non-Farm | Rural-Farm |
|---|---|---|---|
| Total | 8,217 | 7,770 | 447 |
| Head of Household | 5,639 | 5,367 | 272 |
|   With relative in household | 2,336 | 2,161 | 175 |
|   With no relative in household | 3,303 | 3,206 | 97 |
| Living in Household of Others | | | |
|   *Relative's* | 2,111 | 1,942 | 169 |
|   Together with own children under age 18 | 47 | 37 | 10 |
|   Without own children under age 18 | 2,064 | 1,905 | 159 |
|   *Non-Relative's* | 287 | 281 | 6 |
|   Together with relatives | 13 | 13 | 0 |
|   Without relatives | 274 | 268 | 6 |
| Inmate of Institution * | 145 | 145 | 0 |
| Living in Hotel, Dormitory, etc. | 35 | 35 | 0 |

* Estimated by the Statistical Bureau of the Metropolitan Life Insurance Company.
Source: Bureau of the Census, Current Population Report, Series P-20, Nos. 114 and 116.

A recent cross-cultural study of people aged sixty-five and over in America, England, and Denmark has produced some interesting results. "In all three countries, it is unusual for three successive generations to share a common household. In Denmark, approximately five percent, in the United States eight percent, and in Britain thirteen percent of the respective samples live in such households" (Stehouwer, 1968). About a quarter of the aged population in Denmark (twenty-eight percent), in Britain (twenty-two percent), and in the United States (twenty-two percent) live alone. One third of the elderly population in Britain, and slightly less than half in Denmark and in the United States, live as married couples, in a household of their own, without other members. The remaining of the elderly, twenty-seven percent in Denmark, forty-five percent in Britain, and thirty-five percent in the United States live in households which have a more differentiated structure. Most of these households include an adult child, especially an unmarried or previously married child" (Stehouwer, 1968:184).

An interesting comment made by Jan Stehouwer (1968:185), the author of the above quotation, is of significance for the study with which this book is concerned:

*"For the generation of older people represented in the three national samples, the last child normally would have left the parental home as the parents approached their late 50's. Nevertheless, approximately 14 percent of all married elderly couples in Denmark and in the United States and 23 percent of those in Britain, live with an unmarried child. Among those who are widowed and divorced, 15 percent in Denmark, 11 percent in Britain and 20 percent in the United States live with an unmarried child."*

Only seven percent of the Danish unmarried women (meaning single, widowed, and divorced, most of whom at the age of sixty-five and over are widowed) live with siblings or other relatives, but the proportion is as high as thirteen percent in Britain and twelve percent in the United States. In the case of Americans, these relatives may be a parent, niece or nephew, or grandchild. Nine percent of the Danes who fall in this category, five percent of the Britishers, and five percent of the Americans live with other people who are not relatives. Five percent of the Danish unmarried women, seventeen percent of the British, and fifteen percent of the Americans live with married children, which means that they share a residence with more than one person (Stehouwer, 1968:208). The explanation of the residential pattern differentiating Denmark from the other two societies rests upon a tradition of independence in all spheres of life and on the help given by the country through "public care for the aged and a general pension system" (Stehouwer, 1968:224). Each generation is financially independent of the other, and cooperative movements, as well as voluntary associations, attract the active participation of the elderly. Despite such differences and despite the fact that Americans are more likely to live with others than Danes are, the figures also show a strong tendency for older members of this society to reject residence with others. In fact, the household "consisting of a widowed (sometimes a divorced or separated) parent living alone" is one of the major five categories of households which the authors of that study distinguish: "About twenty-two to twenty-eight percent of those aged sixty-five and over" are in this type of household. A second category is that of "households consisting of a widowed (or divorced or separated) parent and married or unmarried children." About nine to twenty percent of those aged sixty-five and over were placed there (Stehouwer, 1968:218).

Independence from adult married offspring does not necessarily imply economic affluence. In fact, the widow who is sixty-five years or older is very likely to be living on an income which puts her below most criteria for the poverty level. Various estimates have concluded recently that "The likelihood of poverty is greater among families headed by a woman than among families headed by a man. The likelihood is even greater if the families headed by a woman are non-white. In 1964, sixty-three percent of the non-white and twenty-nine percent of the white families headed by a woman were poor. The comparable proportions for non-white and white husband-wife families were thirty-two and ten percent, respectively" (Department of Administration on Aging, 1968:1–3). Older people living alone or with non-relatives showed an even poorer income picture. Half of them had 1965 incomes of less than $1,348. This median was only 40.6 percent of the median for people under sixty-five who are not living in families. Those who are old and living in such arrangements include one third with incomes of less than $1,000 and almost three out of five with incomes of less than $1,500 (Brotman, 1968). Part of the reason for such a meagerness of income is the fact that many of the older widows had never received significant incomes or worked in occupations covered by Social Security at that time. Many of the husbands had not obtained the education or achieved the occupational level which would guarantee income-producing investments or a high return rate on some other policy. Many recently widowed and younger persons had work experience producing relatively good incomes, insurance, and some sort of union or work policy which assists survivors, but the older population is often left with no means of support, let alone a comfortable life. A domestic worker married to a chauffeur is not likely to receive much inheritance at his death nor to have other sources of income, if she is physically incapacitated or otherwise unable to keep on doing housecleaning.

Two problems prevent the widowed woman from obtaining a job which offers an above-poverty income. One is her age; the second is her educational background. More younger widows try to work, but this does not guarantee them high incomes. According to statistics of the U.S. Department of Labor, twenty-three percent of all families headed by a woman who was employed in March 1965 had an income below the poverty level in 1964 (1966:1). The Department of Labor also reported that widowed, divorced, or separated women formed forty-one percent of the working population in 1966. These women, however, are not distributed evenly by age, as indicated by the statistics on percentages of previously married women who obtained jobs: fifty-nine percent of those between sixteen and twenty-four years of age; sixty-seven percent of those between twenty-five and forty-four; sixty-three percent of those between forty-five and sixty-four; and only ten percent of those sixty-five and over (U.S. Department of Labor: 1966). There are social as well as financial difficulties for the previously married older woman who does not work; employment provides not only income, but (except for domestics and those in similarly isolating occupations) also a guaranteed source of social interaction. Most older widows find employment in jobs which do not pay great wages, because few have reached high levels of formal education. Almost six percent of the persons aged sixty-five and over (or a million) never went to school at all, and eleven percent (or two million) had less than

TABLE 5: MEDIAN NUMBER OF YEARS OF SCHOOLING
COMPLETED BY PERSONS AGED 65+, BY COLOR
AND RESIDENCE, MARCH 1966 *

| Class | All | Male | Female |
|---|---|---|---|
| Total | 8.5 | 8.4 | 8.6 |
| White | 8.6 | 8.5 | 8.7 |
| Non-White | 5.2 | 4.7 | 5.6 |
| Metropolitan | 8.7 | 8.6 | 8.7 |
| White | 8.7 | 8.6 | 8.8 |
| Non-White | 6.0 | 6.0 | 6.1 |
| Non-Metropolitan | 8.4 | 8.3 | 8.5 |
| White | 8.5 | 8.4 | 8.6 |
| Non-White | 4.0 | 3.4 | 4.7 |

* Source: Herman B. Brotman, "Educational Attainment of the Older Population," Administration on Aging, *Useful Facts* No. 28, September 11, 1967, p. 4.

five years of elementary school. This makes a total of seventeen percent of the aged, or three million people, who are at least functionally illiterate. By comparison, only five percent of the twenty-five to sixty-four age group falls into this category. At the other end of the educational ladder, only about five percent of the older group are college graduates, as compared with eleven percent of the younger segment of the population (Brotman, 1968:3).

The education of the aged population, most of whom are women and a high proportion of whom are widowed, is not evenly distributed in the sixty-five and over group. Whites and urbanites (that is, people who in their youth attended schools in the city) tend to have completed more years of schooling than non-whites and non-metropolitan residents.

All in all, the national figures describing America's older women show them to be relatively uneducated and marginal to the labor force.

## WIDOWHOOD IN CHICAGO

### Demographic Facts

Older people in the Chicago area, many of whom are widows, are not distributed evenly among its seventy-six community areas. The neighborhoods of high concentration are either of older residential character, with small working man's homes and "two flats," or centers for migrants in search of small apartments, residential hotels, or rooming houses. A new form of housing which is useful for the elderly is the "studio" apartment, a self-contained unit consisting of a living-dining-bedroom, with a utility kitchen area and a bathroom. Other limited space developments are created from the breakdown of larger apartments or houses. Enterprising building owners, excited by the prospect of multiple rents, set up kitchen facilities in each room of a formerly larger unit and rent them as separate household dwellings. Bathrooms are shared by the residents but the building is not technically a rooming house.

The area of highest concentration of people aged sixty and over (twenty-nine percent) in the city of Chicago is the "Loop," that is, the very core (Kitagawa and Taeuber, 1963:78–79). Less than one percent of the houses are owner-occupied in this neighborhood; only one percent were built in or after 1950, according to 1960 figures. Sixty-eight percent of the housing is in substandard condition. The median gross rent is $59 a month. Since only six percent of the dwelling units contain more than one person per room and the median number of rooms per unit is one, the conclusion can easily be reached that most of the residents are single. Here the old live among the middle-aged and childless people (forty-one percent are between forty-five and sixty-four) and the young (thirty-six percent are between twenty and forty-four) who are unmarried. They see few children, since less than one percent of the area's population is under five years of age and only three percent is between

ages five and nineteen. The elderly population has increased in proportion to the rest since 1930, at which time they formed only 8.9 percent
of the total. This percentage increased to 11.8 in 1940 and 13.9 in 1950,
until it reached the 1960 total of 28.8 percent. It is possible that the
next census will show a further increase, although there has been some
razing of the older buildings. Seventy-three percent of the population
had lived in a different house in 1955 than in 1960. Twenty-three percent are of foreign stock, meaning that they or their parents came from
outside the United States. Ten percent of the total population is Black,
and one percent is identified as of other races.

A contrasting area of Chicago, also with a relatively high proportion
of people aged 60 and over (21.1 percent), is Auburn Gresham (Kitagawa and Taeuber, 1963:156–157). The community has become increasingly owner-occupied, the proportion rising from 39.7 percent in 1940
to 49.7 percent in 1950 and 53.1 percent in 1960. All age groups are
represented, with 7.8 percent being under five years of age, 20.7 percent
being from five to nineteen years, and 27.0 percent being from forty-five
to sixty-four years old. There is an average population of 3.0 persons
per household, with 5.1 as the median number of rooms per unit. Only
7.4 percent of the population has an income under $3,000, no doubt
disproportionately represented by the aged residents, while 31.8 percent
earn $10,000 or above. The median value of the homes is $17,900, and
44.7 percent of the residents came from foreign stock. Only 41.9 percent
of the males are white collar workers. Thus, this is a generally working
class and lower white collar community with a solid foundation. The
aged are not distributed evenly in the census tracks of the area, ranging
from 18.3 percent down to 10.5 percent. The contrasts between these
two tracks are interesting. The one with a higher proportion of the
elderly has a higher percentage of people with an income of less than
$3,000 (nine percent to three percent), a smaller number of persons in
each housing unit, a lower median value of owner-occupied units, a lower
median gross rent, a lower number of school years completed, and a
higher foreign stock percentage. Throughout the city, a similar pattern
emerges. Areas with a disproportionate number of elderly are poorer,
less educated, black or of a foreign stock background, and contain poorer
dwelling units.

The Black areas of Chicago have proportionally fewer aged persons
than the white areas. This minority group's population died younger, as
discussed previously in connection with United States figures. Furthermore, the elderly are more likely to have remained in the South, on farm
land, or on the periphery of small towns, rather than migrating to the
city. The Chicago neighborhood of North Lawndale, which in 1960 had

a ninety-one percent Negro population, had only five percent of its total in the sixty and over age group (Kitagawa and Taeuber, 1963:72–73). Interestingly enough, there were 3,313 more persons aged sixty-five and over in the 1950's (7.4 percent of the residents, as compared to 3.3 percent in the 1960's) and a much lower proportion of Blacks. The trend seems clear: the older white population, apt to have strong prejudices and fears of economic reversal, moves out as a neighborhood changes in racial composition and goes to another area of small units, but in a white one. Only a few of the older widows remain, if they own homes.

Some of the older widows have been able to find a comfortable residence in the new Chicago Housing Authority's buildings for the elderly. As of December 31, 1967, high-rises constructed specifically for the elderly contained 6,164 persons with an average of 1.2 persons per room (Chicago Housing Authority, 1967). Most of these are widows, since most of the units contain only one room. The buildings often have extensive programs of activities for the residence, organized by the Mayor's Commission on Senior Citizens or volunteer groups.

Most of the white elderly of Chicago do not live in substandard housing; only 16 percent of them are so located. The non-whites are less fortunate; 52 percent of them live in substandard buildings. (Chi-

TABLE 6: HOUSEHOLD INCOME OF OWNER AND RENTER
OCCUPIED DWELLINGS CONTAINING ONE PERSON
ONLY, AGED 65 OR OVER IN THE CITY OF
CHICAGO, 1960 *

| *Household Income in 1959* | *Percent of One-Person Households* | |
|---|---|---|
| | *Owner* | *Renter* |
| *Total Households* | 100.0 | 100.0 |
| Under $1,500 | 59.2 | — |
| $1,500 to $1,999 | 10.7 | — |
| Under $2,000 | 69.9 | 65.0 |
| $2,000 to $2,999 | 11.9 | 12.0 |
| $3,000 and over | 18.2 | 23.0 |

* Source: United States Census of Population, 1960, Vol. 7 (photostatic copies of unpublished IBM tabulations), Table 3.

cago Community Renewal Program, 1964). "Sixty percent of all seniors own their own home," but only fifty-three percent of the non-whites who are sixty-five and over have possession of their dwelling unit. These figures apply to all marital categories.

A report on "The Elderly in Chicago" issued by the Community Renewal Program (1964:56) nevertheless reports that "The rent paid by almost half of the elderly families constitutes over thirty-five percent of their income, while the average rent-income ratio for all families was only about twenty percent." The main reason for the difference is the low median for the elderly.

The following figures of incomes were collected by the Welfare Council of Metropolitan Chicago for both owner and renter occupied dwellings containing one person only, aged sixty-five or over.

Thus, most of the Chicago elderly are living on a below the poverty level income. Twenty-one percent of the Illinois Old Age Assistance Recipients, who are frequently widows and who were part of a national (forty-nine state) study in 1953, had children living elsewhere, and eighty-seven percent of them received no help from offspring (Social Security Administration, 1955: Table 52). This pattern is typical for other states. The figures indicate that having offspring in the state does not guarantee the widow assistance and that the opposite situation of having distant children produces no better financial results.

## The Chicago Area Respondents

The Chicago area widows who were interviewed by a team of National Opinion Research Center trained women were scattered among sixty metropolitan areas in both suburbs and the central city. Since no institutional residential centers lacking private cooking facilities, such as nursing homes, were chosen, all respondents lived in their own dwellings or in the home of others.

The age distribution of the respondents, chosen by a quota system to include 150 aged fifty to sixty-four and another 150 aged sixty-five and over, indicates a bunching under age sixty-five and a relatively low proportion in the category seventy to seventy-four (see Table 7). It is quite probable that this distribution, reflecting a similar skewing in

TABLE 7: AGE DISTRIBUTION OF CHICAGO AREA RESPONDENTS

| Age | Number | Percent |
|---|---|---|
| 54 and under | 39 | 12.9 |
| 55–59 | 40 | 13.2 |
| 60–64 | 72 | 23.9 |
| 65–69 | 46 | 15.2 |
| 70–74 | 35 | 11.6 |
| 75–79 | 42 | 13.9 |
| 80–84 | 16 | 5.3 |
| 85 and over | 11 | 3.6 |

Missouri (Adams, 1969), has more to do with the reported age than the actual one, some women subtracting years. Age sixty-five has strong symbolic meaning in America since so many employers use it as a cut-off time, forcing retirement. The Chicago area respondents have been bereft of a husband on an average of 11.45 years; the average age of the husband at death was 60.10 years. The distribution of their ages at the time the husband died supports the national urban figures and lends credence to predictions of difficulties in remarriage (see Table 8).

TABLE 8: AGE AT WIDOWHOOD OF CHICAGO AREA
           RESPONDENTS

| Age | Number | Percent | Age | Number | Percent |
|------|--------|---------|-------|--------|---------|
| 34 or less | 15 | 4.9 | 55–59 | 52 | 17.2 |
| 35–39 | 14 | 4.6 | 60–64 | 45 | 14.9 |
| 40–44 | 20 | 6.6 | 65–69 | 25 | 8.3 |
| 45–49 | 48 | 15.9 | 70–74 | 20 | 6.6 |
| 50–54 | 52 | 17.2 | 75+ | 10 | 3.3 |

The age at which the wife experiences the death of her husband is a very important feature of widowhood because of the way her life is immersed in other social roles. A woman with several small children at home, at an age herself in which remarriage is possible and employment relatively easy, has a completely different set of problems and adjustments than an older widow who is left living alone. As the figures indicate, most of the widows were between forty-five and sixty-four years of age when the husband died. Eighty-one percent were in pre-retirement ages, and a number had children in the home at the time the husband died.

In fact, fifty-six percent of the respondents still have at least one child at home, with the probability of one and the probability of more than one both increasing as the number of children increases. Most of these offspring are unmarried or at least no longer with husbands; only twenty-two women live with married children. Forty-nine percent of the respondents live alone and an additional twenty percent are heads of the household in which they live. Twenty-one percent of those women who do not live alone are in homes owned or at least headed by an offspring, two percent by a parent, three percent by a sibling, four percent by another relative, and only one percent by a non-relative. This means that women are most apt to be living alone once children marry and leave home, or leave for other reasons. Eight percent of the widows live in the same building as at least one offspring. The figures support the conclusions of the cross-cultural research in Europe and America as to the paucity of households which can possibly be called multi-generational. Further details of residential and contact arrangements with children will be discussed in Chapter Three. Eighteen percent of the respondents do not have any living children, twenty-two percent have one, twenty-six percent have two, fifteen percent have three, eight percent have four, and eleven percent have more than that.

Our interviewers found a high proportion of widows living in houses, forty-one percent of them in single, detached family dwellings, and two percent in attached buildings. Sixteen percent reside in two-family, five percent in three-family units, thirteen percent in apartment buildings consisting of from four to six units, three percent in such buildings with from seven to nine units, and eighteen percent in buildings of ten or more units. Their dwellings were generally (seventy-nine percent) defined by the interviewers as on the same level of maintenance as the surrounding buildings. In spite of the stereotype of widows as women who are not taking care of themselves and living in cluttered, unattractive, if not dirty, dwellings, interviewers who had a chance to rate their respondents by these qualities responded very positively:

TABLE 9:  INTERVIEWER'S JUDGMENT OF THE RESPONDENT'S APPEARANCE IN TERMS OF NEATNESS AND QUALITY OF CLOTHING AND THAT OF HER HOME IN TERMS OF NEATNESS AND CLEANLINESS

| Quality | Grades of Quality | | | | | |
|---|---|---|---|---|---|---|
| | *1* | *2* | *3* | *4* | *5* | *6* |
| Well-dressed | 16.0 | 25.9 | 27.9 | 17.0 | 8.2 | 5.1 poorly dressed |
| Neat | 48.5 | 23.9 | 11.6 | 8.2 | 5.1 | 2.7 sloppy |
| Home neat | 60.9 | 17.1 | 5.7 | 7.1 | 4.6 | 4.6 disorderly home |
| Home clean | 64.6 | 17.9 | 6.1 | 3.9 | 4.6 | 2.9 dirty |

This very favorable judgment of housing quarters as clean and neat was obtained in spite of the fact that the interviews were conducted *cold,* that is, without warning, and that women living alone are not apt to expect many callers. The interviewer simply knocked on a door of a dwelling unit and screened directly from there. The contacts were made at all the usual hours of the day. Interestingly enough, the appearance of the woman's clothing did not produce as favorable impression on our middle-aged, middle-class, and rather chic looking interviewers as did the homes. Either the standards were different or widows are more likely to continue house maintenance even after they are no longer equally careful about self-maintenance.

In spite of the increasing proportion of inner city residents who are black, in Chicago as well as in many other urban centers of America, the age distribution of this part of the population is such as to preclude a high proportional representation in a sample of widows. Very few, of course, are found in suburban areas. Two of our respondents are unclassified, eighteen percent are listed as Black, and the remaining almost eight-two percent as white. Twenty-three percent of these women listed more than one nationality when asked for their background. The largest single identity group was German (twenty-two percent), followed by Polish (eleven percent), English and Scotch (eleven percent combined). Again, these distributions reflect the facts of Chicago's older population. Religious identification is heavily weighted by Protestants, with fifty-two percent of the respondents declaring themselves in that category, while forty percent are Roman Catholic and only five percent are Jewish. The reasons for the relatively low proportion of Jews are dual: movement out of the city and concentration in a relatively small area. The Protestants are contributed to by the blacks, the Roman Catholics by first or second generation immigrants from Eastern and Southern Europe. Most of the Protestants are Baptists (twenty-eight percent) and Lutherans (twenty-

TABLE 10: EDUCATIONAL ACHIEVEMENT OF THE RESPONDENT AND OF HER LAST HUSBAND

| | Self | | Husband | |
| Year Completed | Number | Percent | Number | Percent |
|---|---|---|---|---|
| No school | 11 | 3.7 | 6 | 2.5 |
| 1–4 grades | 24 | 8.0 | 20 | 8.2 |
| 5–7 grades | 41 | 13.6 | 17 | 7.0 |
| 8th grade | 70 | 23.2 | 45 | 18.4 |
| Some high school | 61 | 20.3 | 52 | 21.3 |
| Completed high school | 62 | 20.6 | 48 | 19.7 |
| Some college | 18 | 6.0 | 24 | 9.8 |
| Graduated from college | 8 | 2.7 | 20 | 8.2 |
| Graduate or professional training | 6 | 2.0 | 12 | 4.9 |
| Don't know | — | — | 56* | — |
| No answer | None | | 1* | |
| Percent Base | | 301 | | 244 |

* Not counted in percent base

four percent), the next most frequent being Methodists (sixteen percent) and Presbyterians (eleven percent).

The age and ethnic backgrounds of the widows in this study are also reflected in their educational achievement and that of their late husbands. These achievements indicate that few went beyond grade-school, let alone to college (see Table 10). In comparing these distributions to those of Missouri widows, all of whom were sixty-five years of age or over, we find a much greater proportion of Chicagoans who have some college (eleven percent to six percent) or some high school (forty-one percent to thirty percent). National figures for metropolitan areas show the Chicago group to be slightly higher for all top educational categories than many other cities (U.S. Department of Commerce, 1968:111).

The occupational distribution of the respondents' husbands, fathers, and husbands' fathers show a lack of dramatic difference between generations, an indication of how recent is the rapid upward mobility experienced by Americans (see Table 11). Most of the husbands were craftsmen, operatives or service workers, but a fifth had been managers, mostly of small stores or businesses. One in ten had been a professional. Not surprisingly, none had been farmers, although thirteen men, all black, had been farm laborers. The fathers on both sides were much more apt to have been farmers or farm laborers, a quarter being so listed. There were a few less craftsmen and professionals in that generation than in the husband's. Few of the women are or ever had been in managerial positions, or worked as craftsmen or laborers. More surprising is the fact

TABLE 11: OCCUPATIONAL DISTRIBUTIONS OF RESPONDENT'S FATHER, HUSBAND'S FATHER, HUSBAND, SELF IN BEST JOB AND SELF IN LAST OR PRESENT JOB

| | | | | Self | |
| | | Husband's | | | Last or |
| | Father's | Father's | Husband's | Best | Present |
| Occupation | Percent | Percent | Percent | Percent | Percent |
|---|---|---|---|---|---|
| Professionals | 4.5 | 6.2 | 10.0 | 9.3 | 8.7 |
| Farmers | 14.7 | 17.1 | 0.3 | 0.4 | — |
| Managers | 18.5 | 28.6 | 21.4 | 3.7 | 4.3 |
| Clerical | 2.7 | 1.9 | 5.7 | 33.7 | 25.7 |
| Sales Workers | 3.8 | 3.3 | 5.4 | 3.3 | 4.3 |
| Craftsmen | 18.2 | 17.6 | 24.1 | 4.4 | 5.2 |
| Operative | 15.1 | 9.5 | 16.1 | 21.5 | 21.3 |
| Service Worker | 6.2 | 4.8 | 11.0 | 21.9 | 27.8 |
| Farm Laborers | 9.9 | 8.1 | 4.3 | 0.7 | 0.9 |
| Laborers | 6.5 | 2.9 | 1.7 | 1.1 | 1.7 |
| No Answer | — | — | — | — | — |
| Not Determined | — | — | — | — | — |
| Percent Base | 292 | 291 | 299 | 270 | 230 |

that only three percent list sales as a best job and only four percent as a current or latest occupation. Most widows who worked did so in clerical, operative or service occupations, the latter being mostly domestics.

Forty-four percent of the widows taking part in this study were born in metropolitan Chicago, with thirty-nine percent coming here from other areas of the United States and seventeen percent from outside of the country. The ages at which they entered the Chicago region vary considerably, the foreign women usually coming when they were younger than the native Americans. Their background reflects the migration pattern to this country and the immigration policies admitting people from Europe. Chicago does not have a large oriental population.

The current income of the widow is much lower than the combined family income when the husband was living (see Table 12). The highest income, however, reflects the educational achievement of the husband and, in cases in which the wife worked, her educational background, and their occupations. Only one third of the families lived on $9,000 or over at their best time. Of course, the year of the highest income was likely to have been at a time when the national income was much lower and so was the cost of living. Regardless of the past, the present income situation of the widow is generally bad, falling below the poverty line. Sixty percent of them are living on less than $3,000 a year, fifteen percent of them on under $1,000. Of course, it is possible that their living expenses are minimal if they own homes which are sufficiently inexpensive

TABLE 12: HIGHEST AND CURRENT FAMILY INCOME

| | Current | | Highest | |
|---|---|---|---|---|
| *Income* | *Number* | *Percent* | *Number* | *Percent* |
| Under 1,000 | 41 | 14.9 | 2 | 0.9 |
| 1,000 to 2,999 | 124 | 45.1 | 12 | 5.2 |
| 3,000 to 4,999 | 52 | 18.9 | 49 | 21.3 |
| 5,000 to 6,999 | 29 | 10.5 | 55 | 23.9 |
| 7,000 to 8,999 | 7 | 2.5 | 33 | 14.3 |
| 9,000 to 10,999 | 9 | 3.3 | 26 | 11.3 |
| 11,000 to 15,999 | 7 | 2.5 | 28 | 12.2 |
| Over 16,000 | 6 | 2.2 | 25 | 10.9 |
| No answer | 26* | — | 71* | — |
| Percent Base | | 275 | | 230 |

* Not counted in percent base

to have low taxes. The likelihood is great, however, that their limited financial resources and fear of poverty in the future have constricted their social life space beyond that created by their background deficiencies. Surprisingly, only twenty percent of the respondents report their financial condition to be "really restricted," while twenty-five percent are only "rather short" and a large fifty-four percent are "comfortable," leaving only one percent who admit to being "fairly wealthy." Certainly many are living at a time of high inflation on incomes far inferior to those they enjoyed at the prime of their financial condition.

## SUMMARY

In summary, the widows whose life styles and social roles are being examined form a random sample of women in this marital status who are fifty years of age or older living in the Chicago metropolitan area. They are more likely to resemble widows in other large metropolitan areas than their counterparts in small towns or rural districts. They are relatively uneducated, with, of course, some exceptions, and they tend to have a very restricted family income. They live alone or with an unmarried adult or no longer married offspring. Most are heads of these households. They have been widowed long enough to have made their major role changes, that is, to have re-engaged in society after the period of disengagement which follows the death of the husband. Some have gone through additional role changes voluntarily, or as a consequence of shifts in life circumstances. What is now needed is an in-depth analysis of the major social roles now performed by these women: the vestiges of the role of wife, and the modified roles of mother, kin member, friend, and participant in the community. The presentation in this book deals with these roles in exactly that order, starting with the role of wife.

# 2

# Widowhood As the Last Stage
# in the Role of Wife

## BACKGROUND

Involvement in a social role consists of at least three major stages: that of *becoming* (Becker: 1953; Lopata: 1966, 1971) the social person who will carry out the functional and relational duties of the role; that of *being* the person; and that of *disengaging* oneself from this activity and identity set. The entrance and exit stages may be so distinct as to form separate roles. A sociology major in an undergraduate school performs a role different from that of a sociology professor and from that of a retired sociologist. The role of student is a distinct one, but the stage of retired professor is not really a functional role—just a vestige of the *shrinking circle* phase of the role of professor. The active stage of a role varies by many factors, the most basic being the significance of this role for the social person and for members of the social circle who interact with him as he carries out its duties. The factors influencing variations in the phasing-out stage are still the least studied by sociologists, except in research dealing with retirement.

The process of becoming a social person within a specific role involves several substages which insure that the future participants come into contact, test and accept each other, learn to carry out the duties and to receive the rights, and start the process of relating with each other. Each candidate for a role must either build his own social circle, search out an existing one and convince it of his qualifications, or accept the invitation of people who need a central figure to coordinate their functional inter-action. Testing processes are initiated by representative recruiters, such as employment agencies, or by some segment of the circle, as by patients in the case of a private practice doctor. A decision of mutual acceptance must be reached by the future partners in the relation and should be communicated to all others who are expected to become involved in the role. For example, the mate-selection process in America takes place only between the woman and the man who are making their choices, but members of the society and of their future circle may have some control or at least an indirect influence.

The stage of entrance into a role is often accompanied by a gathering of the necessary objects and symbols and by a preliminary learning process. Gestures indicating movement in and out of this role in the course of daily life become developed and acknowledged, especially when individuals are involved with each other in more than one set of relations. Roles vary in the pervasiveness of the demands they make on participants as well as in their specificity or determinateness. Many factors contribute to variations in role performance by several persons who supposedly carry out similar roles; the function of the social role of medical doctor is to examine, diagnose, and prescribe treatment for preserving or restoring the health of patients, but individual doctors vary considerably in the way they weave their task duties into systems of relations with all segments of their social circles. The history of the role—the incidents and impressions from initial encounters—contribute considerably to the interactional behavior between partners in each social person's social circle. Thus, the becoming stages of trial-and-error and of testing are very important for the way a role develops.

Entrance into a social role requires changes in life style. Other sets of relations within the cluster of each participant must be adjusted to free the expenditures of time, energy, and action that the new role requires. Roles judged important are expected to involve the identities of those concerned. The culture of the whole society, or of the sub-group which shares the knowledge of any social role, contains an image of the ideal or typical role performer, an image which the person has to accept as his own or toward which he must maintain *role distance*. The latter stance, described by Goffman (1961), is one of refusal—communicated to others in various ways—to identify with all or certain aspects of the image of the typical role performer. Thus, housewives in American society frequently declare that they are not typical of the standard social person in that role, and many use other means of *role distance*.

Some social roles require only the token involvement of declared membership, with minimal interaction. A role can atrophy simply by not being called into use, but the stage of leaving it usually requires a new definition of the situation and procedures for the immediate or gradual breaking off of the set of relations that form it. Most circle participants demand a clear declaration of intent to stop carrying out the duties and receiving the rights, and many roles have highly institutionalized procedures for the phasing out of social persons. The effects of having a role may linger for a long time, with duties or status remnants recalling the past at moments. General MacArthur's famous statement that "Old soldiers never die, they just fade away" is symbolic of the gradual process by which some elements of a role may be dropped. Although some situations call for the immediate cessation of a social role, as arrest and imprisonment, or firing from a job, most people are allowed some flexibility in disengaging from all the social relations of a particular social role. This chapter examines the development of the social role of wife and concentrates on the phasing-out stage caused by widowhood, a condition of life experienced by most women.

## THE SOCIAL ROLE OF WIFE: CHICAGO STYLE

### Becoming a Wife
The role of wife is deemed a very important one for women in American society. The waves of studies involving urban and suburban women who are engaged in the complex of wife-mother-housewife roles indicate that the stage of *becoming* a wife was of great personal significance for most of them (Lopata: 1971b). Several other studies (Winch: 1963; Hartley: 1961, 1964; Coleman *et. al.*: 1961; Rose: 1961; Rossi, A.: 1965; Ginsberg: 1966) verify the fact that most girls—from all but the latest vintage—have traditionally seen themselves primarily as future wives and mothers, although with a relation rather than a task focus. Recent trends may be changing the pattern, but most wives in America never planned for a career, for single status, or for competing roles. None of the research indicates that women who enter marriage organize their plans with the expectation of having to phase out of this role through divorce or widowhood.

The process of becoming a wife involves some difficulties, partly due to a dilemma between the personality-focused process of mate selection and the traditional formality of relations expressed in the title of Mrs. John Jones. Most women lead multi-dimensional and independent lives prior to marriage. Such a background was even typical of the widows forming the basis of this book: 74 percent of them had worked away from the home before marriage, and all but a few had gone to school. This means that they functioned in an individualistic manner, establishing and maintaining their own identities and relations. Peer interaction and friendship were focused around a premarital set of identities publicly symbolized by a family name preceded by a personal name. The significance of marriage for the woman is symbolized by the change from her being Miss Mary Smith to becoming Mrs. John Jones. The name is new; it wipes out the woman's past and it camouflages the continuity and individuality of her personal identity.

When asked how the event of marriage changed their lives, the homemakers developed whole lists indicating dramatic shifts in social relations, in life circumstances, and particularily in the self. Getting married was considered by them as one of the *rites de passage* from girlhood into adulthood, bringing responsibility, maturity, and all the symbols of such a status. In retrospect, many tied this event immediately to entering the roles of housewife and mother, which are regarded as two of the consequences of becoming a wife.

### Being a wife

What happens to a woman in the many years of wifehood, in terms of identity, depends on how important that role is to her, the personality of her husband, and the life style that the couple builds out of their resources and interactions. The kinds of relations women develop with their husbands and with others connected with the role of wife vary considerably in American society by social class (Lopata: 1971a; Blood and Wolfe: 1960; Blood: 1969; Komarovsky: 1964). A number of background and life style variables contribute to a great heterogeneity of behavior in this role, even within the same class. Education was a major class factor that separated the Chicago area wives into different categories. The education, occupation, and income of the husband also provided relevant influences, sometimes even offsetting the poorer education of the wife; that is, a highly positioned husband can impose upon his wife or socialize her into higher styles of life than her own schooling would normally enable her to handle. Wives of men in the top occupations tend to be multidimensional in their relations in marriage, more strongly involved in the mate's work, both directly and psychologically, and interacting more in his other social roles. Lower-class, uneducated women tend to be task-oriented, restricted in their involvement in the man's life to his time at home, and hostile to men in general. Racial differences are apparent in this class level because, although lower-class wives of both black and white races tend to be antagonistic, the former complain that men are lazy and unfaithful, while the latter object to attempts to enforce patriarchal authority on them.

Some wives perceive the set of relations in this social role as clearly unique and separated from the roles of mother and housewife; others lump all their sets of obligations in the home into one package, defining their lives as a constant round of work "for the family." The less educated and, in general, the lower-class women either refrain from relational involvement in their husband's work, or restrict it to "nagging him so he gets a better job." They see their main contribution to the family as keeping the men out of trouble or making sure that they take advantage of economic opportunities. As in Mirra Komarovsky's (1967) *Blue Collar Marriage,* communication between husband and wife increases with higher education, even within the lower classes. All indications are that lower-class women participate less than their higher class counterparts in the process of *reality construction,* described by Berger and Kellner (1970), by which self-identities and the symbolic world are redefined by a husband and wife team in constant interaction. Thus, lower-class women seem to be affected in their identities less by marriage than are middle-class women (Lopata, 1971c).

Interaction between an urban husband and wife involves not only home-based activities but also exchanges with neighbors, other couples, and the community at large. Each urban or suburban area develops and institutionalizes its own levels and forms of *neighboring,* influenced strongly by the class of its residents. For example, lower-class wives who are neither members of a tight ethnic community nor long-term residents of a relatively homogeneous area tend to view neighbors with suspicion; thus, if they interact at all, they limit contact to unplanned encounters. Invitations to homes and to planned events such as luncheons are more typical of middle and upper classes. In general, husbands tend to do less neighboring than their wives, restricting themselves to casual meetings or work-connected exchanges. Among the upper three classes they also participate in organized events bringing selected neighbor couples together.

Not only neighboring, but other leisure-time activities are more likely to be carried out in couple companionate interaction as the social class of the husband and wife increases in status. Couple *friendships* are brought into companionate interaction by the wife through her contacts, by the husband from work or associational memberships, or by both from mutual contact in couple-involving events. Such relations tend to be symmetrical among all partners and the activities are shared equally. Sex-segregated interaction still occurs in the middle classes in leisure hours, but for women it tends to be limited to situations of food preparation or removal and for lower-class families certain times are ritualized as "the boys' time" or "the girls' night out." People with newly recognized upward mobility tend to engage in sex-segregated activity more frequently than couples who have been fully socialized into the middle class. The latter are more likely to engage in activities which can be shared by men and women together. In fact, the absence of either a man or a woman unbalances the interaction, so that single people, whether they be never married or divorced or widowed, are often unwelcome in such encounters. Thus, couple companionate interaction with friends or neighbors, forming the major part of leisure-time activity for the middle and upper class women, becomes strained or unavailable if they lose the husband, as we shall see in Chapter Four. The fund of sociability which Nelson (1966) found implicit in Elizabeth Bott's (1957) social network seems to vary considerably for American urban couples, with lower-class wives being more socially isolated than their better positioned counterparts and less involved in the lives of their husbands.

The differences of involvement of husbands and wives in each other's lives by social class are reflected in the orientations women have toward their different social roles. Housewives who were studied prior to the widowhood research were asked to rank the various roles performed by women in order of importance. Those most likely to assign the greatest importance to the role of wife were the very young and newly married, those in their forties, and those married to successful husbands who were themselves holding outside jobs.

If employed, the husband-oriented wife usually has no children or only adult offspring; if she is a suburban housewife, she usually has only one small child and has not as yet shifted to a focus on the role of mother. The suburbanite who consistently places the role of wife in first order of importance, no matter how many children she has, is married to a man with a professional or other graduate degree and a high income. And, finally, the husband-oriented wife tends to be better educated than the woman who ranks the role of mother, housewife, or "family maintainer" as the most important.

In sum, these studies of wives support the conclusion of others (Burgess, *et. al.*: 1963; Blood and Wolfe: 1960; Blood: 1969; Komarovsky: 1953, 1967) that there is a trend toward a companionate and multi-dimensional relation in marriage, experienced most often by the more educated couples who lead middle- and upper-class lives. While this tendency is breaking down formal role interaction and the barriers that have traditionally separated the man's world and the woman's world, it is also increasing the emotional investment of both partners in the marital relation.

Ideally, from the point of view of sociological methodology, the same women interviewed as wives should have been followed into widowhood. Unfortunately, such a research design was not possible. While the prior studies had been of women in the *expanding circle* and the *full-house plateau* (Lopata: 1965; Lopata: 1971b) stages of the role of housewife,[2] the gap in our knowledge about the final stage in the life cycle, that of the *shrinking social circle,* is filled by new respondents.

## BECOMING A WIDOW

### Background Characteristics

The 301 Chicago area respondents and the numerous other women who wrote letters and diaries and who discussed their widowhood at great length, alone with an interviewer or with the help of friends and relatives, were widows at that particular time of their lives. Their husbands were dead, and they had not remarried. The time of life when widows enter the phase-out stage in the role of wife has a great deal of influence upon what they experience because of that event and upon the roles they have to undertake or have available for re-engagement in a society which has so many alternative involvements.

The respondents, half of whom are between the ages of fifty and sixty-four, the other half being older, are not representative of all the women who have been widows, because those who remarried are absent from this study. This means that the respondents who had been widowed during their third decade of life are the survivors of all women who were widowed at that age. The majority (sixty percent) of women whose husband died around 1945 were able to find new mates (Bernard, 1956). This is an important point which must be kept in mind during the analysis; it helps to explain why so many of the respondents who had been widowed early express negative feelings toward their late husband and many other people. Their attitudes kept potential spouses away; the failure to remarry has made them more bitter than women widowed later in life, or they went through more unpleasant experiences than those who remarried or the other persons in our sample who were widowed later in life.

As observed by Bernice Neugarten (1968) and Irving Rosow (1967), age at widowhood is an important factor in determining the attitudes and life styles of women, because the older they were at that time the more opportunity they would have had to rehearse this new life situation. The women whose spouse was one of the first to die in their social environment are likely to find this event much more traumatic than would women who already had some widowed friends. The process of anticipatory socialization prepares people for future life changes, enabling them to rehearse their behavior. There is also the possibility, posited by Cumming and Henry (1961) from a study of residents of Kansas City, that some women who are widowed late in life have a "society of widows" with whom they can pleasurably associate when given freedom from the daily routine of married life. Older women may actually experience an increase in status (Cumming and Henry: 1961) with widowhood, while younger ones may feel a strong drop in social position as they find themselves outside the flow of social life of their married friends when the husband dies.

Widows now living in metropolitan Chicago are most likely to have been in the same or nearby dwelling prior to the husband's death. Half of the respondents resided in the same unit; twelve percent were in the same neighborhood; twenty-five percent in some other part of the same metropolitan area; and only fifteen percent had resided in other parts of the United States. (See Table Set A, Appendix B.) This is a very low mobility rate, in view of their average length of widowhood of 11 years', one contradicting the stereotype of the widow as a person who immediately removes herself from the location containing such unpleasant memories. The fact that such a low proportion of widows had previously resided in other regions is less surprising when one considers that major moves made by female adults are usually connected with shifts in male occupational roles.

Older women also tend to remain in the same residence after the death of the husband more often than do the young, the proportion increasing with age at widowhood. Two-thirds of the respondents who reached widowhood when they were seventy-five years of age or over are still in the same dwelling. The oldest, of course, have the fewest years in which to live as widows and to move, when compared to women widowed in their thirties or forties. The younger the widow, the more apt she is to move to a place where she can start a new life. In fact, the younger the widow, the greater the probability of dramatic changes in life style.

Half of the 148 widows who moved after reaching this marital condition had been living in a house prior to that time. (See Table 2 of Appendix B.) The relationship of residency to ownership points to the fact that those respondents whose husbands survived until the wife was in her sixties were most apt to have obtained ownership of their home. (See Table B of Appendix B.) The likelihood of ownership decreases with age at widowhood, so that only one of the ten respondents who were widowed at seventy-five years of age or over lived at that time in a home she owned. The life cycle of home ownership of these generations of women is indicated by these figures. Women fifty years of age or older widowed young in life were apt to be living in apartments or renting a home, and the very old, to have returned to such a location. At the present time, over a third of the respondents live in a house and only one-fifth are residing in large apartment buildings containing ten or more units. The pattern of residency and ownership indicates that women are not likely to buy homes after the death of the husband. If they ever owned one in their lives, they obtained it after years of saving, but before widowhood.

In view of the known statistics of the study's generations of urbanites, it is difficult to accept the widows' reports on highest family income (see Table 12, p. 52). They do not fit the averages for those occupations, in the year for which they were claimed, nor do they match current funds (although the last-named characteristic is not necessarily dependent upon the other two variables). The problem of weighing reported income by the standard of living figures for the year in which it was earned is complex and beyond the scope of this study. Suffice it to say that almost half of the respondents reported incomes of $7,000 or over at the height of their family earnings, although that was many years ago and although most had been married to men with lower occupational positions and had not themselves contributed evenly or highly to family funds.

## Death of the Husband

Most of the husbands (sixty-two percent) were working at their usual jobs just prior to their death or last illness. (See Table Set B of Appendix B.) One-fourth had already retired and one-tenth were working in other than their usual jobs. Of those who were employed regularly, at usual or new jobs, a fifth had not been ill sufficiently long to have taken time off work, another fifth had been ill for one to thirteen days, ten percent for fourteen days to eight weeks, fourteen percent for three to five months, ten percent for six to eleven months, and twenty-nine percent for a year or more. These figures dispel another misconception about widowhood—that of the husband having been retired and ailing for many years prior to his death. Most of the men had been working full time until their last illness. This does not mean that death occurred immediately, since forty-four percent of the men who were regularly employed had been unable to carry out the duties of the job for varying lengths of time due to illness. In fact, almost one-third of those officially listed as working at their main occupation had been prevented from carrying out its tasks for a year or more.

The illness preceding death of the husband had been handled through hospital or home care, or both. The Chicago area husbands had been hospitalized for the following amounts of time: twenty-four percent for less than a month; fifteen percent for from one to two months; and fifteen percent for three months or longer. The remaining husbands had not spent any time in the hospital prior to their death. In spite of the theory that illness and death have been removed from everyday view to the social isolation of the hospital (Strauss and Glazer, 1968), many of the Chicago area widows had taken care of their husbands at home during the last illness (see Table 13).

Over a half of the respondents (159) did not care for their husbands at home, in eighty-five cases because all of the care took place away from

TABLE 13: LENGTH OF TIME THE RESPONDENT CARED FOR
HER HUSBAND AT HOME DURING HIS LAST ILLNESS

| Length of Time | Number | Percent |
|---|---|---|
| 1 to 13 days | 16 | 12 |
| 14 to 27 days | 8 | 6 |
| 4 to 8 weeks | 27 | 20 |
| 3 to 5 months | 18 | 13 |
| 6 to 11 months | 13 | 10 |
| 1 year or more | 54 | 40 |
| No answer | 6* | |
| Not appropriate | 159* | |

Percent Base = 136
* Not counted in percent base

the home and in thirty-eight cases because the husband died suddenly.
Thirty-six women found the question inappropriate because of unique
features of the husband's death, such as prior divorce or separation, and
six respondents did not specify the length of time they cared for their
husband at home.

The fact remains that forty percent of the remaining widows, or one
sixth of the total, had a sick husband at home for a year or more. Fear
of death prevents public recognition of the high probability of such care
in connection with marital duties. Most women do not obtain any training in the medical care of offspring or spouses until an emergency occurs;
most do not even know the "old-time" home care treatments which
formed part of traditional culture. The current emphasis on hospitalization leads Americans to assume that the ill never have to be cared for
at home, a premise which these statistics show to be false. Hospitals are
often overcrowded and older people are unwilling or unable to go to
them; nursing homes create unpleasant impressions or have highly negative stereotypes surrounding them and are very costly. Thus the family
home remains the only place for many of the ill, particularly for those
with chronic diseases.

Adult children living in separate households can contribute only
temporary relief in the care of an ill parent, while the spouse has the total
responsibility placed on him or her. We asked the respondents how much
help they obtained from their children during the husband's last illness
(see Table 22, Ch. 3). Thirty-one percent of the widows found the question about children's help inappropriate, because the husband had not
required care, because they have no children, or because the offspring
had been too young at the time. Merely half of the only children were
able to help their mothers during this crisis time. Women having more

than one child report that the most help was given by the oldest offspring, but that this aid was not frequent if the offspring lived away from home. Only one-fifth stated that their in-laws assisted often during the husband's last illness, eight percent receiving such help "seldom," and forty-one percent, "never." Thirty percent of the respondents either have no in-laws or found the question inappropriate for other reasons. Thus, most of the widows took care of their late husbands alone, unless there was another adult living in the house at that time.

The probable need to care for an ill husband looms as one of the reasons why some widows do not wish to remarry. The following description of a nightmare of prior care was given by a woman who said "No" when asked if she contemplated remarriage:

> "Well, my husband was sick for eleven years and was in bed for seven and couldn't move, so I didn't have too much (social) life—I could only leave him for a few hours when he was asleep because the doctor said I had to. He said I would go crazy if I didn't. I had a hospital bed in the living room for seven years and I slept on the davenport . . . he had strokes, a lot of small strokes. I don't think he was paralyzed—but he just couldn't move—so I had to feed him and move him so often—and things like that." Question: "Was he able to speak?" "At first a little, not very much, in fact toward the end he got so he didn't know me . . . except once in a while . . ."

Most of the husbands had died of a heart condition or cancer, which can be prolonged ailments, but only one-fourth of the respondents agreed that: "My husband and I pretended we did not know how sick he really was." Twenty-nine percent found the statement inappropriate, presumably because they did not know of the illness, while almost a half found it false. Unfortunately, we do not know if this means that the couple had not known that the husband was so ill, or that they were aware of the facts without a pretense of ignorance. In any case, one-fourth of the respondents lived through what we must assume was a very difficult period of time during which they knew that the husband was seriously ill, while they kept up the game of pretending that nothing was the matter . Some of the in-depth interviews contain rather detailed explanations of situations where pretense was not attempted. Most of the women who were aware of the serious nature of their husband's illness and whose mates were also cognizant of the fact recommended such openness. One respondent specifically suggested that all doctors tell both the husband and the wife, and that they share the burden of such information with each other. The man is then given a chance to arrange his affairs and, if need be, to train his wife for competent management of those aspects of life which had been his province before the illness. Also, such shared knowledge would enable the wife to do those things for her husband which would make his last days more pleasurable or at least less difficult and which would relieve her of part of the guilt experienced by most survivors.

One of the facts discovered by Peter Marris (1958) about new widows of Londoners who had died before reaching the age of fifty was that many felt very angry at the doctor and the hospital staff for not preventing the death. As a result of this finding, the Chicago area widows were asked to respond to the following statement: "I felt angry at the doctor and the hospital for not doing enough for my husband when he was ill." Nineteen percent of the respondents found this declaration irrelevant, presumably because the husband had not been cared for by a doctor or within a hospital prior to his death. An unexpectedly small proportion, twelve percent, found the statement to be true. This pattern of response may be due to the fact that most of the women had been widowed for many years and they may have forgotten or repressed their earlier emotions. It is also possible that this fairly uneducated, older aggregate of Americans simply does not question the established authority of the medical profession. Moreover, many lower-class housewives are fatalistic about death: people die, and there is very little anyone can do about it.

To summarize, the death of the husband had occurred five years ago or more in the case of sixty-eight percent of the Chicago area widows. Many changes in social roles and in life styles have taken place since that time, and almost half have been widowed for over a decade. At the time of the death, however, most of the women were living with their first husband, who was employed at his regular job or at least working full time, although the final illness required some lay-off from work and care at home. The occupations of the husbands were varied, ranging all the way from laborer to professional, with concentrations in craft, operative, service, and managerial positions.

The death of a husband does not automatically dissolve the social role of wife. Duties to the deceased remain; the process of breaking up the total social circle involved in the role takes time; women have to modify their self identifications; all the social roles in which the late husband participated or which were affected by his presence must be changed. These phases are particularly complex in the lives of middle-class American widows who were apt to have been involved with the husband in a multiplicity of social roles. Most members of this society, however, are not accustomed to analyzing their lives in terms of separate role categories—this concept is a sociological invention. Therefore, a women whose husband has died does not generally recognize the fact that all or most of her roles are modified. She simply experiences loneliness or frustration in her relations to others, and only detailed examination of the meaning of such experiences enables us to analyze them into role components.

## Grief

The death of a marital partner, particularly within Western culture, has strong psychological and social consequences upon the survivor. The grief and bereavement effects of the loss of a significant other have been studied by several psychiatrists and psychologists. Parkes (1964a and b, 1965), Maddison and Walker (1967), Maddison (1968), and Weiss (1969) of the Harvard Medical School have been continuing Eric Linde-mann's (1944) analyses of "grief work," with special emphasis upon "bad outcomes" in adjustment to conjugal bereavement. According to Maddi-son and Walker (1967), "A widow is faced with two concurrent tasks: she is required, through the processes of mourning, to detach herself sufficiently from the lost object to permit the continuation of other rela-tionships and the development of new ones; at the same time, she has to establish for herself a new role conception as an adult woman without a partner."

C. Murray Parkes (1965:3) found that "typical reaction to bereave-ment" begins with a period of numbness, followed by wave-like attacks of yearning and distress with autonomic disturbance, which are aggra-vated by reminders of the deceased. Between attacks, the bereaved person is depressed and apathetic, with a sense of futility. Associated symptoms are insomnia, anorexia, restlessness, irritability with occasional outbursts of anger directed against others or the self, and preoccupation with thoughts of the deceased. The dead person is commonly felt to be present, and there is a tendency to think of him as if he were still alive and to idealize his memory. The intensity of such feelings begins to decline after one to six weeks and is minimal after six months, although for several

TABLE 14: LENGTH OF TIME OF GRIEF AFTER THE DEATH OF THE HUSBAND

| Length of Time | Number | Percent |
|---|---|---|
| Less than 1 month | 3 | 1.2 |
| 1 to 5 months | 14 | 5.7 |
| 6–11 months | 29 | 11.8 |
| 12 months | 73 | 29.7 |
| 13–23 months | 6 | 2.4 |
| 24 months | 39 | 15.9 |
| 25 months plus | 31 | 12.6 |
| Always, never get over it | 50 | 20.4 |
| No answer | 56 | 22.8* |

Percent base: 245
* Not counted in percent base

years occasional brief periods of yearning and depression may be pre-
cipitated by reminders of the loss.

The Chicago area respondents were not as consistent as the Harvard
Medical School psychiatrists in their definition of the length of time the
grief lasted or in the specificity by which they ended that phase (see
Table 14).

The time estimations are sufficiently spread out to indicate the lack
of a societally institutionalized period of grief. The statements explaining
the duration of this sentiment are also significant in that they vary considerably in the symptoms used to decide its termination. If the culture
were consistent about the definition of grief, the time and content judgments would be more similar. Some respondents feel that the waves of
grief which Parkes found present after the basic stage was completed are
proof of "perpetual" involvement in that sentiment, while others limit
the definition to the initial period of numbness and consistent depression.
Thus, one widow states "about six months," in answer to the question,
"How long does grief take?"; another responds with, "Well, you never
quite get over it—I wish he was here to tell him things." Thus, grief as
defined by psychiatrists is a set of sentiments most typically following the
death of a significant other or the absence of some important aspect of
life. The components and the length of each stage depend upon the
personal definition of what is a "normal" day-by-day feeling, rather than
upon a set list of symptoms. Such definitions are likely to be part of a
culture in which the definer is immersed and to depend on his perception
of the attitudes of reference groups. The widows' definitions of grief
indicate that, once the severe stage is over, norm expectations control the
situation and institutionalized termination dates or symptoms perform an
important function of moving the person out of this sentiment. Modern
society defines grief as a personal and individualized matter, without
admitting how highly it is institutionalized as a "must." Widows are
often left in undefined situations, thus creating anxiety and interfering
with the "grief work" by which past dependence upon the deceased is
reworked into new life patterns. Of course, there are widows reporting
no feelings of grief over the death of their husbands.

## The Funeral

The one aspect of widowhood which still remains relatively formalized
and specific in role expectations is the funeral, which takes place during
the widow's numbness period (see Gorer, 1965, however, for a statement
regarding the de-institutionalization of even this ritual). One of the
functions of the funeral is to insure that the body of the deceased is
buried or handled in a sanitarily appropriate manner in spite of the ex-

pected emotional instability of the immediate survivors. In addition, of course, the funeral accomplishes other functions: reminding the society of the deceased and building a collective representation (Durkheim, 1947) of him, especially in cases in which he can serve as a symbol of the group; uniting the survivors with new bonds in spite of the death; facilitating disengagement and temporary limbo location of those who are expected to have their lives disorganized by the event; and insuring the living that they too will be remembered. The last function is important. Fear of death is partly due to anxiety over illness and pain, partly caused by a concern over "non-being" and non-experiencing, and, to a fairly large degree, due to the haunting suspicion that no one will really be affected by one's permanent absence. Some of the first organizations started by Polish immigrants in America were insurance groups to which they paid regular fees in order to guarantee a "nice funeral" for themselves. The "Wake" or its equivalent ritual, during which friends and relatives come to "pay respects" to the deceased, accomplishes some of these purposes. Public expressions of grief are allowed at such times. Some societies expect the widow, occasionally with the help of other women, to wail or make other public mourning sounds. In American non-ethnic sub-groups crying is usually done quietly and the time is devoted to talk about the deceased, his life and his last days. The widow is expected to reminisce and to bring to the attention of the visitors any characteristics of her late husband she wishes remembered. The process of crystallizing the image of the deceased begins at this time through a selective attention to certain aspects of his appearance, behavior, and attitudes. The eulogy continues the creation of a positive picture of the life and character of the deceased. The whole process guarantees a continued social existence of the deceased.

The wake and the funeral reaffirm the group identity of the survivors, often with the help of religious collective representations extending all members into afterlife. They are often accompanied with food and drink, which facilitate the feeling of group identity and of shared emotional trauma, while insuring the revitalization of the living. Religious ceremonies emphasize the spiritual and continuing essence of man, and in even nonreligious rituals the "spirit" or essence is seen as hovering protectively over the survivors. The procedures purify the deceased, turning his spirit into a positive force unable or unwilling to harm the living.

The first duty of the widow to the deceased is to carry out the actions of the bereaved person, allowing other people to perform their set parts in the funeral rituals. The widow may be allowed to add idiosyncratic touches to the procedures, but these are not supposed to break the general sequence of events by which the dead are safely entombed. Modern societies use professional or religious roles, such as that of funeral director or priest, to insure that all funeral rituals are followed (Fulton: 1961; Habenstein: 1962; Mitford: 1963). The survivor may be expected to withdraw from active participation, even to modify her appearance in order to serve as a visible symbol of the bereavement; clothing color or style, hair length or arrangement, and other physical features may have to undergo permanent or temporary change. This aspect of the funeral is currently going through dramatic changes, although several respondents mentioned wearing black clothing.

The attempt to extend social existence beyond the physical life can be seen in the various means used to preserve the body of the deceased. The Egyptians developed complex procedures of mummification, but burial in a marked and frequented location, cremation and preservation of ashes, retention and public display of the skull, and many similar actions indicate that the human conception of the spirit is frequently anchored to physical objects. In many societies widows must insure that some symbols of their husbands are retained as reminders of his prior existence.[1]

Geoffrey Gorer (1965) concluded in *Death, Grief and Mourning* that mourning has become de-institutionalized in Western Europe and America. This process has resulted in problems for the survivors. Some of the Chicago area respondents expressed concern about undertaking certain activities, lest they be criticized by neighbors or other members of the community for moving out of mourning too soon.

This study did not go into the details of the funeral or grief as they were actually experienced, since these events often took place in the distant past. All that is now available for research is the memory of this traumatic period, as modified by subsequent situations and the present definitions and attitudes toward the world. This very modification is significant from a sociological standpoint, particularly when analyzed in conjunction with the factors influencing its direction and form.

The respondents were asked about the contributions of two sets of persons to the funeral—the children and the in-laws. Forty percent of the 301 widows did not answer the first question because they either had no children, only young offspring who were not expected to help, or only one child so that they could not compare contributions. Twenty-one percent of the widows had only one living offspring; sixty-four percent of these fifty-nine mothers found that child to have been very helpful, with only eight percent judging him or her of "little" help. Forty-eight of the 181 respondents who had more than one offspring could not decide which child gave the most and which the least assistance. Their refusal is very interesting, since most of them were easily able to evaluate their children's contributions in other aspects of life, and an outside observer could find obvious criteria by which to measure the help given by different persons to funeral arrangements. There are several possible reasons for the unwillingness to differentiate among children's help levels, all of which are connected with the widow's experience during the funeral proceedings. Grief in its first stage, that of numbness, prevents any realistic perception of the actions of others. Also, the ritual itself is effective in moving the widow into an institutionally desired limbo location outside of ongoing life, without which re-engagement in new roles and relations would not be possible. It is likely, also, that she refuses to make value judgments about an event sanctified in memory. A final possibility, one which would be worth testing by future research, is that widows expect, as one of their rights in the role of wife, a certain kind of cooperation from relatives and close friends during times of stress. If the procedures go smoothly, they define everyone as helpful; only deviants are labeled as uncooperative. Thus, judgment in retrospect of help during the funeral may be dependent on the presence or absence of a gap between expectations of help and perceived behavior of others. Children, only or multiple, are usually present and active in some way during the funeral of their fathers. This fact registers on the grief-enveloped widow as a contribution, without need for comparative evaluations.

The above theses concerning help during the funeral are supported by the widow's attitudes toward the behavior of in-laws at that time. In American society, in spite of the weakness of the patrilineal kin line, the family of the husband is still expected to assist in the funeral rites. The expectation that the husband's relatives should function as agents of assistance, although not as the principal actors at the ritual, was not fulfilled in the respondents' memories. Sixty-four percent of the Chicago area widows do not remember being helped at that time by their in-laws. Only thirty-six percent state that they received any help, while twelve women did not answer and twenty-five explained that they had no living in-laws at that time. Some of the widows who were not recipients of cooperative help from relatives of their late husband accepted geographical distances as the explanation. However, many women added comments in answer to the help question which reflected bitterness over the lack of cooperation on the part of in-laws. "They came to the funeral, that's all," stated one respondent who seems to have expected a more active involvement. One of the widows explained that she and her husband had never gotten along with her in-laws while he was still living and that she got no help whatsoever from them after his death. This whole set of comments is sociologically interesting and points to the fact that in this changing society in which old patterns are dissolving, funerals.

like weddings, can be a source of inter-family tension and relational breaks. They are usually seen as performing the function of unifying the family, but the fact that they can serve as crystallizing agents of strain should not be neglected.

## BEING A WIDOW

### Duties and Rights in the Role of Wife in Widowhood

In most parts of the world the widow has the right to expect help from her husband's kinfolk not only during the funeral, but for the rest of her life, unless she returns home or remarries. In addition to their obligations to her, she can usually count on the *in genetricem* rights inherited by her husband's male line, guaranteeing care of the affiliated offspring (Bohannan, 1963). As a result of such arrangements the widow receives support not only for herself, but for the children until they are of an age to contribute substantially to the unit and to the maintenance of their aging mother. In America's past, and in most places of the world, it is difficult, if not impossible, for a widow living alone or with small children to support herself. There are generally only three groups to which a woman can turn to obtain sustenance: her family of orientation, that of her husband, or her family of procreation. The latter consists of her children old enough to produce sufficient economic goods to meet their own needs as well as those of their mother and her younger children.

Some widows in American society who have no children, or very young ones, return to their families of orientation, obtaining economic support or help in child care while they work for wages. However, most of the respondents in the Chicago area did not wish such a shift into dependency, or did not expect help in housing and maintenance from their families. Like the widows studied by Peter Marris (1958) in London, they were even less anxious to turn to the families of their late husband, preferring independence to housing or even financial help. Having become accustomed to running their own homes, they did not wish to become again dependent on parents, and their relations with in-laws never seemed to be sufficiently comfortable to afford that direction of help. In fact, the wish for independence even prevents them from moving into the households of married offspring. "Family," which can mean either that of orientation or of procreation, gave financial help to only twenty-two percent of the widows after the death of the husband. Another four precent borrowed money from their families, but the total certainly does not indicate a wish to lean on kinfolk to solve problems created by widowhood. The changes in family structure and functions seem to have resulted, in the case of a widow at least, in independence from the in-laws as well as from members of her own family of orientation.

The desire for independence from in-laws and the failure by these relatives to assist the widow are both evident in the following table (see Table 15). The in-laws seldom help a woman and her children once the connecting link to them, the husband, is removed. Only one fourth

TABLE 15: PROPORTION OF CHICAGO WIDOWS RECEIVING
DESIGNATED LEVELS OF HELP FROM IN-LAWS IN
SELECTED AREAS OF LIFE

| Area of Help | Frequency of Help | | | Not Appro-priate % | Percent Base |
| | Often % | Seldom % | Never % | | |
|---|---|---|---|---|---|
| With children and home | 7 | 6 | 51 | 35 | 266 |
| By visiting or inviting her over | 24 | 27 | 36 | 12 | 275 |
| By giving her gifts or money | 9 | 11 | 62 | 18 | 273 |
| By giving children gifts or money | 7 | 10 | 50 | 32 | 269 |
| By visiting or inviting children over | 12 | 12 | 43 | 33 | 270 |
| By other contacts, help | 11 | 4 | 62 | 23 | 137 ⁻ |

of the respondents even see their in-laws with any frequency, and thirty-six percent "never" see theirs. Two-thirds never receive gifts or financial assistance from the relatives of their late husband. These figures demonstrate the weakness of the bond of the male line, showing that interaction by a woman with it is dependent upon her husband while he functions as their son and brother. Once he is gone, the woman pushes her roles as daughter-in-law and sister-in-law into the background. Her role of mother does not demand an active inclusion of her in-laws in her social circle.

The lack of in-law involvement in the life of a widow and her offspring is not surprising to sociologists familiar with Peter Marris' (1958) study, but it goes against the traditions of most societies of the world. The distributions accentuate the significance of the egalitarian American family, in that the widow is given the right to maintain herself and to lead a life independent of her in-laws. The fact that wifely duties do not extend to the family of the late husband is a highly symbolic indication of the degree to which the modern urban family is being modified into a nuclear unit. The hostility toward in-laws expressed by many respondents, however, indicates that the trend is not taking place without strain. The conclusion from the answers to this set of questions is that the women have mixed feelings, expecting some help which they did not receive, yet wishing independence in decision-making. It must be remembered that, although most women were widowed in their fifties, many were much younger, and almost all had at that time a living parent and sibling in-law. The fact that so few of the respondents feel that the in-laws helped them with the children must be added to the store of growing knowledge about the modified kinship group with its patterns of help across households. Recent research (see particularly all the contributions to Shanas and Streib, 1965) has exploded the myth of the isolated nuclear family in that kin assistance is documented, but this study questions its existence in the lives of widows and their in-laws.

One of the rights a wife still gains upon marriage in America is financial support for herself and her children by the husband. The culture assumes that this right persists after his death. Although seventy percent of the widows state that their husbands did not leave an estate, because they assume such a term applies only to a formalized will or a large inheritance, relatively many were able to maintain themselves after his death without using outside sources of support (see Table 16).

TABLE 16: SOURCES OF FINANCIAL HELP OBTAINED BY THE
WIDOW RIGHT AFTER THE DEATH OF HER HUSBAND

|  | % Use of That Source | |
| --- | --- | --- |
| *Source* | *Yes* | *No* |
| Continued to work | 23 | 77 |
| Had money on hand | 56 | 44 |
| Family helped | 22 | 78 |
| Borrowed from family | 4 | 96 |
| Borrowed from friends | 2 | 98 |
| Borrowed from bank | 1 | 99 |
| Went to work | 12 | 88 |
| Went on relief, welfare | 6 | 94 |
| Got into debt | 3 | 97 |

Percent Base = 280

Thus, most of the widows were able to survive the death of their husband in one way or another without turning to charity or official lending agencies. Over half had sufficient money on hand to cover the emergency. Yet their current income shows that a vast majority are below the poverty level. The management of finances accompanying the death of the husband thus seems to depend more on a restriction of expenditures than the wise manipulation of ample resources.

The duty to manage the funds inherited from the husband disturbed only a few of the widows, since most were not left with so much money that wise investment was required. One of the widows took a course in financial management in order to understand her husband's investments, but several complained about inability to handle their problems and about the quality of advice they received from others. Many claim to have been cheated of the little money they did get, even by people close to them, because they were so ignorant as to financial matters. Some respondents listed mistakes they feel they made, and an even larger number complained about advice offered by friends. Some reported complete alienation from a friend because of this problem. Others were victimized, by racketeers concentrating on widows, or heard about such situations from other people. They received telephone calls, or even visits from salesmen or people offering services which they did not need or for which they were grossly overcharged. In fact, thirty-nine percent of the respondents agree that "people take advantage of you when they know you are a widow," and eleven percent agree strongly.

The ignorance of financial matters experienced by widows is due to the traditional child-rearing and educational specialization typical of the older generations of American women. In addition, their husbands had often failed to acquaint them with their financial situations. The housewives in Chicago and the Detroit families researched by Blood and Wolfe (1960) present a pattern of financial management in which the higher the income of the family, the more likely the husband is to manage it alone, with the wife being ignorant of most of the arrangements. Even educated women rarely handle or understand investments outside of the household, since they are generally on an allowance system for meeting family expenses. Only in some cases where the husband knew he would not live much longer was the wife trained to take over his part of the financial management. Thus, the division of labor which assigns the husband duties outside of the home makes widowhood difficult.

Even widows who did not have large sums of money to manage often reported strain with friends and relatives over advice in the economic sphere of life. Many women who fear their own ignorance turn to people who are really not competent, because they do not have bankers or lawyers available to them. Others get conflicting advice and do not know which to accept, or make hasty decisions while waiting for help. Whatever action they undertake in such situations is often inadequate, if not completely inappropriate, and the widow feels she has failed her late husband, the children in trust for whom she holds the property, and herself. Awareness of such possibilities increases the widow's anxiety and frustration, which often turns into anger at herself and at the people who did or did not provide advice. In some cases, the widow's anger turns on her deceased husband for leaving his finances in a confusing condition or for leaving her so untrained. Few husbands, even if aware that they are dying, prepare their wives for the financial management of the resources they have accumulated.

However, the obligation to handle the economic wealth left by a husband without sufficient competence to do so does not face many of the older widows of the Chicago area. At least, sixty-nine percent of the respondents found false the statement that: "I did not know anything about our finances when my husband died." Seven percent found the question inappropriate, leaving a still rather sizable one-fourth who found the statement "true."

## Marriage in Retrospect

*"My Husband Was an Unusually Good Man."* The wife's duty to preserve the social existence of the deceased husband in a sanctified form is so effectively undertaken by the Chicago area widows that eighty-seven percent of them find true the statement: "My husband was an unusually good man." It must be remembered that these women form part of the aged segment of the population and that most of them had reached only the level of education and socio-economic status which places them in the social classes with high amounts of hostility toward men. They themselves frequently expressed such sentiments toward their husbands in other parts of the interview. One respondent, for example, repeatedly showed a negative attitude toward her late husband. She felt her marriage had been a mistake, because "My husband liked to go out all the time, and I liked to stay home." She was widowed at nineteen, when her husband was accidentally shot, and never remarried for fear that the second marriage might turn out as bad as the first. Yet even she checked "true" on the husband purification statement.

However, some women refused to bow to the custom of sanctifying the husband, and the relation between that attitude and many others of the "Relations Restrictive Attitude Scale" proved very interesting (see Table I in Appendix C). The woman who refuses to state that her husband was an unusually good man is likely to have had a sex-segregated relation with him—each had their own activities, and the wife knew nothing about their financial situation. She now feels that her friends are jealous of her, and that their husbands make sexual advances. Simultaneously, she agrees with the statement sanctioning sexual relations without plans for marriage. She likes living alone, is sorry for married friends whom she assumes lack freedom, finds this the easiest time of her life, and, in spite of the fact that her adult children make too many demands on her, is now more independent and freer than she was before widowhood. Women who do not think they had unusually good husbands also reject the idea that they have more in common with widowers than with other men they date.

By contrast, the woman who believes that her husband had been an unusually good man shared many activities with him while he was alive, knew their financial arrangements, does not like living alone, rejects the idea that other women are jealous and that their husbands are sexually aggressive toward a widow. She is much less likely to think that married friends should be pitied and does not find her current life easier than before or herself more independent and freer. She rejects the idea of sexual relations without marriage and does not complain that children demand too many favors. She believes that widows should not move soon after the death of their husband, that it is hard to make decisions alone, and that the greatest help she received in her period of grief was from her religious faith. Her attitudes toward others are not necessarily positive, since she thinks that people did not help her in the crisis following widowhood and that she must not depend on others. Her sanctification of the husband is carried over even to the sexual relations with him prior to his last illness, and she considers her marriage above average to the extent that no other marriage could match it. Thus, she tends to look on her past life as more desirable than the present and to resent her widowed condition. It is quite possible that her idealization of the past is contributing to her problems in facing the present.

There are some women who. although they agree with the majority concerning the excellence of their own late husband, do not follow the other attitudes. Almost half of the respondents who agree that their husband was exceptional like living alone; one quarter of them now feel sorry for their married friends, whom they assume to be lacking the freedom they are experiencing; and 103 out of the 247 now feel freer and more independent than in marriage. Also, there are forty-eight women who say the husband was good, but that the marriage was not so much above average that no second one could match it, and twenty-one who refuse to comment on the second statement. It can be assumed that the forty-eight hope to be able to find a second husband as good as the first.

One of the beliefs prevalent in American society is that the widow most likely to favor remarriage is one who was happy with her late husband. Yet the study of Chicago area widows indicates no significant difference between the women who feel obliged to declare their late husband as exceptionally good and the ones who do not, in terms of a desire for re-marriage (see Table 17). Only one-fourth of those now sanctifying their husbands want to marry another man.

Even women who refuse to state that their husband was an unusually

TABLE 17: AGREEMENT WITH THE STATEMENT "MY HUSBAND
WAS AN UNUSUALLY GOOD MAN," BY EXPRESSED
WISH TO REMARRY

| Husband Good Man | Row | Sums | Wish to Remarry | | |
| | | | Yes | No | No Answer |
| --- | --- | --- | --- | --- | --- |
| True | N | 254 | 53 | 201 | 8 |
| | % | | 21R | 79R | 3R* |
| | % | 92 | 96C | 90C | 81C* |
| False | N | 23 | 3 | 21 | 1 |
| | % | | 9R | 91R | 4R* |
| | % | 8 | 4C | 9C | 11C* |
| No answer | N | 13 | — | 13 | 2 |
| | % | | — | 100R | 15R* |
| | % | 5 | | 6C | 22C* |
| Column | N | | 55 | 222 | 9 |
| Sums | % | | 20 | 30 | 3 |

Percent base = 277
R stands for Row, C stands for Column
* Not included in percent base

good man reject remarriage. They explain that they do not like marriage
or that they are now free and independent and fearful of losing these
pluses in life.

Attitudes towards excellence of the late husband, categorized according
to the age of the respondent at the time she is widowed, reflect a puzzling
pattern which is recurrent in other attitude trends. In all but the oldest
years, women in the early years of the age decades are the least likely to
state that their husbands were exceptionally good. The reason for this
trend remains only a hypothesis, which should be tested by work specifically designated to isolate this tendency. This study indicates that
women who become widowed earlier than "normal," and particularly
while they are in the early years of a decade, either had poorer marriages
than women whose husbands survived longer or left them closer to a later
decade of life, or else they reevaluate the marriage in negative terms
because of being left alone at these stages of their life cycle. For example,
women widowed in their early forties are much lower than the average
in their estimation of the excellence of their husbands, and lower than
women widowed in their late forties or even late thirties. The trend is
even stronger in answer to the marriage evaluating question. Women
widowed in the early part of each decade are much less likely to agree
that "My marriage was above average and no second marriage could

match it" than women whose husbands died when they were approaching the next decade in age (see Table III in Appendix B).

*"My Marriage Was Above Average and No Second Marriage Could Match It."* The obligation to sanctify the husband does not necessarily carry over into a purification of the marriage. Only sixty-five percent of the total group of respondents agree that no second marriage could match the above-average quality of the first one (compared to eighty-seven percent who characterized their husband as "an unusually good man"). Ten percent cautiously refrain from any judgment, and twenty-five percent find the statement false. Again, the women who define their prior marriage as above average do not believe that a second one could not match it and are consistent in their responses to the "Would you like to remarry?" question (see Table 18).

TABLE 18: DISTRIBUTIONS OF AGREEMENT WITH THE STATEMENT "MY MARRIAGE WAS ABOVE AVERAGE AND NO SECOND MARRIAGE COULD MATCH IT" BY THE EXPRESSED WISH TO REMARRY

| Marriage Was Above Average | | Row | Sums | Wish to Remarry | | |
| --- | --- | --- | --- | --- | --- | --- |
| | | | | Yes | No | No Answer |
| True | N | 191 | | 26 | 165 | 5 |
| | % | | | 14R | 86R | 3R* |
| | % | 72 | | 53C | 77C | 71C |
| False | N | 73 | | 23 | 50 | 2 |
| | % | | | 32R | 68R | 3R* |
| | % | 28 | | 47C | 23C | 28C |
| No answer | N | 26 | | | | 4 |
| | % | | | 23R | 77R | 15R* |
| | % | 10 | | 12C* | 10C* | 57C* |
| Column | N | | | 49 | 215 | 7 |
| Sums | % | | | 18 | 81 | 3 |

Percent base = 264
R stands for Row, C stands for Column
* Not included in percent base

Thus, most widows who do not expect a second marriage to be comparable to the prior one do not want to remarry. Although less than one fifth of the respondents declare a wish to remarry, almost twice as many of the women who feel their marriage was not so superior are willing to try again. The specific explanations of why widows do not wish to remarry are interestingly related to the statement "My marriage was above average and no second one could match it." There is a definite tendency for the more favorable attitude toward remarriage to be expressed by women who either define their past marriage as not above average or who expect the next one to be able to match it. The past relation is sanctified by seventeen percent of those who answer the remarriage statement by "No, nobody would want me," twenty percent of those who state "No, I don't want to," forty-two percent of those who answer "Maybe," sixty-five percent of those who state "Yes, I hope so," and fifty percent of those who have definite remarriage plans.

The widows defining their former marriage as above average and not wishing to remarry explain their decision in many ways, including: "You can't trust the men available for remarriage," "Remarriage is no good," "It is not good for children to have a stepfather," "I don't want to care for another ill man," and "I'm free now." The reasons given may be rationalizations, that is, societally acceptable reasons for behavior which has other functions, rather than "true motives." Of sociological significance is the fact that the women who did not remarry because complex life circumstances prevented such action, need to explain to themselves and to others this fact. The reasons supplied give insight into the symbolic world of the widow, with explanations varying by social class and by the individual belief system. That a culture provides the generalizations which serve as justification for certain behavior is indicated by ethnic variations in the explanations. Widows living in communities in which there is a strong belief that remarriage is likely to turn out badly will be much more hesitant in looking for a next husband than women living among people who think mature marital relations are bound to be better than a single existence. For example, the Polish American widows in the Chicago area who were interviewed during the exploratory stage consistently expressed the belief that remarriage is bad, particularly if either partner has "any money," because then each is reluctant to spend it on the other or feels exploited. Rejection of a new husband is explained in such a situation as part of the duty to save the former mate's acquisitions for the offspring, rather than spending them in the enjoyment of a new marriage.

Several other attitudes about social relations tend to be connected rather strongly with the judgment of the late marriage (see Table I in Appendix C). The statement that "My marriage was above average and no second marriage could match it" seems to be oriented more toward the present life circumstances than the statement "My husband was an unusually good man." The current situation is seen as a drop in status from marriage, as financially restricted, and as problematic because of the need to make decisions. The woman who now feels that her marriage was good was generally older at widowhood than her attitudinal counterpart and has not experienced sexual propositioning from husbands of friends or jealousy from the wives (see Table III in Appendix C). It is interesting to note that widows who express dissatisfaction with their prior marriages are the most likely to be sexually propositioned by friends' husbands and to face jealousy, or at least to imagine that these are problems. Although wishing strongly for male companionship, the respondents who had good marriages believe that remarriages bring unhappiness.

*"My Sexual Relations With My Husband Were Very Good Until His Last Illness."* A third attitudinal question, aimed directly at the late marriage relation and bound to disturb traditionally reared older women, read as follows: "My sexual relations with my husband were very good until his last illness." In spite of the high proportion of women who declared that their husbands were unusually good men, only six out of ten of the respondents were willing to declare good sexual relations at that stage of marriage. One reason for this relatively low proportion is that twenty-two percent of the respondents refused to make any value judgment in this area of life. Hypothetically, these are likely to be women who did not enjoy their sexual relations or who would not admit such feelings. This leaves one-fifth who do not agree with the statement. The proportion of those who disagree is lower than the proportion evaluating marriage negatively, simply because so many widows refused to answer the question. Proportionally few felt sufficiently obligated to their late husband's memory to declare that one of the most intimate aspects of their marriage was excellent.

The age at widowhood of those women who found the statement about sexual relations to be true is again interesting in terms of decade and segment of decade fluctuations. The youngest and the oldest women were the least likely to define their sexual relations with the deceased as good prior to his last illness.

Agreement with the statement that sexual relations were good does not necessarily lead to a desire for remarriage, but the trend in that direction is very high (see Table 19).

Those widows who wish to remarry are more apt to define their sexual relations with the late husband as good than the women who do not want to re-enter the role of wife. The numbers within each cell are often too small to make conclusive generalizations, but the details of the answers suggest at least some hypotheses about the reasons women give for their stances. For example, the woman who feels that sexual relations with the late husband had been good is the most likely to reject remarriage because

TABLE 19: AGREEMENT WITH THE STATEMENT "MY SEXUAL
RELATIONS WITH MY HUSBAND WERE VERY GOOD
UNTIL HIS LAST ILLNESS," BY WISH TO REMARRY

| *Sexual Relations* | | | | *Wish to Remarry* | | |
| *Were Good* | | *Row* | *Sums* | *Yes* | *No* | *No Answer* |
|---|---|---|---|---|---|---|
| True | N | 172 | | 42 | 130 | 7 |
| | % | | | 24R | 76R | 4R* |
| | % | | 76 | 86C | 73C | 78C* |
| False | N | 55 | | 7 | 48 | 2 |
| | % | | | 13R | 87R | 4R* |
| | % | | 24 | 14C | 27C | 22C |
| No answer | N | 63 | | 6 | 57 | 2 |
| | % | | | 10R | 90R | 3R* |
| | % | | 28 | 12C | 32C | 22C* |
| Column | N | | | 49 | 178 | 9 |
| Sums | % | | | 22 | 78 | 4 |

Percent base = 227
R stands for Row, C stands for Column
* Not included in percent base

"No one would want me now" rather than for other reasons. None of the
respondents who explained their lack of wish to remarry in this way defined their sexual relations as not good. Since many had been widowed
for years, their self-perception in terms of aging might have led to a
feeling of sexual unattractiveness. Other women who praise their past
sexual relations are apt to be already planning on marriage or at least
not giving up their home. Women who refuse to judge their past sexual
relations are also likely to refuse to give a reason for not wishing to remarry. Finally, those women who now define their sexual relations with
the last husband as good, but who do not wish remarriage, include widows
who feel that "No man could be as good" and those who do not want to
repeat the experience of caring for an ill man.

Thus, in spite of the problems of widowhood, especially loneliness, most
widows learn to make the necessary adjustments to the extent of not wishing to re-enter marriage at this stage of life or not having much hope for
that possibility.

## PROBLEMS OF WIDOWHOOD

In spite of the extension of some elements of wifehood into widowhood,
the loss of the social role of wife and the cessation of interpersonal rela-

tions with her marital partner, as well as his removal from multi-dimensional involvement in her life, are bound to create major problems for the survivor. In fact, the higher her social status and the more she is representative of our modern, urban, industrialized and complex society, the more disorganized her life will become upon the death of her husband. This conclusion does not necessarily mean that her life will remain highly problematic or disoriented. In fact, while membership in a companionate marriage leads to greater transitional disorganization after the death of the spouse, the personality characteristics which led to that type of relation are likely to serve as a resource for new life styles. Before examining the various life styles of women phasing out of the social role of wife, it is necessary to study in greater detail the problems and compensations of widowhood as defined by those who are experiencing them. The respondents were asked: "In thinking over all your experiences since you have become widowed, what do you think is the most important problem of widowhood?" After the answer to this question had been fully probed by the interviewer, the following was asked: "What is the next most important problem of widowhood?" The coding of the answers utilized a set of categories developed out of the exploratory studies and included: loneliness, financial difficulties, problems in rearing children, etc. Early in the analysis of the answers it became apparent that the simple category of "loneliness" was insufficient, because of the great range of forms this sentiment took in the experiences of different women.[2] It finally became necessary to examine the content of the statements in greater detail. Some respondents were talking of missing their husbands as total persons with whom they had shared a very close and intimate relationship, while others were concerned with the absence of a partner in an activity or even of just a depersonalized presence around whom work could be organized. Whenever possible, the various forms of loneliness expressed by the respondents were listed separately. Unfortunately, since realization of the complexity of this sentiment was derived only inductively from the answers, sufficient probing of its meaning had often not been made in the field, so that many statements proved difficult to code.

Loneliness involves a dissatisfaction with the present level of social interaction, a definition of social relations as inadequate in quality or quantity. *Situational* loneliness tends to be experienced most strongly by people who had been involved in more intensive relations in the past, but who have not been able to retain or reproduce that level nor to modify their expectations of such interaction. In some cases no adjustment is possible, because of barriers in personality or circumstances which prevent the transformation of causal interaction into the desired closer relation, or because of an unwillingness to substitute partners. Most people in modern American society experience situational loneliness. Of course, people can be lonely because they are not involved in an imagined or expected level of interaction which they have never experienced. The outsider, the person fearing a stigmatic position, and the isolate who has not developed the ability of bringing people closer to him can be *chronically* lonely. A woman, lonely in marriage, who believes Cumming and Henry (1961) when they say that there is a gay society of widows waiting for her after the death of her husband is likely to find only continued loneliness. The young, the old, and the socially unskilled may in the highly integrated years of life dream of social interaction at a level or of a type which makes the available love and friendship seem unsatisfactory.

These facts of human loneliness exist in spite of a culture which still portrays the lonely as the deviant and the maladjusted, while "normal" people are supposed to be permanently enmeshed in fully satisfying relations with others. The result of this belief system is a lack of societally developed techniques to ease the periods of situational loneliness and to reverse chronic loneliness.

Widows who are situationally lonely report one or a combination of the following forms of missing a previously experienced level of social interaction. They are lonely for the husband as: 1) a total individual, a unique person; 2) an object of love; 3) the person making them an object of love; 4) a partner or companion in activities; 5) an escort in couple-companionate interaction; 6) "someone" with whom to talk; 7) a partner in a division of labor within the home or tying her to the economic or social world; 8) "someone" around whom work and time are organized; and 9) "someone" around the house. In addition, many widows feel lonely for a whole life style previously enjoyed or because they are unable to establish a new type of relationship or retain the level of one previously shared with friends. The interpersonal and very private loneliness which misses the husband for himself as a unique human being, not for what he contributed to the wife, is expressed very strongly by the more articulate respondents. Some women specified the fact that they wanted someone to love, or that they missed the man who treated them as something special and who loved them in a way children and friends do not. A widow whose husband had been ill for a long time misses his love prior to these last years: "Here I am so big and fat, and sometimes I'd be reading and would look up and he'd be sitting there looking at me. And I'd say 'What are you thinking about?' and he would say, 'Oh, I was just thinking how pretty you are.' " On the other hand, many widows miss having an escort and a companion in activities away from home. They do not like going out alone or with other women, since many public places in America cater to couples or to men, but frown upon unescorted females. Whatever the policy, the woman accustomed to being accompanied feels unhappy in situations which seem to her to demand an escort who is no longer available. Single women develop methods of obtaining escorts or of handling themselves efficiently without companions, but the widow has habits and feelings developed in marriage which make both solutions difficult.

Living alone, with no one with whom to discuss daily events, is hard on many persons accustomed to frequent conversational interaction. Interestingly, a rather large number of women miss having a person around whom they can organize their work. "I miss my husband, I am lonesome," states one respondent, who upon prodding adds, "I'm alone all the time . . . even when he was alive, we didn't go anywhere or do too much, but at least he was there to cook for, take care of. . . Now there is just me." Dinner-time becomes particularly difficult for widows, since wives organize their work in anticipation of the scheduled arrival of husbands. The right to have someone within the home to help in the tasks of its maintenance, which forms another side of the duties of the role of wife, is disrupted by the death of the husband. Not only does widowhood deprive a woman of an object for her duties of cooking and cleaning, but it removes the individual with whom the rights to reciprical action had already been established. While she cleaned, he repaired, solved electrical problems, and cut the lawn. The woman is left either with having to take over her late husband's duties or with finding someone else who will carry them out. Since other people in her social circles have already established their social relations with a component balance of rights and duties, the sudden demand that they undertake new duties for the widow may cause role strain. The person asked to do something for the widow has to change his work rhythm and may get into difficulties with people whom he or she served before. A daughter-in-law may resent her husband's sudden assumption of his father's duties to his mother in the home maintenance sphere. An additional factor which makes the removal of the work associate difficult for the survivor is the reluctance of many women to ask for help from others. A marriage is, in some ways, a bargained balance between duties and rights. Widows often have little to offer other people to attract them into a new relation meeting their needs. The needs of a married son or daughter or a friend are already met through arrangements similar to those she has just lost. Financial limitations may restrict the widow's ability to hire people to carry on the work previously done by the late husband. All these problems are summarized as "loneliness."

Also, the division of labor in traditional homes often resulted in passive dependence on the part of the wives. "Lonesomeness, for the kind of life you've had . . . your husband made all the decisions and took care of all the financial things, and [now] you have to take care of your own checks and banking and bills, and this is a problem, when you've never done this." This form of loneliness is very different from the one experienced by the "fat" lady quoted before, but it is very real to some women. Finally, the Chicago area widows, just like those studied by the Harvard Medical School Team (Maddison and Walker, 1967; Parkes, 1964, 1965) and by Peter Marris (1958), miss having "someone around," a presence in the house; someone moving around and available in case of emergencies. This is literally the fear of being alone.

The most lonely and frustrated respondents are the ones who expect someone to take over the relational or task duties previously performed by the husband, and who are without such help. The least desolate (Townsend, 1968) are those who have automatic immersion in a primary group, such as a kinship web, or who have satisfactory relations created newly in widowhood. The latter either redistribute the rights, duties, and sentiments focused on the husband among new subjects, or they create new relations which are more than substitutes for the past life styles. The type of woman able to build a new life is usually the more educated, middle-class or upper-class widow with a breadth of perspective and an initiating manner of role involvement which permits her to change her life to meet new needs.

Almost half of the widows list loneliness as their most serious difficulty, and a third name it as the second. Since each form of loneliness was coded separately, more than one reference may come from the same woman who can, for example, miss her husband as an escort to couple-companionate events and as a person. Widows are particularly lonely if they had to lower their self-image by taking a job inferior to a previous one, if she feels other forms of status loss, and if they wish for more male companionship. A satisfactory marriage relation seems to result in feelings of loneliness, but not necessarily in a rejection of remarriage. The concern is with being able to find as good a second husband.

The forms of loneliness which were most often mentioned by the respondents specify missing the husband as a person and as a partner in activities. In spite of the inadequacy of coding clues, patterns of emphasis emerge when the forms are run against background characteristics (see Table 20).

The most heterogenous group is the one which is subsumed under the "person" category, because the typical comment "I miss Jim" is an all-encompassing statement meaning different things to different people. Those using such a personal description of loneliness are apt to be widows of college graduates or respondents who are themselves service workers.

TABLE 20: FORMS OF LONELINESS LISTED AS A PROBLEM
OF WIDOWHOOD

| Lonely for: | First Mention | | Second Mention | |
|---|---|---|---|---|
| | Number | Percent | Number | Percent |
| Person of husband | 58 | 26 | 22 | 18 |
| Partner in activities | 63 | 28 | 35 | 29 |
| Someone around | 23 | 10 | 21 | 18 |
| Talking to someone | 14 | 6 | 5 | 4 |
| Someone to care for | 15 | 7 | 9 | 8 |
| Someone to do things for | 6 | 3 | 1 | 1 |
| Other people shun me | 29 | 13 | 19 | 16 |
| General loneliness | 13 | 6 | 8 | 7 |
| No answer | 1* | | 9* | |
| Not appropriate (not mention loneliness) | 79* | | 172* | |
| Percent Base = | 221 | | 120 | |

* Not counted in percent base

The explanations themselves vary by depth and degree of articulateness, since this category became a catch-all.

Those who miss having a partner in activities form a more homogeneous group. They had been dependent upon their husbands as companions in social interaction outside of the home and now do not have the skills, money, or self-confidence to undertake multi-dimensional activities on their own. Interestingly, women who are concerned with this aspect of loneliness are apt to have also lost a father or a sibling since becoming widowed and to have come from large families. Their constricted social life space is attributed to the absence of the husband not only as an activity-companion, but as its leader.

Those missing having "someone around" the house tend to be over-represented by black widows in the age decade of the forties and by those with only one to four years of formal education. They do not interact regularly with neighbors, are dependent on accidental contacts, believe that they "seldom" received help from their in-laws since the husband's last illness, and that remarriage is not good because "men can not be trusted." They want a "live body" in the house, rather than active interaction, but list independence as a major compensation of widowhood.

Those who miss having someone around with whom they can talk are expressing a more active desire for interaction. They are disproportionately represented by high school drop-outs, whose husbands had the same amount of formal training. Only a "couple" of their friends are also widows, and they fear living with married children because they do not trust themselves to avoid criticizing or overreacting emotionally to the behavior of the other generations. These seem to be women experiencing status decrystallization, in that they fit into more than one social class in different aspects of their lives, who wish for an associate with whom situational strains can be "talked out." Finally, mention should be made of widows who find loneliness a major problem because of missing someone around whom their work can be organized. They are most likely to be white, in their forties, with several living siblings seen only occasionally and without interaction with their neighbors. The overall image is of rather lower-class, quiet, and non-initiating women, who are basically task-oriented and have problems in taking on new social relations or roles.

Other problems besides loneliness are listed by the Chicago area widows. These include financial difficulties, child rearing, decision-making, shortage of time, and self-pity. Black respondents are twice as apt as their white counterparts to find widowhood entirely lacking in problems (thirteen percent compared to six percent). The younger women and the blacks of most ages find money a problem, and the latter category of respondent is worried less about loneliness than is the white. One reason may be that these women were less emotionally dependent on the husband, as evidenced by their report of more strains in marriage. Money was listed as the major difficulty by one-fifth of the respondents and as the second problem by another third. The most likely of all categories of population to list this as a problem of first magnitude are the blacks in their sixties, women with five to seven grades of completed education, those who worked most of the time during marriage, widows who changed their working pattern during the husband's last illness, and respondents who went to work after widowhood at the same level of job as they held before this event. These women took specific actions to alleviate the financial problems, which were acute. The proportion of respondents worried about finances goes down as the late husband's educational achievement goes up. None of the wives of Jewish men expressed a concern about money as the major problem of widowhood, while one-quarter of the widows of Protestants, and a similar proportion of widows of men of any religion who considered their affiliation "very important" focused on this problem. Not surprisingly, women who had to care for their husband at home, who had no money on hand upon his death, and who define themselves now as financially "rather short" or "really restricted" find money to be a major problem of widowhood. Only a few of the respondents who define their current finances as "comfortable" mention money in answer to the problems of widowhood question. This distribution is consistent with that of the reported highest income. There is a steady decrease of the proportion of women listing money as a problem of widowhood as the amount of the highest past income increases. One-fourth of those who did not know anything about their finances at the time of the husband's death and of those who led sex-segregated lives in marriage stress economic problems. In summary, this concern is prevalent among women who never had much money, who experienced a drop of income, and who led traditional and restricted lives in the past. Inadequately trained, they found the maintenance of the family without its main breadwinner a heavy burden of widowhood.

The most likely to judge raising a family as a major problem of widowhood are women whose husbands died suddenly in accidents or when the wife was in her forties and the children were young; these women did not experience anticipatory socialization for widowhood. Only nine percent of the total group of respondents mention this problem, but they are disproportionately women with a high level of education whose husbands obtained a professional or other graduate degree. The same women are likely to see the post-funeral changes in themselves as increased activity and independence. The distributions are not surprising. They were widowed during the full-house plateau stage of the role of housewife. Their high educational achievement and socio-economic status made them very aware of the difficulty of rearing and socializing children without the help of the father. After widows pass this stage of life, they find their existence easier and look upon the past with a realization that their concern with motherhood has left them little time to feel lonely.

The few respondents who state that widowhood brought no problems are distributed unevenly among the various sub-categories of Chicago area women. Blacks now in their eighties in age, for example, are disproportionately represented in this group. They expected to be widowed, because of the high male death rate in their community, and found no unanticipated difficulties in dealing with this change in their life circumstances. Women who believe that they have learned to take advantage of the freedom of life afforded by widowhood are also apt to define this marital situation as relatively problem free. Service workers and respondents with no formal education are disproportionately represented in the category of those who answered "none" to the questions about first problems of widowhood. The picture is generally one of lower-class women who had been working most of their adult lives, who had not developed strong companionate relations with their husbands, who belong to societal sub-groups with a high hostility between the sexes, and who had anticipated widowhood.

Definitions of a second problem of widowhood were given by only forty percent of the respondents, but they also reflect differences in background. In comparison to first problems, these tend to stress money and the lack of a provider, someone to earn for the unit, with less frequent reference to loneliness. As mentioned before, the two sets of answers are not mutually exclusive. The forms of loneliness which are mentioned as a second problem are different than those mentioned first and are given with less prodding. Widows who first listed loneliness for the husband, in any of its forms, then shifted into other problems, while widows who originally selected a different area of difficulty were also less personal in their second answers. The respondents who listed loneliness as a problem of second magnitude are represented disproportionately by those who completed only five to seven grades of schooling and by over half of those who finished only between one and four grades. These widows have several living children who seem not to be able to fill the loneliness gap and lack helpful in-laws. Interestingly enough, although they do not live with their married children, they are more apt than other categories of women to see no problems in such an arrangement. Not even their telephone calls offset these feelings, since the highest proportion mentioning loneliness as a second problem talks with someone at least four times a day. There is a possibility that the phone calls, because they are with people still married, do not alleviate loneliness. One indication of this is the fact that an unusually large proportion of those listing loneliness as a second problem have no friends who are also widows. The whole profile of those who refer to loneliness as a second problem of widowhood points to women who lack a satisfactory level of contact with people in a similar stage of life. Regardless of whether they miss their husbands as persons or find other problems uppermost, these women are lonely now for human contact. They seem to hold mixed sentiments: wishing remarriage, yet feeling it can cause nothing but trouble; being lonely for people, yet listing "peace of mind" as the most important compensation of widowhood.

Respondents who complain about the lack of a breadwinner as a second problem in widowhood are, strangely enough, likely to have themselves worked most of their married life. Isolation seems less of a problem to them because most of their current friends are widows. As a compensation of widowhood they mention "less work," indicating that the problem of not having someone work for you is partly compensated for by having less work oneself.

The few women who list raising children as a second major problem of widowhood are likely to be very frequent telephone users, talking to someone at least six times a day. They do not know their neighbors and are not sure if they want to remarry. Their best job was as craftsman. In general, this picture suggests the top segment of the blue-collar group, which is family oriented.

Money is a problem of secondary importance to one-third of the 120 women who list more than once source of difficulty. It is of particular significance to women eighty years of age or above, those who dropped out of high school, those who married men with an equal amount of schooling, and those who identify as Jewish. (No Jewish women had listed it in the first place.) The husbands of financially concerned respondents had been working at other than their usual jobs just before death. The widows expect trouble in living with married children because of their own anxiety over noise and commotion. Accustomed to active participation, they define their current social life as quieter than before because of financial restriction and fear of going out alone. As is true of those who listed money as the first major problem, those listing it as a second problem feel financially restricted, or at least "rather short."

## COMPENSATIONS OF WIDOWHOOD

Whatever may be the major problems of the Chicago area widows which they attribute to the death of the husband, at least half of them enjoy some compensations, an admission which goes somewhat against the grain of the American value system. Within this culture marriages are portrayed as either bad, and properly ended in divorce or suffered in silence, or good in the sense of "living happily ever after." Widows are expected to be devastated, even years after the death of their husband, and this marital condition is not defined as having any advantage over marriage. Yet, in spite of some tendencies in that direction, most women do not become fatally ill, commit suicide, or become institutionalized in mental hospitals after the death of the husband. Regardless of the amount of shock and grief, the human capacity to adjust and reconstruct reality asserts itself and life continues, either in passive acceptance or in assertion of a new life style. Half of the respondents now agree with the statement: "I like living alone" (see Chapter 3 for details for this attitude), and although some women find the removal of the person around whom they organized their work to be the major source of loneliness, half of the respondents find the release from such duties to be a major compensation of widowhood. One third of them list this as the major or first compensation. Sixty-seven of the 116 women who mention a second compensation list less work; and a fourth of the respondents list independence. Finally, seventy-nine of the eighty-eight women who list three advantages refer to independence, while most of those who had troublesome or chronically ill husbands list peace of mind. One respondent still grieving for a husband who died one and a half years ago lists several compensations: "You don't have to cook if you don't want to; your time is your own; you can come and go as you want; you don't have to be home if your husband isn't there." This quotation illustrates the degree to which housewifely duties are recognized by the elderly woman as part of the role of wife. Older widows who specify cooking as part of the role of wife do not connect this task to the maintenance of home and the self. This may be one of the reasons why even women who have cooking skills become nutritionally deficient when they can not cook for other people. Better educated women, widowed in the full-house pleateau stage, tend to deal with the role of housewife as separate from those of wife and mother.

The importance of cooking as a symbol of the role of wife is very interesting. Like eating, it is mentioned throughout the interviews. The worst time for loneliness is connected with the dinner hour. Eating alone is avoided by arranging for company or even by sitting in front of the television set. One of the respondents copes with the feeling of loneliness at meal time by leaving her house and doing all her errands at that hour of the day so that she does not return until prime television shows are on. She even stopped her home delivery of the mail to give herself the job of picking it up in town. "Meals on wheels" programs by which volunteers bring precooked food to physically incapacitated people living alone are in great demand, partly because they provide the warmth of personal contact. For women living with their husbands in urban apartments or small houses, cooking remains one of the few individuated tasks offering opportunity for service and creativity. Finally, the preparation and giving of food has many symbolic qualities which psychiatrists have recognized for centuries. Older widows often show symptoms of behavior which some medical authorities ascribe to malnutrition rather than to old age. The same is true of older men living alone. Since isolation and malnutrition often go together, Mayor Daley's Commission on Senior Citizens is currently experimenting with a program in Chicago of bringing the elderly to a central location for regular meals and a program designed to break down their social barriers.

An important aspect of the role of wife is its rhythm. Husbands, particularly if they are still employed, and most of those whose widows were interviewed in this study had jobs up to the time of their last illness, want meals at specified hours. Thus, release from the role of wife is often felt as the removal of time restrictions. The frequency with which widows speak of freedom and independence indicates that, in their minds at least, wifehood imposes limitations on their actions. At the age of most respondents the duties and rights of wifehood probably do not refer to constant demands for sexual response. This probability is supported by the very high proportion of women who found the question: "Is it all right for a widow to have sexual relations with a man without planning on marriage?" to be false or inappropriate. This indicates that the forty-two percent who found true the statement: "I feel more independent and free now than before I became a widow" refer to other aspects of their lives. The reasons women give for their lack of wish to remarry also indicate a rejection of restrictions imposed by the schedule of another person who has decision-making rights. Only one-fifth of the 290 women answered yes to the question: "Would you like to remarry?" and the highest single reason given for rejection of a return to the role of wife was "I'm free and independent now."

Some circumstances of the death of the husband may result in an absence of grief or even in a feeling of relief on the part of the widow, especially if she had been performing nursing duties for an extended period of time. Caring for a significant person who is ill creates a state of constant anxiety from which death finally releases the wife. Thus, the process of becoming a widow may include the removal of specific sets of duties or restrictions on time or movement, of a supervisor making decisions and thus curtailing independence, of anxiety and even of hostility. One respondent whose husband was an alcoholic with whom she apparently fought expressed both relief and sadness at his death. Ambivalent attitudes are present in many marriages, so it is not surprising that they exist in widowhood. One 53-year-old widow was first married for six years to a man "I was very much in love with." This husband, who was the father of her two children, shot himself accidentally in the leg while on a hunting trip and did not obtain medical care in time; the leg became infected and he died. She married her second husband because she thought he would help her in raising her children, but stated that she "shouldn't have married a man so much older." Asked what are the "advantages a widow has which a married woman does not have?" she replied: "A whole lot of advantages. I didn't have to lay in bed till 2:00 or 3:00 o'clock in the morning and listen to lectures like I'm a little child, for one thing." The interviewer reports that this widow even debated killing her husband: "He was so mean to her and her children that she said she felt relieved and free after he had died."

The fact that so many women feel more independent and free now than before becoming a widow and that one-third of them agree with the statement: "This time of my life is actually easier than any other time," while a fourth even find true the sentence, "I feel sorry for some of my married friends who have little freedom to do as they please," does not necessarily mean that they were unhappy with their marriage. Many were unhappy, but an undetermined number of others simply closed that stage of life and adjusted to living alone without necessarily redefining their past as too restrictive or lacking in compensations.

## THE IMPORTANCE ASSIGNED THE ROLE OF
## WIFE BY WIDOWS

Many insights into the meaning of different sets of relations in the lives
of American housewives had been obtained by asking for a ranking of
the social roles carried on by women in order of their importance. The
method of giving a respondent a preselected set of roles to be numbered
according to their rank, instead of the alternative method of getting the
judgments through open-ended questions, was used in the widowhood
study because of its comparative ease. The first hypothesis guiding the
use of the role-ranking question in this study is that older widows would
tend to rank the role of wife in the first place in order of importance
more often than women with living husbands and in the full-house-
plateau of the roles of mother and housewife (Lopata, 1966 and 1971b).
There are several bases for this expectation. Rosow (1967) and others
(Cumming and Henry, 1961) have indicated that familial roles increase
in importance with aging, and other sociologists have posited that women
in the first phase of the shrinking circle stage of the role of housewife,
that is, those whose client segment of children had already removed itself
from major involvement with the mother, would turn renewed attention
to their husbands. This shift is expected before the husband's death, which
happens usually after the "empty nest" has been reached. In addition, the
sanctification obligation could be expected to increase the emphasis on the
wife role in the case of widows.

The second hypothesis underlying this aspect of the research is that
widows with different social characteristics, especially those from separate
social classes, would tend to place the role of wife in divergent positions.
If the conclusions of the housewife study have stood the test, widows
should rank the role of wife higher than married women do, but the
characteristics which differentiated the more husband-oriented married
women from those ranking other roles first should also operate among
the widows.

Detailed analysis supports both hypotheses. Forty-five percent of the
widows ranked the role of wife first, compared to twenty-eight percent
of the suburban housewives whose husbands are still living and who are
in an earlier stage of the life cycle. The characteristics of the widows
who are still oriented toward the role of wife are very similar to those
of husband-oriented married women. For example, whites are much
more likely to rank the role of wife in the first place than are blacks,
regardless of marital status. The most apt to give this role priority is
the widow of a man with a professional degree, who had been active in
a professional job, especially if she is now living at a level she herself

defines as comfortable. Educated women are more husband-oriented than uneducated ones, even in widowhood. So are Jewish women who identify themselves as ethnically Russian. The least husband-oriented widow is black, in her seventies, and living on a restricted income. She had little education and either held no job or worked in menial jobs. The woman who does not know her husband's educational achievement is also not likely to place her relation to him very high when compared to her other social roles. Even among whites, the wife's education, the husband's occupation, and her satisfaction with her current income are the main factors which distinguish the husband-oriented widow from the woman of the same color who ranks other roles first. The proportion of respondents giving primacy to wifehood decreases as age increases, the women in their fifties having a twenty point higher proportion than widows in their eighties. Of course, these figures reflect all the other changes in the lives of women. Some other interesting combinations appear when the tendency to rank the role of wife first is cross-tabulated with characteristics such as the age of the husband. Women who had been married to men younger than themselves are more likely to give the role of wife second place; those whose husbands were of the same age distribute this role evenly between the first and the second ranks; those with husbands who had been older are the most likely of the three groups to give it first rank. This is interesting in view of their likelihood not to mention loneliness for the husband as frequently as wives of same-age husbands.

The ranking patterns reinforce most of the previous conclusions that upper-class women, or at least upper-middle class ones, are the most likely to value their role of wife above that of mother, housewife, worker, community member, or daughter, and that ethnic and religious backgrounds play an important role in role ranks below those class levels. The same patterns emerge when all of the references to this role and to relations with the husband are combined into a "role of wife" scale. Obviously, and unlike the scores achieved in the other social roles, this scale does not measure current involvement in relations to the husband. Rather, it is based on references to past activities, attitudes toward the marriage, etc. It is more of an attitudinal scale than the other role scales (see Table IV in Appendix C).

Prior analysis prepares us for the categories of widows who deviate from the percentages expected by their representation in the population (see Table V in Appendix C). Less educated women married to less educated men in lower prestige jobs are less likely to be husband-oriented than other respondents. Women who came to Chicago in their early thirties from another location are apt to have low scores in the role of wife scale, possibly because they had been too involved in trying to help children adjust to the move. Those who moved in their fifties may have already shifted their concern toward the husband, or they may have been widowed more recently. The Jewish widow of Russian ethnic background again emerges as the most conscious of her role of wife, the black woman as the least. There is a strong tie between black race and the occupation of farm laborer on the part of the husband, devaluing the role of wife. A relatively high current income and the widow's estimation of comfort in her present situation form an important combination, disproportionately increasing the probability of husband orientation. We find a strong emphasis on loneliness as a major problem of widowhood among widows who focus on the role of wife, leading to the assumption that they had been more deeply involved with their husband than ones with a low score on the role of wife scale. Again, the woman who is oriented toward this role is more likely to want to resume it, being more willing to remarry than the respondent who scored low in this role.

## THE CASE OF THE BLACK WIDOWS

The answers to various questions dealing with the role of wife by respondents with a black racial identity indicate either the presence of a subculture of antagonism to men or a convergence of personal experiences resulting in a devaluation of the role of wife. Moynihan's report (Rainwater and Yancey, 1967) makes this conclusion obvious, but what the literature neglects is the fact that the black lower-class woman is apt to be socially isolated from many social relations and to have gone through experiences which make her attitudinally restrictive toward not just men, but the world in general. The matriarchally organized group constantly surrounding her with pleasant relations, forming part of the black myth, is simply not there through a major part of her life. Neither is her husband, often because of the high male death rate.

The distribution of respondents by race considering the role of wife to be the most important for women finds twice as many whites as blacks placing it in the first position (see Table 21). Of the fifty-two black women, twelve refused to rank it at all, and the three bottom positions in the six-rank table are disproportionately apt to be chosen by widows of this race.

The life histories of the black widows help to account for much of this tendency to downgrade the role of wife. There are several aspects of this history which are relevant: hostility between the sexes, the high rate of desertion and divorce, and the frequency and early age of widow-

TABLE 21: THE RANK ORDER OF THE ROLE OF WIFE AS ONE
OF SIX ROLES MOST IMPORTANT TO WOMEN, BY
THE RACE OF THE RESPONDENT

*Rank Order of the Role of Wife*

| Race | | Row Sums | Most Impor- tant | Second Impor- tant | Third Impor- tant | Fourth Impor- tant | Fifth Impor- tant | Least Impor- tant | No Ans. |
|---|---|---|---|---|---|---|---|---|---|
| Black | N | 40 | 9 | 12 | 7 | 8 | 2 | 2 | 12 |
| | % | | 23R | 30R | 18R | 20R | 5R | 5R | 30R* |
| | % | 15 | 8C | 14C | 22C | 48C | 29C | 33C | 44C |
| White | N | 229 | 112 | 74 | 25 | 9 | 5 | 4 | 15 |
| | % | | 49R | 32R | 11R | 4R | 2R | 3R | 7R* |
| | % | 85 | 93C | 86C | 78C | 53C | 72C | 67C | 56C |
| No Ans. | N | 5 | 5 | — | — | — | — | — | — |
| | % | | 100R | .0R | .0R | .0R | .0R | .0R | .0R* |
| | % | 2 | 4C | .0C* | .0C* | .0C* | .0C* | .0C* | .0C* |
| Column | N | — | 121 | 86 | 32 | 17 | 7 | 6 | 27 |
| Sums | % | — | 45 | 32 | 12 | 6 | 3 | 2 | 10* |

Percent Base: 269
R stands for Row, C stands for Column
* Not counted in percentage base

hood. Much of the current literature neglects this last factor when dealing with black households headed by women (Rainwater and Yancey,
1967). Among the fifty-two black Chicago area respondents, twenty-
seven women, or fifty-two percent of the total, ended their first marriage
before reaching their forties (see Table 22), due to early marriage and
its dissolution through death or divorce. Half had married for the first
time below the national average of twenty years (Leslie, 1967:265). Five
had been married at thirteen years of age. Eighty percent of the husbands
were older, some by as much as twenty years, which accounts in part for
the young widowhood.

Twenty-two of the widows, or forty-two percent of the total, married
more than once, as compared to sixteen percent of their white counterparts. Those who did not remarry often spent most of their lives in
widowhood. The first marriages of those who later remarried ended in
divorce in sixty-eight percent of the black cases and in only forty-six
percent of the white cases. One black and two white widows had first
been divorced, then widowed. This means that only twenty-seven percent
of the blacks, but fifty-four percent of the whites, who remarried, were

TABLE 22: AGE AT MAJOR LIFE EVENTS OF BLACK WIDOWS

*Age*

| Event | Under 10 | 10–19 | 20–29 | 30–39 | 40–49 | 50–59 | 60 | Don't Know | Total |
|---|---|---|---|---|---|---|---|---|---|
| Came to Chicago | 4 | 9 | 11 | 12 | 5 | 4 | 5 | 1 | 51 |
| First marriage | | 29 | 13 | | | 1 | | 9 | 52 |
| End first marriage | | 6 | 10 | 11 | 7 | 5 | 10 | 3 | 52 |
| Second marriage | | | 9 | 9 | 1 | 2 | | 1 | 22 |
| End second marriage | | | 2 | 1 | 6 | 6 | 7 | | 22 |
| Third marriage | | | | 1 | 3 | | 1 | | 5 |
| End third marriage | | | | | 1 | 2 | 2 | | 5 |
| Birth first living child | | 11 | 17 | 5 | 1 | | | 2 | 36 |
| Birth last child | | 1 | 8 | 9 | 1 | | | | 19 |

widowed by their first husband. The second marriage ended in divorce for eighteen percent of the black women, but for only five percent of their white counterparts. An additional twenty-nine percent of the black women who had two marriages were separated at the time of the second husband's death. Finally, twenty-three percent of the black and thirteen percent of the whites married a third time.

Not only were the blacks less likely than the whites to live out most of their adult life with the same husband, but, in spite of their youth at first marriage, they were apt to have spent many years with no husband in the home, because of widowhood, separation, or divorce. In fact, eighteen out of the fifty-two black widows have been without a husband for twenty years since their first marriage, and another twenty-one for more than ten years but less than twenty, leaving only three widows husbandless for ten years or less. The exact number of years without a husband was often hard to determine, because several of the respondents were unable to outline their autobiographies in the standard middle-class framework of calendar years. Those with minimal or no schooling, but not necessarily of older age, frequently could not recall the dates or the number of years of their marriages. One reason for this was uncertainty as to the official breaking-off point of the relation, but another was unfamiliarity with the habit of dividing life into stages clearly demarcated by external events such as calendar dates. Several tried to establish time periods in terms of other biographical events, such as the birth of children whose ages they could remember. The uncertainty as to marital termination resulted in confusion over the concept of widowhood. Interviewers had to be careful to select only those respondents whose husbands were truly deceased, since the word "widow" is often used in situations where the husband is absent from the home in any of several ways. Widowhood carries more prestige than desertion, but in both cases the husband is dead to contact.

The marital history of the Chicago area black widows indicates that, regardless of the condemnation by the society at large, death, separation, and divorce necessitate an independent stance on the woman's part to insure survival. In fact, only thirty-seven percent of these respondents, compared to sixty-one percent of the whites, agree that "the hardest thing for a widow to learn is how to make decisions."

As the divorce figures indicate, many of the black marriages were not happy, and some of the widowed respondents still express hostility to the deceased. Although the black women comprise eighteen percent of the total sample of widows, they form only eight percent of the high scorers, fourteen percent of the medium scorers, and thirty-eight percent of the low scorers on the "role of wife" scale. The scale combined the widow's ranking of this role in a hierarchy of role importance with several sets of attitudes and sentiments about the deceased. By contrast, the eighty-two percent of women who are white form ninety-two percent of the high scorers, eighty-five percent of the medium, and sixty-two percent of the low scorers.

Strong attitudes of hostility toward one or more husbands permeated some of the interviews with black women. One of the NORC interviewers was so struck by the vehemence of a widow's feelings that she explained in the margin: "This woman went on about how little she thinks of men. Let me tell you, she hates them!" This respondent had tried marriage twice and was miserable both times. "There is nothing good I can say about it. I would go to bed unhappy and cursing while my husband was alive. After he died, I could say my prayers and go to sleep in peace. Women in those days married a man and stuck it out, going about their routine of washing, ironing and cooking regardless of how miserable they were. But the Lord did me a favor and removed my husband, so I would live out the rest of my days in peace." Not all of the women who were unhappy in one marriage found the situation equally bad in another such relation. One had been unhappily married twice, but finally met a man whom she loved. "People thought I and my husband were childhood sweethearts because we seemed so perfectly. matched."

Some of the problems of black marriages were aggravated by the life circumstances of the couple. Most of the fifty-two respondents had been married while still in the South, to sharecroppers, farm laborers, or farmers with minimal acreage. One, a bitter woman of eighty-seven, did not grieve when she learned of the death of her husband, who had been cared for in his final illness by a sister, so that the wife could continue working: "I was out in the field, picking cotton so hard I just forgot about it. I was sick and tired of that farm and was trying to get away from down there. My husband wasn't a good man. I had to work so hard my life was almost a living hell." The highest they ever cleared from the farm was $274 for a season. Another left her husband when she became pregnant again in her forties. She came to Chicago to have her sister take care of her and the child: "It's too hard to pick cotton when you're pregnant." Her husband remained on the farm and died later, but she didn't even go to his funeral. Nine, or seventeen percent of the black respondents, came to Chicago only after the death of the husband, but most migrated with him in his search for a job.

The lower-class sub-culture and the hardships of life produced anger in the women which became directed against the spouse. It persisted in some cases even after his death and prevented conformity to the general American norm of referring to the deceased with respect. Eighty-seven percent of the total group of widows agreed with the statement that "My husband was an unusually good man," and only five percent refused to to make a statement though the interviews themselves contained a frequent spouse-directed hostility. The widows of both social races are heavily over-represented in the three lower social classes, which harbor many openly negative feelings toward the other sex. The obligation to sanctify the dead operates, however, much more consistently in the white community, ninety-four percent of whom saw their husbands as good men, and only four percent who refused to commit themselves. Among the blacks, only seventy-six percent agreed with the statement that the husband had been unusually good, and eleven percent refused to declare themselves.[3a] Judging from the combination of attitudes toward various social relations, refusal to answer usually means rejection of a statement, combined with an unwillingness to declare this publicly. Differences also exist in reactions to the following statement: "My marriage was above average and no second marriage could match it." Only sixty-two percent of the blacks, but seventy-six percent of the whites, share this sentiment, not necessarily because they want to remarry.[3b] Most of the black women are very strong in their refusal to consider remarriage at this late date, though not out of any feeling of obligation to the deceased. Most black women do not want to remarry either because they do not expect to find a good man or because they "can't be bothered," as one respondent put it. The first reason expresses a very negative view of the older black men who would be available for marriage. "The men today are more trouble than they are good," responded one woman. The widows who "can't be bothered" were unhappy with a prior husband or do not want the work connected with maintaining a home for a man or taking care of him in his illness. Others feel that they had a good husband and are dubious of a future one. All in all, seventy-two percent of the blacks, compared to forty-nine percent of the whites, believe that: "Many widows who remarry are very unhappy in that marriage." [3c]

Although a relatively large number of the black widows lost their husbands while the men were relatively young, only fifty-seven percent of the blacks, compared to eighty percent of the whites, found true the statement: "My sexual relations with my husband were good until his last illness." [3d] One widow who was deserted by her husband before his death explained that she "liked being a widow, since I don't want no more husbands. When you got a man that's no good, you is miserable. I don't want to be bothered. I'm doing very well. Well, I'll tell you, the change of life was still working on me. I wouldn't let my husband bother me if he wanted to go to bed with me, I wouldn't let him. You're not supposed to do those things at that time. I didn't have any more relations. I just worked on my job. A married woman has to be bothered with her husband and his sex wants, but a widow don't have that problem unless they want to." Forty-one percent of the black respondents, compared to six percent of the whites, agree that "It is all right for a widow to have sexual relations with a man without planning on marriage" [3e] More of the former also perceive opportunities for entering such relations, since forty-five percent of the blacks, compared to only eighteen percent of the whites, agree that "Widows are constantly sexually propositioned, even by the husbands of their friends" [3f] and fifty-nine percent of the blacks, as compared to thirty-nine percent of the whites[3g], agree that "Other women are jealous of a widow when their husbands are around." Both groups are more likely to experience or expect jealousy from women than advances from their husbands.

Unfortunately, middle-class reticence and anxiety about antagonizing lower-class respondents already fearful of the investigators who might affect their financial situation, prevented a more complete examination of both the black and the white widows concerning other meaningful relations with men which did not end in marriage. Several interviews contain references to men as "friends" who helped the widow recover from her grief or rear her children, or who gave her money during crisis periods. The arrangements mentioned or alluded to seem to involve rights and duties different from the middle-class relations of married people described in Morton Hunt's new book, *The Affair* (1969), but not enough material is available in the interviews to warrant any generalization. There were also black respondents who made it a point not to have any "men in my home and let my children be around things like that. I kept a good home for my children."

In general, the picture of relations in the black community between women and their husbands is not drawn in sentimental or multi-dimensional terms. That these widows tend to belong to the lower classes, which have minimal communication between spouses, is witnessed by the following figures: forty-two percent of the black respondents, compared with fourteen percent of these identified as white, do not know how long their husbands attended school (see also Komarovsky, 1964). Thirty-two percent of the remaining black respondents, compared to sixty-five percent of the whites, declared that their husband had reached a level of schooling above the eighth grade, but all of the widows knew how many years they themselves attended school. We can hypothesize that those who did not know how much schooling their husbands received were married to men who had not been highly educated. The ignorance of the husband's background extends to his father's occupation and the location of his kinfolk. It reflects lower-class culture in more ways than just lack of communication between husband and wife. Life tends to be lived day by day, and the past is forgotten unless it contains unusual events. Small differences in the amount of schooling have little effect on present life and are not tied to plans for the future. Both past and future have little to be savored, and school is seldom a significant memory to be shared with others as an accomplishment. Thus, it is not spontaneously offered as information about the self.

Marital life in the black community tends to be more frequently sex-segregated than in the white community. This may be a function of education, but it is a fact of life for older widows. Fifty-four percent of the black respondents, as compared to twenty-four percent of the whites, agreed with the strong statement that "My husband and I did not do too many things together; he had his activities and I had mine." [3h] (see Table VI in Appendix C). This distinction does not carry over to an admission of ignorance on the part of the two groups of widows about their financial situation. Only twenty-nine percent of the blacks and twenty-five percent of the whites agree that "I did not know anything about our finances when my husband died." As mentioned before, women are more apt to be involved in family financial matters when the income is so low that most of the expenditures are directed toward everyday living than if invested in business ventures. In addition, a high proportion of black women had been working or were separated from the husband at the time of his death, so that they naturally were knowledgeable about their economic situation.

Table VII (Appendix C) contains a summary of the percentages of widows in each race who agree or disagree with statements relevant to their involvement in the role of wife in retrospect, or to their current attitudes toward men. It indicates, in general, a less positive attitude toward men in the black than in the white community. Combined with the history of marriage in the two Chicago samples and the respondents' scores in the role of wife, they show that this relation has been less positively meaningful for black widows than for white ones, involving fewer years of continuous interaction, a more restricted relation, and frequently a more negative effect. This does not mean, of course, that all marriages in the former community contributed to the wife's relational problems or resulted in her social isolation, but only that black women were more often deprived of satisfying relations with their husbands than the white ones were. What remains obvious in all these statistics is that the black marriage problems and attitudes are a direct result of the educational and cultural background of both wives and husbands. All but one of the black respondents had been born outside of Chicago, mostly in Southern rural areas. There is a direct relation between race and place of birth.[3i] This means that the black respondents were the most likely to be deprived of an educational and cultural background which could equip them for life in the modern urban setting. Although there is no significant difference between the black and white races as to current income of the widow, there is a strong racial association with highest income in the past. The Negro woman is very unlikely to have ever had a high family revenue.[3j] She is likely to have been working for money prior to her husband's death, to have continued to work when she became a widow,[3k] and to have had insufficient funds on hand at that time to tide her over.[3l] Nor was she able to get help from her family,[3m] so that she has had a history of independent survival on her part.

## SUMMARY AND CONCLUSIONS

In spite of the rapid industrialization, urbanization, and increasing complexity of the social structure of American society, the basic cluster of social roles available to, and chosen by, its women has been that of wife-mother-housewife. This fact imposes some serious problems upon the last stage of their lives, similar to the problems of retirement in the lives of men who had concentrated upon their occupational roles. The wife-mother-housewife often finds herself with children who are grown, absent from her home, and independent of her as a basic part of their lives; her husband has died, and her household no longer contains a client segment. The traditional woman had been involved, at least in myth (see Shanas, 1968), in a three generational family circle, surrounded ideally with her husband's family of orientation and her own family of procreation. The absence of her husband would be less dramatic under circumstances of an extended kinship group than when he is the only other member of a working, living, and companionate team. Americans put great emphasis upon the role of wife, adding many new features to the traditional orientation in this direction. The mobile and function-oriented society within which this exceptionally long-term and multi-dimensional relation operates places a heavy burden of sentiment and self-involvement on the marriage. Other social relations have become more fleeting or restricted. Institutional segmentalization of most of life and the removal of most social roles from the home have resulted in the separation from one another of the various social circles in which an individual is involved. Economic, religious, educational, recreational, political, friendship, and kin roles are no longer performed within the same circle of human beings.

As kinship decreases control over the lives of its members, and as education and democratization make strong patriarchal authority impossible, the role of wife inevitably undergoes strong modifications. Personal sentiments and interpersonal interaction of husband and wife have increased in significance as familistic obligations to a large kin group have decreased in importance. The man and woman selected each other for marriage on the basis of personal attractiveness, without much attention to the values advised by older people; the relation thus developed lacks the protective cushion of complex primary relations with people able to control its content. The man belongs to a work group with which he spends much of his waking and thinking hours, but occupational mobility and increasingly leisure-oriented mentality have contributed to a lessening of its importance. A counterpart of the London man who works and drinks with men whom he has known since childhood is not likely to be found in many Chicago area offices or factories (Bott, 1957). Like Wilmott and Young's (1960) migrants to a kinship-lacking suburb, the American male is likely to interact with different people during work hours than he does around his home or than he will see five years hence. Contact with his parents and siblings continues after marriage, but in a much modified form. The man's one consistent companion in most non-work activities becomes his wife. The same shifting of basic relations has occurred in the life of the American women. Though her early years of marriage are often focused on the role of mother, it does not take long before her husband becomes the only "client" of her activities and her only companion in the daily cycle.

The American urban woman experiences changes in her life and even in her personality as a result of marriage. This event is a major step in her life, toward which she prepared for many years, not necessarily in learning task duties, but in the development of a marriageable personality. Popularity among peers and eligible males is a major goal of the young woman, and task duties in the role of wife or housewife are learned only after the return from a leisure-oriented honeymoon. The ideal of romantic love is described and embellished in every woman's magazine, from *True Story* to *Ladies' Home Journal*. The image drawn does not romanticize stable love among partners of long-term marriages, except as a prelude to major tragedy. Little is known even among sociologists of marriage in the middle and older years, although much speculation is now taking place about "the empty nest" stage, when, without her children, the woman is expected to withdraw into depression, seek excitement in drink or adultery, or turn to her husband with renewed interest. Yet much of recent literature keeps reminding the reader that marriages are varied in the degree to which their partners are involved in mutual inter-relations, in terms of roles and sentiments. Some women never become husband-oriented after the children shift them from an earlier concentration in such a direction. Ambivalent feelings toward the husband are experienced by many wives, but some simply are never committed to this relation to the extent of being so involved. Lower-class women, enmeshed in a frustrating and anxiety-producing life, feel hostile to men either because they are subjected to autocratic authority or because they do not receive cooperation in meeting the daily problems of life. Involvement in the social role of wife thus varies from woman to woman, depending on the centrality of this role in her cluster, the multi-dimensionality of the social life space, the segment of the social circle toward which she is oriented, her relation-versus-task approach, and the other aspects which distinguish her participation. Wives of successful husbands are much more likely to make the marital relation of central importance, even placing the role of mother in second rank. The modern trend in marriage is for increasing multi-dimensional involvement of the woman and the man in each other's lives. Couple-companionate relations replace sex-segregated friendships and expand into increasing amounts of time, constricted only by the professional activity of the few men who remain as individual entrepreneurs. The couple becomes not only a basic residential, but also a recreational, political, associational, and kin-engaging team. Such multi-dimensional involvement of the husband in the life of the wife makes widowhood a serious problem in middle-class America. Death of the man removes the major segment in the social role of wife and reduces the social circles of mother, friend, housewife, neighbor, etc., often modifying these roles beyond the woman's ability to resume her past behavior. The widow experiences loneliness with the death of the only other person who shares her residence, her home-maintenance work load, and leisure activities. She misses the man around whom her daily work was organized and with whom she exchanged small talk and more significant conversation. Some widows miss the husband as a total personality whom they loved and who returned the sentiment; others simply feel a drop of status. The feeling of a lowering of her social position through the death of the husband is one which only sixteen percent of the Chicago area widows admit in their reactions to the statement: "Women lose status when they become widows—they lose respect and consideration." However, the higher the husband's social position, the more likely his surviving partner is to indicate during the interview that she misses her former style of life and that she cannot reproduce it. One reason for the feeling that widowhood does not carry the same status as the married condition is the couple-based structure of American social life. Women miss companions or escorts whenever they go to public places or to evening events with friends. This is particularly true of women widowed young, when others within their various circles are still attached to their partners.

Some duties of the social role of wife extend themselves beyond the life of the husband, but they are minimal in this society with weak patrilineal rights. The duty to preserve the social presence of the mate is current and includes the obligation to sanctify his personality. Only widows who found their marriages highly unsatisfactory fail to carry out this duty. More women state that their husband was an "unusually good" man than found their marriages above average and without possibility of duplication. The women who were widowed at a young age and who did not remarry are much more likely to express hostility toward the husband, the marriage, and even the sexual aspects of the relation than women whose husbands died at a more "normal" time in the wife's life cycle. Most widows officially state that they do not want to remarry, explaining this decision by their enjoyment of present independence, the belief that such unions are unsuccessful, or the fact that they are simply too old to even think about remarriage. Part of the unwillingness to consider having a second husband may be the feeling of obligation to the first one to remain "faithful." While widows who report good marriages with the late husband are more willing to enter a new relation of this type than are survivors of poor marriages, few expect that they will be able to find another husband. In the case of one-fifth of the respondents, the next husband would be the third or fourth one. Twenty-seven widows had been widowed once before, thirty-four ended their first marriage in divorce. Sexual relations with men whom they do not plan on marrying are also rejected with great unanimity.

The duty to affiliate children with the husband's family and the right of maintenance by that kin have decreased in America to such an extent that many widows maintain only minimal contact with their in-laws or cease it altogether. Whatever the degree of mutual assistance during the life of the man, it diminishes dramatically after the funeral, and the majority of in-laws do not even help with that event. The grandparents obviously can not be a major influence upon the behavior of the youngest generations, since they do not have frequent contact, let alone patriarchal control.

A third of the respondents did not know anything about the couple's finances when their husband died, due to a division of labor that left decision-making in this area in the province of the male. Some husbands knew that death was imminent and were able to train their wives in management of the economic goods they had accumulated. However, older widows are not likely to have been married to men who had sufficient assets, formalized in a way their widows defined as an "estate." The last illnesses diminished goods, yet half of the women had sufficient funds on hand to enable them to continue life without going into debt or obtaining help from their families. An equal proportion either went to work or continued in their job after the husband's death. There is obviously some overlap between these two groups. Half of the respondents now consider themselves to be in a "comfortable" financial condition, but one-fifth is really restricted. One fifth have an annual income of $5,000 or over per year, but fifteen percent are living on less than $1,000.

In spite of the fact that half of the Chicago area widows live alone and most of them like it, an equal proportion mention loneliness as the greatest problem of their present status, and a third consider it a second problem, often listing different forms of this sentiment. Half of the respondents admit to the compensations of free time, independence, and decreased work load.

All the respondents of the Chicago area indicate that being a widow is not a role with a functional base, even that of maintaining status distinctions in interaction with non-widows. Because of the much married nature of American society, being a widow places many women in a rather stigmatic relation with others, self-consciousness modifying many interactions. Duties of the widow depend on the individual rather than upon external regulations; such formlessness can make this experience uncomfortable for the former wife. Identity ties between the self and the husband, and between the self and the role of wife, are possible only in memory, which may be one of the reasons older widows dwell on the past, much as retired men do. The general impression left by the interviews is that many widows consider the role of wife to have been a very important one and that they lack another major role upon which to focus their current personality. For some, of course, the role of mother provides such an identity locus, but they are apt to have been so directed even prior to the death of the husband. Women who are still oriented to the role of wife in widowhood tend to have concentrated on that role when the husband was alive and to have had companionate and multi-dimensional, rather than task oriented, relations with the spouse. They are also the most likely of all the respondents to face strong disorganization in their lives with the death of the husband and to experience very personal forms of loneliness for him as a unique individual. However, as we shall see, they are the same women who have the resources to restructure their identities and their lives after the period of grief is mainly over. They know how, and have the self-confidence, to enter new roles and social relations. Their less educated counterparts, who had been engaged minimally in their roles of wives, are the most apt to be socially isolated when even this link of engagement in societal life dies.

## NOTES

1. The widows of the Ganda in Africa who already had children were assigned the duty of taking care of the grave of the husband (HRAF 1: Mair, 1934, Ganda, p. 220) and many societies required of them the preservation of visible symbols of the deceased.
2. The concept of loneliness has not been dealt with sufficiently in sociological literature. Frieda Fromm-Reichmann points out in "Loneliness" that even psychiatrists have avoided the topic (see Warren G. Bennis et al., *Interpersonal Dynamics,* Homewood, Illinois: the Dorsey Press, 1968, pp. 121–139). Some of the studies of aging bring out the social isolation and feelings of loneliness of such people. (See particularly Jeremy Tunstall, *Old and Alone,* London: Routledge and Kegan Paul, Ltd., 1966, and Peter Townsend, "Isolation, desolation and loneliness," in Ethel Shanas et al., *Old People in Three Industrial Societies,* New York: Atherton Press, 1968, chapter 9.) References to loneliness and explanations of what it means were so frequently made by the Chicago area widows as to warrant separate analysis. (See Helena Znaniecki Lopata, "Loneliness: forms and components," *Social Problems,* 17 (Fall, 1969): 248–262.)

3. The statistical associations between rate and each of the attitudinal or background characteristics are so significant that they are included here:

    3 a. $x^2 = 15.98$; d.f. $= 1$, p. $< .001$

      b. $x^2 = 4.59$; d.f. $= 1$; p. $< .05$

      c. $x^2 = 42.67$; d.f. $= 1$; p. $< .001$

      d. $x^2 = 10.41$; d.f. $= 1$; p. $< .01$

      e. $x^2 = 187.84$; d.f. $= 1$; p. $< .001$

      f. $x^2 = 14.84$; d.f. $= 1$; p. $< .001$

      g. $x^2 = 6.56$; d.f. $= 1$; p. $< .01$

      h. $x^2 = 12.6$ ; d.f. $= 1$; p. $< .001$

      i. $x^2 = 84.51$; d.f. $= 4$; p. $< .001$

      j. $x^2 = 34.37$; d.f. $= 14$; p. $< .005$

      k. $x^2 = 10.04$; d.f. $= 2$; p. $< .01$

      l. $x^2 = 11.87$; d.f. $= 2$; p. $< .01$

      m. $x^2 = 6.06$; d.f. $= 2$; p. $< .05$

# 3

# Widowed Mothers

## BEING A MOTHER

In 1890, the average age of an American woman when she gave birth to her *last* child was 31.9 years. Her age when this child married was 55.3 years and by that time she had been a widow for two years. By 1960, the average age of the woman when she gave birth to her last child was 25.8, her age when this offspring married dropped down to 47.1 years, and she was not widowed until 63.6 years (Leslie, 1967:265). This means that the first segment of the *shrinking circle* stage of a typical family life cycle, when all the children are gone, but before the death of the husband, then spanned 16.5 years. The second segment of the *shrinking circle* stage, when even the husband is absent, spans another fifteen years (Duvall; 1967, 15).

These statistics make it difficult to justify the traditional meaning of life for women which prepared the girl for the role of mother only during the *expanding circle* and the *full house plateau* stages. Her identity and feelings of fullfillment were focused on being a mother of *small* children, leaving her with thirty years of existence made meaningless by this value system. Women are living longer, are healthier and more energetic, but their main function, that of bearing and rearing children, ceases more than thirty years before her life ends. Interestingly, however, the insistence that the girl should become mainly a mother not only results in inadequate preparation for other social roles, such as work or career, community participation, and even friendship, but fails to produce even a careful and adequate training for motherhood. The girl "falls into" the role of mother simply by giving birth and performs it by trial-and-error methods. Consequently, American women report great problems in the role of mother, in spite of their increasing competence in other roles.

The role of mother in modern society is difficult for several reasons. One does not just "learn to be" a mother and repeat the same behavioral process over and over in the relation. When the role was more institutionalized than it is now, the process of its modification with the growth of children was clearly delineated and reinforced by cooperative action of all circle members. The de-institutionalization means that there are no established packages of behavior acceptable both to parents and to the young.

Traditional cultures immersed the role of mother, like that of wife, in a whole set of other viable familial roles, so that the rights and duties now forming the set of parental relations were distributed among several people. The extended family, even the whole community, felt responsible for the rearing of all the young to be future members of the group. Direct teaching, presentation of models, discipline and praise encouraged conformists and punished deviants in guilt- or shame-producing ways. The mother was not the sole watcher of children and disciplinarian; she was aided by family members and, in some cases, paid servants. Thus, the mother was seldom held responsible for the final product. The assumption of inborn characteristics and of inevitable illness and death also eased the burden of the mother's role.

Modern society is simplifying the basic family structure and, in spite of cross-household kinship assistance (Shanas and Streib; 1965), it places increased burdens on the spouse and parent. Very few persons in each household are now held responsible for the care and rearing of children. Older offspring are no longer available for such tasks, since their major obligation is to prepare themselves for occupational and other adult social roles. Unmarried aunts, widowed or married grandparents, and servants are no longer assisting the mother and the father in child-rearing.

Besides decrease in the size and functionality of the residential family, changes in the social structure affect the role of mother before and after widowhood. The community has grown in size to such an extent that informal socialization and control by it as a unit are difficult, if not impossible. When away from home, anonymity makes one child indistinguishable from another, while cultural heterogeneity creates constant strains between the mother, her neighbors, and the representatives of law and community order. Bridges between age groups have been weakened, and growing up is no longer a process of patterning oneself after established models. The youth sub-culture and social mobility have lessened the bonds of common interest and symbols of communication between a mother and her children. The tension in role relations at any age outside of housebound infancy makes motherhood very difficult in our modern urbanizing, industrializing and mobile society.

Most of the housewives studied in the previous research (Lopata, 1971b) felt they are coping with the role of mother, although those with higher levels of education were strongly aware of its importance and complications. One of the main satisfactions of the older mothers was that "the children turned out all right." One almost hears sigh of relief in that phrase. An additional difficulty for the modern housewife is the increasing realization, brought about by the dissemination of psychological and sociological knowledge, that personality and even intelligence are not inborn, but developed. The modern mother thus feels not only responsible, but ego-involved in making her child as "successful," popular, and brilliant as possible. As Bettleheim (1960) has pointed out, such awareness places a heavy burden on the mother. In spite of the increasing responsibility and self-awareness, most mothers, particularly older ones, lack the tools for carrying on the role of mother in developmental ways.

## BECOMING A WIDOWED MOTHER

Most women in the United States and in other societies, for that matter, become mothers. The number of children born to each and the number surviving until she becomes a widow at fifty years or older are not evenly distributed among the Chicago area respondents. The total of 301 widows averages 2.1 children per woman, but fifty-four do not have surviving offspring. This brings the total number of mothers down to 247 with an average of 2.6 children. Finally, fifty-nine widows have only one surviving child, so that the remaining 188 respondents have a total of 583 offspring, with an average of 3.1. The average for the total group, which is relatively low when compared with national statistics, is due partly to the older and poorer women's health problems, producing sterility, and partly to the high infant death rate.

Some children of the Chicago area respondents had died after their mothers became widowed, but the distribution of offspring at the time of the interviews was generally reflective of the group. Having been accustomed to the role of mother as dependent upon the presence of a father, many widows experienced and reported great changes in relations with their children after the death of the husband. On the other hand, there are respondents who had been so estranged from their husband, or so little dependent upon him in their role of mother, as to experience little modification in those relations.

### Loss of the Father

The role of mother was bound to change with the loss of the father, if he was at all active in her social circle. The void caused by his absence could be filled by the mother attempting to undertake all his duties and rights, by the children undertaking segments of the father's roles, by people outside of the nuclear family serving as substitutes, or by some aspects of the father's role being dropped completely. The role of mother is also changed immediately, or in the long run, by other changes in the life of the woman and her family as a result of the man's death. For example, they may become impoverished and have to move to a poorer neighborhood, meeting new problems and leaving behind the friendly neighbors who had formed a cooperative segment of the mother's social circle.

The role of father is so complex in modern societies with their conjugal nuclear families as to make virtually impossible the widow's fullfilling it and the role of mother at the same time. All known societies are concerned with the fate of the young generation which insures their continued existence. The care of the newborn and the growing youth is often assigned to large kin groups, so that the absence of a father is not crucial to their welfare. In this society only the two adults care for and socialize the young, and they are totally responsible for "breadwinning." In the division of labor typical of America, the mother maintains the home, the father brings economic goods to it and covers its cost. His death thus deprives the family of income, unless he had anticipated such an event with adequate insurance or investment. Few men seem to have done so. The most frequent solution for the mother is to go to work herself. This means that she can not perform the mother duties during the hours she is gone, which immediately modifies her role relations with her children and with other members of her social circle, such as teachers.

The loss of the father produces other changes besides those in the function of breadwinner. According to Evelyn Duvall (1967) and others, the modern American father is a personally significant contributor to the socialization and emotional gratification of the family. Women widowed when their children are small express much concern over child-rearing. They are part of the culture in which the division of labor in the home refers not only to task but to affective specialization. They were trained to be the expressive parent, their husband the instrumental, task-oriented contributor. Mothers are traditionally expected to be protective, forgiving, concerned with the sentiments experienced by the child, and not with the problems of society in maintaining its standards. Young widows find it difficult, if not impossible, to be "both father and mother." These two stances toward children are so mutually exclusive and their own training so one-dimensional that the dilemma of changing the approach from one to the other creates real strain. In addition, many widows find themselves incompetent to act in ways they had been carefully trained to avoid, feeling "unfeminine" when attempting such demeanor. They also experience guilt and provoke public criticism by their unwillingness or inability to be strict disciplinarians.

The absence of the father creates additional problems for the mothers of more than one child. Another adult in the household can pay special attention to one offspring, releasing the mother to give individual attention to another or to other tasks. In widowhood, she remains the only object of competitive attention. Finally, having sole responsibility for decision-making worries the widow.

The father's death may necessitate the children's taking over some of his duties to them by becoming more independent and disciplining their own actions or by accepting changes in the behavior of other members of the mother's social circle. They may have to deal with a lawyer in place of their father or make arrangements for their education without his help. If they do not fill some gaps, they must adjust to someone else taking over the father's former function, thus affecting their relation with the mother. For example, police officers may step in as disciplinarians.

The mother may introduce substitutes for the father. Such replacements are facilitated by the presence of a viable kinship group. Male siblings or uncles may undertake some of the duties of the father. Friends, camp counselors, teachers and other males may serve as role models and "dutch uncles" for both girls and boys, although in different ways. The Chicago area contains branches of *Parents without Partners,* an organization founded explicitly to help those in such a situation. Members of these groups get together with the children for social events and compare notes as to problems and solutions in child-rearing. A few of the respondents attempted to join such groups, but most of them had been widowed before the local branches came into existence or after they had no special need for their manifest function. One McHenry respondent mentioned going to branch meetings in search of male companionship, but she found them too heavily attended by divorced women; she was obviously not interested in getting child-rearing help.

A very important modification in the relations between a mother and her children is introduced when the death of their father is simultaneously the death of her husband. The significance of this point is documented by differences in the situation when the mother had been divorced from the father and remarried, and when she was still living with the father. In the latter case the death of the man leaves the woman deprived of a husband who was functionally involved in her life in roles besides that of father. He often maintained her financially, acted as her companion at home and in leisure-time or other role situations, gave her love, was her sexual companion, work-sharer, etc. The children may be expected, or may undertake on their own, to fulfill a number of these duties. If they do not fill some of the gaps in her life, they must adjust to her having these needs satisfied in new ways. She may demand their time and attention, depriving them of their own leisure time, or she may bring in outsiders to whom they are expected to relate. Thus, the death of her husband introduces many changes in the life of the mother. She may not become so much dependent on her children as on male companionship which is separated from her role of mother. Some of the Chicago area widows report that their offspring resent any man who enters the house as a companion or potential marital partner of the mother. Respondents carefully explain that they would not subject their children to a step-father or even to the presence of a male lover, others that their children made things so difficult when men came for dates that they ceased such activities.

There are many factors which affect the ways in which a mother's relations with children and with others in her social circle, indeed her total life style are modified by the death of the husband-father. Basic are the ages and special characteristics of the children. At the end of the woman's life cycle, the changes depend on her age, health, and ability to maintain herself. The average age at widowhood in America, the age of 56, points to the fact that most women lose their husbands after they have reared their children and before they wish to become dependent upon them. They live in a society that does not force them to accept the guardianship of a son or other male; they do not want to live in the homes of married children, and usually they are not involved in a complex household with anyone else. As Rosenmyar and Kockeis (1963) conclude from their study of the elderly of Vienna, they want "Intimacy at a distance" from their adult children.

Other factors besides the age of the survivor affect how the role of mother is changed by the death of the father. Ethnic, religious, and racial sub-cultures influence the roles a woman considers undertaking in addition to that of mother and all that it entails. A very important factor is the educational achievement of the widow, since it affects her ability to cope with the world, utilizing its facilities to help the child grow and offsetting its limitations so that he will not be hurt or "turn out bad." It will also affect her life style after the re-engagement which follows the death of the husband. The widow's financial situation determines the location of the household and determines whether she must leave her offspring in order to earn more money. The presence of a cooperative kin group, neighborhood or friendship clique affects her role of mother, as do the roles in which she is engaged with her children outside of the home. Thus, the changes brought to the role of mother by the death of the father are complex, as are the factors which influence the way this set of relations is redeveloped after the initial disorganization of its basic components.

## Help Patterns of Adult Children

Many widows of the Chicago area obtained help from their children in dealing with the problems arising immediately and at long range after the death of their husband. The kind and amount of help an offspring can give his widowed mother is dependent on the match between the child's abilities and the mother's needs. A child can modify its relation to the mother or at least change the interaction in three basic ways: (1) by serving as an object of her attention, care, and work, by being present, and requiring services from her which were previously provided by the father; (2) by performing tasks previously handled by the father in the division of labor, including the provision of a household income; and (3) by maintaining close interpersonal relations with her—relations which acquire new elements as a result of the husband's absence. All three contributions can be made by a child of either sex, although a daughter seems to attend to more details. They can most easily be performed by someone living in the same dwelling unit. Older children who are unmarried or no longer married can help and enter into close relations with their mothers more easily than the very small or those with their own families. At least, these are the offspring frequently listed as being the "most" helpful to the mother in several areas of life (see Table 23).

TABLE 23: SEX OF CHILD GIVING MOST AND/OR LEAST AMOUNT OF HELP IN SELECTED AREAS, TO WIDOWED MOTHERS OF MORE THAN ONE CHILD

| | Most | | | | Least | | | Can't | Not Appli- |
| Area of Help | M | F | ?* | M | F | ?* | Decide | cable |
|---|---|---|---|---|---|---|---|---|---|
| During husband's last illness | 13 | 27 | – | 18 | 14** | 9 | 33 | 35 |
| During funeral | 28 | 18 | 2 | 20 | 14 | 11 | 57 | 10 |
| With finances | 22 | 10 | 2 | 19 | 13 | 4 | 19 | 63 |
| By being close | 20 | 47 | – | 29 | 24 | 10 | 43 | 7 |
| When feeling blue | 12 | 38 | – | 24 | 21 | 7 | 40 | 24 |
| By giving advice | 28 | 28 | 1 | 24 | 24 | 6 | 34 | 26 |
| By performing services | 24 | 31 | 4 | 29 | 25 | 2 | 39 | 13 |
| Inviting her over | 19 | 20 | 2 | 22 | 12 | 7 | 42 | 32 |
| Coming to see her | 15 | 30 | 3 | 25 | 18 | 7 | 37 | 24 |

?* Means that the mother cannot make *one* of the decisions, either about who was most, or about who was least, helpful. The column headed "Can't Decide" is used if she refuses to discriminate at both levels, and the one headed "Not Applicable" is used if she finds this area of life not requiring help from her children.

   This answer may mean that no help is needed or that the children are not the likely source of it.

** The totals for "most" and "least" are not the same in all areas of help because of frequent multiple listing.

Of the 108 children unmarried at the present time, ninety-three still live with the mother, but the number who were unmarried at the time of widowhood was much larger.[1] Unfortunately, we did not ask the ages at which the children married, so it is impossible to determine with accuracy how many of those listed as the "most" or the "least" helpful at the time the mother needed such assistance were then unmarried and living at home. Residence in the same unit may not, however, be of any help to the widow, if each inhabitant lives in a different rhythm or life style. One woman claims she "never" sees her spinster daughter, because their work schedules result in a shift use of the apartment.

The questions asking for differentiation between the most and the least helpful of offspring in selected areas of life indicate a specialization of relations to the mother by sex, and, to a significant extent, by birth order. Sons are apt to be mentioned by the mothers as managers of funeral arrangements and as financial advisers or providers. Daughters are most often listed as helpers during the father's last illness, as the main source of comfort when she feels "blue," and as being emotionally close. They perform specific services and are more frequently visitors than are their brothers. There is no distinction between the sexes concerning non-financial advice or the extension of invitations to the mother to visit them. Interestingly enough, in view of the above, sons are also often listed as the least helpful in making funeral arrangements, and middle daughters are often declared as the least likely to be "close."

Small children are sometimes listed as of great help because they keep the mother so busy that she does not have time to mourn or feel depressed. Assistance from older offspring does not seem to be desired to the level of dependence, as many of the respondents pointed out. Many, regardless of age, also stated that they do not let their children know when they feel "blue." Women with more than one offspring tend to find the eldest most helpful in giving advice or performing services. A middle daughter is occasionally listed as being the closest, helpful in times of depression, visiting the mother most frequently, or performing services, but children in that birth order are not apt to draw frequent attention at either level of assistance. The youngest daughter is particularly apt to be described as close and helpful. The oldest son is least likely to be identified as the closest of the boys, and the youngest child of either sex is not apt to be defined as the contributor of many services. The closest is not necessarily the most helpful in the task-based activities.

The help patterns reinforce some of the stereotypes of sexual identification in American family relations. Daughters are considered more helpful than sons in the sense of emotional closeness and comfort. A major factor in this identification with their children of the same sex is that widows aged fifty and over are likely to have been brought up and married in a sex-segregated world in which men participated in family relations instrumentally and women expressively (Parsons and Bales, 1955). Sons of those generations were part of the male world; they were expected to take over the father's duties—to give advice, to handle finances, and to make arrangements with the outside world. The mother, later the widow, was expected to turn for understanding and similar identity to her daughter, particularly after the latter has joined her in a set of roles as a wife and mother. After sons leave home and become involved in jobs and outside relations, including those of husband and father, they are expected to be increasingly removed from the mother. The lifetime continuance of sex-segregated relations by women contravenes the modern concept of family life, but the older women were not socialized into the new pattern. The offspring whom these widows considered the most helpful definitely indicated identification with daughters.

However, certain comments of widows with male children would delight Freudians. Some widows receive help which makes them the object of semi-flirtatious attention. Other respondents seem to have reached a "prima donna" position in their families after the death of the patriarch, but it is possible that mothers who are the only women in the family receive such attention even while their husbands are living. Widows surrounded by sons who pay them special attention appear to go through something equivalent to a secondary widowhood when these boys marry and move away.

Basically, though, sons are expected to assist in task-oriented duties connected with their mother's immediate and long range problems. The twenty eldest sons of the 301 widows who failed to carry out this function to the satisfaction of their mothers are clearly listed in their minds as being the least helpful. They are not expected to be of help in other areas, and their failure to accomplish the minimal obligations is clearly recorded. An additional characteristic of the mothers which is of sociological interest is that fewer have problems in deciding who was the most helpful than in determining who was the least useful. The expected level of contribution is remembered as help, while the lack is only labeled negatively in extreme situations. This applies to all children. Those who are in the sex or birth order positions which are traditionally responsible for helping widowed mothers in certain areas of life and who fail to meet these expectations draw negative judgments; they are usually the oldest or the youngest rather than the middle children.

Some widows refused to discriminate among their children, in all or in certain areas of assistance. Although financial help is the kind least required by the mother, two-thirds of them finding that question "not applicable," it drew the fewest "undecided" answers: widows know specifically which children give them the most and which the least monetary aid. The invitations to the child's home and visits are not in question when all of the children are still at home or the mother has an immobilizing incapacity. The latter situation accounts for the difference between the frequency of "inappropriate" definitions of invitations and visits. Those who found the question inapplicable as to help during the husband's illness obviously did not themselves care for him, either because of sudden death, prior marital separation, or care in the hospital.

Often a widow will acknowledge that one child helps her more or less than another and then feels obligated to explain the reasons for this lack of symmetry, even though the question did not call for comments. Most justifications fall into one of the three categories: physical distance, special characteristics of the offspring, and role competition. Most frequent is the explanation that a child lives too far away to be of much help and comfort. This comment is interesting, since many areas of help a widow could receive do not require physical proximity. Financial assistance, "being close," and emotional comfort can be undertaken through the mail, the telephone, and prolonged visits. However, this generation of widows finds more direct contact helpful. Some widows are able to "take the role of the other" in relation to their offspring sufficiently to understand why they are relatively neglected or not assisted by one or another child. One respondent explained that her son was blind, another has a handicapped daughter who can not help in selected areas of life. Role conflict on the part of the offspring, particularly in relation to her or his family of procreation, interfered with help to the family of orientation, including the widow. "He has ten small children; he can't help," is a specific statement of this frequently given excuse for a child. In many situations, the justification included not only the number of grandchildren, but the stages in their life cycle, and it was often accompanied by expectations of greater help in the future. The role conflict was sometimes defined, sadly or with hostility, in terms of the offspring's spouse, who is seen to be the true cause of non-help. Widows often feel that their own children would be of more assistance than they are, if only the husband or wife did not block such action. This attitude keeps them from feeling anger at the offspring, directing it instead at a comparative stranger or outsider, but it undoubtedly contributes to the strain in the interaction between generations.

Questions concerning helpful versus unhelpful, closest, or emotionally most supportive children were often disturbing to the respondents because of the implication of favoritism. In egalitarian American society, siblings, grandchildren, and particularly children are to be "loved equally." This attitude is not universal, even within this society, since lower-class black mothers have traditionally favored female children, while the Judeo-Christian tradition focuses upon the eldest male as the natural recipient of the greatest attention and identification. Other societies, such as the Indian, have built into their cultures the norm that mothers and fathers should select one child for favorite treatment. It is possible that extended families living in shared headquarters can allow open favoritism, because any child who is allowed to live can find some relative for whom he can be the favorite, but the more likely explanation is that these cultures assume inequality in all social relations. The anxiety evoked by the topic of favoritism, particularly among Americans of middle-class background, indicates that asymmetry of feelings and identifications is present, but sufficiently against the norms to be personally disturbing. When deprived of a cultural justification for favoritism, the American parent of a small number of children may pretend that variations of feeling and self-projection do not exist. Such a problem may be particularly acute in one-parent families. The de-institutionalization of open favoritism may be difficult not only for the widow, but for the non-favored child, who may conclude that there is something basically unlovable or "wrong" with him or her.

In spite of the fact that many mothers refused to identify one child as "closer" or more emotionally supportive than another, the majority found no such problems. Fewer had problems identifying the closest than the least close.

*"Sons are More Help to a Widow Than Daughters."* The various comments of widows concerning the relative contributions of different children which were tapped during the exploratory research led to the inclusion of the following statement into the "relations-restrictive attitude scale": "Sons are more help to a widow than daughters." The results support the conclusions drawn from the help chart. Only seven percent of the respondents agree strongly with this attitude, and another fourteen percent simply agree. The remaining seventy-nine percent were distributed as follows: forty-two percent disagree; thirteen percent disagree strongly; and twenty-four women find the statement irrelevant, because they personalize it and they do not have any children of their own, have only one offspring, or have either all girls or all boys (see Table VII in Appendix C).

Women who do not find sons more help than daughters are more family-oriented than those who agree with the statement, in that they also rank higher on the sibling scale. They do not date, or, if they do, they make no distinction as to the marital status of their escorts. They make no claim that their sexual relations with their husbands were good until his final illness, and they do not wish more male companionship right now. Thus, except for the few daters, they reject male relations more than women who find sons of greater help than daughters. At the same time, women who prefer their male offspring hold many negative attitudes toward a variety of people. They are not the "normal" or happily adjusted mothers of this sample. They believe that sharing one's home causes trouble for widows, that women lose status when their husband dies, that relatives are "your only true friends," and that married friends were not much help to them during their period of grief. They lived sex-segregated lives with their husbands and were unfamiliar with family finances, pretending also not to know how ill the man was in his last years. They express an interestingly conflicting set of feelings, agreeing both with the statement "I wish people wouldn't try to get me to go out and do things all the time" and with "I would do more things outside of the home if someone would come and pick me up." The combination is one of rejection of many people, in spite of a passive adherence to traditional stances. It indicates the need of widows to relate satisfactorily to daughters; if they reject or feel rejected by the female offspring, they also find other relations unsatisfactory.

*"One Problem With Adult Children is that they Always Want You to Do Favors for them: Baby-sit, or Sew, or Things Like That."* One reason why mothers become dissatisfied with their relations with one or more children is that they feel the balance between their rights and duties is unjust. Often the older widow has decreased her level of work around the home to a comfortable level and resents being asked to work for others, even for her adult children. Some of the favors demanded or timidly asked by offspring cause inconvenience and even irritation. Another reason is their relative independence and the competition of other roles. Modern women are likely to have children in the hectic *expanding circle* and *full house plateau* stages of their family of procreation cycle, while they themselves are still young and full of energy. The grandmother who re-engages in a multi-dimensional and busy life after the death of her husband often resents demands made upon her by adult children not because she wants to sit quietly, but because she wants to do other things. She put in her "stint" as a family woman and now she wants to engage in leisure-time activities. Particularly in the middle and upper classes grandmothers have been released from the traditional automatic acceptance of work. As servants become scarce in society and fewer young women are able to afford them, they turn to the mother for help. The more affluent mothers never had to do such work because they had

servants, the newly comfortable do not want to return to it. The revolt of the grandmother against work in the home of her adult children is also evidenced by her belief that the main compensations to widowhood are: less work and more free time.

This unwillingness to undertake obligations toward married children was expressed so often during the exploratory research as to warrant its inclusion in the relation-restrictive attitude scale. The Chicago area widows were asked to express agreement with the following statement: "One problem with adult children is that they always want you to do favors for them—baby-sit, or sew, or things like that" (see Table VIII in Appendix C). This is a relatively strong statement, negating the traditional functions of the gladly helpful grandmother. The respondents are older women, mostly minimally educated and thus in the old-fashioned mold. However, eight percent agreed strongly with the statement, twenty-four percent agreed, thirty-eight percent disagreed, and only fifteen percent disagreed strongly. Another fourteen percent refused to make any judgment, presumably because their lack of experience made it impossible to judge parent-child relations. Thus, one-third of these widows agree that adult children make unwarranted demands on their parents.

The respondents who hold this attitude toward children are likely to be socially isolated and not as apt to have a high contact score as those who feel more positively toward their role of mother. Their other attitudes are also restrictive of social relations. Indeed, this attitude distinguishes significantly between the women who are at the extremes of these three scales. A widow who thinks children demand too many favors tends to be low on the role of mother scale and to have a low average frequency of contact with her offspring. Thus, there is a relation between her attitudes and her actions. She does not even uphold the obligation to purify her husband by making him an unusually good man. Although wishing more friends, she is angry at her current associates, whom she judged as unhelpful in her time of grief. She also felt angry at the doctor and hospital for not saving her husband. She did not know the family finances and states that her present income makes it impossible to retain friendships. She thinks sons are more help than daughters, that relatives are one's only true friends, and that people take advantage of widows; she experienced a status drop after the death of the husband and says that sharing a home causes nothing but trouble. Finally, she wishes people wouldn't bother her by trying to get her to do things outside of her home. This is a strong combination of the more negative statements in the relations-restrictive scale.

One of the services included in this question drew especially negative statements, not only in this part of the interview, but throughout, and that is baby-sitting. Although there are many widows who enjoy going to the home of their children and "sitting" with the grandchildren while the middle generation goes out, or having the young ones dropped off at their own houses, many find it to be an imposition. Although usually enjoying contact with their grandchildren, many widows feel that "baby-sitting" is really an irksome duty to their children rather than a pleasant privilege. There are several characteristics which deprive this activity of relational pleasure. In the first place, baby-sitting has become a paid occupation, usually performed by unskilled teen-agers, and many widows feel their children should spend the money for such help. Baby-sitters are usually used to release the parents for social events at which the single widow would feel uncomfortable or which she envies; she is therefore resentful. Why should she work so that they can play? As currently institutionalized, the role of baby-sitter is also a passive one, not allowing active socialization of the young into established styles of life or even punishment for transgressions. The person is expected to literally sit and watch the child, performing only actions which keep the child healthy and happy. Such watered-down "grandparenting" is not fulfilling, particularly to women accustomed to "authority" and "respect" from the young.

The rights and duties uniting a widow and her married children do not always end with agreement as to what is a just balance. Some women expect from their children help or at least attention of a type or degree they are not receiving; others are bothered by what they consider excessive demands. Whatever the overall pattern, most widows do not obtain a great deal of financial aid from their children during the time immediately following the death of their husband. The interviews indicate that few depended upon their offspring at the time when they had to re-establish life into a more or less comfortable pattern. In fact, the rate of self-sufficiency in widowhood is surprisingly high when it comes to finances (see Chapter Two). The current reported income indicates, however, that a number of respondents were rather short or really restricted at the time they were interviewed. Probably what happens is that immediate needs are solved by short range methods, enabling children to relax about their need to contribute to the newly widowed mother. As the years go by, funds become exhausted, work is no longer available, and the widow gradually loses her financial strength. Usually the process is slow and does not result in a sufficiently dramatic event to call for a re-evaluation by adult children. Children seem to assume that once the social and financial problems following the funeral are settled, new needs are not likely to arise. The widow had the funds then, so she is not helped later. A final consideration is that the modern widow really does not want economic dependence upon her children, preferring to be restricted rather than to turn to such a solution of her problems. There seems to be an undercurrent of anxiety that a plea of help will diminish the level of pleasure of interaction now available, so that the widow prefers to keep quiet than to ask for additional assistance.

## RESIDENTIAL ARRANGEMENTS OF WIDOWS

### Living Alone
The independence of widows is reflected by the fact that forty-nine percent of them are able to live alone, and that sixty-nine percent of those who have someone else in the home are the formal heads of such households, either because they are the owners or the main renters. In only twenty-one percent of the cases is the headship in the hands of the offspring; two percent live in parents' homes, three percent in those of siblings, four percent in those of other relatives, and two percent in homes belonging to non-relatives. Twenty-nine percent of the total number of respondents live with only one other person, twelve percent with two others, and ten percent with more than that. The last group is not necessarily composed of three-generation families, as a closer analysis shows. The total number of people with whom the 153 respondents who share a residence are living is 277. Eighty-nine of these co-residents are under the age of twenty-one, but only forty-four of them are her children. Thus, forty-five of the youngsters are less directly connected with her, as grandchildren, nephews, or nieces. Two-thirds of the people with whom a widow lives are thus adults (277 minus 89). In general, sixty-seven percent of the total number of widows do not have an offspring in the house, young or adult, but the larger the number of children a woman has the greater is the probability of her having one under the age of twenty-one who is still living in the home.

The greatest proportion of children with whom the widows are living are unmarried (see Table IX, Appendix C for total number of children by marital status). Only twenty-two live with married children and their families; one-third of these are black, although this race consists of only one-sixth of the sample. Eight respondents live with separated or divorced, and six with widowed offspring, and a high proportion of these are black. The total sample has 108 unmarried children, and ninety-three of these live with the widowed mother. A disproportionate number of the fifteen who live away are black. Thus, black widows are much more likely than their white counterparts to live with now or previously married children, although this sharing is not a continuous pattern. More of the whites live with unmarried offspring.

Women who live alone are likely to have a limited number of children or no surviving offspring. Thus, mothers of only children are not likely to be living with them at the age of fifty or above, whereas respondents with four or more living children usually have one in the house who has not yet reached marital age, or who delays starting his own family. Race is not a significant factor differentiating the proportion living alone, but this is mostly because of the high proportion of black women who have no living offspring. When widows with no children are left out of consideration, the black woman is more likely to be living with an offspring than the white woman is. Ethnic differences are pronounced. All of the Greek women are living with married children and declare this to be part of their culture. Only half of the Polish women live alone, while seventy-six percent of the Germans, seventy-seven percent of the Italians, and seventy-eight percent of the British live alone. In general, the figures support the tentative conclusion that women with strong ethnic affiliations and lower socio-economic backgrounds are more likely to live with their children, partly because they have more of them and are widowed earlier, but also partly because of an inability to maintain themselves alone. This capacity is cultural, because women are not expected to be independent, and also realistic, since they cannot fend for themselves in an urban environment. The assumption that widows move to the Chicago area from other locations in order to live with their offspring is not borne out by the statistical distributions. Those most likely to be living alone are women who migrated in their teens; those least likely are widows coming in their fifties.

Age is the most important variable influencing the probability of solitary residence (see Table 24).

Thus, widows are most likely to live with one or more children when

TABLE 24: THE NUMBER OF CHILDREN LIVING WITH A
WIDOW BY HER AGE IN DECADES

| Number of Children in Same Dwelling Unit | Total N | Total % | Age in Decades 59– % | 60–69 % | 70–79 % | 80+ % | Total % |
|---|---|---|---|---|---|---|---|
| None | 203 | 67 | 21 | 42 | 30 | 7 | 100 |
| One | 73 | 24 | 26 | 36 | 23 | 15 | 100 |
| Two | 18 | 6 | 61 | 33 | — | 6 | 100 |
| Three | 4 | 1 | 75 | 25 | — | — | 100 |
| Four | 2 | 1 | 100 | — | — | — | 100 |
| Five | 1 | 0 | 100 | — | — | — | 100 |
| Percent base | 301 | | 79 | 118 | 77 | 27 | |

they are young and the children are still unmarried, or later when the mothers are very old and unable to take care of themselves. However, even the women who are eighty years of age or over are not likely to be living in the children's households, as only one-fourth share a residence with one or two offspring. Fifty-six percent of them still live alone, almost the same proportion as in the youngest age group, fifty-four percent of whom are already alone. That is, although this table supports conclusions drawn from other life-cycle studies, the stereotype which assumes that the elderly always live with offspring is not borne out, partly because they tend to outlive their children, but partly because of their continued insistence on independent housing.

Cross-tabulations of residential sharing by evaluations of the importance of the role of mother indicate that widows living with one child are the most likely to list the role of mother in the first place. Women with more children in the dwelling are likely to rank it second, after that of wife, and women living alone give it second or even third place. It is, of course, impossible to determine the emotional significance of such ranking patterns. Those who live alone may be more removed from the role of mother because of physical distance, so that it plays a less significant part in their lives; or *vice versa,* they may be unwilling to live with offspring because they do not value the relation highly. All six of the women who rank it in one of the two bottom of the six positions are living alone.

Widows—especially home-owners—living with someone else are the least likely to feel that sharing one's residence with others creates trouble. Twenty-two percent of the respondents are living in residences which are headed by someone other than themselves, but only thirteen percent of these agree with the statement. This may be merely the caution of not biting the hand that feeds, but it is also quite possible that the respondents willing to move into the home of another person are the least likely to expect and experience trouble. Women sharing a residence with someone else, however, are more apt to believe that they lost status with the death of the husband than those who live alone; this tendency is particularly strong among those living not with a child, but with a sibling or other relative. It is also possible that having to move into the home of a non-child is more humiliating than having a child willingly share living quarters. Also, those who live with someone else are the most likely to feel that "My present income makes it impossible to maintain old friends."

In sum, women living with children are apt to be in their own homes with unmarried offspring and to be in the youngest age group studied, that in the fifties. Many work or receive some economic help from the oldest child in the residence, but they have minimal incomes for this age group. Those with several children are more often Catholic in religion and of minority ethnic or racial status. Women with higher incomes and more education are more apt to be living alone. Those with no schooling have at least one child in the home. A relatively high proportion of the children who live with their mothers are of marriageable age or older, but many will marry later in life, so that widows in their seventies tend to lose even adult children from the household through marriage and movement away or death. Within this decade are located a disproportionately large number of solitary residents.

Of the twenty-two respondents who live with married children, all but five live with daughters, and eleven, or half, live with the eldest female offspring. The sex is not significant in shared residence with unmarried offspring, but women who are widowed, divorced, or separated are slightly more likely to live with their mothers than men (eight to six). This means that seventy-two of the children of various marital statuses living with their mothers are women and fifty-seven are men. This distribution reinforces the previous conclusion, that widows feel closer to their daughters than to their sons, or that the daughters feel a greater obligation. In addition, more women than men live in the same building as their mothers, but in a different dwelling unit (nineteen to seven). Fourteen of these girls are married. The sexual difference becomes less pronounced as the distance to the mother increases. Whatever their distance, more daughters (eleven) than sons (four) have reached widowhood.

*"I Like Living Alone."* The conclusion that older widows live alone out of a desire for independence and freedom is supported in a more detailed examination of agreement with the statement: "I like living alone." Almost half of the respondents agree, thirty-six percent disagree, and eighteen percent abstained, presumably because they already live with someone. Those expressing agreement are not necessarily the widows who are solitary residents, or *vice versa* (see Table 25), but a much higher proportion of those living alone feel this way than of those sharing a residence.

In general, the larger the number of people with whom the widow is living, to the number of four, the less likely she is to agree with the statement "I like living alone." One-third (forty-two) of the solitary residents answering both questions do not like this living arrangement, and there are forty-seven respondents who live with other people, yet claim to like living alone. Actually very few women live with more than two other persons, only eight percent of the total being in such circumstances. The fact that relatively few widows who live with two, three, or four other people would prefer living alone indicates either that the problems of

TABLE 25: AGREEMENT WITH THE STATEMENT: "I LIKE
LIVING ALONE" BY THE NUMBER OF PEOPLE IN
THE HOUSEHOLD, INCLUDING THE WIDOW

| | | I Like Living Alone | | | | | |
|---|---|---|---|---|---|---|---|
| Number in Household | Total | True | | False | | No Answer | |
| | % | No. | % | No. | % | No. | % |
| One (alone) | 57 | 97 | 70 | 42 | 30 | 9 | 6 |
| Two | 24 | 27 | 46 | 32 | 54 | 29 | 49 |
| Three | 11 | 8 | 29 | 20 | 71 | 7 | 25 |
| Four | 3 | 2 | 33 | 4 | 67 | 5 | 83 |
| Five | 3 | 1 | 14 | 6 | 86 | 4 | 57 |
| Six | 1 | 0 | — | 3 | 100 | — | |
| Seven | 1 | 1 | 50 | 1 | 50 | — | |
| Eight | 0 | 1 | 100 | 0 | — | 1 | 100 |
| Nine | 0 | 0 | — | 1 | 100 | — | |
| N | | 137 | | 109 | | 55 | |

Percent Base = 246
* Not counted in percent base

sharing a residence are exaggerated in the minds of other women or that
the self-selection system is operating well. The latter alternative refers
to the possibility that women who like to live in large households are the
most likely to agree to such arrangements. Women living with only one
other person are the least apt to be satisfied with such an arrangement.

The younger the woman at the time she becomes a widow, the more
likely she is to agree that she likes living alone (see Table X in Appendix
C). This tendency indicates both adjustment to solitary residence and
the possibility that women widowed at different ages respond to different
implications of the statement. Those younger at widowhood may either
be expressing satisfaction with independence or thinking of other men
as residential companions. Those who were very old at that time may be
less desirous of independence and more lonely without their husbands.
The fact that the older the woman, the less likely she is to want to live
alone throws into question the dis-engagement theory (see Cumming and
Henry, 1961), according to which people willingly shrink their social life
space in old age.

Cross-tabulations between the statement "I like living alone" and other
relations-restrictive attitudes indicate a rejection of that position by
women who define their husband as an unusually good man (see Table
XI in Appendix C). Having been ignorant of family finances prior to
the husband's death, the widow who now likes living alone was helped
to recover from grief by her faith rather than by friends and is resentful

of this alleged lack of assistance. She has finally achieved a feeling of freedom and independence and an easier life, none of which she wants to lose by sharing a home. She holds an interesting set of attitudes toward men, denying that she wants more male companionship, while stating that it is all right for widows to have sexual relations without planning on marriage, that husbands of friends proposition widows, and that the wives are jealous. There are only twenty-five women who like living alone and who wish for more male companionship, while twenty-two of the respondents contravene a strong norm of their generation of Americans by approving sexual relations without marriage. It is possible that older widows who never remarried, although they had been deprived of a husband early in life, hold attitudes which prevent pleasant interaction with members of the opposite sex.

## REASONS FOR NOT LIVING WITH MARRIED CHILDREN

The fact that few widows aged fifty and over would be living with their married children, and that this is a consequence of choice rather than coincidence or unavailability of offspring was anticipated from research of other cities and countries. Rosenmayr and Kockeis (1963) found that the elderly of Vienna, Austria, wanted independent living from their children, but "intimacy at a distance." Several teams of sociologists working with Ethel Shanas (1968) also concluded that living apart from married offspring is the choice of older people in the United States, England, and Denmark (see also Kosa *et. al.*, 1960). The data are somewhat surprising in view of the Western European culture, particularly its family ideology. Until recently, women were strongly discouraged from living alone; many would seem ill-equipped by training and socialization to maintain themselves alone in a complex urban center. Yet the contributors to *Old People in Three Industrial Societies* (Shanas, 1968) concluded, from research of family history on both continents, that few families had actually been able to carry on three-generational households even prior to industrialization and urbanization (Winch and Blumberg, 1968). That so many relatively uneducated residents of Chicago and of small towns of Missouri (Pihlblad and Rosencranz, 1968; Adams, 1969) are living alone may be less a proof of their competence to exist in the modern world and more a result of the strong wish to live independently; a reversal of factors can be anticipated for future generations.

The unwillingness of widows to live with their married offspring is primarily a consequence of the shift of home management and was investigated through interview questions. The first of these read: "Have you ever lived with any (other) of your children for longer than a month?" The hypothesis behind this query was that changes in living arrangements are expected to be sufficiently traumatic, or their attempts sufficiently difficult, as to make them subject to experimentation and change. We expected some widows to have tried living with their married children, but to have found the arrangement unsatisfactory to the extent of changing residence. The study proved that this type of experimentation and shift was very rare. Only nineteen percent of the widows not now living with children tried that type of housing in the past. This means that twenty-two of the 301 respondents now live with married children, fifty-four have no living offspring, and forty-seven of the remaining lived for an extended period of time with one of their offspring and then terminated the arrangement.

The second question in the series directs itself to the length of time of such a residential arrangement, and the third to "What factors influenced you to move to another place after living there?" Most of the forty-seven women who stated that they had lived in the homes of married children in the past explained carefully that the arrangement was designed from the beginning to be temporary. The child or the mother had crisis needs which required the sharing of a household and led to a separation once the problems were solved. Those admitting relational problems gave reasons interestingly similar to those elicited by the next query: "Many women say that there are problems in living with children after they are grown up and married, no matter how nice everyone is. What (is/do you think would be/was) the most important problem in the situation? PROBE FULLY. And the next most important?" The similarity of answers indicates either that the "sub-culture" of the widowed contains realistic estimates of relational problems, or that situational anticipation becomes a "self-fulfilling prophecy" when women live with married children.

American culture provides explanations of why parents should not live with married children: "Two women in the same kitchen are no good," "The generation gap; they have their ideas, I have mine," "Young people like to be alone," and "I want to do my life my way." The formulas prevent the situation from becoming too personalized. What the widow is saying is: "It is not me they hesitate to have live with them, but all generations have different needs," "I am not a problem to them, just modern life," or "I am not an 'unnatural mother' for not wanting to live with them, but older people need quiet." If fully believed, these statements not only prevent attempts at living together, but also prevent feelings of guilt or rejection. Since cultural change brings strains between expectations and actions, such systems of belief bridge the gaps. We can

predict that the family institution in urban, industrial, and complex societies will increasingly incorporate proverbs, legends, and admonitions
which warn widows from living with their married children. As of now,
the frequency with which such statements are used and the degree to
which they are actually believed are not necessarily matched. It seems
that, although fifty-nine percent of the responses are couched in such
depersonalized terms, with twenty-six percent referring to the generational
gap and eighteen percent to the inability of two women to run the same
home, the following secondary statements are still very personal. Only
sixteen percent of the respondents feel that there are no, or would be no,
problems when widows live with their married children. A disproportionate number of such judgments are made by black widows, reflecting
another aspect of the black community's life.

When really pressed, most respondent interpreted the question about
problems of living with married children in very personal terms. They
list specific difficulties of their own interactional situation or they project
from the concrete into the hypothetical future, from short encounters
into permanent co-habitation. The difficulties they visualize can be classified as involving one or several separate roles: housewife, mother, mother-
in-law, grandmother, and friend. The complexity of these responses is
not surprising in view of the multi-dimensionality of modern role patterns.
When several people live together, the combination of their relations can
create a multiplicity of problems, particularly if the basic unit has developed a system of interaction which does not include an outsider. When
explaining problems they expect to have in such situations, widows often
assume that "instant" living together is accomplished by other people.
The American dreams of non-conflict and perfect personality are believed
sufficiently by widows for them to assume that their fears are unique.

The foundation of all problems for a widow living with married children is her position in such an arrangement. Traditionally, the mother
became the center of a household, even in patriarchal societies; one or
more children remained and gradually or formally took over its management at a certain stage of life. Lines of territoriality and authority remained in her hands until the transfer, and vestiges remained. If two
women were judged capable of running a household owned by a man,
formal regulations established who was the "housewife" on the basis of
marital, age, or other priorities (Ross, 1961; Freedman, 1965).

Modern societies, organized along identity and authority lines other
than familial, modifying residential inheritance and permitting neolocal
residence, have confused traditional family roles. Children move away
and establish their own households, usually before the death of the father.

A combined residence later in life can usually be accomplished only if the widow is willing to give up her house and move into one under the authority of a younger woman, daughter or daughter-in-law, and her family. The new wife had married with the assumption that she could establish her own home, supported by her work and by the income of her husband. Since the dwelling was not inherited, she does not feel an obligation to sacrifice any control to the older mother.

Thus, the main area of conflict between a widowed mother and her daughter or daughter-in-law focuses upon the management of the household, and this area contains several different problems. One of these concerns the right to determine how the work in the home is divided and accomplished. The main housewife assumes the right of control over the possessions belonging to her and her family. She can tell a maid, children, or even her husband how they should contribute to the management, based on her definition of their abilities and needs. She makes the decision and has the right to complain if they do not complete the tasks according to her wishes. Such a division of labor includes the assignment of a task, specification of procedures, rhythm, and product; and the right to judge the end result. The younger woman's inability to demand a certain flow of work or to criticize the older woman living in her home would leave her powerless and frustrated. The older mother, on the other hand, resents the reversal of the relation from earlier years of her daughter's life or from traditional authority of the matriarch in her own home.[2]

Another aspect of the real or anticipated conflict between a widow and the daughter or daughter-in-law into whose home she would have to move, if she decided not to live alone, relates to her feeling of status loss in giving up the role of housewife. Young women, influenced by the new "Women's Liberation" movement, or trained for other occupational roles, devalue the role of housewife; older widows often find this role of great importance and identity. They hate to give up being the "mistress of the house." A possible solution, of course, would be for the older woman, who still wishes to be a housewife, to manage the home, while her daughter or daughter-in-law could happily participate in the larger society without giving up her rights in the roles of wife and mother. The intertwining of these three roles makes this ideal difficult to attain. Also, as mentioned before, many widows do not want to do that much work, particularly when the household contains several people.

The opposite side of the household management picture can also create problems. Some daughters or daughters-in-law refuse to share the role of housewife with the mother when the latter moves into their homes.

Such a position is usually justified as being for the benefit of the widow, but the result can be a feeling of complete uselessness. One respondent explained why she finally moved out of the home of her son: "I don't like to be a bother. I had nothing to do. She wouldn't let me *do anything*. She was overly kind." Others complained that the refusal of the mistress of the house to allow them to participate in the work flow accentuated their position as an outsider and minimized their feeling of being competent human beings.

Other combinations of strains causing irritation and even competition are reported or expected by the widows. Tension scenes produce feelings of rejection and accentuate their feelings of insecurity. Generally speaking, it is the widow who is the most likely to suffer in the competition of housewife role performers. She is the invader in a home organized and managed by the younger woman, whose husband and children are likely to take her side in arguments.

The concept of territoriality is related to the role of housewife and house occupant. An on-going family has an operating use of space and rights over it. Sleeping, eating, and even bathroom space is assigned to residents for certain times, to be used in a manner judged appropriate. The rhythm is broken by the introduction of another person into the household, causing irritations of which the stranger is apt to be aware. Use of the bathroom is symbolic of spacial rights problems, and references to overcrowding, in combination with noise and commotion, are frequently made by widows. The allocation of even incomplete rights over certain spaces to the widow usually deprives someone else of their rights. These problems are sometimes solved when the family of the married child moves to a new location when the mother decides to live with them. In the new residence, spacial rights are allocated with her in mind, so that the rights she gains are not obtained at the cost of former owners. Such a solution prevents irritation on the part of the family and saves the mother from feeling that she is impinging upon others' territorial rights.

Difficulties in working out a satisfactory set of relations in the role of housewife between a woman managing a home and the mother or mother-in-law who moves into it are expected to occur in American urban centers under the following conditions:

1. If it is the home of the younger woman;
2. If that woman is a daughter-in-law or a daughter with whom the transmission of authority lines is difficult to accomplish;
3. If one or the other woman does not want to work out a new division of labor because of possessiveness, lack of trust in the other, or personality rigidities;

4. If the home does not require enough maintenance by two housewives as to enable each to derive a sense of worth from her independent contributions;
5. If the level of competence in the role is unequal and visible;
6. If the interpersonal relations interfer with task allocation of performance, and blockage comes from other members of the household;
7. If individualism and familism are differently represented in the
   perceptions of the role of housewife by the two generations;
8. If neither woman has alternative role specializations.

The most difficult situation occurs when the widow has to break up
housekeeping before she is psychologically ready for it, and she moves to
a home which is culturally different from the one she managed, due to
the rate of cultural change, the social mobility of her offspring, or marriage by her child outside of her identity group. The highest level of
problems is imposed upon the living arrangement if there is an emotional
reaction on both sides to the division of labor or the manner in which
the tasks are carried out. Even small areas in the role of housewife may
become symbolic of basic differences or difficulties, as when irritation
arises repeatedly over the content and timing of meals.

The relation between the widow and specific others in the household
can create problems in other social roles besides that of housewife. The
role of mother is a source of actual or anticipated strain for Chicago
area widows contemplating life with their married children. The problems vary according to the sex and the connection of the offspring with
the mother. There are four types of relations in the role of mother to
married children:

[Model of Mother-Child Relations]

|  | Offspring | In-law |
|---|---|---|
| Daughter | 1 | 3 |
| Son | 2 | 4 |

This study indicates that mothers presently living in the homes of married children, those having had that experience in the past, or those considering it for the future are most concerned about their daughters-in-law.
Sons-in-law are also mentioned, but not as frequently. The fear, sometimes very strong, is interesting when compared to the situation of the
traditional matriarch of China, or even India, who looked forward to the

time her son brought his wife home, because she would take over much of the burden of work. The Chinese system was hard on the daughter-in-law (see Goode, 1963:309), but the modern American system makes the widow hesitant to enter a home managed by the wife of her son. How much of this attitude revolves around a competition for the son in a patriarchally-founded system is hard to determine. An excellent summation of the widow's attitudes is contained in the following: "Well, I could never live with my son, because his wife is not friendly to me."

Other widows, however, worry over the possibility of conflict with their own offspring in a situation of shared residence. Asked what are the problems of living with married children, one stated: "I think they ought to be separated. I think a son is not a son after he gets married." Another stated the situation somewhat more directly: "Children change so; they change so after they get away from their parents; their character and personalities change; they're more difficult; they get set in their ways; they don't always agree with you." These statements express the feelings of two mothers who witnessed their child changing with the addition of adult roles, a transformation which they interpret in relation to themselves. They want small children, not adults, in personal interaction. Feelings of alienation are particularly prevalent in American society, which socializes children to be different from their parents. Here the rate of cultural change and upward mobility are so great that people can easily develop a style of life and a personality quite different from those into which they had been socialized by mothers and fathers. "Children change so after they get away from their parents," is thus a realistic appraisal of the situation, yet it indicates sadness and disappointment, especially when it implies a rejection of the mother's values and norms. In addition, the increased independence of offspring can disturb authoritarian parents.

According to Robert Winch's (1962) theory of identification, parents with many advantages, who can continue to offer married children rewards for interaction, are the ones with whom continued identification can be expected. The respondents who felt uncomfortable with their adult children tend to be lower-class women whose children had become successful.

Even without status decrystallization between generations, there are universal changes in the mother-child relations as the children undertake new roles away from the home. In America these modifications are not comfortably institutionalized, as evidenced by repeated observations of generational "gap" and conflict. At the same time, mothers often report an increase in identification of their daughters with them and a mutuality of interests, as the latter undertake the roles of wife and mother.

One area of interaction between a widow and her adult children and their families can be broadly defined as "impingement upon the rights of others to lead their own lives." Naturally, the problem has two directions of flow: the widow impinges upon the life style of her children and their families, or vice versa. An area of interaction which is frequently mentioned in such terms is that of advice-giving or criticism. "I don't believe in living with children. The biggest reason would be that parents should not interfere in their children's lives," is a general statement of the problem. A much more specific one comes from another respondent: "The compulsion to give advice. Advice is always resented, and I think the resentments would build." The process of advice-giving, felt to be detrimental to relations between married children and their mothers, has several aspects. It assumes that the advice-giver knows how to analyze a problem and find solutions better than the person toward whom the advice is directed. Such a stance is often demeaning to the recipient. Sometimes the situation in question is not regarded as problematic by the recipient, because of differences in values. Value conflicts are often contained in the solution itself. A solution "obvious" to the observer of partial scenes may ignore other factors of which the recipient is aware, but which he does wish to bring to the attention of the adviser.

Many widows recognize some of the problems of the adviser stance and yet continue to give advice. Part of this syndrome is a consequence of the role of mother, which generally acknowledges her position as a situation-definer and behavior-determiner. Such rights in relation to small children are difficult to leave behind when the offspring become adults who are able to see their own world with greater perception than an outsider. Even mothers who define their own behavior as "meddling" may feel duty-bound to offer advice and criticism when they think their children are acting in ways detrimental to their welfare. They identify with their offspring and find it impossible to follow the "minding my own business" rule.

An area of disagreement between widows and their married children, frequently defined as a major problem in intergenerational living, is child-rearing. Most societies assign great importance to the role of mother, and most women have definite ideas as to the norms of behavior in this role. Not only its importance, but its rate of change in modern urban centers, produce great differences and intergenerational tensions. Old patterns have become dramatically de-institutionalized so recently that the older generation often can not cope with the behavior of modern mothers, fathers, and children. The Chicago area widows aged fifty and over were especially upset about the child-rearing methods of the middle generation, that is, over the behavior of their own children and in-laws toward the grandchildren. The interviews indicate that this is an area of higher emotionality and tension than the actual behavior of the grandchildren *vis-à-vis* the grandmother, although that, too, can be a problem.

The problems with the third generation are often symbolized by the widows in terms of "respect." This concept encompasses aspects of deference and demeanor (Goffman, 1956) which have undergone dramatic changes in modern urban America. Traditional means of showing "respect" in social relations have been modified, and this aspect of interaction has often been replaced by a more informal egalitarianism. In addition, the new concept of children's individual dignity makes many young people feel that their rights are not being respected by the older members of the kin group. That is, grandmothers do not grant the youngest generation either traditional or modern rights of respect, while feeling themselves deprived of the accustomed symbols of dignity. Generally, grandmothers who complain most about this aspect of their relations with grandchildren are the ones who have not had frequent, close, and direct contact with the youth, seeing them usually in the presence of the intermediary generation.

Conflict between husband and wife is often embarrassing for an outsider to witness, especially the mother of one of them. The protective habit of motherhood makes an impartial or non-interfering stance difficult.

Impingement upon the rights of individuals by the actions or expressed attitudes of outsiders comes from both directions. A rather large number of older widows fear that they will lose their own independence if they move in with their children. "I never took orders from my husband, and I sure as hell couldn't take orders from the children," is a strong explanation of why one widow lives alone. When probed, the importance of independence seems to focus upon the right to "get up and go when I please" and not having to "wait until they decide what they are going to do, and then fit in." The woman wants the right to make decisions as to her own life rhythm, activities, finances, and even cooking. This does not necessarily mean that she wants to engage in activities which would meet the disapproval of her offspring. Most respondents even disclaim the desire to have more male companionship, and all but a few disagree with the statement that a widow can have sexual relations without planning on marriage. They just want to plan and carry on their lives at their own speed, without comments from their "efficient" children.

The right of a woman to express herself freely is often stated as part of the whole concept of independence of identity, rather than just as a source of concern over relational tensions. This freedom of spirit shows that widows are not as dependent as often portrayed, or as their educational and income backgrounds might indicate (see also Marris, 1958). Many may not have the skills to reorganize their lives dramatically by making new friends and re-engaging in society; they may sit and wait for children to visit or take them places, but they are generally quite sure that they want to remain mistresses of their own homes. Lonely at times, they prefer this to being a dependent or peripheral person in the home of a married offspring.

A major reason a widow may not be living with her children is seldom stated directly and openly. One respondent who lived with an offspring for six months gave the following explanation for moving: "I think you're better off alone, if you are older. Children kind of get on your nerves at times, and I didn't feel I had the right to correct them. And I felt, if I moved, it would be better. I know I was welcome there by my daughter and son-in-law. This move was strictly my choice." However, when asked what the problems of living with married children are, she said: "I feel that it's the widows that live with children are the ones that have imaginary problems. *They imagine they're not wanted,* that they have to do too much and have to help with children. They feel they are not wanted. Young people feel they want to discuss things, and they don't want anyone around or anyone else's opinion."

It is impossible to determine the prevalence of anxiety on the part of the widow that she is simply not wanted by married children from the data collected for this study. Allusions to such anxieties are often expressed so indirectly as to preclude an estimation of their strength. Interestingly enough, no one mentions, even by indirection, the fear that the offspring might be hurt by the widow's refusal to move in with them. Thus, rejection is seen as a one-way street, re-emphasizing the older widow's feeling of a drop in personal value. Nor is it possible as yet to really measure the balance between the desire of a widow to spend her remaining years without work, noise, commotion, tension, and conflict and her unconscious fear of rejection. We can not ignore the fact that thirty-six percent of the respondents believe that "This time of my life is actually easier than any other," and that forty-two percent agree with the statement: "I feel more independent and free now than before I became a widow."

## DISTANCE FROM CHILDREN

The geographical distribution of adult children of the Chicago area widows reflects the family decrystallization trends in this type of society.

Traditional societies developed institutionalized procedures by which off-spring dispersed from the parental homestead upon reaching some age symbolically significant of adulthood and upon achieving resources for self-maintenance away from the family. In agricultural societies, all, or designated, sons remained on the land of their parents. Even the visiting patterns of older parents and their offspring were socially delineated. Factors such as social class, number and sex of living children, occupational availability, and marriage customs influenced the distance children settled from their older parents and the contact maintained with them. Offspring were socialized to expect to live in specified locations in relation to their parents, and parents knew that some of their children would have to move away, usually upon marriage.

Industrialization has changed and is continuing to change the system. Men, and later women, became economically emancipated from parental training, work, and dependence upon tools of sustenance. The scarcity economy and the Protestant Ethic combined to justify a child's moving from his parental home in search of a better job than the one locally available. Migration from the land of socialization eventually included movement to different societies and parts of the world. Men usually initiated cross-border moves, thus contributing to the breakup of the patrilineal and patrilocal residence unit. It is possible that a gradual transformation occurred at that time in the relation of a mother to her sons and daughters. No longer able to depend on her son as the only off-spring to remain in the home, she gradually shifted her allegiance to the daughters. In the past, daughters could not be depended upon in patri-local societies to provide continued contact; now sons ceased to be called on for constant help and support. Of course, even daughters might move away as their husbands seek greener economic fields, but the mother can keep on believing that they did so involuntarily, that they would have preferred to stay near her. Duty to the husband, and dependence upon him, form a justification for neglecting the duty to the mother to continue being geographically close.

The movement of the offspring from the home territory into the labor force has had a second important influence upon the family, and that is status decrystallization even within the same generation. The different children do not necessarily move into the same occupation or career pattern; brothers and husbands of sisters tend to go diverse ways occupationally and to reach varied levels of socio-economic success. Many interviews with widows emphasize that one or another of her children is, by her set of standards, "a success." Such offspring are generally seen less often than those who retain the same style of life and neighborhood as the mother, but they are often mentioned. The distance between their homes and the mother's is justified in terms of such success, though the details of the occupational mobility are not always understood by the less-educated widow. A general aura of pride or resentment reflects the feeling of social distance.

The concept of time-distance is being used here in determining the subjective sense of distance between the mother's residence and the children's home. "How long does it take to get there?" varies by available transportation and financial resources, as well as by the world perspective of the widow. Gary, Indiana may seem a great distance from Chicago to a widow who does not drive and is dependent upon the cheapest available transportation. An uneducated woman can not relate distances proportionately. For her the familiar world consists of very limited territory. Time-distance helps explain visiting patterns.

The dispersal of the family of procreation of the older widow is reflected in the figures of Table 26 (p. 192). As mentioned before, thirty-two percent of the respondents have one or more children in the same dwelling. A much higher proportion was expected to have an offspring in the same building, but in another unit, or at least in the same block. These figures are very low. On the other hand, sixteen percent of the respondents have at least one child in the neighborhood. The categories are not mutually exclusive, as the same mother could have a child in the house and one in the "soup carrying area" by which Townsend (1957) defined the neighborhood.

At the other extreme of time-distance, one-sixth of the respondents have at least one child a day or more away, and a fourth, more than one hour, but less than a day away. The most likely location of adult children is within an hour's time-distance from the mother. All the figures indicate that most children are within Chicago or its suburbs, but that the dispersal is great and the widow is located asymmetrically in relation to her several children.

The location of only children in time-distance from the mother is very interesting. Twenty-two percent of the respondents have one child, twenty-six percent have two, fifteen percent have three, and one-fifth have more than that. Over a fourth of only children live with the mother, few are in the same building, block, or even neighborhood. One-third are in the city or a relatively close suburb, and only six percent live very far away. By means of contrast are the mothers of three children, among whom twenty-four percent have one child, and twenty percent have more than one child at a distance requiring long travel. Thus, only children are very apt to be sufficiently close to reach the mother in less than one

TABLE 26: PERCENTAGES OF WIDOWS WHO HAVE DESIGNATED NUMBERS OF CHILDREN LIVING IN THE SAME DWELLING, IN THE SAME BUILDING, IN THE SAME BLOCK, SOMEWHERE ELSE IN THE NEIGHBORHOOD, ONE HOUR OR LESS, OVER ONE HOUR, OR OVER ONE DAY AWAY, BY NUMBER OF LIVING CHILDREN

*Percentages of Widows Having Children at Designated Time-Distances*

| Total Number of Children | N | % | Same Dwelling No. of Children | | | Same Building No. of Children | | | Same Block No. of Children | | | Same Neighborhood No. of Children | | | Less Than One Hour No. of Children | | | Over One Hour No. of Children | | | One Day or More No. of Children | | |
|---|---|---|---|---|---|---|---|---|---|---|---|---|---|---|---|---|---|---|---|---|---|---|---|
| | | | 0 | 1 | 2+ | 0 | 1 | 2+ | 0 | 1 | 2+ | 0 | 1 | 2+ | 0 | 1 | 2+ | 0 | 1 | 2+ | 0 | 1 | 2+ |
| None | (18) | 100 | 100 | — | — | 100 | — | — | 100 | — | — | 100 | — | — | 100 | — | — | 100 | — | — | 100 | — | — |
| One | (22) | 72 | 72 | 28 | — | 95 | 5 | — | 98 | 2 | — | 89 | 11 | — | 71 | 29 | — | 88 | 12 | — | 94 | 6 | — |
| Two | (26) | 61 | 61 | 26 | 13 | 90 | 9 | 1 | 99 | — | 1 | 82 | 18 | — | 44 | 35 | 20 | 84 | 11 | 5 | 86 | 11 | 2 |
| Three | (15) | 62 | 62 | 29 | 9 | 96 | 4 | — | 98 | 2 | — | 82 | 18 | — | 38 | 33 | 29 | 67 | 20 | 13 | 56 | 24 | 20 |
| Four | (8) | 48 | 48 | 28 | 24 | 80 | 20 | — | 100 | — | — | 72 | 12 | 16 | 28 | 16 | 56 | 64 | 24 | 12 | 92 | 8 | — |
| Five | (5) | 57 | 57 | 28 | 14 | 71 | 28 | — | 93 | — | 7 | 64 | 21 | 14 | 14 | 28 | 57 | 64 | 14 | 21 | 71 | 28 | — |
| Six | (1) | 25 | 25 | 75 | — | 100 | — | — | 100 | — | — | 25 | 25 | 50 | 75 | — | 25 | 50 | 50 | — | 75 | — | 25 |
| Seven | (3) | 30 | 30 | 50 | 20 | 90 | 10 | — | 100 | — | — | 40 | 20 | 40 | 50 | 10 | 40 | 30 | 50 | 20 | 60 | 10 | 30 |
| Eight | (2) | 40 | 40 | 40 | 20 | 100 | — | — | 80 | 20 | — | 60 | 40 | — | 20 | — | 80 | 20 | 60 | 20 | 40 | 40 | 20 |
| Number | | 203 | 203 | 73 | 25 | 278 | 22 | 1 | 296 | 3 | 2 | 249 | 40 | 12 | 170 | 71 | 60 | 238 | 44 | 19 | 252 | 33 | 15 |
| Percent | | 67 | 67 | 24 | 8 | 92 | 7 | — | 98 | 1 | 1 | 83 | 13 | 3 | 56 | 24 | 20 | 79 | 15 | 6 | 84 | 11 | 5 |

hour. Unfortunately, we do not know if this is a consequence of her having moved close to them or of their having decided not to move too far from the mother.

## CONTACT WITH CHILDREN

Research by family sociologists indicates that patterns of interpersonal interaction between family members residing in different households varies in response to several influences. Five basic sets of factors affect the frequency of contact among people living apart: the functions they perform; the facilities available for carrying them out; the procedures institutionalized to begin, engage in, and end them; the social space in which they take place; and competing relations and actions. The more important the function of the contact for its participants, the more likely they are to try to maintain it. Thus, as predicted by Robert Winch (1962), families offering members greater rewards—social status, mutual help and pleasurable company—will be more likely to keep up interaction than families who have little to offer members in competition with others sets of social relations. The functions or benefits derived from contact compete among each other and with other sources for obtaining them; in modern society pleasure is frequently derived from couple-companionate relations with non-kin friends (see Robert Weiss, 1969). On the other hand, interaction across generations may provide different types of satisfactions than those obtained from peers, so that adult children may go out of their way to see the older generation and to expose their children to kin encounters. Judgment of functions performed by different relations varies according to the definition of what is important in life and of the ways in which its goals may be reached.

The functions respondents feel are being met by interaction between them and their adult children include the intrinsically personal satisfactions of "primary relations." Not all people define both the family of orientation and the family of procreation as functional on the primary level, once adulthood is reached. Contact is often so filled with "generational gap" strains as to be devoid of intimacy and pleasure. In other groups, the relations are so formalized as to be secondary in nature and sentiment. The Chicago area widows express all of these sentiments: desire to see children because they enjoy the contact or because ritual demands it, and discomfort over any interaction. The same woman sometimes feels comfortable with one offspring and his family, while trying to avoid frequent contact with another or to depersonalize it into exchanges of services. Depersonalization is difficult in a family culture which demands that family members be sentimentally important to each other in pleasurable ways.

Some benefits which may be derived from family interaction were characterized by Cooley (1909) as *secondary* (see Chapter Four for further discussion). These have consequences other than pleasure of association and meet external goals through task-oriented action. Much of family interaction meets such secondary goals; services are exchanged, duties performed, and tasks accomplished beyond the socializing interchanges. Sometimes these interfere with the primary interaction, but usually they are woven together. For example, afternoon baby-sitting by the grandmother can end in a family dinner which is enjoyed by all parties and not considered a mere exchange for services. Some interaction is limited to secondary goals, like when a son comes over to repair a leak in the roof and then leaves immediately. As Litwak (1968), Sussman (1968), and others contributing to the Shanas and Streib volume (1968) have pointed out, most families do exchange help, money, and other services. These require at least a minimum of contact and may actually by needed to guarantee occasions into which primary sentiments can be woven.

The procedures for initiating, carrying on, and completing interaction vary considerably among different people and even within the same family. Tradition often required that the more prestigious person initiate the contact and indicate its termination; this procedure insures that the encounter will take place. Modern life has made spontaneous contact difficult over a distance. Multi-institutional life makes absence from the home frequent for all but the very young and the very old. The possibility that someone will not be home prevents many a person from driving several hours on an impromptu visit. Therefore, arrangements must be made beforehand, a time set, the direction of movement established, and inclusion rules set. Such procedures are necessary for event-planning. American families have also worked out some ritualistic contacts which guarantee a Sunday dinner or at least holiday contact. Generally, except for people who live close to each other, the more institutionalized the procedures, the more likely that the contact will be regular. Sporadic interaction tends to be rarer than the once-a-week or even once-a-month planned events.

The facilities needed to maintain patterned contact between a widow and her adult children must include some means for covering the distance. Time, money, and transportation problems are often mentioned by Chicago area women as restricting interaction. The ability of the person to mobilize resources to accomplish this goal varies also by motivation. Some widows with very little income still manage to arrange visits to children's houses with greater frequency and regularity than others who have more money and less distance to travel. Most of the respondents do not drive a car, and they have to rely on public transportation or on relatives and friends to take them on visits. For example, about two-thirds of the 143 widows who have an eldest child visit him or her by car, a similar proportion traveling to see other children, if they have more than one. The offspring may have to come and pick up the mother, which means that the distance is doubled and frequency of contact is influenced. Eighteen percent of the widows visit their eldest child by local bus, seven percent by train, and thirteen percent by airplane.

One of the decisive factors in social interaction between a widow and her offspring is the location of the contact. Upper- and some middle-class women are likely to attend events with their widowed mothers—concerts, lunches, meetings, etc. They also arrange for formal events in the home of one or the other generation. Such interaction varies again by many factors, including household size and composition. Widows with small apartments are often unable to entertain their families. There tends to be a gradual shift back and forth during the life-cycle of many of the widows. Widows maintaining relatively large residential units, who are in a good financial position and in full health, often bring the children and grandchildren together for regular Sunday or at least holiday dinners. If, however, the children are in a stage of their own life cycle which makes transportation of the whole unit difficult, the widow may end up going to their home for such events even before she is made incapable of entertaining by health or finances. Some women have the resources to invite their children's families to public resorts, paying all expenses for such holidays. Other facilities for insuring contact may be summer cottages which become gathering spots for the extended family during appropriate seasons.

As the widow ages and is less able to move around easily, the interaction scene changes. Adult children, especially daughters, who no longer have small children confining them to the home start visiting her during the day. Work may interfere, however, since many middle-aged women are now returning to regular employment and cannot visit their mothers with ease. Several of the Chicago respondents explained the lack of frequent contact with one or more children in terms of such role conflict.

In general, contact with offspring tends to be asymmetrical, in that widows see some of their adult children more often than others, and the contact tends to take place more in the home of one of the interactional partners than in the other's. In fact, most widows (eighty-four percent) do not see any offspring who live away from the home at a frequency of

TABLE 27: PERCENTAGES OF WIDOWS WHO HAVE THE
DESIGNATED NUMBER OF CHILDREN RESIDING
OUTSIDE OF THEIR HOME, WHOM THEY SEE DAILY,
WEEKLY, MONTHLY, A FEW TIMES A YEAR OR LESS,
BY NUMBER OF LIVING CHILDREN

*Frequency of Contact*

| Number of Children | Daily No. of Child. | | | Weekly No. of Child. | | | Monthly No. of Child. | | | A Few Times a Year No. of Child. | | | Less Than That No. of Child. | | |
|---|---|---|---|---|---|---|---|---|---|---|---|---|---|---|---|
| | *0* | *1* | *2+* | *0* | *1* | *2+* | *0* | *1* | *2+* | *0* | *1* | *2+* | *0* | *1* | *2+* |
| None (18) | 100 | — | — | 100 | — | — | 100 | — | — | 100 | — | — | 100 | — | — |
| One (22) | 86 | 14 | — | 78 | 22 | — | 89 | 11 | — | 95 | 5 | — | 91 | 9 | — |
| Two (26) | 84 | 9 | 8 | 54 | 29 | 16 | 85 | 13 | 2 | 89 | 11 | — | 82 | 15 | 2 |
| Three (15) | 82 | 13 | 4 | 49 | 31 | 20 | 80 | 18 | 2 | 67 | 22 | 11 | 51 | 33 | 15 |
| Four (8) | 76 | 20 | 4 | 32 | 28 | 40 | 60 | 24 | 12 | 84 | 8 | 8 | 76 | 16 | 8 |
| Five (5) | 78 | — | 21 | 29 | 14 | 57 | 71 | 28 | — | 57 | 14 | 28 | 78 | 14 | 7 |
| Six (1) | 75 | — | 25 | 25 | — | 75 | 100 | — | — | 75 | 25 | — | 75 | — | 25 |
| Seven (3) | 40 | 40 | 20 | 20 | — | 80 | 40 | 10 | 50 | 70 | 20 | 10 | 60 | 20 | 20 |
| Eight (2) | 40 | 40 | 20 | 40 | — | 60 | 20 | 80 | — | 40 | 40 | 20 | 40 | 40 | 20 |
| Number | 252 | 33 | 22 | 187 | 60 | 54 | 249 | 40 | 12 | 257 | 31 | 13 | 242 | 43 | 16 |
| Percent | 84 | 11 | 6 | 62 | 20 | 18 | 83 | 13 | 4 | 85 | 10 | 4 | 80 | 14 | 5 |

once or more a day. This group naturally includes those who have no
children and all of those whose offspring still live at home; the proportion
decreases as the number of living children increases. Women with many
children have a relatively high probability of seeing at least one of them
daily . In fact, the best way a woman has of guaranteeing contact with
adult children after she becomes a widow is by having many children.
Only twenty-two percent of those having only one child see him or her
weekly, while forty-five percent of the mothers of two children see at least
one at that frequency, and the proportion increases steadily by increase
in number of children.

At the other extreme, fourteen percent of the respondents see at least
one child, and five percent more than one, very seldom, "less than a few
times a year." One respondent explained that she had not seen her two
boys since 1945; another that her daughter ran away from home at eighteen years of age and has not been heard from since. More of such comments would have helped to fill out the contact picture, had we realized
their possibility prior to the study. Face-to-face contact with children
living at great time-distances or even outside the range of easy interaction
tends to be limited to long-planned and formal trips and to be much more

systematic and frequent on the part of middle- rather than lower-class women. Mothers of many children are likely to see at least one at rare intervals.

In summary, older widows' contact with adult children is neither as frequent nor as rare as family sociology might lead an observer to expect. Eighty-four percent of the respondents see no child outside of the dwelling unit at a rate of once a day or so, sixty-two percent see none weekly, eighty-three percent see none monthly, eighty-five percent see none at the rate of a few times a year, and eighty percent see none more often than that. The extremes of contact are thus infrequent, when all the children are considered. The greater the number of living children a woman has, the greater the probability that at least one will be seen at frequent and regular intervals, and the greater the probability that at least one will be lost to frequent interaction. In general, large families become scattered, but geographically and/or socially isolating time-distance is more apt to occur in lower socio-economic groups than in higher. Most widows see one of their children more frequently than the others.

In fact, the *average* frequency of interaction with adult children living away from home on the part of Chicago area widows tends to be low, when computed from the frequency for each child, divided by the total number of living offspring. A total of forty-seven percent of the respondents, or 142 women, do not have any child outside of the household or see those living away at an average of a few times a year or less. This includes the fifty-four who have no living offspring and the forty-nine who are now living with their children, leaving thirty-nine widows, or thirteen percent of the sample, who have children residing away from them whom they see very rarely. The only situation in which this average could be obtained in conjunction with frequent contact with one child is in families with many offspring, and there are very few of these. Thus, we can be pretty sure that there are women with living children whom they see only on unusual occasions, and that most of the respondents can not build their whole lives around interaction with the next generation. One-fifth see their offspring on an average between once a month and a few times a year. Those widows who see children living on the outside on the average of at least two times a month comprise just over one tenth of the total. Average weekly contact with all children is not as frequent as Table 27 might lead us to expect, since only eighteen percent have such a total, with four percent seeing their children on an average of several times a year, and only five percent less than that. The figures for average contact thus support the conclusions drawn from Table 27 that most widows see one child more often than others, and this lack of multiple interaction pulls down the overall frequency.

The youngest and the oldest widows are the least likely to have children living outside of their home whom they see very often. That the younger widows have a low average of contact is partly due to offspring in the home and partly to role competition. They are active at work or in other sets of relations, and their children are deeply involved in their parental and housekeeping or occupational roles. The frequency of contact between the mother and her offspring outside of the home increases in the next decade; more children move to outside locations and the widows expand the attention they can give children because of the diminishing competition of their other roles. The seventies bring widows a slow-down of contact with children, as the needs of these offspring are expanded into other sets of extra-familial relations and as their mothers, lacking expansion facilities, begin to be faced with a shrinking of their social circle. The last age group shows passive stances on the part of the widows and an increased concern on the part of the children, resulting in asymmetrical relations. It is impossible to predict, however, whether this trend will continue in the next generation of widows, because the very old in this sample are also the least educated and they are incompetent to maintain the social life space of many sets of relations.

Widows with physical disabilities which they define as limiting their activities are apt to be seen by an offspring at more frequent intervals than widows who do not feel such limitations. Definitions of income adequacy play an even more important part in the success of contact maintenance. The three women who report their financial condition as "fairly wealthy" see their children at an average of at least once a week. Both white and black widows in lower economic circumstances are likely to be at one of the two extremes of the contact average: those who have children nearby see them often and those whose offspring are at a greater distance see them very rarely. As in friendship interaction, higher income facilitates easy transportation, the use of entertainment rituals, and other means of maintaining socializing contacts. Women who feel restricted in income or who live in socially limited worlds, because of lack of education or other disadvantages, are not likely to interact with their children with regular frequency. Unless provided with easy means for contact with other people, they tend to be socially isolated. The poorer women are not only the least likely to maintain contact with geographically distant children, they are also the least likely to have living offspring. Their social isolation is thus a consequence of many factors. These facts dispel the myth that the women most needing contact with children, of personal and of secondary functionality, are the most likely to have it. Quite the contrary is true. The women able to retain a relatively high average of contact with their offspring are the ones who "need" it least from the vantage point of social isolation. Need, rather than leading to fulfillment, often results in restrictions of effort and affect, and *vice versa*. Contact is related more to the ability to maintain it than to the function it could perform in the life of the widow, with the exception of the few widows who are suffering health problems.

Visiting with people varies considerably not only in frequency, but in length of time. Assuming that family contacts are very different when they involve staying overnight than when they are limited to coming and going for a part of one day, we asked the respondents if they had stayed overnight in anyone's home during the past year. Fifty-eight percent said "yes." They were then asked in whose home they had stayed; fifty-six percent of the 172 widows slept in a residence of their children, while others listed different locations. In addition, twenty-six percent had been in several homes, many undoubtedly staying part of the time with children. The length of the visit ranged from less than ten nights a year for twenty-four percent of the respondents, to from 10 to 30 nights for twenty-three percent, and longer than that for nine percent. Generally, however, the expectation preceding the study that many widows would travel much of the year, visiting one child or sibling, then another, has not been borne out. Almost half did not visit anyone, and another quarter did so for only ten nights in a whole year. Additional information weakens the hypothesis that widows visit primarily the children who live a great distance away. Most explanations of overnight visits indicate movement restricted to the city and the neighboring areas. A son or daughter living in a suburb or even at a time-distance of less than one hour will come on a Friday and pick up the mother for a weekend visit. Such arrangements require sleeping space and a willingness on both sides to put up with temporary inconvenience. Mutual desire or convenience incline the widow to spend more time with one child than with the others.

The widow is likely to receive more overnight visits than she makes, although the proportion is not as high in Chicago as among small town Missouri residents (Pihlblad and Rosencranz, 1968; Adams, 1969). One reason is the shortage of space in the residences of many urban respondents, who moved to a small apartment after the children left or after the death of the husband. Missouri widows are apt to live in their own homes with several extra rooms and to be visited from a distance, since most have only one, if any, child in the vicinity. However, as many as sixty percent of the Chicago respondents are able to accommodate an overnight guest. There is an interesting difference between the people whom a widow visits and those who visit her. Only sixteen percent had children stay with them, although a few more children are undoubtedly included in the most general category combining several types of visitors, who were entertained by twenty-three percent of the respondents. The widow is likely to be the one who visits her adult offspring, while she herself is visited by other relatives. The latter are most frequently younger members of the family—grandchildren, nieces, or nephews. They come to keep the widow company or to do some favor for her and in return they obtain her undivided attention and accomodations when they are venturing out from their own homes. Thirty-three percent of the respondents had overnight visits for less than ten nights a year, eighteen percent for between ten nights and one month, and only seven percent for more than one month. Eight women had visitors who stayed a total of three months or thereabouts.

In summary, the women who maintain frequent contacts with their children are of two major types. One is in the upper part of the lower class, probably an eighth-grade graduate. She defines such contacts as important, has several children, and sees at least one of them with frequency. She is not strongly involved in competing social roles, and neither are her children. The second type, having a high average contact with all children, but a relatively low frequency with any one, is of the upper and upper-middle class. She makes the effort to see her children at more formalized and rhythmic events. She also maintains a complex communication sequence, meeting outside of the homes, organizing activities with pre-arranged dates. She has the funds to visit distant offspring and the facilities to be able to receive them in turn. The very lowest, socioeconomically, of the widows tend to represent extremes of contact situations, often seeing offspring who live nearby, but rarely seeing those who live at greater distances. In this class, conflict with offspring is also either more frequent or more openly expressed, and there are cases in which contact is not even attempted by one side or the other.

In all socio-economic groups, some widows wish more direct contacts with children than available, either of a primary nature or as service receivers. They do not like situations in which they feel that they are "interfering" or being "used," and often the life-style and the demeanor of younger generations result in such interpretations by the widow. The Chicago area interviews are spotted with comments which indicate varying degrees of dissatisfaction with the location, amount, and type of contact with adult children who live outside the mother's residence. Some of the respondents are very bitter over what they define as neglect; others offer complex rationalizations with undercurrents of resentment for infrequent contact.

Direct face-to-face contact is not the only way widows are involved in the lives of their children, although it is the preferred way, particularly on the part of lower-class older women. The telephone has become a major means of communication between people who live or work apart and who have trouble in getting direct interaction as frequently as they desire. One of the respondents reports seventy calls a week; another, forty calls; and a third, thirty. One the other side of the picture are the women with no living children (eighteen percent) and those who either do not communicate with those they have as often as once a week or do not have a phone (twenty-four percent). Some call only for holidays or special events, and a few cannot get ahold of their offspring because they are traveling, usually with the armed services, or are institutionalized or without phones of their own. Telephone conversations can be a significant part of the woman's life, if she is able to retain a feeling of identity with her children through them, but they do not fill much of the available time for most respondents. Only thirteen percent really use the phone often, eight to fifteen times a week, and four percent are on it even more frequently, that is, sixteen times a week or more. Assuming that four calls in a seven-day period is a minimum for close contact with at least some offspring, we find that sixty-one percent of the Chicago area widows have minimal or no telephone contact with any offspring.

We did not inquire how often the widow wrote letters to her children, but we did ask how many letters she wrote to anyone during that period of time. Fifty-one percent of the respondents wrote no letters weekly, sixteen percent wrote one letter, and eleven percent wrote only two or three letters. Most of the respondents make no effort toward active involvement in this manner in the lives of people living far away, be it their children, other relatives, or friends. Since an average of three letters a month would be minimal for one interaction, this means that this form of contact is insignificant for these women, many of whom were not educated to use the written word as a means of maintaining relations.

## THE IMPORTANCE OF THE ROLE OF MOTHER

Widows who see their children at relatively frequent intervals are much more likely than non-interactors to rank the role of mother as first in order of importance in comparison to those of wife, housewife, worker, daughter, and friend. This fact may be due to two trends in the history of the relation: they may value this role because it is now the major source of their engagement in society or they may have made it the focus of their role-cluster for many years, building and maintaining facilities to make contact possible. Those who rank the role low may do so because they never had the opportunity to be involved in it or because something happened to the relation. Since most life patterns are a gradual outgrowth of small decisions (with, of course, dramatic exceptions), the probability is that the orientation of widows toward the role of mother is a result of several tendencies which mutually stimulate each other. Women oriented toward the role of mother go out of their way to interact with children, not only often, but in a mutually pleasant manner. They push aside other roles, and their engagement in the familial institution precludes movement into other dimensions of societal life. Previous studies of married women living in suburbs and the city and of housewives currently employed indicated the importance of the hierarchical positions assigned by people to their different social roles (Lopata, 1971b). Such a classification of the order of importance was mentioned in Chapter Two, with special reference to the allocation of the role of wife and the characteristics of women who build such a hierarchy. Some insight may be obtained from a similar analysis of the location of the role of mother in the role-cluster of widows.

Forty-three percent of the 281 women who responded to the rank question in the widowhood interview gave the role of mother first place, and forty-two percent, second, leaving only twelve percent who felt it deserved no better than third rank, and one percent who assigned it to one of the three positions below that. The distribution is interesting in terms of assumptions underlying the study which came from established sociological literature. One hypothesis is that in widowhood, release from the competing social role of wife would increase concentration on the mother role. This hypothesis was not borne out, for a lower proportion of widows than of married women rank motherhood as the primary obligation of their sex. The opposite hypothesis was that they will value the role of mother less than younger housewives in earlier stages of this and the housewife roles, because they are older women, two-thirds of whom have no living children in their residence. This assumption is actually supported by the figures. Suburban housewives with pre-high school children were much more likely than the older widows to list the role of mother high on the scale. Only working women living in the city came close to the proportion of widows who list the role of mother in first place. Of course, there are several factors operating here. The older widows are more likely to have been brought up in a patriarchal culture. Also, many may feel obligated to sanctify the role of wife, as indicated in Chapter Two. The combination of factors works against top priority for the mother role on the part of women living in a society heavily oriented toward this set of relations.

The next question is: "Who are the widows who focus on the role of mother instead of on alternative sets of relations available to women?" The various cross-tabulations between the first-place ranking of this role and selected characteristics bring out some interesting tendencies. Not surprisingly, in view of their disproportionate rejection of the role of wife as of greatest importance, black women are more likely than their white counterparts to assign the role of mother to the first place. This reinforces the thesis that the strongest tie in the lower-class segment of the black community, where the older widow is likely to be, is between mother and child rather than between husband and wife (Rainwater, 1967). White women born outside of the United States are slightly more prone to value highly obligations to children than women born in America. Some ethnic and religious differences are also significant. For example, Polish women married to Polish men are more apt to rank the role of mother above that of wife, with German and Greek women following suit. The number of Greek women is small in the sample, but during our exploratory research all of the Greek respondents showed this preference, as does the literature concerning the traditional family of that national heritage (Campbell, 1964). English widows of the Chicago area are less frequently focused on the role of mother.

In spite of the stereotype of the "Yiddisher mama," Jewish widows consistently list the role of mother in the second place, usually following the role of wife. Catholics rather than Protestants are apt to list the role of mother as the most important to a woman; and those who find their religion, whichever it may be, of extreme importance also rank motherhood first. A strong relation exists between orientation toward the role of mother and homogeneity of friendships by religion and even by ethnic background. The combination indicates that those women who are ethnically identified with less prestigious minority groups are apt to be oriented toward the role of mother as the most important one a woman can perform.

Education and role-ranking combines into two distinct patterns. The widow highly oriented toward the role of mother is likely never to have gotten beyond the seventh grade or else to be highly educated. The former traditionally assigns importance to motherhood, particularly if she is in an ethnic group with such a tendency, the latter is conscious of the importance of motherhood's developmental function. The most likely combination of age and education giving high rank to the role of mother falls to the oldest respondents who have completed between four and seven grades of school. The very educated are few in number.

It is possible that women who felt they had to work while their husband was living resent in retrospect having had to leave their children, and they devalue the contribution the role of wife made to their lives. The occupational distribution of the workers indicates that those who were in low paying and low prestige jobs are much more likely to downgrade the role of wife and upgrade the role of mother than the few women who were in more prestigious occupations. This fact indicates the importance of differentiating why women work and how their jobs affect their family lives. Women who feel they must work to help support the family may be more oriented to the role of mother and less positive about the role of wife than women who have mixed reasons for seeking employment. Many of the workers are black. Wives of prestigiously occupied husbands place the role of mother second to that of wife. Finally, the more children a woman has, the more likely she is to value the role of mother as the highest in the role-cluster available to her.

The importance assigned the role of mother and the problems cited as the most important in consequence of the husband's death are strongly related. Only thirty-three percent of the women who rank the role of mother first found loneliness to be the major problem of widowhood, out of the total proportion of forty-three percent who gave it that rank. Rather, "raising a family" and "having no one to share work and maintenance" were seen as the major effects of being left without a husband, and being "shunned by others," as the major form of loneliness. These women are likely to have been widowed relatively early in their life cycle, at a time when they were still deeply involved in child-rearing. This fact explains the otherwise contradictory trend of better educated women being likely to rank the role of mother first. The women who are highly educated were either widowed young and placed the role of mother first, or they were widowed later and in that case they definitely ranked the role of wife as the most important. Decision-making and the absence of someone for whom the widow could perform caring functions are the next set of problems for widows who rank the role of mother first. This type of woman does not want or expect remarriage. Other types of social relations are often not available to her because of her limited education, and children are not always at a comfortable distance for maintaining closeness. Although in contact with one offspring, she is not sufficiently surrounded by family to fulfill the nutrient functions she values so highly. These facts indicate that not all widows strongly oriented toward the role of mother are actually in satisfactory contact with their offspring. Generally speaking, however, orientation toward that role, positive sentiments in its connection, and actual interaction form a consistent package.

Thus, women who rank the role of mother above that of wife, housewife, career builder or worker, daughter, and friend tend to be very conscious of their obligations to rear children, because of either culture or life circumstances. This rank order does not necessarily spell hostility toward the husband or the role of wife, but such tendencies are sometimes combined. Interestingly enough, European immigrants who came from traditionally patriarchal cultures are often more oriented toward the children than toward the husband. This tendency may be a direct consequence of loosening patriarchy or it may be a consistent trend. It is strongest among the black women, because of the slave situation and later emancipation circumstances. Several studies indicate that upper-class women are more husband-oriented or at least cyclical in their role identifications (see Chapter Two). The still assimilating or culturally disorganized women may be rebelling against strong male dominance by turning their attention and identification toward their children. This factor may thus be a contributing force toward the child-orientation of the American society. Gradually, as husband-wife relations become modified by education and the importance of the husband's occupation affects the life style, the woman becomes more oriented toward him, once the intensive years of child-care are over. The wife whose husband dies at that stage of her identification cycle may retain this orientation throughout life; the one whose husband is still around after the children leave home may shift back to a stress on the role of wife.

## DEGREES OF CHILD ORIENTATION

A very obvious question which arises from the attempt to determine the relative importance of various roles in the lives of respondents is the relation of the formal declaration to actual behavior. Women, or anyone else for that matter, can declare one social role as of utmost importance only because the culture demands such a hierarchy. It therefore became important for us to combine such a rank system with all other references to any role, attitudes toward components, and actual behavior in relation to it. The combined effort became labeled as the "social role of mother scale." Those scores obtained by women who are mothers were then separated from the attitudinal combinations obtained by women with no living children, and the scores of the former were collapsed into three levels of involvement. The collapsed levels of the role of mother scores were then cross-tabulated by some of the variables hypothetically expected to be of significance to the role.

Women who are active in the role of mother tend to have high interaction scores with other people, and *vice versa* (see Table 28). Those proportionately isolated from living offspring tend to be also isolated from other human beings.

Thirty-eight percent of the widows scoring high on the role of mother scale also have a high total rate of contact with others. Only eight percent combine involvement in motherhood with low participation in inter-

TABLE 28: SCORES IN THE ROLE OF MOTHER SCALE BY
FREQUENCY OF CONTACT SCALE

| | | Total | Score, Role of Mother | | | |
|---|---|---|---|---|---|---|
| | | | High (30–50) | Medium (17–29) | Low (01–16) | No Children |
| High | N | 29 | 9 | 16 | 4 | 6 |
| (50–80) | % | | 31R | 55R | 14R | 21R* |
| | % | 12 | 38C | 12C | 3C | 11C |
| Medium | N | 112 | 13 | 66 | 33 | 21 |
| (26–49) | % | | 12R | 59R | 29R | 19R* |
| | % | 45 | 54C | 49C | 37C | 39C |
| Low | N | 106 | 2 | 52 | 52 | 27 |
| (01–25) | % | | 2R | 49R | 49R | 25R* |
| | % | 43 | 8C | 39C | 58C | 50C |
| Column | N | 247 | 24 | 134 | 89 | 54 |
| Sums | % | | 10 | 54 | 36 | 22* |

Percent Base: 247
R stands for Row, C stands for Column
* Not included in percent base
Gamma = .50; Chi-square = 31.98; d.f. = 4; p <.001

action outside of this role and only four of the high interactions are
minimally involved with living children. These facts make it difficult to
believe the old stereotype of the woman as specializing in the role of
mother to the exclusion of other social relations. In fact, fifty-two women,
forming a fifth of the mothers with surviving children, score low on both
the role of mother and the contact with others scales. This rather large
proportion of minimally involved women represents almost half of the
low scorers in the role of mother and almost three-fifths of the low scorers
on the general contact scale. In fact, except for the middle ranges in both
scales, which naturally draw heavy concentrations, this is the largest group
produced by the cross-tabulations between the role of mother and the total
contact scales. Part of this distribution is due to the fact that forty-three
percent of the respondents are low-contact women, that is, their total
score of interaction with a variety of people is low. The image of the fully
socialized "merry" widow is thus open to serious question. Contact with
children at least guarantees safety from social isolation for many mothers,
but not for all women. Those widows who have no children are likely
to be social isolates, in terms of frequency of contact with other people.
Having adult children helps pull widows into the mainstream of societal
life or at least into familial institutions.

The social role most closely related to that of mother in terms of the scores of respondents is that of sibling[2a] (see Table XII in Appendix C). Women without children are even more likely than the high scorers in the role of mother to see siblings often and to value positively this relation. The roles of wife and neighbor are less relevant to the role of mother. Vestiges of the role of wife do not influence how much a woman will involve herself in the role of mother, indicating that involvement in one role does not either guarantee or prevent participation in other sets of social relations. There is a negative association between the score in the role of mother and agreement with the statement that married children ask too many favors, as indicated before.[2b] Two other statements produced high gammas, but low chi squares with the role of mother scores, mostly because of blanks in some of the cells and high medium concentrations. The mother role is associated negatively with the feeling that widows must make their own lives and not depend on others.[2c] None of the widows who have a high score on the role of mother scale agree with the statement "It is all right for a widow to have sexual relations with a man without planning on marriage." [2d] Thus, women strongly involved in the role of mother, holding positive attitudes toward children and interacting with them frequently, are not interested in establishing an independent life and experimenting with non-marital sexual relations. They do not mind doing things for their children, or at least they interpret the interaction as symmetrical rather than as requiring them to do one-sided favors such as baby-sitting, sewing and such.

The scores on the role of mother scale combine many attitudes, references to children as helpers in solving problems of widowhood and as contacts. It is therefore not surprising that there is not a complete overlap between them and the rank given by the respondents to the six basic roles of women (see Table XII in Appendix C). Although there is a strong tendency for mothers who rank that role first to have a high score on the role of mother scale, one third of the low scorers also assign that role first place, indicating that they are not able to convert their values to actual interaction.

Those who score poorly in the role of mother, although they have living children, are more apt than other women to give the role of wife first or second place, and they even emphasize the role of daughter. Women with no living children are not likely to give the role of mother first place, assigning the role of wife that rank more frequently. They also stress the importance of the role of housewife more often than do mothers, and they are the only category of women to place the role of worker in first rank with any frequency. In general, women without children downgrade the role of mother (see also Shanas, 1962), since only sixty-three percent rank it in first or second place, compared to ninety-nine percent who score high on the role of mother scale, ninety-two percent who score medium, and eighty percent who score low.

Interestingly enough, there is no tendency for the women valuing their obligations to offspring to define the opposite flow of relations with equal vehemence. That is, they do not value the role of daughter anywhere near that of mother.

Thus, women with no living children are, not surprisingly, less concerned with family roles and more highly involved in sets of relations outside of the family of procreation than their more family-oriented counterparts. The roles of sibling and daughter gain greater emphasis for women without children, but the strong differences are in the roles of neighbor, housewife, and worker. This means that women without children are more apt to become dramatically involved at the extremes of the roles of neighbor, housewife, and worker than are women who have been engaged in the role of mother.

The relation between age and attitudes of widows toward the role of mother and their levels of involvement in that role are also interesting. The respondents most likely to have a high score in the role of mother are in their sixties (see Tables XIII and XIV in Appendix C). Widows still in their fifties are likely to have children who are independent of their care, while they themselves are working or engaged in other social roles. Thus, they are not as likely to be oriented toward the role of mother as are women below them in age. By the time they reach the sixties age decade, work roles are less exciting and other forms of social engagement do not draw their attention to the same extent as in prior decades. Thus, they may be shifting from an expectation of remarriage (regardless of how realistic it is) to an increased dependence on the role of mother. The next two decades might support the disengagement theory, if it were not for other factors. Widows in their seventies and over are apt to have children who are no longer in the expanding circle and full-time plateaus of their roles of mother and housewife. The grandchildren are grown, at school, or even away from home, and they have returned to work or become engaged in other non-familial activities. Widows who are not so involved, or who are at ages when full activity schedules are less available, may have children who are too busy to drop over or extend invitations. Also, they are less needed by these offspring. A final consideration may be that, as age increases, health and financial limitations make involvement in any role, including that of mother, more and more difficult.

The widow's age at the time she came to Chicago proved a significant influence on her current involvement in the role of mother. Her score is apt to be high if she came during the middle years of her twenties, thirties, and forties, but low if she came as a teenager or after her children were grown. Women who migrated in their teens to the Chicago area may be experiencing strong status decrystallization in relation to all or some of their children, while the older widow is likely to have left some offspring behind and not to be able to see them often. Women who arrived in the city during the early years of their children's lives may have had to devote so much attention to the role of mother as not to be able to build alternative investments. Many details of the study indicate this possibility.

As prior conclusions would lead us to believe, involvement in the role of mother varies among different racial and ethnic groups of Chicago, although it often goes contrary to established stereotypes. Many black respondents are less involved in this role than are their white counterparts, although they give formal deference and are matriarchally assumed to focus on this role. Blacks are sixteen percent of the respondents answering both questions, yet form only eight percent of the high scorers, fourteen percent of the medium scorers, and twenty-one percent of the low scorers. One-fourth of the black respondents have no surviving children, but the remaining mothers do not fit the Moynihan picture of the black family. The scores in the role of mother are due to the fact that, although they tend to live occasionally with one child or another, they do not consistently maintain frequent contact with all their offspring; and the movement of people in and out of their households does not leave them with a high total contact score. A few are closely tied to their children's lives, but they are exceptions. Irish, Italian, and Polish mothers score high on the role of mother scale, those with an English background are more likely to fall in either the low or the high end, seldom in the middle. They are also less likely than the other groups to be childless. German mothers are disproportionately apt to be missing from the high scorers in the role of mother scale. Protestant widows are likely to have low scores in the role of mother, whereas Catholics have high scores. The former, composing 52 percent of the population, are represented in the various levels, ranging from high to low, in the following way: 42, 48 and 62 percent, respectively; while the latter have a 54, 40 and 30 percentage, respectively. As shown by previous tables, Jewish mothers do not have high scores; none of them are at the top, and they form seven percent of the medium category and six percent of the low category.

Women with no formal schooling have high scores in the role of mother more frequently than those with more education, mostly because they have more children, can not live independently, and have a restricted social life space. Eighth grade finishers are evenly distributed among all levels of the scale and, in fact, education beyond this point does not seem to be a significant factor influencing scores. The same is true of the relation between this score and the husband's achievement, except that widows of professional men are likely to be high in the role of mother scale. The three highest scores in that role are recorded for women whose husbands had no education, finished high school, and hold a professional degree. The contrasts are interesting. Other features of the life styles of these three educational groups suggest that there are different reasons for strong involvement in the role of mother on the part of women in these varied situations. The widows who did not know the schooling achievements of their husbands tend to be disproportionately low scorers in the role of mother, although they did not do much better in the role of wife. Only 14 percent have high scores, 20 percent, medium, and 31 percent are in the low range. Childless women are also apt to be ignorant of the number of years their husbands completed in schools. Thus, the picture of social relations on the part of women who never found out the educational background of their husbands, or of women whose late spouses never finished more than the minimum, indicates that these women are not strongly wife- or mother-oriented. These facts go against all the stereotypes of lower class family styles in the white community. A major reason for the scores is the fact that lower-class women are the most likely to have lost contact with several children because of death or physical and thus social distance.

Wives of professional men, who generally scored high on the role of wife scale, were disproportionately frequent among both the high and the medium level scorers on the role of mother scale. One reason that they scored this way on the scale which combined various aspects of mother-child relations is that they declared and felt identification with their husbands, while maintaining constant and positive relations with their children. Lower class women expressed a frequent hostility toward males and were unable to maintain a high score of interaction with children, simply because they lacked the facilities for systematic relations. Few widows of men who had been employed in professional jobs have no surviving children; on the other hand, few have large families. Thus, they tend to be highly husband-oriented while deeply concerned with the role of mother and able to retain constant, if not frequent, contact with offspring who are rather independent and geographically scattered. The most child-oriented widows had husbands who were operatives or service workers; the ones most represented in the low end of the scale of the role of mother are also most likely to have been widows of service workers and laborers. Thus, women who shared the life style available to male service workers are likely to be at the extremes of the role of mother scale; they are either strongly interactive with locally available children or likely to have infrequent contacts with distant offspring.

Current income does not seem to have as consistent an influence on the role of mother score as expected. Most widows strongly involved in that role are located in the medium levels of reported income. Women living on between $1,000 and $2,999 represent forty-six percent of the population, but only thirty-three percent of the high scorers on the role of mother scale. At the other end, only one of the twenty-five widows whose income is $7,000 and above has a high score, seventeen having middle scores. The in-between group, with an income between $3,000 and $4,999, comprise only eighteen percent of the sample, but thirty-three percent of the high scorers. These differences are significant. Self-definitions of financial condition support this pattern, with the "comfortable" widows being medium scorers, the "rather short" ones being the high scorers, and the "really restricted" ones very apt to be found at the low end of the score continuum. Not only financial restrictions, but physical ones lower the ability of a widow to participate fully in the role of mother. Forty-four percent of the respondents feel their health prevents full involvement in activities, and only thirty-eight percent of them have high scores, while forty-seven percent are in the low score end. Still, the differences are not dramatic, indicating that even those women who find it hard to move around can manage to be strongly involved in their role of mother, if they wish. They are frequently the recipients of visits rather than the visitors, but their attitudes do not constrict their social life space.

In spite of expectations, recent widows, that is, those whose husbands died less than one year before the interview, are not necessarily the high scorers in the role of mother. Eighty percent of them are medium scorers. The proportion of high scores reaches fifteen percent for those widowed five to six years, and seventeen percent for those who husbands died from ten to fourteen years ago. The highest proportion of low scorers are those widowed thirty years or more, although they often rank the role of mother in first place. Even two or three years of widowhood do not produce strong tendencies toward involvement in the role of mother. Of course, if the widows whose husbands died recently had children who were older at that time, they were not so easily able to concentrate on the role of mother as those whose husband died when the children were small and still at home. As indicated before, contact with children increases slightly in the first year of widowhood, but not enough to offset habits of non-involvement in the lives of offspring living away from home. Women widowed recently may have children who are so geographically scattered or so involved in other social roles, such as jobs or family of procreation obligations, as to make sudden involvement in the lives of the mothers impossible.

The fact remains that many widows do not want to become deeply involved in the role of mother after the role of wife diminishes in importance. Even those who are high scorers in the former role do not necessarily wish to become completely immersed in relations with children. They prefer "intimacy at a distance" to the problems anticipated in sharing a household with married offspring or with anyone else over whom they do not have the kind of influence they had in the past in their own families. Women who personally expect trouble from living with their child, and who declare specifically such anxieties, are much more apt to be low scorers in the role of mother than women who use generalized descriptions of such difficulties. Low scores of involvement in the role of mother are not surprisingly related to reported or expected tension in relations with married offspring.

The combination of the scores a woman achieves in the role of mother after she reaches widowhood and in her different sets of relations and other involvements is certainly influenced by her ethnic background, her education, her race (because of the other factors), and her family structure. These characteristics are generally stereotyped in social class packages, but hopefully new research will segregate the contribution of different variables to her life style.

## SUMMARY AND CONCLUSIONS

The trends toward industrialization, urbanization, and increased societal complexity have modified the role of mother not only during the *full-house plateau* stage in family life, but even in widowhood. A very dramatic change in this role is that women whose husbands have died and whose children have married and left home tend to live alone. The fact that a society allows women to live alone or even among strangers is a strong indication of the changes which are occurring in urban centers. Agricultural communities tie the older people to the family upon which they are heavily dependent.

Separate living on the part of a widow and her married offspring is a consequence of the increased independence of both from each other. The child is able to obtain a job independently of the parents and to live in a new separate residence. The older mother does not have the power to force these children back to her home after the death of the husband. On the other hand, she does not wish to give up this household and the role of housewife even in old age in order to become a peripheral member of the household managed by another woman. She prefers to run her own home, with independence of movement and freedom to organize her own work rhythm. She anticipates no major problems if never-married, separated, divorced, or widowed offspring move back into her home, and occasionally she is willing to move into a residence which lacks a housewife, but few of the places in which she settles contain more than one woman.

Not only the wish for independent control over her own home, but anticipated problems in several social roles keep her from moving in with a married offspring. The problems are seen in all major roles: housewife, mother, mother-in-law, grandmother, and even friend. They are very specific but can be summarized as involving conflict over authority and the flow of household activity, impingement on the right of others to live their lives without advice or criticism, and concern over the mother's efforts to do as she pleases. The desire for independence and for freedom from conflict and tension is sufficient to offset loneliness and the difficulty of living alone. Those who actually live with their married children often define this setup as a last resort. On the other hand, there are widows living alone who wish for shared residence, although rejecting some solutions of this problem and not knowing how to institute procedures for satisfactory living together.

Although there is a growing sub-culture which institutionalizes solitary life for women who have become independent and which justifies rejection of residence with married children, it is not fully accepted by the older widows. Some agree strongly that there is a "generation gap" and that "two women can't live in the same kitchen"; others mouth the proverbs but take very personally their relational strains with their children. Some assume that only they have such problems, and that other women are happily immersed in relations with their families.

The fact is that even "intimacy at a distance" is not achieved by most older American urban widows. Daughters have been able to return to an identification with the mother once their lives become similar to hers. Although widows obtain help during the funeral and in financial arrangements from sons, they are most apt to believe that daughters are emotionally closer and of more comfort when they feel blue. Again, this pattern is not surprising to modern Americans, but it is a change from patriarchal and patrilineal patterns in which the widow is dependent upon sons, while daughters are expected to become absorbed into the families of their husbands. Help offered to a Chicago area widow by children in various areas of her life is usually defined in terms of expectations somewhat organized by birth order and sex. One child seems selected for greater interaction and help than the others, but the spirit of independence permeates the relations of women with adult offspring. The respondents do not want to become dependent upon their children, they do not receive help or obtain much assistance or even interaction from the relatives of the deceased husband, and they seldom list siblings as significant others. By far, the role of mother is more important to them than any other familial role except wife.

The widow seems also reluctant to become too involved in the lives of her children for reasons other than the wish for independent residence. She tends to think that she has done her work, raised her children, and is deserving of rest. Many consider themselves imposed upon by their offspring by being asked to perform too many favors; they do not define "baby-sitting" as an opportunity to interact with grandchildren as much as a service to the child. Intergenerational strains are expected over the behavior of the youngest generation, but particularly over the child-rearing practices of the middle generation. Widows are glad to return home to the quiet of their own residence after a visit to younger families, although they enjoy the visit itself. The form and frequency of interaction between a widow and her offspring varies by the social class of the participants. Middle-class women tend to be middle scorers in the role of mother, combining attitudes and actions in periodic, but not immersing, contact with children with their other social roles. Lower-class women tend to be located at either end of the role of mother scale, seeing children who live nearby at a high frequency and not keeping steady contact with those whose distance makes it too difficult. Middle-class women use several forms of contacting their children, including the telephone and correspondence; lower-class women tend to restrict themselves to face-to-face interaction. The cycle of contact does not necessarily follow the idealized "life cycle" (Leslie, 1967), as many women have children living at home after the average age for marriage, and their involvement in the role of mother tends to be affected by life circumstances. For example, although this does not happen very often in the lives of white women, widowhood or the divorce of a child may bring him or her back to the home of the mother for certain periods of time. The general impression left by the widowhood interviews is that the women are not highly involved in the role of mother, although there are great variations of affect and contact by many factors, and a lack of symmetry in relations of each widow to her different children. The younger widow has children at home, the very old or physically handicapped and some members of ethnically or racially identified minority groups continue residing with family members throughout life. In general, however, few widows live with their married children and their families.

# NOTES

1. Ethel Shanas, *et. al.*, *Old People in Three Industrial Societies, op. cit.*, especially Chapters 6, 7 and 8. Variations in residential arrangements of widows occur with size and complexity of community and cultural configurations. (See Helena Znaniecki Lopata, *et. al.*, "Social Relations of Widows in Urbanizing Societies," paper given at the International Sociological meetings, September 1970, in Varna, Bulgaria and "Social Relations of Older Widows in City and Small Town," mimeographed in June, 1970).

2. a. $x^2 = 18.75$; d.f. $= 4$; $p < .001$; Gamma —.28
   b. $x^2 = 11.81$; d.f. $= 2$; $p < .005$; Gamma —.28
   c. $x^2 = 5.14$; d.f. $= 2$ not significant; Gamma —.46
   d. $x^2 = 5.00$; d.f. $= 2$ not significant; Gamma —.40

# 4

## Social Roles in Kin Groups

### BACKGROUND

In patriarchal societies, especially in those with strong patrilineal tendencies and patrilocal residence, the male members of the family identified mainly with each other. The man looked on his grandfather, father, son, and grandson as his most significant relatives. The women were in less important positions *vis-à-vis* him, because it was not through them that the lineage status, authority, work assignment, and inheritance were transmitted. The women had two groups of allegiance, their family of orientation until marriage and then the families of their husbands. Even the children they bore were considered part of the husband's family.

The dramatic changes in the social structure and functions of the family, as experienced with urbanization and industrialization in America, freed each procreational unit from both of their families of orientation. The husband-wife-and-young-children unit is now the focus of life for all its members. It is expected to live independently, with the roles of son or daughter, brother or sister, pushed into the background of importance. The ideal of independence is understood as a process to be built into relations between parents and children, as well as among siblings. Roles outside of the home soon pull even the very young into sets of relations over which the parents have little control, and they seldom include a sibling. The decrease in the size of the sibling group and individuation in the treatment of each offspring, who is no longer responsible for the others, has increased and institutionalized "sibling rivalry." Status and life-style decrystallization usually lead brothers and sisters in different directions.

The official breaking point between the parents and any offspring, whether a son or a daughter, is marriage and the setting up of a separate household. The relational movement is dual: independence and the purposeful relegation of roles in the family of orientation to secondary importance. Some exchange of services and gifts with both background families does occur (see Sussman's, Litwak's and Shanas' chapters in Shanas and Streib, 1965), but it is not expected to favor either side or to lead to a loss of independence.[1] Interaction is designed to be almost on an equality level, with parents refraining from controlling their married children. This focus upon the family of procreation is expected to continue through life. Most people do not return to the parental home in the role of dependent child, even in widowhood (see Marris, 1958 and Lopata, 1971e) or in divorce, particularly among white families. American black families of the lower class are often not financially stable enough to maintain separate households in crisis situations. Even the older parents understand that their children must place obligations to spouses and offspring ahead of those in the role of son or daughter (Shanas, 1962).

Thus, the American society expects mothers to continue focusing on their family of procreation even after widowhood and the departure of offspring; yet the children are not expected to reciprocate by focusing back on the mother. This situation has a high potential for relational strain for older women, especially widows, who had usually been brought up in much more patriarchal homes. The shift of attention in the culture from the old to the young makes this historical generation lose at both ends of the life cycle. In childhood, they had to tolerate being subservient to older people in the family, being socialized into venerating them, but they expected the same attitudes to be directed toward them when they finally reached the appropriate age. Although becoming themselves much more oriented toward their families of procreation than their parents had been, they are mixed in their responses toward their offspring, who focus downwardly and "neglect" the older mother in favor of their own children and grandchildren.

Several factors have helped to orient women toward the roles of mother and wife rather than those of daughter or sibling. In the first place, the dramatically changing American culture is oriented toward the young as "the knowledge generation," the hope of the future, the proof that progress is being made. Secondly, the ego of the American adult is more basically involved with children than with siblings or parents, unless the latter bring unusual status, life-style, or interpersonal rewards (Winch, 1962). The children are "her product" not only because she is their biological mother, but because modern society has placed on her shoulders the burden of insuring their life, growth, and development. She is the one blamed if they become "juvenile delinquents" or "unsuccessful" children in some way. The housewife in the "shrinking circle" stage of the role of mother, after the offspring have established themselves independently, is apt to declare that the major satisfaction of her life is that "the children turned out all right."

By virtue of the same trends, the modern mother tends not to look back in strong identification with her own mother. In the first place, her ego is not involved in how her parents "turned out." She may be embarrassed by the gap between her style of living and theirs, but this is an acceptable aspect of American society, found difficult only if the upward mobility of the middle generation was very dramatic, such as a light Negro's "passing" into the white society. However, she can not be held responsible for her parents; they were already there before she had any influence on them or their environment; they were powerful, and her inability to change them is not considered to be a failure of her intelligence or psychic strength. Because of the ideology of American society which encourages upward mobility and the acquisition of symbols of success, the middle generation woman is more apt to identify with her even more successful children than with the less prestigeful older parent. Status decrystallization among her collateral relatives also makes many siblings and cousins unavailable for comfortable or desirable contact.

Thus, a whole combination of factors direct an adult woman's attention toward her children rather than backward toward her own family of orientation. Anxiety in the role of mother combined with ego involvement (see Bettleheim, 1962, for a discussion of problems in such emphases); identification with success, and youth orientation of the culture encourage the pushing aside of kin roles not directly connected with the children. It also decreases the value given to roles outside of the home such as worker and member of the community.

In spite of the devaluation of the role of daughter in modern society, the adult woman usually tries to fulfill her duty of seeing, or keeping in contact by phone or letter, with her older mother. The relation is often, but not necessarily, personally warm, since both generations have experienced a similar life cycle of marriage and motherhood. Relations with siblings tend to be selective, or restricted to special occasions. In this society, as in England (Bott, 1957), the older woman often insures contact among her offspring by arranging for family events. Siblings who have moved outside of easy contact distance are seen sporadically.

The emphasis on younger generations may not extend to grandchildren, the independence of each residental unit from the extended family having influenced strongly the role of grandmother, by removing the youngsters from frequent and easy contact. Cultural change and the "rationalization," democratization and "scientification" of child-rearing procedures make the knowledge acquired by the older grandmother from traditional culture and her own experience irrelevant, if not judged harmful. Strains in relations between the older widow and her offspring over the subject of child-rearing, besides the "generation gap" in values, contribute to a potential of discomfort in the role of grandmother. Other strains are reported by younger generations in interaction with older aunts and uncles, who are likely to have different values and styles of living than their parents.

It is the function of this chapter to examine, at least partially, the trends in social relations between an older woman in an urban center and her parents, siblings, grandchildren, and more peripheral kin members. The analysis suffers from the fact that the research was not basically oriented in this direction, on the sociologically derived assumption that these relations do not form the core of a widow's life in this American location.

## RELATIONS WITH PARENTS AND THE
## ROLE OF DAUGHTER

The basic conclusion reached by the analysis of data from several studies of urban women is that, although personal relations with parents form a significant part of life for several adult women, the social role of daughter is not a source of identification or emphasis for Americans after entrance into the roles of wife and mother. The way that the Chicago area widows evaluate the role of daughter indicates the complexity of three-generational definitions which, as mentioned in Chapter Three, are difficult to understand. That is, the way the mother defines the role of daughter leaves some doubt as to whether she is referring to her obligations to her parents or to those of her children to her. In either case, it is an underplayed role, more likely to be mentioned by women in unusual life circumstances than by those involved in relatively normal situations.

The one-and-a-half hour interview asked for various role perceptions and definitions of life-changes on the part of widows at this stage of life. The length and depth of interaction with the interviewer allowed plenty of opportunity to mention parents as significant others, reference persons, or contributors to major life events, in the past or present. Fathers were mentioned very seldom, either because their significance is not great in the lives of women fifty years of age or older, or because they died before the husbands and thus did not affect the respondent's adjustments to widowhood. Mothers are mentioned more often and in several ways: as persons who helped the respondent when she was faced with widowhood problems, as a companion, or as a significant other whose death occurred in recent years. Mothers helped daughters who were widowed when young by welcoming some of them back home, caring for their children, or strengthening their will to build a new life. Most daughters did not move back home after having moved away, but crisis situations on the part of either generation can create opportunities for increasing the intimacy at a time when there is need for it. Some respondents mention obtaining comfort from the knowledge that the parents are available for interpersonal interaction or comfort. However, more turn for such response to their adult children rather than to their mothers, at least they make much more reference to such action. The most frequent mention of parents, particularly of mothers, is in terms of desolation (Townsend, 1968) produced by their death. Sometimes the woman cared for her mother or other kin during their illness, and the process may have reaffirmed the closeness, tying it in with memories of close associations of the past.

The death of a parent may not be remembered by an older widow as an event changing her life significantly, if they had lacked close contact in intervening years since her childhood, or if the relation had decreased in intimacy. A woman who moved to Chicago several years ago and who had not seen her mother since that time, reports feeling little effect of her death. Sometimes this particular event was combined in the memory of the respondent with several similar losses so that it does not stand out as having strong consequences. Death of a parent can be experienced as a release by the survivors, especially if they had been involved in prolonged care or if the alternatives of senility or total incapacity were judged as worse. On the other hand, the death of one parent may force care of the remaining one on an offspring, adding to already present burdens. A Mexican respondent reports having to bring her mother to her home, since the death of the father deprived her of the only English-speaking person in the parental household. Some respondents benefitted by their parent's death by inheriting money or a house. Asked how her life had been changed by the death of a mother who lived with her, a widow guiltily admitted that she is happy, because she can finally own a cat. Some respondents expressed real hostility toward their parents in answer to this question. One reports that she was not affected at all by the deaths of several members of her family of orientation: "They never did anything for me."

The attitudes toward living or deceased parents on the part of women aged fifty and over and living in an urban center depend on memories of childhood and the intimacy of the relation in ensuing years. The intimacy is based on the history of the relation, geographical closeness, and frequency of contact and *vice versa*. Women who report feeling close to their mothers attempt to see them more often than those indicating indifference or hostility. Many of the respondents are migrants to the city, having left their parents behind in Europe or in other parts of the United States. Often, the move formed a symbolic leaving behind of a whole style of life about which many negative judgments and sentiments are still felt. The resentment concerning having had a "difficult" childhood can slide over into a resentment against the parents for not having prevented it, or for having directly contributed to it. As in the case of other social relations, the more uneducated and poorer of the widows did not retain frequent or systematic contact with relatives left behind, nor express positive sentiments toward many of the members of their family of orientation. There were even some complaints over demands for financial help, seen as impositions. In sum, if any member of the family of orientation is mentioned with tenderness or sentiments of intimacy, it is not likely to be the father, but the mother or sister. The female parent is spoken of as a companion, helper, recipient of services, or sufferer from male dominance or neglect. The death of a parent can leave a daughter with a feeling of desolation, accentuated in cases in which she was already widowed and the relation with the parent had been significant to the end, or had been recalled in memory by the event. However, there are situations in which the death of a parent is met with nothing but indifference, worry about a modification in life circumstances, hostility, or relief.

## THE ROLE OF SIBLING

Most of the Chicago area widows either have no living siblings or are in minimal contact with the survivors. There are exceptions of women who are in frequent interaction with one brother or sister, but the average contact with all such relatives is very rare, less than a few times a year, and often limited to "family affairs," such as weddings and funerals. At the same time, the life cycle of such relations is interesting and supports the Sussman (1968), Litwak (1968), and Shanas (1968) thesis that there is a modified extended kin system operating in America. That is, women are often able to turn to their siblings and receive real help, in terms of services, finances, or comfort. In fact, the very knowledge that there is a group of people or even one individual with whom one has permanent ties seems to provide security for a widow. Even status decrystallization and the development of different life styles do not necessarily lead to a complete cutoff from potential interaction or sentiments of identification. In this respect, such relations differ from friendships, which tend to lose viability over time and distance. Kin relations are potentially available as life circumstances change, in crises, or when other events activate them periodically. Contact during emergency situations is reported by many respondents, who belong to the generations in which there are apt to have been many crises due to illness, death, and economic insecurity. It is at these times that siblings turn to each other for assistance, often obtaining many-leveled help.

Although brothers are not likely to be specifically listed as the closest sibling, or as the most helpful in times of need, they contribute much as do sons, in making funeral arrangements, offering financial assistance or advice. Some widows have a whole set of actively involved siblings, and references to brothers are more frequent in their cases. The sibling helper most frequently reported is a sister, and she is also the most likely to be listed as "close." Part of the feeling is one of remembered intimacy in childhood, but most of it seems to grow out of a similarity of life experiences. A sister is often reported as the one person who helped most in the difficult period following widowhood. The form of assistance is one mainly of companionship, including even a temporary sharing of households. Sisters also help care for each other, and for each other's children, during times of illness. Many of the respondents have lived most of their lives in poverty or on its borderline and have not been able to afford extensive medical care, hospitalization, or nursing attention. During illness they had to depend on relatives in the home, or ones making other kinds of arrangements. The ill person moves in with a sibling, or *vice versa*, or a sister comes over for a few hours a day to attend to her needs. Such contact with siblings is frequently reported among blacks and immigrant women, who are the most likely to need it desperately. As soon as the crisis is over, the siblings tend to return to their own lives, with little contact unless the time-distance between them is minimal.

Siblings often contribute to the migration of families. One brother or sister will come to Chicago and, after obtaining enough residential space and income, will send for another. They share housing and expenses until the newcomer obtains sufficient resources to establish his or her own home. The first move is likely to be near the first sibling, but future life circumstances tend to take them further and further apart. Among the respondents, those who migrated to Chicago recently are the most apt to be still living relatively close to a sibling. This is particularly true of the Mexicans in the sample.

Since older widows have not been habituated to contact through correspondence, few mention letter writing among family members. Siblings living far away, even at the other end of the city, are either seen rarely, at special occasions, or almost not at all. Yet several widows report very close and active interaction with a sister. One sees her sibling daily, goes on walks and shops with her, talks on the telephone whenever she feels blue, and receives assistance in the form of advice and encouragement. The sister appears to be the leader in the relation, the respondent passively waiting for suggestions of action. Few sisters, however, live together, even if they are in similar situations of having children grown and gone and being now husbandless. It is probable that the same constrains restricting the sharing of residences with married children or friends are operating here: the fear of interactional problems, and the wish for freedom of action, independence, and lack of work.

## Number of Siblings

Twenty percent of the respondents have no living siblings, but the proportion varies considerably by class, place of birth, and similar factors. Among residents of Chicago, the death rate is much higher in the black community than in the white. All but one of the black respondents had been born outside of the city, usually in the rural and agricultural South; the migrants are more apt to be without living siblings than the native-born Chicagoans. The blacks form sixteen percent of the respondents, but twenty-five percent of those have no surviving brothers or sisters. Respondents who are the only remaining offspring are much more likely to be located in the lower levels of educational achievement than those who still have siblings. Those who do not know how much schooling their husbands finished, and the widows of men who obtained no, or little, formal training lack siblings, but the pattern is uneven after that level of the husband's education. This is not surprising since the death rate of the wife's family relates to her background, not to that of her husband, so that only extremes are relevant. Protestants are more apt to be siblingless than Catholics or Jews. Part of this is due to the fact that most blacks are Protestants. Only Germans and the English, of all the ethnic identities, are disproportionately lacking siblings, and this is mainly because they are the oldest women in the sample. Twenty-nine percent of our total sample is under 60 years of age, but only fourteen percent of the survivors of sibling groups are of that age. The relative proportions begin to reverse after that age: forty-one percent of the total, but thirty-two percent of the siblingless are in the seventies; and six percent of the total, but twenty percent of the siblingless are eighty years of age or over. The length of widowhood does not prove to be significantly related to the proportion of widows who have no surviving brother or sister.

Those without siblings are likely to have been married more than once, to farm laborers, service workers, or craftsmen. Again, their marital instability, due to divorce or widowhood, reflects their social class. They are apt to define their current economic condition as really restricted, and their income, in fact, is most apt to be under $3,000. Whether because of health anxieties or the effect of a poor childhood environment, those who have no living siblings also find their activities limited by physical disabilities.

There are also attitudinal differences between women without siblings and women with living siblings. The former consider themselves as having been ignorant of financial arrangements at widowhood, define their previous marriages as sex-segregated, and refuse to declare them as above average. The siblingless are also apt to express pity for married friends, because of their supposed lack of freedom, and a desire for more friendship, despite feeling that sharing one's home causes trouble and that living alone is good. Widows without brothers or sisters wish more male companionship but think that people take advantage of widows. They do not wish to remarry and do not expect to be able to find a new husband, often because of health problems. The probability that they do not have anyone intimate to share troubles following widowhood is reflected in their lack of perception of change in themselves or in their limiting such a change to "increase in worry." Those who lack such kin are not as likely to consider free time a compensation of widowhood as women with brothers and sisters are, but they stress independence and being "one's own boss" more often. "Peace of mind" is listed only by them and by low interactors in the role of sibling. The women lacking siblings are the most likely of all the respondents to assign the role of community member to the last position and to put the role of worker in fourth or fifth place, out of six, while the other women either place worker at the bottom or much higher. This pattern reflects the lower socio-economic class background of women with no living siblings.

The death of a sibling was often listed in answer to the questions: "Did you have any close relatives who passed away after you were widowed?" "If yes, who was that?" and "In what ways was your life changed by (his/her/their) death?" The death of a sibling was psychologically upsetting to the widow, because it left her alone in terms of family, because it sometimes culminated a series of deaths, or because of its special circumstances. Respondents often reported feeling sad when really they meant guilty, because the sibling had died before contact was re-established after years of distance and before they undertook some symbolic action of sisterly love. Loneliness is a consequence of the death of a sibling with whom personal association had been maintained. Also, positions in the family structure may change due to the absence of one member, usually the eldest. On the other hand, some widows experience no difference in their lives upon the death of a sibling, having lost contact with him or her years ago, or not feeling any personal identification with relatives, or with that one in particular.

At the present time, twenty-two percent of the respondents have one living sibling, nineteen percent have two, sixteen percent have three, and twenty-three percent have more than that. Four women actually have nine brothers and sisters, but they do not see them often.

### Average Frequency of Contact With Siblings and Feelings of Closeness

Only six of the 301 widows have at least one sibling and see them daily, and five of these have only one brother or sister (see Table I in Appendix B). The greater the number of siblings, the lower the average contact frequency with them. This fact indicates a great dispersal of the sibling group. Four women see their siblings at an average frequency of daily to weekly, eighteen visit weekly (eight of them have only one sister or brother), and fifteen weekly to monthly. Sixty-three percent of the total number of respondents see their siblings at an average of less than a few times a year, leaving twenty-three percent whose average is between monthly and "a few times a year" visits. The most apt to have an average contact with siblings at least once a month have four or five of such relatives. The average drops for those with fewer siblings and for those with more. The figures certainly do not disclose a picture of close and highly interactive older siblings in the Chicago areas. The contact situation is somewhat similar to that with adult children, except that the latter interaction is much more frequent. Lower-class widows have fewer siblings and are less apt to see theirs at regular intervals than are upper- and middle-class respondents. Geographical dispersal has been experienced by both types of families, but the former are less able to cover time-distances than the latter. Whites are more apt to have siblings and to interact with them more frequently than the blacks are. Although the numbers are small, the average frequency of contact tends to decrease as the age of the widow increases, partly due to the death of siblings (see Table 29).

The differences in frequency of contact with siblings are not significant when the length of widowhood is considered, with one exception. The widows who have been without a husband over five years are much more apt to see their siblings fairly often than those who are recently bereaved. It is possible that they planned their residential changes with consideration of a location near a sibling in the same life circumstances. Such decision-making seems, however, more apt to be undertaken by women with at least some high school education. Those with less schooling are the respondents who see their siblings on the least frequent average.

TABLE 29: AVERAGE FREQUENCY WITH WHICH RESPONDENTS INTERACT WITH THEIR SIBLINGS, BY AGE DECADE

*Frequency of Contact*

| Age | Row | Sums | Daily | Day to Weekly | Weekly | Week to Monthly | Month to Few a Year | Few a Year to None |
|---|---|---|---|---|---|---|---|---|
| 59 and less | N | 79 | 2 | 2 | 10 | 3 | 29 | 33 |
| | % | | 3R | 2R | 13R | 4R | 37R | 42R |
| | % | 26 | 33C | 50C | 56C | 20C | 42C | 17C |
| 60–69 | N | 118 | 2 | 2 | 7 | 8 | 28 | 71 |
| | % | | 2R | 2R | 6R | 7R | 24R | 60R |
| | % | 39 | 33C | 50C | 39C | 53C | 40C | 38C |
| 70–79 | N | 77 | 1 | 0 | 1 | 4 | 9 | 62 |
| | % | | 1R | 00 | 1R | 5R | 12R | 80R |
| | % | 26 | 17C | 00 | 6C | 27C | 13C | 33C |
| 80 plus | N | 27 | 1 | 0 | 0 | 0 | 3 | 23 |
| | % | | 4R | 00 | 00 | 00 | 12R | 85R |
| | % | 9 | 17C | 00 | 00 | 00 | 4C | 12C |
| Column | N | — | 6 | 4 | 18 | 15 | 69 | 189 |
| Sums | % | — | 2 | ; | 6 | 5 | 23 | 63 |

Percent Base: 301
R stands for Row, C stands for Column

The different nationality groups are represented in all average contact frequencies in relations with siblings, but the Polish and the German respondents are the most likely to have daily contact, and those in the least frequent category are disproportionately non-Europeans and Scandinavians. The proportion having a high average frequency of contact increases as income and self-definition of a comfortable financial condition increases. The proportion who see all their siblings on an average of *less than a few times a year* decreases from a high of seventy-six percent among those receiving under $1,000 a year to sixty-four percent of those between $1,000 and $2,999, fifty-six percent for those between $3,000 and $4,999, fifty-two percent for those between $5,000 and $6,999, and twenty-eight percent for those between $7,000 and $8,999. The figures above that are too small to generalize. There is a definite parallel between definitions of financial condition and frequency of contact with siblings. The same is true of physical disabilities. Those who feel they have limitations on their activities as a consequence of some physical condition are the least likely to have daily, weekly, or even weekly to monthly contact averages, while the figures are heavily weighted in the other direction by respondents who feel healthy. Part of the reason, as mentioned before, is that the less healthy have fewer surviving siblings whom they can see; but in addition, this relation is not as vital for most women as that with children, and so is more apt to be affected by physical limitations.

In order to determine if widowhood had an effect on the relationship between the woman and her siblings, we asked each respondent if she found true the following statement: "My brothers and/or sisters became much more important to me after I became a widow." Only thirty-one percent of the widows found this statement true, fifty-one percent disagreed with it, and eighteen percent abstained, presumably because they have no siblings. This attitude is significantly associated with the belief that a widow must be independent of other people, that she should not move from the home she shared with her husband too soon after his death, that she would prefer living near other widows than in other locations, but that she should not share a residence (see Table 30). This is an interesting combination of attitudes toward the home on the part of

TABLE 30: PERCENTAGES OF RESPONDENTS FINDING TRUE
THE STATEMENT "MY BROTHERS AND SISTERS
BECAME MUCH MORE IMPORTANT TO ME AFTER
I BECAME A WIDOW," BY OTHER ATTITUDES,
WITH GAMMA ASSOCIATIONS

| | | Siblings More Important | | | | |
|---|---|---|---|---|---|---|
| Other Attitudes | N | True True | False True | True False | False False | Gamma |
| Widows have to make own life | 246 | 95 | 89 | 5 | 10 | .35 |
| A new widow should not move | 238 | 88 | 74 | 12 | 26 | .45 |
| Sharing a home causes trouble | 218 | 67 | 50 | 33 | 50 | .33 |
| Widows prefer living near widows | 226 | 44 | 29 | 56 | 71 | .31 |
| I wish people would not try to get me to go out | 237 | 31 | 19 | 68 | 81 | .33 |
| My faith helped me most | 270 | 87 | 78 | 13 | 22 | .31 |
| I have trouble being nice to those who did not help | 263 | 14 | 8 | 86 | 92 | .27 |

women whose siblings increased in importance to them in widowhood. The passivity of the stance *vis-à-vis* the world of sibling-oriented women is implied in their agreement with the statement "I wish people wouldn't try to get me to go out and do things all the time," and with "My faith helped me more than anything else after my husband's death." It is even reinforced by the association between closeness with siblings and the feeling that "I have trouble being nice to people who did not help during my period of grief." On the other hand, there is no significant association between sibling closeness and evaluation of the late marriage and husband, attitudes toward friends, or general community orientations. Those respondents who were most apt to reject the sibling statement were much more oriented toward friends and had stronger attitudes toward men.

Women who feel that their siblings became closer to them after the death of their husband are much less likely to be at the low end of the "frequency of contact scale" than those who feel no change in such relations (see Table 31). There is a strong association between this sentiment and active social interaction with several people. The contact is not likely, however, to be with children or friends, but with neighbors. Again, this reinforces the prior conclusion that women who feel that they are closer to their siblings in widowhood than in marriage are home-based in their attitudes. By the same token, feeling of closeness to siblings does not guarantee protection against social isolation. Ten percent of the respondents who feel more psychologically involved with their brothers and sisters nevertheless score high on the social isolation scale, the proportion being the same as for those who report no change. Not surprisingly, the attitude toward siblings is reflected in contact with them. Women who feel no closer now actually do not have much contact with the parallel members of their family of orientation. The association is strong and the score itself is dependent upon contact and the reporting of siblings as helpers in emergency situations and as associates in activities.

## Levels of Involvement in the Role of Sibling

Only twelve of the 301 Chicago area respondents scored high (sixteen to twenty-four points) on the role of sibling scale, which combined living with a sibling, average frequency of contact with sisters or brothers outside of the dwelling unit, references to such relatives as helpers in the re-engagement process or as people whose death affected the respondent, and expressions of feeling of closeness. The whole interview was combed for indications that siblings are important to some women. Sixty-one respondents got medium scores (eight to fifteen points) and 167 got low scores (zero to seven points). Fifty-nine women have no living siblings,

TABLE 31: PERCENTAGES OF WIDOWS WHO FIND TRUE THE
STATEMENT: "MY BROTHERS AND SISTERS BECAME
MUCH MORE IMPORTANT TO ME AFTER I BECAME
A WIDOW," BY SCORES IN THE DIFFERENT SCALES

| | | | | *Scores in Roles* | | | | | |
|---|---|---|---|---|---|---|---|---|---|
| *Siblings More Important* | | | | *High* | *Medium* | *Low* | *Total* | *Gamma* | $x^2$ |
| | | *N* | *Relations-Restricting Attitudes* | | | | | | |
| Siblings Closer | True | 247 | | 12 | 69 | 19 | 100 | −.07 | .36 |
| | False | | | 14 | 68 | 18 | 100 | | |
| | | | *Social Isolation Scale* | | | | | | |
| Siblings Closer | True | 247 | | 10 | 67 | 23 | 100 | −.18 | 2.70 |
| | False | | | 10 | 74 | 15 | 100 | | |
| | | | *Frequency of Contact Scale* | | | | | | |
| Siblings Closer | True | 247 | | 15 | 56 | 29 | 100 | .36 | 12.54 |
| | False | | | 11 | 37 | 52 | 100 | | |
| | | | *Role of Wife Scale* | | | | | | |
| Siblings Closer | True | 247 | | 34 | 51 | 15 | 100 | .04 | 1.05 |
| | False | | | 35 | 46 | 20 | 100 | | |
| | | | *Role of Mother Scale* | | | | | | |
| Siblings Closer | True | 206 | | 12 | 51 | 37 | 100 | .06 | 1.32 |
| | False | | | 8 | 55 | 38 | 100 | | |
| | | | *Role of Sibling Scale* | | | | | | |
| Siblings Closer | True | 223 | | 9 | 39 | 52 | 100 | .55 | 19.82 |
| | False | | | 3 | 17 | 80 | 100 | | |
| | | | *Role of Friend Scale* | | | | | | |
| Siblings Closer | True | 247 | | 14 | 45 | 42 | 100 | −.17 | 3.42 |
| | False | | | 15 | 55 | 30 | 100 | | |
| | | | *Neighboring Scale* | | | | | | |
| Siblings Closer | True | 247 | | 13 | 34 | 53 | 100 | .34 | 7.94 |
| | False | | | 6 | 23 | 70 | 100 | | |

d.f. $= 2$ $x^2$; p. $<.001 = 13.8$; $<.01 = 9.2$; $<.05 = 6.0$

as mentioned before, although most of them had some during their lifetime.

Widows in the younger age decades of life, that is, below fifty-nine,
are much more apt to have high scores in the role of sibling than are the
older ones. None of the women aged seventy and above are able to maintain contact with their siblings (see Table 32). Part of this difference is

TABLE 32: SCORES IN THE ROLE OF SIBLING SCALE BY AGE
OF THE RESPONDENT IN DECADES

| | | | | Scores in Role of Sibling | | | |
|---|---|---|---|---|---|---|---|
| | *Total* | | *No Sib-ling* | *High (18–24)* | *Medium (8–15)* | *Low (0–7)* | |
| *Age in Decades* | N | % | N* | % | % | % | *Total* |
| Below 59 | 71 | 29 | 8 | 7 | 35 | 58 | 100 |
| 60–69 | 99 | 41 | 19 | 7 | 24 | 69 | 100 |
| 70–79 | 57 | 23 | 20 | 00 | 19 | 81 | 100 |
| 80 plus | 15 | 6 | 12 | 00 | 13 | 87 | 100 |
| N | 242 | | 59 | 12 | 62 | 168 | |
| % | 100 | | | 5 | 26 | 69 | |

\* Not counted in percent base

due to death of siblings. Health and income limitations operate here, because siblings are apt to be geographically dispersed and difficult to reach. The very old widow may be visited by children, but she and her siblings have the same problems and often find it difficult to get together. Length of widowhood produces a similar distribution because of its connection with age, but those widowed less than one year also have low scores since it usually takes three or four years to build flourishing relations. The pattern is reminiscent of that of neighboring (see Chapter Six) and may indicate a tendency of older women to limit themselves to people of their own age who are members of the family or who live near the home. More contact is maintained with sisters than with brothers. Age at migration to Chicago by those who were born outside its limits is also an important factor. The most likely to have high sibling scores are the natives, and the only migrants who have high scores came during their thirties. Those who came with their siblings see them often, those who came alone lose contact. The age difference at migration is not as important, however, as the difference between the natives and those who were born elsewhere, indicating that many migrants did not come as total families of orientation, that they have negative feelings toward people with whom they spent their childhood, or that status decrystallization has resulted in a scatter within the metropolitan area. The natives have a three times greater probability as the migrants to have high scores, a time-and-a-half probability to have medium scores, and are only two-thirds as apt to have low scores.

A disproportionate number of the high scorers either obtained some high school education or graduated from college. The latter group retains an even flow of event-focused interaction, the former try to live near their siblings. The medium scorers completed high school or went on for some college education. A disproportionate number of women with a professional training and those with less than eight grades of schooling have low sibling scores. Both of these very different segments of the sample are apt to be only children, but their lack of contact with survivors of a multi-child family is due to different factors. In spite of the stereotype of the lower class woman as tied into a kinship group, the figures indicate that she is the most apt to be isolated from siblings. Women who had been married to men with eighth grade educations and those who do not know his schooling are more apt to be at the low end of the score than those who completed high school. Blacks are apt to be at the extremes of interaction with siblings, scoring either high or low, with few in the middle, while whites are most apt to maintain the median of contact. The black scores are partly due to the fact that all but one of the respondents had migrated from the rural South, often not bringing any siblings with them.

Roman Catholics are most apt to have a disproportionately high score and to be least likely to be at the low end of the continuum, an exact reversal of the Protestant tendencies. The Jewish respondents are also low scorers. Those who identify themselves as Germans are medium scorers, the Poles being high scorers. Those who do not consider themselves as members of ethnic groups accumulate few points in the role of sibling. Women married more than once seem to have experienced so many geographical, social, and identificational shifts that their sibling relations have decreased to a minimum. Eighty percent of those who remarried fall in the low end of the sibling scale, while this score is shared by only sixty-nine percent of the total sample. Women who took care of their husband at home prior to his death have a high score, possibly because of the help they needed and obtained from their siblings. Widows who are currently financially restricted are the most apt to be non-interactive with brothers and sisters. Those who are "rather short," that is, in the next level up, are most able to maintain a medium level of contact; those who are "comfortable" are the high scorers. However, the high scores do not necessarily have the highest income; widows now living on between $1,000 and $3,000 outdistance them in this respect. It is possible that this income category contains many respondents who live near their sisters or who come from large families. Those with high incomes are apt to be involved in a multi-dimensional social life space, with relations with siblings forming only part of the interactional scene. Physical disabilities operate to reduce sibling scores; combined with financial restrictions at the bottom level, they prevent a sizable number of widows from having frequent contacts with their sibling groups.

The high scorers report that they are lonely for their husbands as persons and as partners in activities. Although most widows do not wish to remarry, the low scorers are less apt to reject the idea (seventy-two percent) than the high scorers (ninety-two percent). Seventy-five percent of the high scorers, thirty-nine percent of the medium scorers, and fifty-one percent of the low scorers see no advantage to widowhood, indicating that high involvement in the role of sibling is not necessarily seen as a substitute to relations with the husband. Less work and more free time are also seen as major or secondary compensations by women who do not see their siblings often.

The ranks assigned to different social roles performed by women combine interestingly with scores on the role of sibling scale. Only eighteen percent of the high scorers, nineteen percent of the medium scorers, but thirty-two percent of the low scorers place the role of daughter in one of the first three positions. Thus, those who are not close to their siblings are apt to find the role of daughter important more frequently than the interactors. The role of housewife is differently evaluated by the three groups, the high scorers being much more apt to give it one of the first three positions of importance. The proportion decreases from their high of ninety-one percent to a seventy-four percent for those with medium scores and sixty-three percent for those with low scores. Thus, an increase of involvement in the role of sibling is associated with an increase in the importance assigned the role of housewife. This supports the emphasis on the home of previous statements. The role of worker is not placed in any of the top positions by any of the high scorers, and only eight percent of them so rank the role of community member. Twelve percent of the medium scorers, on the other hand, give the role of worker one of the top three positions, and nineteen percent assign the role of community member to one of these ranks. Eighteen percent of the low scorers assigned the worker role and ten percent assign the community role to the top three positions. Thus, women who interact with their siblings with a medium level of frequency and closeness are more likely than the others to be oriented toward a broader social world, while the high scorers are strongly oriented toward the home and family, and the low scorers are concerned with work as a means of obtaining needed income—the lack of which they find constricts their interaction with brothers and sisters, children and friends.

Several statements on the relations-restrictive attitude scale are significantly associated with the score on the role of sibling scale (see Table 33).

The distributions reinforce previous conclusions. Widows who are close to their siblings nevertheless believe that faith helped them more than any person after the death of their husbands. They do not think that

TABLE 33: PERCENT DISTRIBUTIONS AND TESTS OF
ASSOCIATION OF THE SCORE ON THE SIBLING
SCALE AND *AGREEMENT* WITH ITEMS ON THE
RELATIONS-RESTRICTIVE ATTITUDE SCALE

| *Attitude* | No Sib- ling N | \multicolumn{3}{c}{Score on Sibling Scale} | | | *Gamma* | $x^2$ |
|---|---|---|---|---|---|---|---|
| | | N | High % | Medium % | Low % | | |
| Sharing one's home causes trouble | 24 | 210 | 2 | 20 | 77 | −.46 | 12.36 |
| My faith helped me after widowhood | 39 | 230 | 6 | 29 | 64 | .67 | 10.51 |
| Widows feel like a fifth wheel | 26 | 224 | 3 | 31 | 67 | −.01 | 7.31 |
| Wish people wouldn't try to get me out | 14 | 224 | 2 | 40 | 58 | .22 | 7.15 |
| I wish I had more friends | 24 | 222 | 5 | 16 | 79 | −.33 | 5.97 |
| My husband was an unusually good man | 49 | 232 | 6 | 26 | 68 | .44 | 2.45 |
| OK for widows to have sexual relations | 7 | 217 | 00 | 16 | 84 | −.48 | 3.87 |
| Widows are sexually propositioned | 10 | 209 | 4 | 17 | 79 | −.36 | 4.49 |
| I feel sorry for some of my married friends | 11 | 215 | 7 | 24 | 59 | .27 | 4.10 |
| Income makes friendship impossible | 12 | 222 | 4 | 19 | 77 | −.25 | 2.22 |

$x^2$ with d.f. = 2;   p < .001 = 13.8;   p < .05 = 6.0
Gamma significant at .25 or above

sharing a home causes trouble, that widows feel like a fifth wheel, or that it is all right for a widow to have sexual relations with a man without marriage. They do not want more friends, do not think that their lack of funds is sufficient to restrict existing friendships, nor do they agree that husbands of friends proposition widows sexually. On the other hand, they feel sorry for some of their married friends because of an alleged lack of freedom experienced by them in such relations, while stating that they themselves had an unusually good husband. They do not like being convinced to go out of their home to engage in more diversified activities. The picture is of a woman rather immersed in a sex-segregated life, in past and present, with little contact with husbands of friends, leading to a lack of experience of sexual propositioning and the absence of the "fifth wheel" syndrome. The freedom in widowhood which they experience is one of non-action or a lack of change of level of involvement, rather than a freedom to engage in society at a broader level than in the past.

At the same time, the women active in the role of sibling are not socially isolated from other sets of relations. There is a significant correlation between the scores on the role of sibling and the frequency of contact[2a] and the isolation.[2b] This means that involvement in the role of siblings is connected with interaction with other people. Women lacking such contact are also apt to lack other forms of social relations. At the same time, a low score on the role of sibling scale does not automatically guarantee social isolation, since only twelve percent of the low scorers have a high isolation score, seventy-two percent of them being medium and sixteen percent being low. People without siblings are much more apt to be socially isolated than any of the women with surviving brothers and sisters. A basic reason for this is the low socio-economic background of these respondents, influencing both the death rate and social isolation. The really high correlation is with the frequency of contact scale. It must be remembered that this scale combined all frequencies of contact with references to weekly and weekend activities shared with people, etc. One could not get a high contact score from association with siblings alone. This means that women who interact with siblings also go out of their way to associate with other people.

The degree of involvement in relations with siblings is associated with a home and family orientation, in that the high interactors in that role also score highly on the role of mother (see Table XV in Appendix C) and neighbor (Gamma .32). There is no association between the role of sibling and friendship, orientations to the role of wife, or community participation.

## THE ROLE OF GRANDMOTHER

Eighteen percent of the respondents have no children, and eleven percent more have no grandchildren. Thirty-six percent of the widows have at the most five, twenty percent have between six and ten, and twelve percent have over ten grandchildren. The average number of such relatives per woman is 6.8, when those with no grandchildren are disregarded. Since there are 218 grandmothers with 1,452 grandchildren, we had assumed a large number of great-grandchildren, but these turned out to be relatively rare. Twenty-nine percent of the respondents have no grandchildren to supply the next generation, and forty-six percent more do not have any great-grandchildren, leaving eighteen percent with five or less, four percent with six to ten, and only two percent with more than ten great-grandchildren.

We asked each respondent who has grandchildren: "Do you feel particularly close to (one or more of) young grandchildren?"; and if she answered "Yes," we asked: "Why do you suppose that's true?" The same

TABLE 34: PERCENTAGES OF WIDOWS WHO HAVE A
FEELING OF CLOSENESS TO SOME OF THEIR
GRANDCHILDREN AND GREAT-GRANDCHILDREN

| Answer | Grandchildren | | Great-Grandchildren | |
|---|---|---|---|---|
| | Number | Percent | Number | Percent |
| Yes | 120 | 56.9 | 25 | 35.2 |
| No | 91 | 43.1 | 46 | 64.8 |
| No Answer | 2* | — | 1* | — |
| Not Appropriate | 88* | — | 229 | — |
| Percent base | 211 | | 71 | |

\* Not counted in percent base

set of questions was repeated for great-grandchildren (see Table 34).
Interestingly enough, none of the respondents or the interviewers objected to the question of differential closeness to different grandchildren,
while, it must be remembered, there had been objections to questions
asking for favorite offspring. American culture admits that grandparents
may have favorite grandchildren, although it rejects the idea that a
mother may feel closer to one child than to another.

Half of the respondents state that they do feel closer to some grandchildren than to others. We found, when screening the interviews, that
women who state that they feel equally close to all their grandchildren
are not close to any, since there is a strong tendency for this generation
of grandmothers to develop a fondness for one child or the offspring of
one family. There are basically four reasons given by the widows for
feeling particularly close to some grandchildren: frequency of contact,
absence of interference in the interaction, special circumstances of the
child, or special attention given by the child to the older woman. Of
course, the last named reason usually has a history of building up the
relation, which may be dependent on the other three factors. Frequency
of contact with young children is a product not of the youngest, but the
middle and eldest generations. Women oriented toward the role of grandmother would tend to go out of their way to live near, come into contact
with grandchildren, and perform services which would involve them.
For example, they are more prone to accept baby-sitting invitations and
to arrange their schedules so as to have the appropriate time free for
such activities.

Mothers who want their children to interact with their grandmothers
also provide greater opportunity for so doing. Whatever detailed explanation the respondent gave for having favorites among grandchildren,
the opportunity to get to know them in interpersonal relations comes out
strongest (see Table 35). One reason a grandmother may be given a

TABLE 35: REASONS GIVEN BY RESPONDENTS FOR FEELING
CLOSER TO SOME GRANDCHILDREN AND
GREAT-GRANDCHILDREN

| | Grandchildren | | Great-Grandchildren | |
| *Reason* | *Number* | *Percent* | *Number* | *Percent* |
|---|---|---|---|---|
| See and Know | 50 | 42.0 | 15 | 60.0 |
| Child's age | 2 | 1.7 | None | — |
| Boys—Girls | 3 | 2.5 | None | — |
| Other | 29 | 24.4 | 7 | 28.0 |
| Equally to all | 35 | 29.4 | 3 | 12.0 |
| No answer | 1* | — | None | — |
| Not Appropriate | 181* | — | 276* | — |
| Percent Base | | 119 | | 25 |

* Not counted in percent base

chance, or practically forced, to get to know a grandchild can be the
special circumstance of the latter's life. Several of the women report that
one of the children has a special health problem that requires the care
which she can perform easily, thereby relieving the mother to care for
the rest of her family. The death of a child's mother or her illness or
withdrawal from this role for other reasons may leave the child needing
a mother substitute. There are widows who moved into the homes of
their sons or sons-in-law to replace the mother of the children. Desertion,
divorce, or widowhood in the life of a daughter may result in the sharing
of households with the widow or even with the mother when the father
is still living. Disproportionately many black respondents report such
situations. The daughter moves into the home of her mother with small
children and then gets a job while the mother takes care of the offspring.
"I raised them," and "They lived with me when my daughter lost her
husband," are sufficient explanations in the minds of several widows asked
why they feel closer to some grandchildren more than to others.

The women who feel particularly close to one or more of their grandchildren are most apt to have been widowed between the ages of sixty-
five and seventy-four; those least likely to be identified with some member
of the third generation sufficiently to feel close were widowed at the age
of thirty-four or under. In all likelihood, the former group was home
when the grandchildren were young, and thus available for frequent contact, while the latter went to work and were too busy to develop really
close contact in later years with their children's children. The middle
generation is also more apt to have developed so much independence
under these circumstances that they do not call the grandmother to perform the interactional favors which make contacts frequent enough to

result in a feeling of closeness. Interestingly enough, it is the great-grand-child who is the object of close feelings on the part of women who were widowed early in life. Having lost the chance to develop intensive inter-action with the prior generation because of the factors given above, the women finally retired and started devoting more time and attention to the generation now young. Only thirty-five percent of the widows feel close to great-grandchildren, but sixty-seven percent of those widowed at the age of thirty-four or younger, fifty percent of those widowed be-tween thirty-five and thirty-nine, and sixty-seven percent of those widowed between the ages of forty and forty-four are in this category. Most older widows do not feel particularly close to their great-grandchildren, if they have any. The factors of social distance due to class, age, and historical differences of culture help explain the fact that so few have sufficient contact of pleasurable and interpersonal variety to produce feelings of closeness.

A lack of close relations with any grandchildren is reported by quite a few respondents and often explained in terms of physical distance. However, since others who are also separated from their offspring and their families manage to see them and feel close, one suspects that other factors are operating. One is the tension in relations with the middle gen-erations, discussed in Chapter Three. Social relations take time to de-velop and are highly influenced by trust and mutual respect. A few of the older widows bluntly stated that their own children would not let them get close to the grandchildren. The middle generation of Americans has gone through a revolution during their lives, purposely leaving behind the culture of their parents in the ghetto, ethnic community, and work-ingman's areas. They migrated from other areas of America or descended from migrants. Many have been successful and developed or joined the post-World War II "other-directed" (see Whyte, 1956 and Riesman, 1954) middle-class culture. They turned to experts trained in medicine and psychology in their attempt to raise their children "scientifically" or at least "developmentally." They simply do not trust their own parents to reinforce this outlook on child-rearing, and they are not secure enough to allow for the inconsistencies which are bound to crop up as a result of three-generational contact. Therefore, they intervene in the interaction between grandmother and grandchild to an extent which diminishes the rewards and increases the frustrations of each situation. The result is a lack of feeling of closeness. Not surprisingly, grandmothers who feel close to some grandchildren usually get plenty of opportunities to see them alone, without the middle generation. "They live next door and they are in and out of here all the time," says one respondent who very much enjoys this informality. Thus, the "distant" grandmothering found by Neugarten and Weinstein (1964) to be one of the modern styles may simply be the consequence of lack of opportunity to really interact as full personalities who are not afraid to openly express their feelings and reactions. The same restraint may, of course, be operating on the side of the grandchildren. Parental attitudes may impress on the grandchild the idea that he must treat the older generation in a manner that is unnatural for him, so that he avoids contact whenever possible. Since there is a cultural gap, brought about not only by the difference in time at which most of the socialization took place, but also by social class differences, the barriers must be broken down for a relation to develop. Frequent interaction from infanthood habituates the grandchild to behaviors of the grandmother which are not typical of the middle-class world in which he is growing up, but become objectionable only if downgraded by his peer group. Infrequent contacts emphasize the differences and, when compounded by any discomfort due to parental cautions or other forms of interference, they may prevent any but superficial interaction. Stereotypes of the aged usually do not help unless they contain traits which are positively valued by the young.

Thus, there is a great range in the relations of widows with their grandchildren, basically influenced by the degree of comfort of contact and by the behavior of the intervening generation.

## RELATIVES IN THE NEIGHBORHOOD

The known (Rosow, 1967) dependence of older widows' social interaction upon physical distance to possible associates, led to the question as to how many respondents have relatives living in their "neighborhood." No attempt was made to delineate the boundaries of a neighborhood. One-hundred-and-thirty-six of the 301 Chicago area widows have no kinfolk in their neighborhood (see Table 36). When asked to specify the type of relative who lives nearby, the remaining respondents usually listed adult children. At that, only fifty-one widows, or one sixth of the sample, have only children in the area while eighteen more have a combination of child and sibling, and seventeen have a combination of child and some other relative. This makes a total of eighty-six women, or one-fourth of the sample, who have an offspring in the neighborhood. Fifty-one widows, or a sixth of the total, have a sibling in the area. Other relatives tend to be nephews or nieces.

Widows who have no relative living in their neighborhood form forty-five percent of the sample, and they are most likely to have been in their residence for twenty years or more, or for five years. They are apt to have

TABLE 36: RELATIVES LIVING IN RESPONDENT'S
        NEIGHBORHOOD

| Relative | Number | Percent |
|---|---|---|
| Children | 51 | 31.9 |
| Siblings | 24 | 15.0 |
| Other | 32 | 20.0 |
| Child and siblings | 18 | 11.3 |
| Child and other | 17 | 10.6 |
| Siblings and other | 9 | 5.6 |
| All | 9 | 5.6 |
| No Answer | 5* | — |
| Not Appropriate | 136* | — |

Percent Base                                     160
*Not included in percent base

moved after the death of the husband. Those who did not move after that event and those who are in their homes less than two years are the most likely to be living near relatives. In fact, women who have moved within the past year are very apt to have several relatives around. Although only thirty-six percent of the whole sample have one to six relatives in the immediate vicinity, seventy-five percent of those who have lived in the area less than one year are close to that many kin members. A cycle of role involvements is suggested by these figures. The stable residents are likely to be living in older sections of the city and to be the last of their family to be so located. Adult children are not likely to move close to them. Widows who move, and who try to be around their relatives often find that these people disperse in less than five years. A young widow tends to be more oriented to other roles, particularly work, and not to make the effort to settle near kin members. Those who have children in the area are mothers of not yet married, or formerly married offspring or those who moved themselves to be near already married offspring. The dispersal is relatively rapid but is usually followed by another attempt by the various relatives to live not far apart. This second clustering is not as successful as the first, since fewer widows have relatives in the neighborhood after having been in it between ten and twenty years than after being in it between one and two years.

## SUMMARY AND CONCLUSIONS

Widows aged fifty or over are not highly oriented toward the role of daughter, even if they have a feeling of closeness for their mothers. Even those who have living parents do not refer to obligations to them, nor to rights received from them. The role of daughter also does not enter into many descriptions of past life or events. The few who mention a parent are much more apt to be talking of the mother than the father. Mothers are referred to as helpers, sources of comfort or of sadness brought about by their death. The role of sibling is also not very involving for most of the respondents at the present time, although references to it are made in the past. One reason is that one-fifth of the widows have no living sibling, and another, that many of the others are not in geographical proximity to a brother or sister. About one-sixth have siblings living in the neighborhood and twelve of these respondents engage in frequent interaction. An additional sixty-two women have at least a median score of interacting and feeling of closeness to a sibling. This leaves 168 respondents who have at least one brother or sister and who interact with that sibling at a minimal level or not at all. The rhythm of involvement in the role of sibling is uneven, the consequence of life events rather than the result of a purposeful attempt to stay close. Although the average of frequency of contact with all living siblings at any period of time is very low, one such relative, usually a sister, may be seen more often than others, and emergencies may dramatically increase contact. Siblings are sources of comfort and of more pragmatic help in time of need more so than friends who are no longer in easy interaction distance. The family bond is better able to weather the interruption of contact than friendship, and crises bring the family together.

Relations with grandchildren are of significance to older widows only if the social distance between the generations is cut down by frequent contacts without interference from the middle generation and if these contacts are conducted in a manner building trust and mutual respect. Grandmothers and grandchildren are not so frequently close and free of problems as idealized in the literature. Many widows familiar with the concept "generation gap" use this as a reason or excuse for not wishing to live with grandchildren or even to baby-sit for them, which is an action generally defined in the middle generation's terms. A feeling of closeness to grandchildren may be due to the special circumstancs of the latter's life, but inevitably it is associated with frequent and direct contact. Of course, the contact is usually facilitated by a wish for such a relation, but it may be forced on the partners because of the absence or problems of the middle generation. Usually, great-grandchildren are not seen frequently enough to bring about a feeling of closeness. There are some women who did not have a chance to be close to their grandchildren, because they were widowed young and involved in many roles, including work, who now find pleasure in relating to the next generation.

Over half of the respondents have some relative in the neighborhood, children being the most likely to live near their mothers (one fourth of the sample). With these people the widow is apt to interact fairly frequently. However, non-offspring relatives are not likely to be living nearby and are not seen very frequently. The more geographically and socially distant siblings and grown grandchildren come into contact with the older woman very seldom, and then usually at family events such as weddings or funerals.

## NOTES

1. Most of the pioneer work destroying the image of the nuclear family as a unit isolated completely from kin was done by Eugene Litwak and Marvin Sussman. (See Litwak's "Geographical Mobility and Extended Family Cohesion," *American Sociological Review*, 25 (1960): 385–394; "Occupational Mobility and Extended Family Cohesion," *American Sociological Review*, 25 (1960): 9–21; and the "Use of Extended Family Groups in the Achievement of Social Goals," in Marvin Sussman, ed., *Sourcebook in Marriage and the Family*, Boston: Houghton Mifflin Company, second edition, (1963): 477–484; and Sussman's "The Isolated Nuclear Family: Fact or Fiction," in Robert Winch, Robert McGinnis and Herbert Berringer, eds., *Selected Studies in Marriage and the Family*, New York: Holt, Rinehart and Winston, 1962, pp. 49–57; Lee Burchinal, "Kin Family Network Unheralded Structure in Current Conceptualization of Family Functioning," in Bernard Farber, ed., *Kinship and Family Organization*, New York: John Wiley and Sons, Inc., 1966, pp. 123–133 and "Parental Aid to Married Children: Some Implications for Family Functioning," *Marriage and Family Living*, 24 (November, 1962): 320–332.) The presence of cross-household interaction among kin members is stressed in arguments against Talcott Parsons, who reputedly denied its existence. Careful analysis of Talcott Parsons' comments on the family indicate the possibility of strawman exaggerations on the part of others. (See Talcott Parsons, "The Kinship System of the Contemporary United States," *American Anthropologist*, 34 (January–March, 1943): 22–38.) At the same time, the tendency to see the kin as a viable component of daily life or even of life styles may be a simple swing of the pendulum in the opposite direction. The same conclusion was reached by Geoffrey Gibson in a paper entitled, "Kin Family Networks: Overheralded Structure in Past Conceptualization of Family Functioning" (Mimeographed).

2. a. $x^2 = 35.65$   d.f. $= 4$ or p $< .001$
   b. $x^2 = 9.09$   d.f. $= 4$ or p almost $< .05$

# 5

# Friendship in Widowhood

## BACKGROUND

Human beings relate to each other in a variety of ways, with different sentiments and along a whole range of intensities, influenced by assumptions of what are "natural" relations and partners and the procedures institutionalized by each culture for their development. They can respond to each other fleetingly or permanently; superficially or with a strong sentimental involvement; with one major sentiment, ambivalently, or with a whole bundle of feelings; through a broad social life space or within restricted role limits; as a means of fulfilling themselves or in an open exchange of gains; from an ascribed base or through individual achievement; consistently or intermittently; etc., etc. Each child learns not only the behaviors appropriately directed toward different members of his community, but the attitudes and sentiments which form their base. He becomes socialized into the assumption that love or friendship, hate or avoidance are permissible only toward certain individuals and never toward others. In addition, each member of a community usually has some choice of people whom he can bring into closer intimacy or push back to the most distant limit of the allowed level. Thus, everyone is not located in the same closeness to everyone else, not only because of custom but also because of choice. Also, a definite life cycle of social relations is usually tolerated, if not demanded. People move closer during certain periods in an individual's life, through a series of intimacy-developing steps, and then they phase out or at least change their relation.

Most of the known literature of the world assumes that the closest social relations among people are contained in the family circle (Ibn-Khaldun, Fischel, 1967; Gumplowicz, 1899; Hume, 1874; Cooley, 1915). Relations which were judged to be almost, but not quite, as close were named "fraternal" or "sororal," and highly developed rituals such as "Bruderschaft" (Znaniecki, 1965: 138) were devised to convert non-family persons into members of the kinship group.

Members of larger societies enter into social relations with people out-side of the close group in order to achieve some external goals which can not be met by it. Such relations—with virtual strangers, passing acquaintances, or formal role partners—became more necessary and their importance more apparent as urbanization, industrialization and increased societal complexity brought people out of the close circle into a variety of interactions. These became stabilized as client relations, colleagueships, job subordinate-superordinate encounters, supplier and service exchanges, etc. The dichotomy between relations which are deemed close, involving the total personality and intrinsic criteria, and those entered extrinsically for other purposes became conceptualized by Charles H. Cooley (1915) as that of *primary* and *secondary* relations (see also Durkheim, 1947; Tonnies, 1957; Weber, 1930 and 1964).[1] The American culture contains in it an assumption, implicit also in Cooley's terminology (see Orbach, 1970), that the former relations are more "natural" and basic than the latter, in spite of the fact that social life could not continue without either. An additional assumption makes interaction difficult in urban centers, and that is that close, personal relations such as friendships can not be developed in secondary settings with virtual strangers, for whom external goals serve as the basic reason for interaction. Americans tend to divide the world into the person-oriented and the task-oriented segments, often ignoring the fact that these are not mutually exclusive. For example, modern marriage is idealized as a primary relation, while its secondary features are judged as unfortunately interfering with its basic aim (Bur-gess, *et al.,* 1963). Yet, despite the simplistic dichotomy, most relations in American society contain a combination of these forms of interaction. A more realistic classification of social relations would contain the follow-ing five types:

1. *Primary,* that is, focused on itself with no extrinsic goals; role strain is expected to be resolved in such a way as to preserve individual and relational, not task, concerns.
2. *Secondary,* or "business," "bureaucratic," etc., in which the major purpose of the interaction lies outside of its personal features; it is goal-oriented, logical, objective, and "functional," that is, directly beneficial to the participants or to larger units. Primary relations are discouraged.
3. *A mixture of primary and secondary* in a system which pretends to ignore, but tolerates, the presence of interaction scenes which are not part of its foundation. Each set of relations is classified as basically located at one extreme, and warning whistles are blown if it goes too far toward the inappropriate end. Most offices and

factories actually operate in this bargained manner, but within task-oriented role limits. Modern companionate marriages are the opposite of these.

4. *A mixture of the two,* in which the primary or interpersonal is manipulated in order to reach secondary ends. The ballroom dance studio (Lopata and Noel, 1967) and many other business organizations use a variety of encounter scenes to build personal sentiments in order to shift them later to objects and services not normally vested with such feelings. American society generally considers such a manipulation of primary sentiments for secondary gains as dishonest, but clever.

5. A final way of *blending primary and secondary relations* is by defining them as mutually compatible within the same situation. In social groups attempting such a mixture there is an intertwining of intrinsic judgments of members, a flow of relation and task orientation, and a multi-dimensional interaction. Many friendship-based voluntary associations attempt such balances, and any encounter will flow back and forth among all three types of social relations: the task-oriented, the relation-oriented, and the blended. A particular relation in such a system may move out of the original contact situation and flourish independently.

According to most observers, the two social relations which are viewed in America as the closest to the primary end of the scale are those of erotic lovers and of friends (see Znaniecki, 1965: Chapter 7). The former, if isolated from the function of reproduction and the task aspects of the roles of husband or wife, mother or father, and the rest of the marriage complex; and the latter, if detached from co-worker obligations or enforced service-exchanging, are entered into for the sheer pleasure of interpersonal response, with no superordinate goal. The fact that such relational partners are not concerned with the external functionality of their association has usually made them the objects of a variety of social controls. Some societies have tried to prevent or at least restrict certain members from becoming partners in such relations. Frequently, they have been placed in a peripheral location *vis-à-vis* more functional roles.

## FRIENDSHIP

The relation of friendship has an interesting history in American society and varying significance within its sub-groups. Most of its cultural components are still embedded in a non-mobile small town or settled neighborhood life in which the pool of eligibles is limited to same sex members known for many years. Thus, the rituals of bringing another person into the "best friend" category are designed to start with already known semi-friend positions and to begin early in life. These characteristics have made the development of a new friendship extremely difficult in modern urban centers, where it must start from mere acquaintance or even some candidate-searching action through the whole life cycle. Traditionally, the culture of all but the upper classes does not contain such friendship-building mechanisms. In fact, their development has been hampered by a village-like distrust of all strangers and the assumption of permanency and ascribed nature of "true friends." Life in modern America, with its known situations of manipulative use of primary relations and sentiments for secondary purposes, has deepened the distrust. Many Americans in the cities carry with them a strong suspicion of "the ulterior motives" of anyone who befriends them and withhold their own sentimental overtures for fear of bringing mistrust upon themselves.

New forms of friendship have been emerging and can be classified in the following way.

ILLUSTRATION I: MODEL OF FRIENDSHIP RELATIONS

| Degree of Permanence | Range of Choice of Partner | |
|---|---|---|
| | Ascribed | Achieved |
| Permanent | brothers who are also friends, etc. | friends individually chosen for "a lifetime," etc. |
| Transitional | debutants, army buddies, etc. | neighbors, club members, etc. |

The major changes in friendship have been from dependence on ascribed relations, which are considered permanent, to individually achieved ones, which are acknowledged as temporary. A transitional ascribed relation is often found in large groups whose members are going through rituals of life or dramatic events and are expected to feel strong friendship sentiments toward each other. Boot camp bunk mates, or any individuals thrown into close proximity and sharing a temporary lot, are expected to develop close ties which dissolve when life circumstances change and choice allows the selection of partners (see also Stouffer, *et. al.* 1949). More permanent ascribed friendships can develop among brothers or neighbors in non-mobile locations. Originally they may be forced by the larger group but later develop a life of their own. An increasingly large segment of American social life also centers around transitional achieved friendships, which are based on the assumption that once geographical or social mobility separate the freely chosen partners, their contractual and sentimental involvement will discontinue (Dubin, 1956; Whyte, 1956; *Practical Builder,* 1966). The decreasing permanence and increasing freedom of choice have broadened the categories of candidates for such friendships. Awareness of the relation's potentially temporary status has shortcut the stages of its development and lessened fears of being burdened too long with one too hastily formed. At the same time, only people who know the procedures for converting secondary relations into primary ones have such friendships potentially available; societal members, particularly of an older generation, may refuse intimacy to others contacted in secondary locations.

## FRIENDSHIP OF WOMEN PRIOR TO WIDOWHOOD

The expansion of friendship to more people more easily met has not permeated through the whole society, nor is this relation assumed to have the same characteristics for all people and for all stages of the life cycle. The high period of friendship orientation is expected to be youth, when the "important functions" of on-going societal life need not be met. Friends help each other in the socialization process and into transition stages. What happens after this stage of life, particularly when marriage, parenthood, and male work roles are added, varies considerably in this heterogeneous society in response to many factors. There are several different ways in which the husband and wife can be involved in friendships outside of the marriage unit:

1. *Sex-segregated companionate relations* in which the husband and wife participate in different groups, as described in working class boroughs by Elizabeth Bott (1957), Michael Young and Peter Willmott (1957). "Men have friends, women have relatives," is the way Bott (1957: 68) describes this combination.
2. *Sex-segregated companionate relations* in which the husband is attached to a clique, while the wife is relatively isolated. The women married to clique members do not form a separate group, as exemplified by lower-class Mexicans described by Arturo and Genevieve De Hoyos (1966) in "The Amigo System and Alienation of the Wife."

3. An alternative *clique connection,* in which the wife is the only one who is strongly involved, is a friendship which prevents couple-companionate relations from becoming primary in importance to her, as reported by Nelson (1966) in his description of a residentially stable segment of New Haven, Connecticut.

4. *Sex-segregated companionate relations* connected with the *male kin line,* as exemplified in patriarchal, patrilineal, and patrilocal societies. Both sets of friendship groups are ascribed, the male having been born into one and the wife joining its female counterpart upon marriage. Anthropological literature abounds with descriptions of such arrangements.

5. *"Couple only" companionate relations,* in which the husband and wife lack sex-segregated friendships and engage in leisure activities only as couples, appear rather rarely, even in modern literature. The honeymoon period in American marital relations draws the attention of the partners to each other, and other units are not usually portrayed as part of the activity, although "vacations with" another couple may set up such temporary relations. The romantic love ideal assumes that no external friendships are needed, that the relation is "total," but many studies indicate that this is only part of the fantasy woven into this "romantic fallacy." London professional couples are portrayed by Elizabeth Bott (1957) as close to this ideal, since they are supposedly separated from sex-segregated friends; but several commentators have felt this "social network" to be inadequately studied or explained (Nelson, 1966; Weiss, 1969). We simply do not know the prevalence of this pattern.

6. *"Couple plus" sex-segregated companionate relations* seem to be most frequent among middle- and upper-class Americans, including the Chicago women who are married. The form they take, the source of either couple or sex-segregated friendships, and the activities they involve vary by social class, residential area, and idiosyncratic factors. The "couple plus" concept refers to relations of modern husbands and wives which include both couple socializing and same sex friendships developed by each partner out of current life. Lower-class couples are apt to have none or fewer of these, most contacts being limited to sex-segregated or asymmetrical relations. The patterns tend to be dependent upon individual selectivity, with age and the generation to which the respondent belongs as contributing factors to the form they take (see Lopata, 1971b).

Generally speaking, the friendship relations of an increasing number of urban Americans are expected to be pushed into a background of importance with marriage and parenthood. They are never supposed to compete with the obligations and identifications of those other sets of relations. One way such a move has been facilitated is through the addition of the role of friend to the set of relations binding the husband and wife to each other. Another is by transforming the highly involving same-sex friendship into a more shallow couple-companionate, or leisure-time activity with a circle or "crowd." Married women tend to define their best friends as the female partners of the couples with whom they socialize on weekends (Lopata, 1971b).

Of interest to sociologists has been the source of friendships of modern couples, the conclusion generally being that the husband contributes more than the wife (Babchuk *et. al.*, 1963).[2] The *Occupation: Housewife* research discovered that the contributions of both mates to the pool of friends depends upon many factors, basic among which are education, role involvements, and stage in life cycle. The following illustration indicates the possible sources of couple-companionate or sex-segregated friendship relations of couples which were discovered in that research.

ILLUSTRATION II: MODEL OF COMPANIONATE RELATIONS, COUPLE AND SEX-SEGREGATED BY ORIGINATOR AND DEGREE OF CHOICE, CHICAGO HOUSEWIVES AND WORKING WOMEN *

| *Participant* | *Originator* | | | |
|---|---|---|---|---|
| | *Wife* | | *Husband* | |
| | *Ascribed* | *Achieved* | *Ascribed* | *Achieved* |
| *Husband* | *As Couple* | | *Friend or Clique* | |
| | Matriarchal kin and spouses | Wife's friend clique, and their husbands | Patriarchal kin (especially sibs) | Friend, clique group |
| *Wife* | *Friend or Clique* | | *As Couple* | |
| | Matriarchal (especially sibs) | Wife's friend voluntary group clique | Patriarchal kin and their spouses | Husband's friend, clique group |

* Helena Znaniecki Lopata, *Occupation: Housewife*, (Oxford University Press, 1971b)

# FRIENDSHIP IN WIDOWHOOD

Most of the Chicago area respondents had been widowed in the middle years of life or later. If they followed the typical patterns of friendship-formation, their more middle-class representatives were involved in couple-companionate relations. Unless the woman worked, many of the friends were brought into the unit through the work-contact of the husband. Lower-class women were less apt to have friends and more likely to be sex-segregated in their relations. In general, the lower the socio-economic class, the more dependent the woman on ascribed interaction, particularly with kin members in sex-segregated scenes. The higher the class, the more likely the wife to be engaged in couple-companionate, achieved friendships to which the husband was a major contributor. As this chapter will indicate, it is this second type of widow who experienced the greatest strain in her friendship relations as a result of the death of her husband.

A large majority (seventy percent) of the Chicago area respondents had known their friends before they themselves became widows. The twenty-three percent who met their friends after the death of the husband also form an important segment of the population. They are most likely to be women who moved after widowhood, who found association with married friends so difficult as to purposely introduce changes in associates, or who undertook new roles providing opportunities for new relations. Only two percent explained that they have associates met both before and after widowhood; six percent listed other situations. Forty women found the question inappropriate, for unknown reasons, but only seven admit to no friends at all. Housewives, too, tend to claim friends, even in cases in which they could not give the names or community location of such supposed associates. Although American society insists that friendship is of secondary importance to family and work roles, an admission of a lack of friends must raise considerable anxieties. The researchers studying older people in small towns of Missouri (Pihlblad and Rosencranz, 1968) found respondents who claimed the whole community to be "friends."

When asked what proportion of their friends are now also widows, only four precent answered "all," and eleven percent "none," nineteen percent "most," twenty-one percent "half and half," twenty-eight percent "a few," and fifteen percent "one or two." These figures are highly significant, particularly in view of the stereotyped image of the widow, created in part by the Cumming and Henry (1961) picture of Kansas City women, eagerly awaiting the occasion to join "the society of widows." The Chicago study indicates that most widows continue to consider some married friends as close to them, and very few limit their contacts to women of the same marital status as their own.

Statistically, one would expect the proportion of friends who are also widowed to increase with the respondent's age at widowhood. This generally is the case. Although four percent of the respondents restrict their friendship to widows, fifteen percent of those who lost their husbands at the age of forty to forty-four fall into this category. The highest proportion of "all" widowed friendship is for women over seventy-five years of age (forty percent), and the proportion rises with each decade from twenty-four percent of those widowed between sixty-five and sixty-nine, and thirty percent of those widowed between seventy and seventy-four. At the same time, those women who claim no widowed friends are most likely to have experienced their marital change when they were thirty-four years or under, forty to forty-four, fifty to fifty-four, and sixty to sixty-four. Again, the women who were widowed in the early years of their respective decades show a pattern different from those whose husband died when they were in the latter years of their decade. This tendency reinforces some of the conclusions of Chapter Two concerning the difficulties experienced by women widowed after they had entered a new decade of life. The older the woman at widowhood, the more likely she is to have known her friends prior to the death of her husband. A high proportion of those who met their friends after reaching this marital condition had been at that time thirty-four years of age or younger (seventy-two percent, compared to the average of twenty-three percent), and the proportion drops dramatically to thirty-eight percent in the next older age category and declines steadily after that. Again, this means that most women continue to see old friends who are still married or at least consider these people their friends.

TABLE 37: THE PERCENT OF FRIENDS OF RESPONDENTS WHO ARE OF THE SAME RELIGION AND NATIONALITY AS THE RESPONDENT

| | Same Religion | | Same Nationality | |
|---|---|---|---|---|
| Proportion | Number | Percent | Number | Percent |
| All | 51 | 17.5 | 56 | 21.5 |
| Most | 112 | 38.5 | 55 | 21.1 |
| Half and half | 53 | 18.2 | 42 | 16.1 |
| A few | 46 | 15.8 | 55 | 21.1 |
| One or two | 16 | 5.5 | 13 | 5.0 |
| None | 7 | 2.4 | 34 | 13.0 |
| Don't have friends | 6 | 2.1 | 6 | 2.3 |
| No Answer | 3* | — | 13* | — |
| Not Appropriate | 7* | — | 27* | — |
| Percent Base | | 291 | | 261 |

* Not included in percent base

In attempting to learn more about the composition of the friendship groups of widows, we asked what proportion of their close associates were of the same nationality or the same religious group.

The figures in Table 37 suggest that women find people whom they consider friends in situations of frequent contact. This conclusion reinforces the findings of many other researchers (Rosow, 1967; Lopata, 1972a) that people depend upon being brought together regularly by social groups or work situations in order to be able to maintain primary relations. This is particularly true of the older American, who is constricted by a lack of education and middle- to upper-class resources for friendship maintenance. Most women go to church more frequently than they attend meetings of groups of their national culture society or other associations; many simply do not belong to such organizations or are not strongly identified with a specific ethnic group. This point is supported by the fact that only two percent of the widows have no friends in their own religious group and that seventy-four percent have at least half of their friends of the same faith, while thirteen percent have no friends of the same nationality, and only fifty-nine percent have at least half of their friends in the same ethnic group. Both sets of figures support the conclusion that older urban widows tend to have a restricted social life space. In fact, one-fourth of the respondents restrict all their friends to members of the same national group, while a slightly smaller proportion see only friends of the same religion. The ethnic community is still viable for a surprisingly large number of widows, but the figures again lead to the suspicion that "friends" may not be people necessarily seen often.

Friendship within an ethnic group is somewhat surprising in view of the self-identification of the respondents. When asked to classify themselves by national origin, half of them had responded "American," while only five percent listed another ethnic group, twelve percent used a hyphenated term (such as Polish-American), and thirty-two percent referred to themselves as descendants of a foreign group (such as Americans of Polish descent). The others found the question inappropriate, presumably because of being identified as Negro, rather than as Afro-American, a term more popular among the young and more highly educated, and the rest gave mixed backgrounds. The identification question was followed by the one asking for the proportion of friends of the same nationality, so that the figures do indicate in-group identification, but often of marginal status.

The older the woman, the more likely she is to claim that all her friends are of her nationality. Twenty-one percent of the total group so classified their friends, but only fourteen percent of women fifty-four years of age or younger limit all their friends to one group, while thirty-one percent of those in the age bracket of eighty to eighty-four are located here. There is again a slight dipping pattern, with women in the early part of each decade having a greater tendency to limit their friends than ones in the latter part. As to religion, the older the woman, the more likely she is to have friends only of the same religion, and even in the same denomination. The women who do not share a religious identification with their friends tend to be younger.

Thus, older widows are restricted in their friendships to women of the same marital, national, and religious background and current marital status, while those in the very eldest categories who were widowed late in life are the most apt to see only other widows. At the other end of the extreme are women who after widowhood have added new friends not necessarily of the same religion or nationality.

## CHANGES IN SOCIAL LIFE SINCE WIDOWHOOD

Since so much of American "social life" is dependent upon contact with friends, we asked each respondent how this aspect of her life changed after she became a widow (see Table 38). Actually, we had expected a

TABLE 38: CHANGES IN QUALITY AND QUANTITY OF SOCIAL LIFE WITH WIDOWHOOD

| Changes | Number | Percent |
|---|---|---|
| None now | 8 | 2.7 |
| Less | 113 | 38.3 |
| More | 34 | 11.5 |
| Different activity | 4 | 1.4 |
| Different people | 10 | 3.4 |
| Same | 126 | 42.7 |
| No Answer | 6* | — |
| Percent Base | | 295 |

* Not included in percent base

much higher proportion of respondents to describe dramatic changes in activity or in associates. The fact that thirty-nine percent feel that their social life has decreased in intensity with widowhood is not surprising; the fact that forty-three percent report no change is startling. Some of the reasons for such answers can be seen when they are cross-tabulated by the age of the respondent at the time when her husband died. Not surprisingly, the older women are the most apt to report no change. Sixty percent of those aged seventy-five and over at widowhood, fifty-six percent of those between seventy and seventy-four years, forty-eight percent of those between sixty-five and sixty-nine, and only forty percent of those between sixty and sixty-four report no change. Women reaching that marital state when thirty-four years of age or younger are highly underrepresented in this group, with only fourteen percent of them defining their social life as stationary. Rather, they are the most likely to report an increase of social activity. Women widowed in the early part of their forties and fifties and sixties are more apt to report their social life as less active than women in the latter halves of these decades, although this tendency is less frequent as age increases. The respondents who report a higher level of social involvement after widowhood also tend to have been in their sixties at the time their husband died. They thus may be the only group who fit the "society of widows" stereotype, since they have a sufficient number of widowed friends, and the health and the money to engage in an active social life. It is quite probable that the women widowed when thirty-four and younger have a different "social life" than those widowed in their sixties.

When prodded, most women explained the aspect of their social life which had undergone modification by references to attendance at public places (fifty-eight percent) or to visiting patterns (twenty-seven percent). Those who report changes in entertaining and being invited to friends' homes were disproportionately located in the fifty-five to fifty-nine age category at the time of widowhood; women who miss being able to go to public places were usually widowed under thirty-five years of age. Ninety-two percent of the widows in that category report change in attendance at public places, with a steady drop to forty-two percent of women widowed in the late fifties. Interestingly, there is a rise to sixty-five percent for women widowed in their early sixties.

There are several reasons given for the change or lack of change in the social life after widowhood (see Table 39). Most of the respondents who report a modification of activity tend to complain that many social events are couple-companionate ones and that they do not want to go or are not invited. Eleven are afraid to go out alone; another seventeen feel it is wrong for a woman to go places unescorted. Those who report an increase in activity include the ten who state that they did not go out much before because the husband refused to take them and the twenty-four who now feel free to have a social life which they did not experience in marriage.

The fact that forty-two percent of the respondents report no change in their social life after the death of the husband indicates the presence of a highly sex-segregated leisure world. Those women who so defined

TABLE 39: REASONS FOR CHANGES IN SOCIAL LIFE SINCE
WIDOWHOOD

| Reasons | Number | Percent |
|---|---|---|
| Did not go out with husband, now do | 10 | 5.9 |
| Freer now, busier | 24 | 14.2 |
| No longer invited | 18 | 10.7 |
| Couple events, does not want to go | 59 | 34.9 |
| Old now, less healthy | 13 | 7.7 |
| Restricted (child in home, etc.) | 12 | 7.1 |
| Afraid to go out alone | 11 | 6.5 |
| Women can't go places alone | 17 | 10.1 |
| Is a homebody | 4 | 2.4 |
| Other | 1 | .06 |
| No answer | 6* | |
| Not appropriate, life did not change | 126* | |

Percent base = 169
* Not counted in percentages.

the effects of becoming a widow are the less educated, who report no
change in themselves in widowhood, and who are more socially isolated
than the women who either report more or less social life. They were
peripherally involved in social relations in marriage and remain so in
widowhood.

The impression created by the explanations of why and how the respondent's social life had or had not been modified by the death of the
husband is of three basic trends: Most widows who had been active in
a multi-dimensional life now experience constriction in many types of
social activities, particularly in those involving couple-companionate
associates. They now spend time formerly so engaged at home alone or in
the company of their families. Few go out on a Saturday night with
other widows and even fewer accompany couples, although they may be
active during the non-weekend day. The second trend is of an increase
in involvement in social situations away from the home as a result of
freedom from the obligation to stay in a restricting relation, the need to
"keep busy," or the development of new friendships, including dating
relationships with men. Relatively few women enjoy this freer style of
life and these are the most apt to report involvement in work and voluntary associations—indications of upward social mobility. The third tendency is for widows to retain the same degree and quality of social life as
before the death of the husband. Those women falling in this category
who are not socially isolated are apt to be involved in high interaction
with kin—with children and grandchildren, more than with siblings and
their offspring.

## RELATIONS WITH FRIENDS

Naturally, the friendship patterns of women in widowhood can not be fully tapped by asking about their "social life," since that term usually refers to couple-companionate exchanges. A relatively large segment of both the exploratory and the more formal interviews was devoted to probing for attitudes and definitions of friendship relations, particularly as they are affected by widowhood. It soon became apparent that friendship styles depend on relations prior to the death of the husband, the strains these undergo as a result of the changes brought about by that event, and the modifications then introduced into the pattern. There are basically three friendship styles exclusively or simultaneously available to widows. The first two are dependent upon sex-segregated situations of contact, which means that they occur during the day and in the middle of the week. Married women generally go out or stay home with their husbands on weekends and evenings. Traditionally, the woman is expected to be in the house when the man returns to it, especially if his efforts on the outside are directed toward providing for its maintenance. The unmarried or no longer married woman is not part of the leisure-time couple ritual of her married friends. Couples who are actively engaged in a "social life" interact with other couples, and even those who spend their leisure time alone or with kinfolk are not comfortable in the presence of an unattached woman.

The first style of friendship available to widows is continued membership in a sex-segregated dyad or woman's clique, regardless of marital status. If relatively permanent, such a group can gradually shift from mostly married to mostly widowed members. The early widows bear the brunt of the role change (see Neugarten, 1968 and Rosow, 1967) and help to anticipatorily socialize their still married friends for greater ease of later transition. The second friendship style is a result of the situation in which widows are gradually dropped from the circle of married women and solve this problem by becoming isolates, remarrying, re-engaging in society through roles other than friendship and finding within them new colleague relations, or joining "the society of widows" (Cumming and Henry, 1961). Colleague friendships are restricted to work situations if the others are married. The fourth of these solutions can result from a purposeful search for widows. Some respondents explain that strain in their interaction with married friends resulted in seeking out former associates who had dropped from the group when they became widows, or in joining clubs to meet new friends. Using the associational meetings as a contact point, they arrange to go with new friends, invite them to their homes, and plan for increasingly frequent "events." It is particularly the middle-class woman who uses voluntary associations to find new friends who are also widows.

One of the exploratory interviews provided insight into the effects of the husband's death upon friendship patterns. Asked about her former friends, this suburbanite who became very active in voluntary associations explained:

*Well, you see, I dropped all my married friends. This I knew before I ever became a widow, of course. My husband had cancer and it was a four-year siege, so I knew. He finally took his own life because he couldn't bear it any more, but I knew this was coming and I read everything that I could read, that I could get my hands onto that I thought would help me . . . and I knew that trying to continue a friendship with another married couple was neither good for them nor me, because you are a fifth wheel and they are kind and they will be for a while but if you don't drop them, they are going to make you feel as though you should go out and look for widows (laugh), you know what I mean.*

Joining "the society of widows," however, offers problems for many women who had participated in a couple-companionate life prior to the death of the husband. American society is geared for couple attendance at public functions which involve polite companionship, and several respondents felt a real status loss in having to enter such places with only women, often to the extent of refusing to do so.

*I feel that. Well, how can I put it in words? Second class citizen, that's true, you do feel that way. Well, I think just the fact that you don't have an escort when you go places—I think that this is very pronounced and very evident if you go out to dinner. I don't like to go out to dinner alone, so consequently you try to get on the phone and call somebody else up and see if they're in the mood to go. This sets you apart, you see a couple of women . . . I can remember down in Miami, I hate Miami for that reason. When I was not a widow yet, you'd see groups of beautifully gowned, elegant looking elderly women, you knew they were all widows. Immediately they were an isolated segment of society in my mind at that time, and I'm sure when we go into a restaurant, maybe two or three or four of us, I'm sure that other people look at us the same way.*

Of course, many women do not have the training or the funds to develop new life styles with widows which involve traveling and theatergoing, dining out or entertaining. Women with less education and wealth have usually been socialized into a more restricted use of leisure and into an inability to enter the sequence of stages required for such friendship styles. They often depend on contacts with other people which are accidental and thus seasonal or sporadic. If living in the "old neighborhood," they are able to develop some informal friendship interaction through such techniques as going shopping at the same hour and in the same places as other widows.

The third type of possible friendship interaction includes the widow in couple-companionate activities, as she was prior to the death of the husband. Many Chicago area respondents, particularly the younger, middle-class ones, indicate a desire, and often an attempt, to carry on such a style of friendship. These tend to be women used to getting together for dinner or a party at someone's home, going out to movies or other public events, having picnics, and so on. They enjoyed these events and they and their husbands built friendship patterns around these activities. They may, or may not, have had simultaneous sex-segregated cliques, but the leisure-time "crowd" formed a very important part of their lives. Many more widows than those who are actually involved in groups of couples had attempted such membership, but finally dropped out, finding themselves too marginal to the group unless they had an escort. The next section of this chapter will examine the difficulties involved in the relations of widows with their married friends.

### Strains In Friendships With Widowhood
Exploratory research revealed that many widows experienced serious strain in their relations with married friends after the death of the husband. The interview schedule was thus designed to reach such feelings through a whole series of questions. In analyzing the results, however, we found four types of Chicago area women who did not experience much change in their friendships after becoming widowed. The numbers were not large, but they cannot be ignored, because they represent an important segment of the older urban population.

The first category of women whose friendships did not change after widowhood are immersed in family life to such an extent that they have no time, energy, or sentiment left for the development of close interaction with outsiders. These are often women who were socialized into a sex-segregated patriarchal culture, and the husband's death made little difference to them personally.

Another type of woman whose friendship role was not modified much by widowhood is the *home-based* housewife who "never had much social life" of either sex-segregated or couple-companionate variety. This type of widow may have casual relations with neighbors or she may limit herself to associations focused in the church. Sometimes her life is very restricted.

The third type of woman whose friendships did not change after the death of her husband is even more deeply isolated and restricted in her social life space. She is likely to be without living children or siblings or with someone "back home" whom she cannot see often. She cannot replace them with friends because she does not have that kind of personality. Highly dependent upon an active husband in the past, she wishes strongly for friends and people to take her places, but she does not know how to overcome her habitual immobility and passivity. She reports her daily, evening, and weekend activities as "nothing" or watching TV.

The fourth type of woman is a social activist, most of whose energy has been devoted to organizational or paid work around which her friendships revolve. The death of the husband does not modify these relations because he was not involved in them in the first place.

Although these four types of women report no strains—because their life did not involve friendships or because the husband's death did not affect this aspect of their social life space—most of the respondents had experienced some difficulties. The severity of strain in friendship as a result of widowhood varies by many factors, as does its aftermath of attitudes and relations in the following years. Most of the respondents did not understand the causes for the strains in friendships and took them as proof of a personal rejection of themselves, reinforcing an anxiety that they are not acceptable friends, caused by past dependence on the role of wife or on the personality of their husband. They complain that their married friends dropped them from their social activities, failed to call, acted awkward in their presence, made them feel like a "fifth wheel," and in general made contact too painful. Exploratory interviews with friends of such widows indicated a feeling of strain on their part, but the blame was placed on the woman whose husband had died. Friends found the widow over-sensitive, lacking in interest and understanding of their problems, and unwilling to cooperate in any projects. Thus both sides of the relation faced difficulties.

*We didn't have a wide circle of friends. We had about 15–18 people that we considered close friends but, oh, I don't know . . . I could feel that they were afraid that 'Now she is alone out there in a new home that needs a lot of taking care of and this and that, now I wonder if she is going to involve us.' Now, maybe I am a sensitive person . . . maybe I am over-sensitive, but I noticed they slacked off coming, and when I would invite them they would come; but it wasn't with the same gusto that they used to come with, so I simply divorced myself from them. A few of them hung on for a number of years, but it was a more casual thing. It wasn't that good warm relationship that we had before. You sense it, you feel it, you know people when you've known them for 20–25 years.*

A detailed analysis of the open-ended responses to strain questions indicates that there are several problematic components in situations of interaction between a new widow and her married friends. Almost inevitably, at least part of the strain revolves around couple-companionate occasions which used to form tħe basis of the friendship. Several aspects of such encounters can cause strain after the removal of one participant: making the plans, transportation to and back, decisions and calculations involved in the process of meeting the costs, table arrangements and specific activities, such as dancing. The whole institution of polite companionship is built either around sex-segregated contact, or especially in America, a symmetry of partners. Anxiety over strain in couple situations may even infect sex-segregated contact among the women.

Most invitations to couple-companionate events are extended by the wife, but in a manner which indicates that she is the social secretary of a household organized around the husband's work. After the husband's death, the widow does not have to meet such time restrictions. Several of the friends that were interviewed complained that the invitations they received from a widowed associate did not fit into their normal course of life. It is possible that the widow, wishing to avoid dates which could conflict with the couple's round of activity, set up events at times awkward for the potential guests. On the other hand, it is equally probable that the recipient of an invitation prefers to go to a home which guarantees the presence of both host and hostess rather than to chance a party which might prove uncomfortable. At least the widow suspects that her invitations are turned down for this reason and may not extend them again, thus contributing to her own isolation from previous coupled friends.

Widows who accept invitations to the homes of friends or to meet them somewhere else often feel awkward about transportation. Seventy-five percent of the respondents do not drive a car, either because they never learned or because its maintenance becomes too much of a burden after the death of the husband. Many women living in older neighborhoods of Chicago are afraid to use public transportation or even to walk outside at night and can only go out if someone picks them up. Such dependence either creates sufficient embarrassment to prevent widows from asking favors or results in so much inconvenience that friends no longer extend invitations. Many associates are living at inconvenient distances from the widow, and hostesses do not like to have their husbands absent themselves before a party to drive to pick up a widowed guest.

Financial arrangements also contribute problems for the maintenance of friendship relations. Couple-companionate interaction is traditionally financed by the males. Widows often do not date, and so payment for social events falls on them and creates strain. The males in the party feel a gentlemanly obligation to pay for themselves, their wives, and for the widows. They are faced with higher bills, and the widow feels dependent. A further financial problem for widows is often a drop of income with the death of the husband. Wives who previously have not had to adjust to a husband's restricted retirement budget are frustrated by their inability to "keep up with the Joneses," who are still living on their husbands' full earning capacity. Previously shared and enjoyed activities are now impossible because of their expense. One fifth of the respondents find their income restrictions so strong that they cannot continue their relations with friends, and many others report curtailment of activities.

There are psychological problems, too. The widow worries that she may embarrass her friends by her very presence, that the interaction will become strained because of her. The friend is fearful of saying the wrong thing, of hurting the widow's feelings, or of creating a wave of grief with its accompanying emotionality. Thus, a relation, built originally on a playful and rather casual round of weekend socializing, becomes a source of problems because of the anxieties and new, unclear needs. Self-consciousness leads to over-acted cordiality, which is experienced by the other as insincerity. Each leaves the incident angry at the other and at herself, yet not knowing how to prevent a duplication of the scene. Such meetings are painful for all partners of a prior friendship, who still have some sentimental attachment for each other. Irritation or outright anger develops, feelings are hurt, friends are rebuffed, and the widow is ignored the next time a social situation is planned. Complex rationalizations are given by the friends in talking with each other, mostly in terms of the widow's problems which make their good efforts ineffectual. These explanations facilitate the closing of ranks without the odd member, in order to continue the round of pleasurable activity which brought the people into the couple-form of friendship in the first place.

Another problem with friendships in widowhood is that both the emotional and the social needs of widows differ from those of married women. Interests change, discussions of marital problems are irrelevant, even painful, and the bonds of sex-segregated relations become weakened by the lack of commonality of life. It is undoubtedly true that many widows want to convert a casual friendship relation into one of much deeper significance or intimacy than the friend desires. Associates do not often want to listen to sad feelings of friends, which were not part of the former relation. As one respondent advises new widows: "Don't cry, it only scares friends away."

The pathos in the experience of many respondents is their feeling of powerlessness (Fromm, 1947). Widows who are in the process of becoming alienated from their friends often fear of doing something that may further the drift, and this concern makes comfortable interaction practically impossible. They are afraid to speak up when feeling left out or when the phone does not ring for a while because this complaining may cause guilt in the already embarrassed friend; therefore they keep the irritation within themselves, though frequently the sentiment is apparent to the friends. After a while, one of three patterns seems to emerge. The period of tenseness may pass, and the relation may resume with fewer strains. Or, the widow may turn to new social roles and relations and decrease her contact with old friends. Finally, she may become increasingly passive and inactive. The last named situation, termed "dis-engagement," is often very painful. The widow spends more and more time alone at home rather than face the possibility of embarrassment. After a while she no longer expects to hear the telephone, receive a call, or be invited to share the pleasures of others. She accepts a passive philosophy of life, made easier if she was socialized into it earlier in life. The formerly active woman who meets rebuffs and constricts her friendships is the most bitter and the frequency of negative statements about relations with friends indicates the presence of many strainful situations.

### Help Received by a Widow from Friends
On the other hand, some widows report helpful friends. Asked who helped most in getting her back into life after the stage of strongest grief, one respondent listed her best friend. "She seemed to sense when I needed someone, and she would call me and have me come over. She seemed to give me strength, and she was so understanding . . . giving me strength. That's the main thing." Another has more than one such friend. "My friends, they'd come over almost all the time. Whatever I wanted to do, they took me wherever I wanted to go. Just by being with me and by inviting me for dinner and so on." An interesting explanation of a friend's help was given by a college graduate: "Just being a friend, we went out to dinner, golf. I mean she tried to treat me as if nothing happened."

In general, friends have helped widows in several ways. In the first place, they keep them occupied with activities which take their attention away from the death of the husband. Such activities vary considerably according to social class, and they not only keep her busy but, if planned beforehand, help her organize time and provide a set of pleasurable anticipations. The second type of help widows list from friends is symbolized as "understanding," "empathy," "being there when needed." Combined with the companionate aspects of this set of sentiments is the feeling of being important to, and of being liked by, a significant other. The mood is of mutual acceptance and quiet support. Thirdly, friends contribute significantly to "grief work" (Lindemann, 1944). Contrary to the prevailing norms of American culture, a widow needs to grieve, to release her feelings, to talk about her late husband, and to rework her world in accordance with the fact that he is dead. Close associates also prevent social isolation—a state which encourages "self-pity." Finally, friends provide the opportunity for a woman to compare her position with that of others, to see certain advantages in her decisions as to future life styles. For example, a Greek woman's cultural values are reinforced by visits from her friends of other backgrounds. "My Jewish friend comes over, has three daughters; says 'two feet can't go in one shoe' (meaning she does not want to live with any of her married daughters). Children want her, she not want to go, says 'want to be free.' Funny, Greek mother want to live with daughter; funny, each person different. I say, 'This is America.' "

Thus, the contributions made by friends to a new widow are support, attention which acknowledges that she is going through social and personal difficulties, active engagement in social interaction, and easement of her transition from one style of life into another. The feeling that she is being helped by her friends is most likely to be expressed by the type of respondent who has really close associates rather than mere leisure-time companions. Such a woman can simultaneously express some concern over feeling like a 'fifth wheel' in social situations involving the husbands of female friends and the sentiment of gratitude for the interpersonal help she receives. The angry and frustrated woman is going through a period of strain in which there is no matching of expectations and behaviors, but this may be only a stage in the transformation of friendship. The long-range angry woman never resolves the problems with prior associates and has not forgiven them for their failure. Thus, there are three situations surrounding the relations of a widow with friends: in the first, the friends help in meeting the needs of the widow, as she defines them; in the second, strain develops, but is resolved over time; and in the third, it never reaches a satisfactory solution.

Our knowledge of the presence of strain in the early days, and even years, of widowhood led to the inclusion of several statements on this subject in the relations-restrictive attitude scale. Of special relevance here is: "My married friends have not been much help to me during my period of grief." Most of the respondents have been widowed for many years, and the statement refers to the period following the death of the husband, yet over one fourth (twenty-seven percent) of the respondents agree with it, with twelve percent refusing to declare themselves on this subject (see Table XVI in Appendix C). Cross-tabulations with other attitudes show that the women who consider that they received little help from friends during the period of grief hold various negative feelings toward other people.

Interestingly enough, over a half of the respondents who are dissatisfied with the quality or quantity of help they received from married friends also agree with the statement: "My present income makes it impossible to maintain old friendships." Unfortunately, it is impossible to determine whether this combination means that they are angry with their friends for not making an effort to see them in spite of their changed economic status, or whether anger over other failures in the relation becomes converted into a financial justification for limiting contact. A widow with this attitude toward friends is also likely to feel that people take advantage of widows, that widows often feel like a "fifth wheel," and that there is a loss of status after the death of the husband. The anger created by the friends' failure to meet expectations may lead to these other attitudes, or *vice versa,* the respondent may be annoyed at friends for not protecting her against the loss of prestige or misuse by other people. In either case, friends are not preventing one-fourth of the widows from feeling a status drop and hostility in the environment, and the respondents are unhappy over such failures. On the other hand, eighty-three of the 255 widows who responded to both statements do not connect their anger over their friends' failure to help with a drop in status.

Only twelve out of the 251 respondents feel that their friends were unhelpful and that they themselves have trouble being nice to such associates; sixty-five women who found friends unhelpful nevertheless find no problem in their own responses. They either did not expect much assistance or feel magnanimous themselves because they do not hold lack of help against their friends. Many of the respondents wish they had more friends, since they now need such relations more than before the death of the husband or are now dissatisfied with former friends, or have now redefined the quality of such associations. Those who feel that their friends have been helpful also agree that "My faith helped me more than anything else after my husband's death." This combination of attitudes supports the Maddison and Walker (1966) thesis that widows who satisfactorily resolve the problems brought about by the death of the husband feel they have experienced support in several parts of their environment.

Women who judge friends as having provided inadequate assistance tend to reject women in general. For example, they feel that sons are more help than daughters. Although women preferring the help of sons form only twenty-eight percent of the total number answering both questions, forty-three percent of those who also feel that friends were not helpful agree with this attitude. Criticism of friends tends to be related to a feeling that adult children demand too many favors, that other women are jealous of a widow, and that widows are constantly propositioned sexually, even by the husbands of their friends. Such a combination points to the possibility that a woman who is accustomed to special attention from males and to being the center of such interaction prior to widowhood finds her present relations inadequate. She feels that she is valued as a helper to others, rather than as a center of their attention. She is likely to enjoy the kind of semi-flirtatious treatment which men direct to some women, and she may be angry with her female friends for keeping her from such interaction. No longer invited to couple-companionate affairs, she interprets the change as a result of jealousy over the remaining husbands. The complex of attitudes is interesting, particularly in view of the fact that so few respondents (only twenty percent) openly agree that they wish more male companionship. The same type of widow is also likely to be angry at the doctor and the hospital staff for not "doing enough" for her husband during his last illness; perhaps she feels that he, too, should have been the center of attention.

Although the feeling that friends were not of much help in grief has a high correlation with other negative orientations to people, it does not lead widows to agree that "Relatives are your only true friends." Only twenty-six women hold both of these sentiments. The majority of respondents reject both, indicating a distinction in their minds between the role of friend and that of relative. Rejection of friends as helpers does not have any association with movement in widowhood toward increased closeness with siblings or to really strong mother-role orientation, indicating support for Robert Weiss' (1969) contention that various interpersonal relations form distinct and non-substitutive categories. Rejection or hostility toward one relation does not necessarily lead to an increased concentration on another. In fact, it may simply be part of a generalized feeling of hostility. There is also no association between the judgment of usefulness of help given by friends and feelings about living alone.

## ATTITUDES TOWARD FRIENDS

There are three specific attitudes toward friends which drew very interesting responses from Chicago area widows. Although not universally applicable, these feelings may form the basis for strain in relations. The presence of such attitudes was evident enough during the exploratory research and encouraged the inclusion of the following statements into the relations-restrictive scale: "One problem of being a widow is feeling like a 'fifth wheel,'" "Other women are jealous of a widow when their husbands are around," and "Widows are constantly sexually propositioned, even by the husbands of their friends." Over half of the respondents agree with the first statement, with eighteen percent agreeing very strongly. The sentiment of being an "odd ball" in social situations may not be entirely due to an expectation of jealousy by women friends, since only thirty-seven percent of the respondents agreed with that statement, with only nine percent agreeing strongly. Sexual propositioning by husbands is less likely to have been experienced or assumed, since only nineteen percent of the respondents agree with this statement, with only four percent feeling strongly about it. Thus, feeling like a fifth wheel has connotations other than sexual, and widows are more apt to expect jealousy from women than propositioning from their husbands.

The way these three attitudes are related to other items of the relations-restrictive scale is also interesting. Women who feel like a fifth wheel in couple-companionate interaction belong to the small minority of respondents who are likely to be dating and who find widowers the most comfortable companions in such situations (see Table XVII in Appendix C). Not surprisingly, feeling like a fifth wheel leads women to a very strong conviction that widows must become independent, although decision-making is difficult and other people take advantage of their vulnerability. Sharing a home with others—probably married offspring—is not a solution for loneliness for women who feel uncomfortable with people who have spouses in the situation. At the same time, widows who agree that women in their marital status are fifth wheels do not necessarily feel that their friends have been unhelpful or that they themselves have lost status after the death of the husband. This last combination of attitudes is difficult to understand, since one would expect the movement into a fifth wheel position to imply a loss of status. It is quite possible that the answer lies in the ambiguous definition of status loss. A woman may feel peripheral to a social situation without interpreting this as evidence of a lack of prestige or respect. Women experiencing "odd ball" feelings, however, reject completely the idea that widows can have sexual relations without marriage and do not think that husbands of friends make sexual propositions. The combined picture is of a person deprived of the protection of the decision-making husband, whose presence served to facilitate social interaction with friends and to prevent exploitation by others. Feeling vulnerable, the widow resents not being part of the symmetrical world to which she formerly belonged. At the same time, she tells herself that she must be independent.

Respondents who do not think widows are in a position of a fifth wheel also reject sexual relations without marriage and even male companionship. They do not feel a loss of status, a restriction of income, or the need for living near other widows. Their friends have been of help and husbands do not proposition them. They seem to have lived, and to continue to live, in a sex-segregated world, so that they experience little change with the death of the husband.

Not surprisingly, there is a very strong relation between the feeling that "Other women are jealous of a widow when their husbands are around" and the belief that "Widows are constantly sexually propositioned, even by the husbands of their friends" (see Table XVIII in Appendix C). Although 126 respondents disagree with both statements, a disproportionately large segment sensing jealousy also expects overtures. These women feel exploited by men who assume that they are hungry for pure sex rather than lonely for multi-dimensional relationships. They see sexual overtures of husbands of friends as relationally false or empty, lacking interpersonal intimacy which they want most. Such overtures do not treat them as desirable individuals.

The feeling that other women are jealous of the widow is also connected with a sense of status drop. Such respondents like living alone, near other widows, and believe that remarriage brings nothing but trouble. They see their past marriage as above average and want more male companionship, while rejecting sexual relations completely. Thus, they seem to miss most non-sexual interaction but think that their women friends do not understand this feeling. One respondent indignantly stated that any time she got near a husband simply to talk to him, his wife would find an excuse for pulling him away. Of course, it is possible that the wives are sensing in the widow a desire for intimate relations with men which the widow will not admit to herself. The traditional American culture does not allow for sexual desire in an older woman. Thus, while she may disclaim any designs on the husbands of her friends, the wives may not trust such declarations and may really feel jealousy. There does not have to be a direct association between what the widow claims to feel, or actually feels, and the interpretation given by her friends.

The expectation of jealousy from women friends is related to the age at which a woman become widowed. Although only ten percent of the respondents agree strongly that other women are jealous, fifteen percent of those who were widowed at the age of thirty-four or less express such sentiments. Interestingly, nineteen percent of those widowed between sixty-five and sixty-nine agree with the jealousy statement. It is possible that they are reflecting their own feelings when their husbands were still living and coming into contact with their widowed friends. Although only thirty-three percent of all respondents agree mildly with such a statement, fifty percent of those between 40 and 44 years of age at the time of widowhood were so inclined. This particular age-at-widowhood group has the highest expectation of jealousy from friends (sixty percent) of both high and mild agreement level.

The statement: "Widows are constantly sexually propositioned, even by the husbands of their friends" is relevant to friendship relations in four ways. In the first place, such an expectation may arouse guilt feelings in a widow. More importantly for the older widow trying to recover from grief and build a new life, sexual overtures may cause "moral shock." Thirdly, during the period of life between being a wife and a widow she may simply wish for more quiet friendships and not be interested in aggressive approaches from others. Finally, such overtures may drive home the realization of her changed social status at a time when she is trying to maintain life as it was. If she is treated differently now by her male and female friends than when her husband was alive, and before she herself is ready to change her life style by returning to open hetero-geneous relations, she may even resent all overtures. It is hard to deter-mine whether she would feel the same way about sexual propositions from men who are not the husbands of her friends, from persons interested in building complex relations with her, or from future marital partners. The rejection of sex, dating, and remarriage implies a total negative feeling independent of the source of propositioning.

Widows who think that women in their marital situation "are con-stantly sexually propositioned, even by husbands of their friends" hold other strongly negative attitudes. The relational-scale items which are associated significantly include: "People take advantage of you when they know you are a widow" (Gamma .75), "Women lose status when they become widows, they lose respect and consideration" (Gamma .72), "It is all right for a widow to have sexual relations with a man without planning on marriage (Gamma .58), and "I wish I had more male com-panionship" (Gamma .45). Interestingly enough, the less likely a woman is to define her marriage as above average, the more likely she is to feel that widows are sexually propositioned (Gamma .34). One of the reasons for this is that both attitudes are felt by widows who were rather young when the husband died so that they were not fully adjusted in the mar-riage. Another reason is that such widows are most apt to be of the black social race. On the other hand, women widowed in their forties, when they could be expected to receive propositions from men, disagreed dis-proportionately with that statement. It is possible that they did not try to continue relations with people seen previously in couple-companionate situations but turned to work or other social roles for friendship.

Finally we explore the question of how the previously examined experiences of widows affect their overall definition of friendship and desire for such relations. Attitudes were tapped through four statements of the relations-restrictive scale: "Relatives are your only true friends," "Old friends cannot be replaced, no matter how one tries to make new ones," "I wish I had more friends," and "I feel sorry for some of my married friends, who have little freedom to do as they please."

The feeling that "Relatives are your only true friends" proved not to be related significantly to many of the thirty-six items of the relations-restrictive attitude scale (see Table XIX in Appendix C). Its strongest association was with the statement "Women lose status when they become widows, they lose respect and consideration" (Gamma .52). The heavy concentration of responses is in the "false-false" category. That is, women who separate the role of friend from that of relative are not necessarily identifying the change from wifehood to widowhood as a status drop, in spite of strains. Very few women identify their present position as a status drop, but thirty-nine percent of those who reject non-kin intimate relations report less status. Thus, the restriction of social relations to family members does not prevent a woman from feeling that she has experienced a status depreciation in widowhood.

Respondents who agree that relatives are the only true friends a woman can have also expect unhappiness in remarriage, exploitation by others, a monetary constriction of primary relations, and sexual propositioning from friends' husbands, while simultaneously wishing for more friends and for someone to pick them up and take them places. They show anger toward past friends, admit an inability to be nice to those who did not help, and believe that they lacked such assistance. Generally, widows who agree with the "relatives are your only true friends" statement continue to identify with the ascribed group and do not seek individualistic separation from it in achieved friendships. Those who find friendship outside of kinship may also have experienced a rejection toward friends and hostility during the early time of widowhood, but they separate the roles and expect a lot from friends. Women who restrict their feelings of intimacy to relatives want to be centers of family life and to have more social interaction with relatives than they currently have. It is possible that they do not reject friendship but rather that they reject overtures as infringement on their privacy. They want consideration but prefer those forms of deference within a sheltered life, making no effort to develop new social relations. This whole set of sentiments is very characteristic of the uneducated woman, and the relation between education and agreement with the "best friends are relatives" statement is highly significant.

If not relatives, then already established friendships are favored by older widows. At the same time, several sentiments such as anger, resentment of exploitation, and discomfort lower the level of correlation between the statement "Old friends cannot be replaced no matter how one tries to make new ones." The combination indicates a rejection of the outside world rather than a warmth of feelings about past relations (see Table XX in Appendix C). Women who do not expect to be able to replace old friends tend to be suspicious toward the world around them and idealize the past. Vehemently believing that widows must make an independent life, they nevertheless find decision-making very difficult and expect people to be trying to take advantage of them. They reject remarriage as a solution to their problems, but do not feel that widowhood brings a loss of status, nor do they think that widows are sexually propositioned by husbands of friends. Those favoring established relations feel they were helped most by their faith, rather than by people, at the time of their grief. Although these women see old friends as irreplaceable, they also yearn for someone who would come and pick them up to do things away from home; the present set of relations does not contain anyone who would perform such services. These attitudes result in timidity in social relations and *vis-à-vis* the world.

The weakness of association between the belief that old friends can not be replaced and the other attitudes in the relations-restrictive scale may be due to its future orientation. Making new friends is not a part of the way of life of many older widows, so that they never compare past relations to hypothetical new ones, much as they do not contemplate remarriage. The past, containing marriage and friendships, is past, and they do not expect to reproduce its good elements. The strong tendency of widows (two-thirds agree with the statement) to believe that old friends cannot be replaced contributes to their restricted social life space. Again, it must be remembered that these are historical generations which do not deal with life through a flexibility of style.

It would be a mistake, however, to assume that belief in the non-replaceability of old friends grows out of satisfaction with the current number of associates, or prevents anger against remaining friends. Almost half of the respondents want more friends than they have now, and cross-tabulations between this wish and other attitudes offer a picture of some very lonely women. One of the basic factors widows blame for an insufficient number of friends is their income-restriction. Sixty-one women want more friends and thirty-five of them are financially limited by their own definition. This leaves twenty-six women who feel they have the money to interact with friends but lack people in such relations. On the other side of the picture are 140 women who have enough money to retain friendships and are very happy with the number they have (see Table XXI in Appendix C).-

The one-third of the respondents who want more friends tend, nevertheless, to be very negative toward such, and other, relations. It is paradoxical that these respondents simultaneously feel that "Relatives are your only true friends," that married associates have not been of much help, and that husbands make sexual propositions. Thus, the new friends they desire seem to be of a different type than the ones they had in the past. They also have trouble relating with those people whom they define as unhelpful during the grief period. In fact, they even resent their children, feeling that they are being asked to do too many favors. Having led sex-segregated lives with their husbands, they reject the idea of remarriage and even sexual intercourse. The general combination of attitudes indicates that respondents wanting to expand their friendships have a passive and negative view of existing relations. Those who need no additional friends may have experienced strains following the death of the husband but are able to rebuild past associations or build new ones.

Although the associations are not high, some of the other combinations of attitudes are interesting. Sixty-seven of the ninety-nine respondents wishing more friends feel like a fifth wheel when with their associates. Seventy-six of these women have no objection to being coaxed out of the home to "do things all the time." These are women who wish to expand primary interaction, yet do not make the effort to do so and resent the type of interaction now available to them.

Women who wish they had more friends are less apt to like living alone than those surrounded by satisfactory associations. Half of the eighty-nine women who want to expand their circle of intimates do not like living alone. Of the 145 who do not need more friends, eighty-six like and only fifty-nine do not like solitary residence. Few of the respondents actually live with friends, even if wishing greater involvement in this role. Part of this is due to the strong belief on the part of women of this age that "Sharing one's home with anyone causes nothing but trouble for a widow." Fifty-one respondents wishing more friends believe this statement, as do the eighty-nine who are satisfied with their circle of intimates. This is surprising in view of the dissatisfaction of many widows with living alone and also with living with children; one would expect them to be more willing to share a residence with a peer with whom work and space arrangements could be developed out of an equality of power. Of course, it is possible that the widow who spent most of her life running a home for her husband and children now wants to maintain it simply for her own pleasure. This fits with her statements that major compensations of widowhood are freedom to come and go as she pleases and release from time and work schedules. She may thus feel that taking a roommate or a housemate would throw her back into the old pattern. Secondly, as mentioned before, many older women, and members of American society in general, wish to avoid all situations of possible conflict and irritation. Calm and relief from a hard and turbulent life are ideals incorporated into the culture. The roommate could also be seen as an impingement on relations with visitors. Another reason why women reject the idea of sharing their homes with even a peer is their lack of trust in fellow human beings. Many respondents feel that others are out to cheat them and take advantage of their vulnerability. This suspicion is strongly ingrained in the lower classes, whose members have faced many life experiences not designed to build trust. The female population now being studied is the least likely to have a history of positive relations with others; the result is fear of having a stranger, or even a semi-intimate, enter and live within the same four walls, day by day, with no guarantee of an easy termination of the arrangement. Finally, many widows who might consider living with a peer simply do not know how to go about finding a satisfactory candidate, how to make the arrangement, or how to develop it along lines causing the least amount of life disorganization. Not knowing how to build pleasant adult home-sharing relations, they simply reject the idea without trial.

In general, the woman who wishes greater friendship in widowhood is a more passive person, oriented toward the family, formerly immersed in sex-segregated marriage and consequently experiencing greater difficulties in decision-making and financial management than her counterpart who is happy with her circle of friends. Her children demand favors without providing satisfactory interaction; she wants friends without trusting people. She does not have the ability to convert secondary interaction acquaintances into more involving and deeper relations. It is quite possible that she has never had many friends. She is not particularly rejective of her married friends because of a supposed lack of help, since she probably had not expected much from them. Also, she does not relate her wish for new friends with the statement that "Old friends cannot be replaced, no matter how one tries to make new ones" (Gamma is only .11). Thus, her shortage of friends does not seem to result from her dropping of former associates. Either she always wanted more friends, even before the death of the husband, or she now feels a void which she would like to have filled by friends. She does not want to live with such associates, and she does not know how to find new friends or expand her social life space.

We tested one of the ideas developed above—that the rejection of friends as roommates is a result of a wish for peace and a lack of schedules —by the following statement: "I feel sorry for some of my married friends, who have little freedom to do as they please" (see Table XXII in Appendix C). This sentiment is shared by forty-three percent of the respondents, although it may be a function of several different factors. Since one-third of the respondents agreed with the statement "I feel more free and independent now than before I became a widow," it is not surprising that these two statements have a high association (Gamma .68). Nor is it surprising that women who supposedly feel sorry for their married friends now find their lives easier than ever before (Gamma .53). Such women do not even want people to drag them out to do things away from the home. They are satisfied with the fact that their faith helped more than people to get them over grief. Widows who do not feel a strong obligation to sanctify the late husband are more apt to feel that their married friends lack freedom than those who now find him to have been an unusually good man. They reject remarriage, seeing it as a source of trouble, also feeling that people take advantage of widows and that other women are jealous. Their independence is asserted by the fact that they like to live alone. Widows who had been in sex-segregated relations with the husband are more apt to regard marriage as a restriction than the women who have been involved in couple-companionate and multi-dimensional relations. In other words, those women for whom marriage had been mainly a round of work are pleased to be rid of it and feel themselves to be in an enviable situation.

Those respondents who do not pity married friends consider their own husband to have been an unusually good man, while at the same time not wishing to remarry. In other words, they are past-, rather than future-oriented. They reject the ideas that they have trouble being nice to people, that married friends were no help in widowhood, that the medical profession did not help the husband sufficiently, that widows are sexually propositioned, and that it is all right for them to accept such relations. They also define their marriages as multi-dimensional, involving even a shared financial knowledge.

The strong emphasis on their current life as one of freedom and independence supports the thesis that the Chicago area widows chose not to live with married children and even with their peers because of this factor. Rejection of such arrangements out of fear of relational strain operates on the other side of the coin. Life is easier now as a result of a decrease of residents in the home, and the widow does not wish to again become constricted in time and work; but loneliness and the desire of friends outside of the household operate at the same time to prevent complete satisfaction of life. The Rosenmayr and Kockeis (1963) conclusion that older people desire "intimacy at a distance" can thus be applied not only to offspring.

## THE SOCIAL ROLE OF FRIEND

All references to friends in terms of social life, daily interaction, trips, help in solving problems of widowhood, and various attitudes were organized in "the social role of friend scale." Just as in the case of other role scales, the scores were collapsed into high, medium, and low levels and then cross-tabulated with other scores, other roles, background, and attitudinal characteristics of the respondent.

Only forty-two women (fifteen percent) scored high on the role of friend scale, 137 (forty-nine percent) scoring medium, and 101 (thirty-six percent) scoring low. The distribution places this role as one of greater interactional significance than that of sibling and neighbor. It is relatively under-represented at the low end of the continuum. This finding is surprising, in that it shows that women interact with friends although the American society undervalues this role for its adults. The traditional judgment is reflected in the fact that even widows who are involved in interaction with friends list the role of friend low on a rank order of women's sets of obligations. If there is competition, the married woman is expected to fulfill obligations toward her husband and children in preference to those toward friends and the value system extends throughout the lifetime. The widow soon learns that her married friends solve their role conflicts by devoting most of their attention to their husbands and, in the upper three classes, to the round of couple-companionate interaction, even at the cost of neglecting relations with her. She is personally hurt by this attitude, yet she does not question its normative rightness. She is herself too immersed in the American culture to question the standard that friends must first be wives and mothers. Interestingly, however, she does not apply a modified view of friendship to herself even after the husband's death and the childrens' movement away from constant contact. The friendship role is seen more as a set of interpersonal interactions than as a societally structured set of relations.

These statements are partially supported by the fact that the role of friend is not significantly related to any other of the roles measured here: wife, mother, sibling, or neighbor. The background characteristics of the respondents are related in several ways to their scores in the role of friend. Involvement generally increases as age increases, possibly because of a decrease of demands from other roles. Women in their seventies, however, are most frequently at the two extreme levels of involvement in comparison to other women. The general trend shows no evidence for disengagement assumptions in aging.

The highest involvement in the role of friend can be found in women who had been widowed one to four years. There seems to be a rhythm of involvement in this role, based on factors external to the relation itself, but connected with the flow of reactions and experiences following widowhood. Those respondents whose husbands died less than a year ago are low in friendship interaction, the frequency of high or medium participation increasing between one and four years, and decreasing after that for a low in the period between five and six years. The first part of this swing supports the conclusion that strains develop in the relations which take the year of grief to dissipate. The reason for the dip between five and six years is unclear; it may be due to expansion in other roles. A high or medium involvement in friendship is not again likely until later in widowhood.

The high scorers in friendship interaction are most apt to have had some college education; the low scorers are apt to be completely devoid of any formal education. Seven of the eleven respondents who have had no schooling are at the low end of the scores. At the other end of the continuum, it is difficult to determine why none of the eight college graduates have a high friendship score and why half of them are even low in their involvement. Other findings indicate they may have experienced strain in trying to retain couple-companionate friendships after the death of the husband, with resultant negative attitudes and a decrease in interaction. Those below that achievement may settle for sex-segregated relations. Uneducated women are isolated in many ways. The achievement of the husband bears a direct and positive relation; the more schooling he obtained, the more probably his wife's score is at the high or at least medium level on the friendship role scale. Those who have low scores had a husband with no schooling or one whose achievement they did not know.

Protestant widows have a greater probability of reaching high or medium levels of friendship than any other religious members. Roman Catholic women are more likely to be low or, at most, medium in score; Jewish women are disproportionately low scorers, and they have a very low probability of being located in the high group. The number of women so identified is small, (fifteen in *toto*), but there is an indication of a cultural orientation minimizing friendship. Nationality identification also seems to influence friendship scores, reinforcing the thesis that cultures differ in the value they assign to the role of friend. German and Norwegian woman are more oriented toward this role than are the others.

Polish and Russian women, some of whom are also Jewish, are the most likely to have a low score. Black women tend to be located at the extremes. The Irish are evenly distributed among all three levels, as are the descendants of other British Islanders, although they tend to be a little under-represented at the low end of the scale.

Women who had been divorced or widowed prior to a later marriage tend to be more friend-oriented than those who lost their one and only husband. Again, this suggests a possible need to develop skills in building relations with people who previously stood at a greater social distance. Widows of men who were older than they tend to be located in the medium range of the friendship role, those whose husbands were younger in the lower ranges, and those of the same age within the higher scores. As indicated elsewhere, companionate marriages are more likely to develop among same age partners and seem to lead to stronger friendship relations outside of the family.

The widows of managers, salesmen, and service workers have the greatest probability of being in the high end of the friendship scale. The last named group is heavily reinforced by the presence of several black women, the more educated of whom have a high chance of being located high in friendship. Although it is difficult to explain the connection, women who took care of their husband at home during his last illness are likely to have high friendship scores, while those who did not perform such duties at all tend to be located at the bottom of the scale. The former may have needed friends more and may have been home, rather than at jobs, long enough to cement such relations.

The financial condition of the widow is a very important factor in her being able to maintain friendships. Present circumstances often reflect a past income which allowed for different life styles. In addition, it takes money to keep in contact with friends and to engage in the round of activity which guarantees frequent interaction. The lower the comfort level of the financial situation, the lower the probability that the widow has a high friendship score (see Table 40). Of sociological interest in the association between the role of friend and the reported comfort of income is the fact that we had previously discovered a lack of association between reported income and the felt financial comfort level. This is undoubtedly due to the presence of other life supports or "fringe benefits" and a divergence in levels of expenditures, but the low self-placement on the comfort index is itself a relations-restrictive attitude. The women who feel restricted financially are often the same respondents who express hostility toward former friends and the world in general. They do not want to deal in terms of current realities, and their expectations outweigh their life circumstances. The complex is tied together, since women

TABLE 40: RELATION BETWEEN THE COLLAPSED SCORES OF
THE ROLE OF FRIEND SCALE AND REPORTED
FINANCIAL CONDITIONS

| Reported Financial Condition | Row Sums | *Role of Friend Scores* | | |
|---|---|---|---|---|
| | | High (10–17) | Medium (05–09) | Low (00–04) |
| Fairly | 3 | — | 1 | 2 |
| Wealthy | — | .0R | 33.3R | 66.6R |
| | .9 | .0C | .6C | 1.8C |
| Comfort- | 162 | 29 | 77 | 56 |
| able | — | 17.9R | 47.5R | 34.5R |
| | 53.8 | 65.9C | 52.3C | 50.9C |
| Rather | 75 | 7 | 41 | 27 |
| Short | — | 9.3R | 54.6R | 36.0R |
| | 24.9 | 15.9C | 27.8C | 24.5C |
| Really | 61 | 8 | 28 | 25 |
| Restricted | — | 13.1R | 45.9R | 40.9R |
| | 20.2 | 18.1C | 19.0C | 22.7C |
| Column | | 44 | 147 | 110 |
| Sums | | 14.6 | 48.8 | 36.5 |

Percent Base = 301
R stands for Row, C stands for Column

who had a hard life are the least positive in their orientation to it and to other people.

On the other hand, the self-reported physical condition of the widow does not appear to be significantly connected to her friendship score. Those reporting health limitations on activities include half of both the high and the low friend groups. Actually, most women reporting physical difficulties manage a medium level of contact, as measured by that scale. The difficulties which they list—arthritis, weak heart, and poor eyesight for the most part—do not necessarily prevent activity in friendship roles, although they are also apt to be used as explanations for total non-involvement. A similar pattern had been apparent in relations between the role of mother scores and declared physical limitations.

Those who rate high on the friendship scale find loneliness as the major problem of widowhood. The medium scorers worry about decision-making, raising a family, and sharing the division labor. This means they were widowed while children were still in the home. Those low scorers who mention loneliness generally miss having "someone" around—a partner in work or an object of care. It is interesting to note the connection between friendship scores and the wish to remarry. Although, as mentioned in Chapter Two, only fifty-five widows openly declare a willingness to marry again, they are disproportionately represented at the extreme ends of the friendship scores; those who would not consider another husband remain in the middle range of relations with peers of the same sex. Those with high friendship scores are also more likely to feel hopeful about finding another husband, although the numbers here are very small. They thus have a positive attitude toward several sets of social relations and a future orientation.

Women who interact frequently with friends are apt to see changes in themselves as a result of widowhood. It is possible that the awareness of change in one's personality comes from the "looking glass" reflections provided by comments of close associates rather than from introspective observation.

The friend-oriented women disproportionately feel that widowhood has no compensation, while medium scorers define it as an increase in "free time," and the low scorers are happy with "being one's own boss" and "less work." The medium scorers join the low scorers in finding the second compensation of widowhood as "being one's own boss," while the low scorers repeat that it means less work. The combination of attitudes indicates that women with low scores in friendship relations tend to be task-oriented, possibly making difficult the development of social relations outside of activities which are work-focused. Task-oriented men and women in occupations with a similar focus can develop friendships as a peripheral consequence of repeated contact, but task-oriented housewives may find this orientation toward life detrimental to the development of primary relations in social situations.

With increase in the size of the building in which the respondent lives, the proportion of medium scores tends to go down and that of extreme scores goes up. The greatest proportion of widows having a high score live in building with ten units or more. This indicates that residents of large apartment buildings either become isolated or develop high friendship scores. Large housing centers tend to increase the potential of friendship by bringing more candidates together, as Rosow (1967) discovered, but they can also increase the fear that overtures will be rejected or may result in an invasion of privacy. Even high density cannot help people with strong anti-social attitudes. The *Occupation: Housewife* study concluded that the fear of privacy invasion among lower-class women is due to their inability to protect themselves and the suspicion that close contact will bring nothing but harm.

There are some very interesting associations between the role of friend scores and specific attitudes in the relations-restrictive scale (see Table 41).

TABLE 41: SIGNIFICANT ASSOCIATIONS BETWEEN THE ROLE
OF FRIEND SCORE AND SOME ITEMS OF THE
RELATIONS RESTRICTIVE ATTITUDE SCALE

| *Attitude* | *Association* Gamma | $x^2$ * |
|---|---|---|
| One problem of being a widow is feeling like a fifth wheel | −.71 | 51.75 |
| Relatives are your only true friends | −.72 | 50.60 |
| Other women are jealous of a widow when their husbands are around | −.64 | 47.60 |
| Widows are constantly sexually propositioned, even by the husbands of their friends | −.48 | 17.89 |
| People take advantage of you when they know you are a widow | −.35 | 12.98 |
| My present income makes it impossible for me to maintain old friendships | −.41 | 11.08 |
| Most widows prefer living near other widows | −.30 | 8.21 |
| Many widows who remarry are very unhappy in that marriage | −.28 | 7.79 |
| Women lose status when they become widows—they lose respect and consideration | −.31 | 7.39 |
| My married friends have not been much help to me | −.29 | 6.61 |

* 2 d.f. $x^2$ significant at p. $<$.001 if 13.8; at p $<$.01 if 19.2; at p $<$.05 if 6.0

Women who score low on the role of friend scale often feel like a fifth wheel and therefore do not retain friendships. These widows are the most likely to believe that other women are jealous, that husbands of friends proposition women in their marital situation, that people take advantage of them, that remarriage brings nothing but unhappiness, that widows have less status than wives, and that friends were unhelpful during the period of grief.

Women who score high in the role of friend scale have the opposite attitudes, being positive in their view of social relations, having a sufficiently comfortable financial condition, and wishing to build and maintain new friendships. It is impossible at this level of analysis to determine whether these positive attitudes toward friends and one's own position in the world is a consequence of, or the major factor in, involvement in friendship roles.

The differences between the low and the high scorers in the role of friend are significant along the lines contained in Table 41. On the other hand, there was no significant association between the score on that scale and such attitudes as "Old friends cannot be replaced no matter how one tries to make new ones," "I would do more things outside of the house, if someone would come and pick me up," "I like living alone," and even "I wish I had more friends." Having a certain number of friends and being involved in relations with them does not preclude, or guarantee, a desire to increase the number of such associates.

In general, the conclusion that women who have friends and are able to retain their involvement in this role in widowhood have more positive attitudes toward social relations than those who are not engaged in it is supported by the cross-tabulations between this role and the relations-restrictive scale scores (see Table 42). The latter scale consisted of thirty-

TABLE 42: RELATION BETWEEN THE COLLAPSED SCORES OF THE ROLE OF FRIEND SCALE AND THE RELATIONS-RESTRICTIVE SCALE

| Relations-Restrictive Scores | Row Sums | Role of Friend | | |
| | | High (10–17) | Medium (05–09) | Low (00–04) |
|---|---|---|---|---|
| High | 38 | 2 | 12 | 24 |
| (13–19) | — | 5.2R | 31.5R | 63.1R |
| | 12.6 | 4.5C | 8.1C | 21.8C |
| Medium | 198 | 31 | 99 | 68 |
| (07–12) | — | 15.6R | 50.0R | 34.3R |
| | 65.7 | 70.4C | 67.3C | 61.8C |
| Low | 65 | 11 | 36 | 18 |
| (00–06) | — | 16.9R | 55.3R | 27.6R |
| | 21.5 | 25.0C | 24.4C | 16.3C |
| Column | | 44 | 147 | 110 |
| Sums | | 14.6 | 48.8 | 36.5 |

| | |
|---|---|
| Gamma | −.29 |
| Chi-Square | 14.60  (D.F. = 4) p <.01 |
| Percent Base = 301 | |

six items, only a few of which were directly connected with the role of friend. The relations-restrictive attitude scale broached a whole range of generality and specificity of sentiments toward different types of social relations. The figures lead to the conclusion that there are four types of widows in terms of the association between their involvement in the role of friend and their attitudes toward the world. The first group, consisting of only eleven women, is very involved in the role of friend and holds an extremely positive view of the world. At the other extreme are the women, twenty-four in number, who are not involved in the role of friend to any viable extent and are full of hostility toward specific individuals and the social environment in general. The third group, which is not surprisingly the most numerous, with ninety-nine respondents, achieves medium scores in the role of friend, while holding mixed attitudes toward people. This leaves a fourth significant category which includes sixty-eight respondents who are not actively involved in friendships, but who are not highly negatively oriented toward others, thirty-one women who are strongly friendship-oriented but are mixed in their sentiments, and thirty-six who are very positive, but only at the medium level of involvement. These last categories show that women do not have to be completely consistent in their attitudes toward their social environment to function actively in it. They may feel anger or at least a rejection in some spheres of life yet not restrict their social life space as a consequence. Those who are medium scorers in friendship may be involved in other roles, so that they build their total social involvement or social contact scores from more than one set of relations. Further reference to the connection between the degree of involvement in various social relations and attitudes will be made in the chapter summarizing community location of widows and in the final chapter.

## SUMMARY AND CONCLUSIONS

The social role of friend does not have strong ideological support for adults in American society, but it is important in the daily lives of many of the Chicago area widows. Only a third of the respondents are extremely low in such interaction and negative in attitudes toward this primary relation. These women are negative in their attitudes toward the world in general. At the same time, even the interactors frequently report strain in relations with friends immediately after the death of their husband. The base for the friendship shifts at that time, requiring modifications. Unfortunately, the process is not understood by the participants, who tend to place personal blame on themselves and each other.

The women who are minimally involved in, or completely lacking, friendships tend to be lower class and dependent on ascribed social relations. If spacial and geographical mobility, death, or any other reason has broken up their kinship, neighborhood, or long-time associations, they are left relatively isolated. They are unable to develop friendships because they are suspicious of strangers and even acquaintances and lack knowledge of the steps needed to convert mere contact into a primary relation. The restricted social life space of such widows is not due to choice but to psychological problems and to a lack of skills when confronted with new situations.

Some of the minimally involved widows, in terms of friendship, had never been active in this role; others decreased their participation because of strains, financial or health problems. Their disengagement from primary relations involves passive adjustment to the environment, which is typical of historical generations socializing people into an acceptance of life as given. Although the proponents of the disengagement theory may find these adjusted widows proof of successful aging, the interviews indicate a very painful history of the withering of the friendship relations and strong hostility toward the environment for not providing resources for continued engagement.

Widows whose lives had been focused on couple-companionate friendships have usually modified these relations or had to build new intimate associations. The strains involved in such transformations grow out of the whole bundle of activities surrounding leisure time in American cities. Unless she is able to find a male escort acceptable to friends, the woman finds herself a fifth wheel in interactional scenes involving couples. Attempting to continue the same round of activity becomes impossible, or in any case difficult, and the initiating widow finally reorganizes her friendships. If she continues contact with former friends, it tends to be on a sex-segregated basis during the week and day-time hours. Often missing male companionship, such a woman at least avoids jealousy from wives and sexual advances from husbands. Many a widow finds association with women in the same marital situation more comfortable or enjoyable. She seeks out former friends who had been widowed before her or uses secondary contact situations to find new friends. The widow who is able to convert acquaintances into friends has to have self-confidence and knowledge of the steps necessary to increase intimacy of interaction.

Women who develop satisfactory friendships, who weather the transitional period and solve its problems creatively, tend to have a higher education, a comfortable income, and the physical and psychic energy needed to initiate change. These are the same characteristics which underlie social engagement in other spheres of life. Friendship is important to the modern urban woman, and it can be expected to increase its significance in this society as more and more educated women reach older age. In the meantime, many women who could have happier lives can not use friendship to expand their social life space. The fact that they are not happy is apparent from all their attitudes and the contrasts between them and the socially engaged women. It is the conclusion of this analysis of the role of friend that the society could contribute to the welfare of its older widows by increasing the opportunity for them to become involved in primary relations.

Three types of changes in the lives of widows must be instituted before the older, less educated woman can build new patterns of socializing to meet her changed needs. First, the society or urban center must organize activities of interest to this population at the hours which they find most lonely and which they are able to utilize. Secondly, the opportunities for contact with people like themselves must be arranged. This means that the activities must be publicized, contact made with potential participants, and transportation guaranteed for the events. Thirdly, the widow must be psychologically convinced that she can make friends and build inter-action to satisfying levels. Counselors, volunteers, and group organizers can contribute to the self-confidence of a widow in many ways and success at each interaction scene helps build a foundation. Until people are socialized into initiating and building upon their own interactional skills, opportunities for repeated contact and involvement in pleasant activities are needed to force the breakdown of suspicion and all the other barriers between potential friends. Physical proximity is not enough, as evidenced by the frequency of social isolation in even high density areas (Rosow, 1967).

American society could also provide a clearing house of information about home or at least meal sharing. Such a system would have to be organized with a set of rules to facilitate easy entrance and exit from such arrangements. A major contribution, however, to the welfare of widows can be the dissemination of knowledge about the inevitability of strains in friendships. If more people were aware of the difficulties in converting friendships of wives into those of widows, a great deal of personal rejection and anxiety feelings could be alleviated.

# NOTES

1. Cooley named the intrinsic relations primary because he considered them basic to human nature and first in time in the socialization cycle. The ideal primary units he defined as the family, the neighborhood, and the peer group. Secondary relations were regarded by Cooley almost negatively, as entered into for purposes other than the joy of interaction and thus as almost "unnatural." Some sociologists (Orbach, 1970) have criticized the use of the

concept of "primary" because of these latent value judgements but it is widely used in American sociology. Much of the literature of large-scale, urban society contains similar biases in spite of a lack of any proof that human beings develop their potential and experience, all the variability of life's resources, any better in village than within complex social systems.

2. Nicholas Babchuk and Alan Bates conclude that the husband contributes most to couple-companionate relations. The housewife and the widowhood studies in Chicago indicate the possible importance of two factors: the stage of the couple's life cycle and the roles in which each partner is involved at the present time and in the immediate past. Women often feel that they are the major contributor to the companionate circle because they select a limited number of friends out of a large pool provided by the husband's work organization. (See Nicholas Babchuk and Alan Bates, *op. cit.*, "Primary Relations of Middle-Class Couples: A Study of Male Dominance," *American Sociological Review,* 28 (June, 1963).

# 6

# Involvement in the Community

## BACKGROUND

Sociologists have been attempting, with varying degrees of success, to define the geographic and social areas within which members of the larger society build their daily lives. The term "community" is often used to designate a village, a small town, or a sub-area of a city, "each of which could be regarded as having a history of its own as a community, a name, an awareness on the part of its inhabitants of common interests, and a set of local businesses and organizations oriented to the local community" (Kitagawa and Taeuber, 1963:xiii). Chicago urban sociologists delineated eighty local community areas in 1928. In 1929 the census bureau prevailed upon E. W. Burgess, one of the originators, to cut this down to seventy-five, thus shifting boundaries immediately. Even the original set of areas included many heterogeneous communities, as evidenced by the Near North which contained what Zarbough (1929) labeled *The Gold Coast and the Slum,* and Bridgeport, which housed a preponderance of working-class families who were, however, ethnically diversified. Boundaries allotted to areas were often not of population splits but of railroads, the river or the canal, industrial sites, etc. In the meantime, these local communities became further fragmented by lines drawn by the Board of Education, the Police Department, and other administrative bodies (Barsky, 1971). So many changes have occurred in American cities as to blur the lines and characteristics of local areas (see Stein, *The Eclipse of Community,* 1960), while simultaneously the concerned society is trying to rebuild itself in community lines. As a result, the various residential areas within modern societies can be located along a continuum according to the closeness with which they match the "ideal typical" characteristics originally identified as forming a community:

1. Members who are bound together by a sense of identity.
2. Members who share the same values.

3. A common language, including its local "patois."
4. An identifiable and known limit or boundary, so that people know who belongs and who does not.
5. A life style influenced by mutual interaction.
6. A system for the production and socialization of its own members.
7. Relatively stable membership without high mobility.
8. A diversification of member roles facilitating relative self-sufficiency from the outside society (see Goode, 1956:194-200).

Obviously, the last characteristic must leave open the definition of self-sufficiency. Very few communities of the modern world could continue to exist in the manner they have developed with no outside support. Regardless of its dependence on the society, the traditional community tends to turn to its own members for the solution of its daily problems and is keenly aware of when it must go outside for help.

A major problem of modern communities is the increasing heterogeneity and mobility of the population; a second one is its expansion into non-community involvements. People are apt to move into a town or area of a city without knowing its identity, basic values, or in-group vocabulary, in fact, without having any intention of learning the local style of life and changing their former orientation. Identification with social groups has become segmentalized, following the diversification of social roles performed by each individual away from the local area, and the feeling of community membership is often an incidental aspect of the self. True, purposeful attempts have been made to create the ideal typical community in some suburbs or "communes," but people in the society generally range considerably in the degree of their involvements, direction and breadth of identification, and in the reference groups whose standards they accept. A decrease in the importance of the local community has been mainly replaced by increase in the importance of the national and cosmopolitan, and ideational communities. The awareness that community identity can transcend geographical boundaries, bringing together members with shared values who are geographically dispersed, is evidenced by definitions of a profession as a community (Goode, 1956).

The process by which people's horizons have been expanded beyond the local community has been gradual and has not affected the lives of all residents of urban centers. There are three basic levels of involvement in Chicago and its local communities by metropolitan residents. One segment of the population, still relatively small in most parts of the world, copes with urban life with an understanding of the basic social systems of the society and of the metropolis; it selects and identifies with a multi-dimensional set of components. Each involvement is chosen on the basis of individuated criteria of preference: the job and the work organization within which it is carried on; the political party and its sections; the religion and the specific church; the educational establishment, including communication media; recreational activities and groups; and other organizations are all selected and the degree of participation in them determined by self-defined needs. Social groups concerned with the broader world, the nation, the city, small areas or professions are joined by such people, and identification with their goals developed with different degrees of commitment. Movement in and out of these involvements is accomplished whenever one or both parties of the relation change their definition and their satisfaction with the rewards it provides. Urban life is basically structured for this kind of person, who is fully trained in logico-bureaucratic procedures for voluntary engagement in primary and secondary relations and in formal social roles.

The small town is quite different in its organization and functioning, with its almost automatic involvement in all aspects of life. In the city, the anonymity of the past and segmentalized role characteristics open up the possibility of experimenting with new social roles at most stages of the life cycle to an extent absent in the smaller community, which forms stereotypes of persons on the basis of their known history. However, the experimentation requires an ability to meet formalized testing procedures prior to entrance into any set of relations. The individual must select a role, prepare himself for it, learning skills and acquiring new characteristics, such as attitude or dress, and bringing himself into contact situations. He must be willing to subject himself to extrinsic tests of performance.

The analogous method of coping with the city, historically the most frequent, and currently stifling much of its life, is one of highly restricted, haphazard, and passive use of its facilities. Entrance into the city, location within it, and selection of various roles come to many people by chance rather than by planning. Knowledge of a unit of the social structure and of how it fits into the larger society is never acquired, and life is spent in activities centered repetitiously around the home, a few streets, and the work place. Identification is limited to the family, a few neighbors and sometimes work associates, but mobility in the occupation prevents even broader involvements in the work group.

A third form of living in the city, carried out by some of the immigrants and their descendents, the "villagers" who initially reproduced in Chicago the restricted life of the "okolica" (Thomas and Znaniecki, 1918–20), included an expansion of this village provincialism. The ethnic communities established by some European, and now Mexican and Puerto Rican, immigrants provide a cushion against the shock of living in a totally unintelligible city and socialize their members to look beyond the family and immediate neighborhood. For example, the Polish-American community was able, through its leaders, newspapers, and voluntary associations, to broaden the villagers' identification from that "okolica" to the Polish national culture society, to the extent that they identified themselves as "the fourth province of Poland" during the World War I years. The ethnic community transcends the local area and unites all the people living in America who identify themselves with the ethnic culture and their fellow nationals. The voluntary associations and mass communication media accomplish this function of keeping the people in touch with each other, freeing them from utter dependence on the face-to-face contacts of a restricted neighborhood. The black population of this country lacked such a community until recent years; involvement in it is likely to be limited to the younger and more educated persons. Religious communities function in a similar way among other urbanites, expanding their identification and reference groups beyond the restricted daily life, varying among each other considerably in the attention they give to child and adult socialization.

Thus, residents of a city differ in the level and degree of multi-dimensionality of their involvement in its life, depending on many characteristics, such as age, occupation, education, and identification with restricted neighborhoods or with ethnic, religious, or professional communities. The social engagement of Chicago area widows aged 50 and over who are the subject of this book was investigated through three social roles: neighbor, participant in voluntary associations, and work in paid employment. Most are found to be highly restricted and haphazard in their use of urban resources to enrich their daily life.

## RESIDENTIAL LOCATION OF CHICAGO AREA WIDOWS

Movement into the Chicago area by the fifty-five percent of respondents who are not native to it, and mobility within it by all the widows, is often only an attempt to escape conditions defined as bad in a previous residence, rather than a rational choice based upon a careful consideration of characteristics and resources. Thirty-nine percent of the widows came to Chicago from other parts of America, seventeen percent from other continents, most from rural and agricultural areas, so that they lacked familiarity with cities, let alone with Chicago. Fifty-one of the fifty-two blacks came from the south, where their fathers, and, in some cases, their husbands had been farmers on small bits of land, tenants, or share croppers. When the migrants came to Chicago they simply settled with or near people they knew, who had selected their neighborhood in an equally non-analytical manner. Most did not choose this particular city and its sub-area because it offered the best opportunity for expanding their social life space or personality. They simply hoped to find less exhausting jobs and an easier life in a city to which family or neighbors had already migrated.

Few of the European-born migrants had lives of leisure before coming here, and their arrival was usually followed rapidly by employment in the first job they could obtain. Settlement in their own place occurred after the pay checks started coming in, and it tended to be in physical proximity to the people who had influenced them to migrate by setting an example. Their location and movement since entering the city, as well as the mobility of most older native-born residents, have been influenced by building deterioration, community changes, such as "urban renewal" or the appearance of newcomers against whom they were prejudiced, and by life changes due to cycle or crises shifts. By the time they were interviewed, fifty percent had moved since the death of their husband. The average number of times they had changed residences after becoming widows was three, and the average length of time they have been in their current location is 6.0 years for the whites and 5.7 years for the blacks. As mentioned in Chapter One, widows generally reside in areas of high concentration of the elderly, either because they remain in their homes, which tend to be in old areas, or because they move to neighborhoods featuring low-rent, small-size units. Forty-one percent of the respondents live in single-family detached dwellings. Only two percent are in single-family attached structures, and sixteen percent in the preverbial Chicago "two flats" of the older workingman's neighborhoods. Eighteen percent live in buildings containing 10 or more units, leaving one-fifth in apartments with from three to nine households. It must be remembered that only complete dwelling units were covered, leaving out boarding houses and retirement hotels in which each unit lacks separate cooking facilities. The majority thus lives in multiple unit buildings, but a sizable proportion maintain a separate home, often of small size.

The interviewers were asked to rank the respondent's residence and the surrounding area through the use of a interviewer rating scale (see also Table 10 p. 35).[1] Words which had been found by prior social research and tested by NORC in other interviews as bi-polar, that is, mutually exclusive but measuring the same general trait, were listed in our scales at the left and right extremes of a piece of paper with six open positions between them. Each interviewer checked how close to either extreme she considers the subject to be located. Thus, the dwelling unit could be judged as falling in any of the six positions between "neat" and "disorderly" (see Table 43).

TABLE 43: RATINGS BY INTERVIEWER OF RESPONDENT'S
RESIDENCE, IN SELECTED TRAITS

| | Positions | | | | | | | |
|---|---|---|---|---|---|---|---|---|
| *Extremes* | *1* | *2* | *3* | *4* | *5* | *6* | *No. Ans.* | |
| *Respondent's Home* | % | % | % | % | % | % | | |
| Neat | 61 | 17 | 6 | 7 | 5 | 5 | 20* | Disorderly |
| Dirty | 3 | 5 | 4 | 6 | 18 | 65 | 21* | Clean |
| Rich | 4 | 12 | 38 | 26 | 14 | 7 | 19* | Poor |
| Relaxed | 40 | 23 | 19 | 9 | 4 | 1 | 26* | Tense |
| *Respondent's Block* | | | | | | | | |
| Well-kept | | | | | | | | Poorly-kept |
| Dwellings | 30 | 25 | 24 | 11 | 4 | 6 | 4* | Dwellings |
| Littered Streets, | | | | | | | | Clean Streets |
| (refuse, glass, etc.) | 3 | 4 | 8 | 13 | 28 | 44 | 3* | (no refuse, glass, etc.) |
| Very Poor | | | | | | | | Very Well-to-do |
| Neighborhood | 6 | 7 | 39 | 34 | 9 | 5 | 2* | Neighborhood |
| Mainly | | | | | | | | Mainly Single |
| Apartments | 18 | 18 | 16 | 10 | 17 | 20 | 3* | Dwellings |
| Open Spaces (Lawns, yards, space between buildings) | 24 | 15 | 25 | 9 | 16 | 10 | 3* | Crowded (no lawns, yards, space between buildings) |
| Mainly Commercial and/or Industrial buildings | 5 | 7 | 9 | 10 | 18 | 50 | 4* | No Commercial or Industrial Buildings |

* Not included in Percent base.

It must be remembered that the interviews were conducted without any prior contact or appointment with the respondent, by experienced, mostly middle-aged National Opinion Research Center women, matched by race to the area they were covering. The fact that so many found the respondent's home neat and clean is a compliment to the widows and, as mentioned in Chapter One, it explodes the myth that older widows who no longer have to maintain the home for the husband or children allow it to fall into a messy and unclean condition. The habits of a lifetime, plus plenty of time and a need to move about and do things, assert them-selves in the condition of the residence. Of course, half of the women have someone living with them, contributing to the unit's maintenance or serving as a judge of the work or a "client." Few of these residences are so luxuriously furnished as to give an added incentive to the house-wife to produce a show place. Only four percent of the dwellings were judged by interviewers to be on the highest level of "rich," and only twelve percent at the next highest. Most of the homes are judged medium in expensiveness of furnishings and, surprisingly, only seven percent are placed at the poor end of this trait's continuum. Most of the dwellings were evaluated as emitting a relaxed atmosphere.

The dwelling units of the Chicago area widows tend to be located in areas judged by the interviewers as falling at the "well-kept" end of the continuum, although one-third are in the middle, and one-tenth are in the poorly-kept category. Only seven percent are judged as badly littered, while forty-four percent—a large proportion—are at the highest position of cleanliness. However, the areas are not likely to be at either extremes of poverty or affluence; most are right in the middle. Thirty-seven per-cent of the blocks contain mostly single dwelling units, and thirty-six percent have only apartment buildings or are heavily so composed. This means that one-fourth of the residences of the respondents are located within mixed areas as far as building size is concerned. One fourth of the blocks are considered by the interviewers as open (i.e. uncrowded), with another fifteen percent as nearly open, and one-fourth as either crowded or almost crowded. Half are in residential areas with no com-mercial or industrial sites and few are completely surrounded by such buildings, leaving forty-four percent in blocks with at least one shop or other income-producing unit.

Very few of the residences of widows are in outlying parts of the suburbs; they are more likely to be in the central core of the town. The interviewer assigned to a pre-test in Libertyville spent days trying to locate even one widow, because she was looking in the newly developed area of high-cost homes. She finally found some widows in the center of town. As the above set of characteristics indicate, most widows live in older and architecturally mixed sections of a town, particularly in the city.

## SOCIAL INTEGRATION INTO THE NEIGHBORHOOD

The social integration of a widow into her neighborhood varies according to several sets of characteristics. There are basically six matches between her and her neighborhood. The first type of widow lives in a community which is contained in one building or a set of a few buildings, usually devoted to people of her own age. Much sociological and political debate has centered around the pros and cons of segregated living for the older segment of the population, but most research indicates that social isolation increases as the density of people in the same life cycle and life circumstances decreases (Rosow, 1967). Several of the random sample and of the exploratory interviews were conducted in the Chicago Housing Authority's buildings for Senior Citizens. Generally, widows in such locations engage in stronger forms of neighboring and feel more a part of a community than widows in the open city. Of course, all of them are not equally involved in the activities of the buildings. The same is true of a retirement hotel which is currently being studied. Two basic factors operate to influence the amount and type of neighboring engaged in by residents of buildings which have a high density of the elderly, and, thus, of widows. One is the form of activity designed to facilitate interaction. Eating together provides some opportunity, but the activities which are most socially integrative have not yet been determined through research. The second factor influencing the degree of social involvement of widows in dense situations is their socio-economic background, with its resultant social and activity skills and degree of self-confidence. Many of the buildings designed for older persons draw or select people in the lower income brackets, which for this age group often implies minimal education. Such people are trained, as mentioned before, to be suspicious of strangers and fearful of becoming too involved in neighboring. They do not like to have others know too much about them and feel anxiety over what they label infringement on their privacy. The lower the socio-economic class, the fewer skills the person has to prevent such invasions and the less likely are their associates to be sophisticated in granting them necessary rights. Even younger lower-class women share these attitudes, since they tend to lack the optimistic view of the world and of their acceptance by others which is so characteristic of people who have successful lives and who have the skills needed to keep social relations within comfortable bounds. The experiments with retirement hotels and municipal housing units indicate the difficulty of involving people who share such non-participant backgrounds, but the success of some activity programs shows that the proportion of participants may be increased by appropriate planning. Migratory communities, composed of "snow birds" who come south for the winter, and the highly interactive Sun Cities or Youngstowns of Arizona, Florida, and California prove that it is not the age of the inhabitants of a neighborhood which limits social interaction. In spite of the fact that social density and a common social status increase the *Social Integration of the Aged* (Rosow, 1967), the social class of the residents and certain characteristics of the activity patterns institutionalized or attempted by the community retard or facilitate the involvement of large numbers of inhabitants.

A second type of match between a widow and a neighborhood occurs if she has been a relatively long resident of a stable area which she defines in positive and fond terms. One such woman estimates that there are many widows in her area because "They made their lives here and then stayed after they were widowed." She interacts with them frequently. Another states "I think, for one thing, they've lived here so long that they just stay here because all their friends are here and its too difficult to start over at an older age," as the reason her area contains many widows. A major characteristic which influences the attitudes toward a neighborhood is safety, a feature about which many urban inhabitants of America are very concerned. Convenience for shopping and transportation are added pluses of an area in which the widow feels particularly comfortable, because she is not apt to have a car or to be habituated to suburban patterns of infrequent shopping ventures. However, stability and acceptance of the neighborhood do not necessarily lead to high forms of neighboring, as some such areas develop norms of only casual interaction. Even long-time residents do not actually do much socializing. Such institutionalized non-interaction is more typical of the older apartment buildings than of areas of private homes, but it exists even in the latter.

A third type of widow can be located in any of a variety of neighborhoods, but her participation is restricted by the presence of offspring or other relatives who keep her company and occupy her time. This situation ranges from the case of a respondent who has so many relatives in the area that she has never had a chance to meet others residing there, to one who restricts all her social contacts to her daughter. Half of the respondents live in a neighborhood inhabited by relatives. These women tend to interact more often with kin members than with other neighbors, even in stable communities. White women, as mentioned in Chapter Three, are likely to be living in their own homes with unmarried children who are often sufficiently adult to provide companionship and partnership in ventures out of the area. Black women more often live with now or formerly married children and many are employed, the role of neighbor competing unsuccessfully with those of mother and worker.

A fourth kind of neighborhood situation in which Chicago widows are located is one of changing populations. It is often a prior ethnic community of which the respondents form the remnants, as new migrants to the city start moving in and the more successful ethnics move out to areas of secondary settlement. Originally such areas had provided warmth and identification for the woman, with the mother tongue being spoken in stores and churches and contact with people from the same village bringing reminiscences through visits or club meetings. As the area changes, the old churches no longer provide sanctuaries and the women become afraid to go out alone. Old friends have died or move away, sometimes to live with married children at a great distance. Those who remain have all their earthly possessions invested in their home, which could never be sold for enough to facilitate the purchase of another residence (see also Gans, 1962). Many do not speak English well, some hardly at all, and they feel frightened and deserted in a hostile world. One respondent, who does not speak English, spends much time sitting in her window watching her neighbors throw cans and bottles, the children breaking the slats of her fence. When she goes out to clean up her yard, the children poke fun of her ignorance and appearance. The changing ghetto areas also make life difficult for the widow who moves into them because she can not continue living in her previous location.

A number of widows, particularly those of lower socio-economic status who are first generation migrants to the city from rural areas and who then experienced mobility within it, are living in disorganized and hostile communities in which neighboring is a rare phenomenon. A number of the black women report: "I don't know neighbors, I don't belong to groups. I don't have any friends in Chicago." Another states: "I don't know any of the neighbors, I stay in most of the time." She belongs to no voluntary associations and does not even have a telephone in her home. A mother who was able to rear her illegitimate son finally had to give him up because the neighborhood in which she lives is so "bad, the boys are bad."

A final category of widow does not know her neighbors and does not interact with them because she moved into the home of an adult child or other established person. If the basic family is of a generation younger than the widow, she is likely to find herself in an area without people in a similar life situation. A seventy-three year old woman lived with her son for three months, but returned to her old community: "I missed my other children and my friends." She defines the difficulty of living with married offspring as: "From my experience, I think the problem is that you miss your own age group. I am much happier to be with my own friends." A major difficulty in such situations is that the older mother may be an immigrant from another country or rural area, much less educated and generally of a lower class than her children. Moving into their home results not only in strain between the generations immersed in different social classes, but also in a mismatch with the neighborhood. Young or even middle-aged couples living in middle-class suburbs provide an environment in which the lower-class mother is uncomfortable.

As mentioned before, there are two sets of characteristics which influence the level and forms of neighboring: the characteristics of the area, and the abilities of the widow. Two cases of widows will be presented here to exemplify in greater detail the processes by which a woman can select and utilize the resources of a community, a process discussed at the beginning of this chapter. One widow has managed to develop a full life, although she lives in a rather distant suburb, which according to her is really a small family-oriented town without many facilities for integrating women in her marital state. She feels strongly that widows have to make an independent life for themselves and finds very difficult the manner in which others treat her now that her husband is no longer around. Asked how widows become re-engaged in society she replied:

> "*I think we do it ourselves. We get together in groups. We had a bridge club of eight of us for quite a while, and getting eight women together at one time is no mean feat. But we did it rather successfully for about three or four years. One of them is now in a home up in Woodstock and another one moved away, so we kind of gave it up. But I think widows, I think they can do it themselves. In the big city, you can have organizations; you can have clubs and rent space, but I don't think there would be enough of us out here. I think if people just treat us fairly—that's all—treat us like you treat another person. Don't isolate us, don't put us in a different strategy (sic) of society, because we are still a part of all this and we want to be part of it. I don't want to be isolated. This is the first thing people think of—she's alone, and they think of her as something apart from the mainstream of society. And I resent that, because I feel I'm contributing almost as much as anyone else. I burn as much electricity, I have to eat and I have to buy clothes and I'm contributing economically, and until I become a burden on society, I feel I'm still a part of the mainstream and that's the way I want to be considered.*"

This respondent feels that, if she lived in a larger community, her "oddness" would not be apparent and she would have greater freedom to participate in society, but she considers herself tied down by her home.

Another widow, living in a luxurious apartment on the "Gold Coast," has gradually become so disenchanted with Chicago as a community of identification that she has broadened her horizon to include other American cities and Europe, feeling more comfortable away from this metropolis than within it. While her husband was alive, she had enjoyed very high status, which she feels completely stripped away by his death. She finds it now easier to establish herself as an individual in communities with which she has not been connected through such a history. While the interview was taking place, she received a call from a New York furrier asking when she could pick up her new hats. She replied that she was going to Boston for an "opening" the following week and would drop in to get them on that Friday. Although not highly educated herself, she had been married to a very successful and "deeply studied" man, who familiarized her with world history and culture by guiding her through many countries, so that she gained a sophistication facilitating movement in and out of these lands, always in their upper classes.

At the other extreme from this wealthy cosmopolite are widows who do not know the names of their neighborhoods and who are completely unfamiliar with the history, present organization, and facilities of the city in which they reside. Some have never been downtown. Most tests administered such women to measure "mental alertness" are so culture-bound that they measure nothing but their social life space. For some widows, facts such as that today is Tuesday and that a particular man is mayor of the city are of no importance. Some no longer leave the home because of health or other limitations; others depend on a son or other associates to drive them to the doctor, somebody's home, or a store. Trained to be passively responsive to actions of others and formerly married to men with little more knowledge of the community than they have and with little communication of abstract information in the inter-action process, they have sometimes lived all their lives within a very restricted social world, much like that described by Thomas and Znaniecki as typical of the Polish peasant in Europe. Some of the older women do not speak English or read in any language, let alone that of their secondary residence, so that they are cut off from all means for learning. The bits and pieces of data about Chicago beamed through the mass communication visual media do not cumulatively build a system of knowledge, since the widows lack the foundation for sorting and anchoring them. For these women the city remains a vast mystery of incomprehensible organization and threatening danger, which they are powerless to control. A history of such involvement in the city is presented by a woman who is now happily living in a Chicago Housing Authority building. She entered the country at the age of 17 to live with an aunt in Chicago, in place of her sister who was afraid to cross the ocean. At a later date she moved into the southern part of the city, "and then the colored came in and we had to get out of there. So I had a job at a clock factory north, and one of the ladies that worked with me had a cousin that had a grocery store right on Damen, and I used to stop there for lunch, milk, etc. So, I knew I had to get out of 74th and Green, so I asked this fellow if he would help me try to find a flat. So within two weeks she called me up to tell me about this three-room apartment with a nice back porch. So I moved over there, and it was kitty-corner from the shop where I worked. So for those three years that I worked—I worked there seven years all together—but for the last three years, I didn't have any bus fare to spend." Her next move was also haphazard, rather than a result of familiarity with the city and a careful analysis of needs and resources. She was still working, but her husband was becoming increasingly ill; he had one lung removed, operations on both eyes for cateracts, and was really failing. "And my sister told me I should stay home with him, that he really needed me at home. So then I rented this place, she's the one who put an application in for me, to the precinct captain. That's how I got in here so fast."

Most of the literature about *Why Families Move* (Rossi, 1955) assumes, by statement or implication, a rational process of eliminating unavailable or undesirable areas and gradually focusing on a few alternative communities. Not only the widows, but most of the housewives studied in the previous projects do not proceed logically to find new housing. They are not familiar with the city and move to get away from a bad situation, or to be closer to children or to work. They hope for the best result out of a limited and not fully investigated set of choices.

The urban center and the society at large bewilder many of the older widows socialized in rural areas, villages, and small towns. The news they hear on the radio or television frightens them out of all proportion to their own danger. For example, rape is very unlikely to happen to an older widow, yet it is precisely she who is most afraid of it. The lack of knowledge and fear of the world at large is exemplified by one respondent, a European refugee interviewed at length during the exploratory period. She greeted the principal investigator at the door with a letter in English from the Chicago Housing Authority in hand. This was a "final notice" that she should evict the woman in her basement, because it was against the law and public safety to have anyone living there. She explained in Polish that she had tried to tell them she can not evict the woman because the latter has no place to go, and she herself could not exist without that tenant because the latter knows some English. All around her she sees Puerto Rican families with several persons in the basement and she feels persecuted. She had been trying to communicate these facts to the housing bureau for months but could not, because no one at the telephone number given in the letter speaks her language. A call to the bureau by the interviewer resulted in arrangements for a Polish-speaking social worker to come and see her. The investigator then tried to calm the respondent by saying that the government was trying to make the area safer, but that the process was slow. "Government," she exploded, crying and shaking. "What has government done for me? Government took my husband and killed him, government took my son, and I don't even know where his grave is. Government took me to work in Germany. Government is taking away my house because I have a friend." It turned out that the Russian forces occupying Poland had taken her husband during World War II and inducted him into their army, in which he died during the German campaign. The Germans forced her son into their service, while they deported her to a work camp in the interior of their country. She finally left at the end of the war and managed to get over to America, where she and a sister, now dead, worked twelve hours a day to save money for a rather attractive, brick house. They took boarders and gradually established an equity. Now the "American government," in the form of the city housing department, was threatening her with confiscation of this home, if she did not comply with the directive to evict the boarder living in the basement. She sees the influx of Puerto Ricans into her neighborhood as the same kind of invasion that she experienced from the Russians and Germans, and she hates them as enemies. The American government which permits this occupation seems to her to be also an enemy set on destroying her.

In general, many of the Chicago area older widows do not regard their city or neighborhood as an opportunity to become engaged in a broad social life space and to develop relations which would alleviate loneliness. Their view of their area and their interaction in it varies by level and content.

## NEIGHBORING

Studies of neighboring forms and levels in metropolitan Chicago indicate that each small social area develops its own institutionalized pattern of interaction among those considered to be "neighbors." Even this concept varies by community, extending sometimes to all those within its political boundaries, sometimes only to people living on the same block or across the street from each other. By the same token, each resident is socialized or habituated to a pattern of neighboring, and the relation she develops with people around her depends upon the matching of the two sets of procedures—the community's and her own. The types of interaction which are available in neighboring are: casual conversation outdoors, where contact occurs as a consequence of other actions; borrowing and lending or service-exchanging; informal "dropping over" to the neighbor's home, requiring interpersonal ease and familiarity; invitational visiting, involving pre-arranged dates and "event" socializing; attendance together at meetings of the same organization; and going out together to the same leisure events away from the area. Any of these activities may be sex-segregated or tied into couple-companionate interaction, but communities and people differ considerably in the degree to which any of these exchanges form a part of their life.

The study of the older widows in the Chicago area indicates that many are not socialized into the kind of neighboring which is dependent on the conversion of comparative strangers into persons with whom any of the above listed forms of interaction may be carried on comfortably. In fact, most of the informal neighboring of modern America since World War II, which has drawn the attention of so many observers, is restricted to new suburbs of middle-class people and does not engage the widow. In many new suburbs, friendships and neighboring become intertwined with couple-companionate interaction, which makes it very difficult for widows who remain after the death of the husband. Those who moved at that time, as half of the respondents did, whether from suburbs or residences within the city, are often unable to form new relations because they are located in areas of "institutionalized non-interaction" and even "anomic non-interaction." The former pattern involves a mutual agreement not to socialize; the latter is based on the rejection or at least the ignoring of the neighbor's value system and a refusal to engage in friendly exchanges.

The figures obtained from the Chicago area interviews indicate that the most frequent form of socializing with neighbors is dependent upon sporadic contacts occurring outside of the home—when both are working in the yard, walking, or going back and forth from their homes to other places (see Table 44). Of course, the contact may not be completely

TABLE 44: PERCENTAGES OF WIDOWS WHO ENGAGE IN SPECIFIED FREQUENCIES OF INTERACTION IN THE SEVEN FORMS OF NEIGHBORING

| Form of Neighboring | Frequency of Neighboring | | | | Not Appropriate Number | Percent Base |
|---|---|---|---|---|---|---|
| | Fre-quently | Occa-sionally | Seldom | Never | | |
| Talk casually outside | 45.9 | 36.9 | 15.7 | 1.6 | 46 | 255 |
| Borrow or lend | 2.4 | 10.6 | 17.7 | 69.3 | 47 | 254 |
| Drop into each other's home | 14.6 | 30.3 | 25.2 | 29.9 | 47 | 254 |
| Visit by invitation | 9.0 | 29.8 | 27.8 | 33.3 | 46 | 255 |
| Go to club meetings together | 5.1 | 10.6 | 6.7 | 77.6 | 47 | 254 |
| Go out together | 3.9 | 13.3 | 10.6 | 72.2 | 46 | 255 |
| Other activities | 6.4 | 12.8 | — | 80.9 | 207 | 94 |

unplanned, as women can organize their shopping and gardening to fit the schedule of their neighbors. Whole communities can be informally organized by age groups in terms of the ebb and flow of movement in and out of the home and public places. Several respondents mention that shopping is a major event in their daily life, since it is intertwined with causal contact with neighbors on the way to and from community stores. However, even this limited form of socializing, the only one available to the majority of women with any frequency, is engaged in often by only about half of the respondents, leaving the remaining widows able to maintain it only "occasionally" or "seldom." For them, this aspect of social engagement is not sufficiently strong to fulfill complex interactional needs.

Borrowing or lending, the traditional reason or excuse for neighboring, is not popular in the Chicago area. At least, two-thirds of the widows never engage in it, and only two percent so interact frequently. The preponderance of the "never" response indicates a new norm among such women—one discouraging or at least disclaiming exchanges of services with those living nearby. One respondent explained that every time she got close to her neighbors, she was asked to baby-sit; she feels that her younger neighbors befriend her only to make use of her in solving their problems in the role of mother.

The informal "dropping over" to the homes of neighbors, so often mentioned in William H. Whyte's (1956) *Organization Man* and David Riesman's (1954) *The Lonely Crowd,* is simply not a major part of life for most widows: only fifteen percent have that kind of relations with neighbors with any frequency, while a third never engage in it. Visiting by invitation is also rare, in fact, more so. Almost four times as many widows never engage in it as those who are frequently involved with their neighbors in this way. Even less likely are the other forms of neighboring: eight out of ten respondents never go together with neighbors to meetings and seventy-two percent are never accompanied by people living nearby to leisure-time events away from the area. Only a fifth of the respondents ever undertake other activities with people living in geographical proximity.

The proportion of widows who do not frequently engage in neighboring, in spite of their discontinued obligations to small children and a husband, is much greater than that found among suburban housewives, black working women, and urban housewives of both white and black communities. There are several specific reasons for the difference, the basic one being that children, rather than being a barrier, are an asset to neighboring; they restrict the movement of mothers and bring them into contact with each other. Also, the younger mothers are more edu-

cated and middle-class than are the older widows. The same characteristics affect the rate of neighboring by the different kinds of widows.

## Characteristics of Women Engaging in Different Levels of Neighboring

The previous research indicated that the highest level of neighboring
occurs when couples are young, with young children, recently moved into
new homes in new communities sharing a middle-class culture. Not
surprisingly, the older widows are not likely to be engaged in heavy
neighboring of this type, since they lack most and often all these characteristics. Age alone affects the level and form of interaction. Generally,
the most likely to know their neighbors and to be involved in several
forms of interaction with them are women between the ages of fifty-five
and seventy, although the distributions shift somewhat in form. Widows
between eighty and eighty-four years of age are more apt than their
younger or older counterparts to be at least acquainted with people
residing nearby, without interacting with them frequently. It is possible
that they represent the last group to remain in areas of old residence and
that their very age insures a feeling of integration; the even older women
have moved to the homes of married or formerly married children, where
they are not acquainted with the community.

Casual talking outdoors with neighbors is likely to involve the younger
women and the proportion decreases consistently after age sixty-nine.
The very old woman is not apt to be outdoors often enough to come into
contact with other people. Borrowing and lending, rare as it is, is disproportionately likely to engage women from fifty-five to sixty-five, and
generally to drop after that. Again, the numbers of women who engage
in this exchange frequently is very small, but "occasional" and "seldom"
scores are higher in age groups under sixty-nine. Dropping over to each
other's home is most likely to happen if the widow is between fifty-five
and sixty-five in age. Younger women are active in many other roles and
drop in only occasionally, and the older ones tend to fall into the "seldom"
or "never" end of the continuum. Visiting by invitation is even more
specifically distributed by age, with the youngest group engaging in it
very seldom, so that the proportionally high scorers are those fifty-five to
fifty-nine and sixty-five to sixty-nine years of age. Club meetings are
rarely attended with neighbors at any age, and no pattern appears in the
cross-tabulations. Leisure-time pursuits outside of the area with those
living close are the specialty of women in their sixties.

Age affects the amount of time and energy available to women for
socializing with neighbors, partly because of the life-cycle entrance into
competing social roles. It also affects such facilitating characteristics as

mobility, financial resources, and the general "libido" or life force. Another very important factor is the length of time a widow has lived in the neighborhood. Half, or 153 out of the 301 respondents have not moved since the death of the husband, and they tend to be more fully involved in neighboring than any of the movers. The next neighborly group is one which has resided in the area for three years or less. This finding is surprising, since we had expected the longer residents to be more active. It is possible that those residing in a neighborhood longer have their scores lowered by age or by the changing nature of the area. The new movers may make special efforts to become acquainted with neighbors. They may feel particularly lonely after having left the home shared with the husband or after other role shifts, so that their need for neighboring is greater than that of the more established widows. Also, they may be living in areas with a high density of people in similar life circumstances. On the other hand, a cycle of neighboring may be operating even here, with a change in residence increasing the desire to know neighbors, and settling down in an area bringing out more passive stances and a lack of interest, especially if the turnover of rentals brings strangers in the place of those acquaintances cultivated during the first three years of living there. In any case, frequent informal interaction increases with length of residence until a peak of fifty-seven percent is reached at three years. This is even higher than the fifty-four percent of women who never moved after becoming widows, whose scores in other forms of neighboring, however, outweigh all movers.

Occasional borrowing is engaged in by twenty-seven women, twenty-three of whom are still in the same dwelling unit as when the husband was alive. Those who did not move are more likely than their mobile counterparts to exchange such services often, or at least occasionally, and to be under-represented in the "never" category. This is a dramatic concentration, showing these non-movers to be in a very different relation to neighbors than movers, retaining an older tradition among people comfortable with each other and not afraid that "People take advantage of a woman when they find out that she is a widow." It indicates that a lack of borrowing and lending may not be a consequence of a woman's self-sufficiency, but rather of her anxiety about imposing on others or being imposed upon.

Residence in the same dwelling as prior to widowhood makes a great deal of difference in the other forms of neighboring. The non-movers form 236 percent of the movers in the proportion who frequently drop over to the neighbors' houses, 283 percent of those who visit by invitation, 225 percent of those who go to meetings with women living nearby and 400 percent of those who go out socially with them. In the latter two cases the numbers are small (nine and eight), but the differences are significant. Thus, although many widows feel obliged to move because of financial circumstances, grief for the husband, or unwillingness to maintain housekeeping in a larger place, those who move are not likely to develop as close a relation with neighbors as those who remain. Of course, it is very probable that different categories of women move from those who stay, and that the least likely to be successfully integrated in any area are the most likely to give up their home for a strange location.

Knowledge that moving away from an area after the death of the husband may have negative effects on social relations, at least the belief that such is the case, is shared by most of the respondents. At least, thirty-six percent agree strongly and forty percent agree that "A new widow should not move too soon from the place in which she was living before her husband died." Those who agree at either level with this statement are not likely to be socially isolated (Gamma −.31), but they tend to hold rather passive attitudes toward their social relations. They are apt to think widows feel like a fifth wheel (Gamma .26), and that it is hard for them to make decisions (Gamma .25). Respondents who don't think widows should move too soon consider their relations with their siblings to have become closer in widowhood, and, if they date, they feel more in common with widowers than with men in other marital situations. The more children the woman has, the less likely she is to insist that moving soon after the death of the husband is not a good idea, either because such a move is a necessity, or because she is less dependent upon her neighborhood in her social relations. The latter can be due to a concentration on the role of mother or worker, or to her assurance that she can build new relations in a new neighborhood.

In spite of the warning about rapid movement away from the home shared with the husband, more of the newly moved enter several types of neighboring interactions than those who broke ties with former neighbors many years ago. This point is sufficiently important to warrant repeating.

Several other aspects of the different forms of neighboring are significant. The Porgy and Bess image of the black woman immersed in frequent and mutually beneficial interaction with neighbors is not representative of the black Chicago area widow. Twenty-one percent of the blacks, as compared to only fourteen percent of the whites, do not even know their neighbors; fewer (twenty percent to forty-five percent) can estimate how many, if any, other widows live in their community. Statistics of widowhood in both communities indicate that black women should expect to find more widows than their white counterparts. More blacks than whites do not enter any form of neighboring, except occasional attendance at meetings and borrowing or lending; the numbers in those activities are still small (see Table 45). Extreme levels of interaction are slightly higher at the "frequent" level for the blacks than the whites in the club attendance category, due to the presence of block clubs in several areas of the black belt.

TABLE 45: PERCENTAGES AND NUMBERS OF RESPONDENTS REPORTING FREQUENT AND TOTAL ABSENCE OF INTERACTION IN SPECIFIED FORMS OF NEIGHBORING, BY RACE

| | | | Race | | | |
|---|---|---|---|---|---|---|
| *Norm and Frequency* | *Total* | | *Negro* | | *White* | |
| | % | N | % | N | % | N |
| *Talk outdoors* | | | | | | |
| Frequently | 46 | 114 | 36 | 15 | 47 | 99 |
| Never | 2 | 4 | 2 | 1 | 1 | 3 |
| *Borrow and lend* | | | | | | |
| Frequently | 2 | 6 | 5 | 2 | 2 | 4 |
| Never | 70 | 174 | 61 | 25 | 72 | 149 |
| *Drop over* | | | | | | |
| Frequently | 15 | 37 | 12 | 5 | 15 | 32 |
| Never | 30 | 75 | 24 | 10 | 31 | 65 |
| *Visit by invitation* | | | | | | |
| Frequently | 9 | 23 | 7 | 3 | 10 | 20 |
| Never | 34 | 85 | 46 | 19 | 32 | 66 |
| *Club meetings* | | | | | | |
| Frequently | 5 | 13 | 7 | 3 | 5 | 10 |
| Never | 78 | 195 | 68 | 28 | 80 | 167 |
| *Go out together* | | | | | | |
| Frequently | 4 | 10 | 2 | 1 | 4 | 9 |
| Never | 73 | 182 | 85 | 35 | 70 | 147 |
| *Other things* | | | | | | |
| Frequently | 6 | 6 | 5 | 1 | 7 | 5 |
| Never | 82 | 76 | 85 | 17 | 81 | 59 |

Intermediary levels not given. Fifty-one women did not answer this set of questions, 46 because they already stated that they do not know their neighbors.

Finally, the forms of neighboring engaged in by Chicago area widows vary by the factor of their education, though in rather strange ways. Two trends are similar to those found among the housewives and working women who formed the *Occupation: Housewife* samples. The first trend is of a gradual increase in the amount of neighboring in most forms, particularly those involving pre-arranged and systematic contact, as the amount of education increases. The second trend is toward a drop of involvement, or a dipping, in intermediary achievement levels. Although college graduates are higher than high school graduates in all but borrowing and lending, college drop-outs are much less apt to be strongly or even occasionally engaged in the various forms of neighboring than high school graduates. The same dip, although slightly less extreme, is found among high school drop-outs. A tentative conclusion reached in the previous study must be repeated here, but the finding was not anticipated and further research is needed to substantiate it. Women who do not finish the education which they started are less self-confident than the finishers, are living in neighborhoods in which their training is inferior to the leaders, or are displaying the same behavioral pattern which led to their dropping out in the first place. Dropping out at less than the grade school level is less significant, possibly because even a grade school education does not offset the lower class suspicion of neighbors. Actually, the woman who has the most frequent, rather than the most multi-dimensional, relations with neighbors is the high school graduate. This means that she depends heavily on informal socializing, seldom undertaking planned contact focused on some specific activity. Her casual exchanges are more frequent than those of the college graduate who builds neighboring into a more systematic set of relations of different kinds. Of course, it must be remembered that only ten percent of the respondents went beyond high school, which is typical for older women, but it makes generalizations about college graduates clearly tentative.

## The Role of Neighbor

The various references in the interviews to the role of neighbor, including the forms of interaction summarized in Table 42, and references to neighbors as helpful in widowhood, as a source of frequent contact, or in other ways as important to life were all combined into a scale for the "role of neighbor." The purpose was to find out what proportion of women are on a high, medium, or low level of involvement in the role of neighbor and what characteristics differentiate widows at these three levels. Few respondents are involved in a high level of neighboring, when compared with other roles and with the involvement of married women. As stated before, suburban mothers of young children are active in neighboring relations. Only ten percent of the older widows obtained the ten to eighteen points classifying them as high scorers. Twenty-eight percent ranked medium in the role (five to nine points) and sixty-three percent scored low (between zero and four points).

Widows with high scores on the neighboring scale, however rare they are, are apt to have very distinctive traits. They tend to be under sixty years of age and widowed only one or two years. Their high score of involvement in neighboring comes from their active participation in several of the activities listed in Table 4. Those widowed less than a year are also high scorers, but their numbers are too low for generalization. These figures certainly indicate that women turn to their neighbors as a source of human contact when they become lonely with the death of the husband. Later in widowhood other relations take over, or the woman withdraws into greater isolation. The respondents who had been born outside of the Chicago area are high scorers only if they migrated to Chicago as small children or in their forties. In other words, they did not experience being newcomers when newly married or while their children were small. Also, they are likely to be at least high school graduates; a disproportionately large number of high scorers have exactly that level of achievement. There is a dip among those who dropped out of college, a tendency observed also among housewives who live in suburbs. Those respondents having more education are involved in neighboring. Those with an eighth grade education or less are low scorers. The husbands of the high interactors were also more educated men, but dropping out of college by the spouse is not a factor affecting the score of the wife. It is not surprising that wives of managers or professional men are the ones scoring high as neighbors. Black respondents fall at both extremes of social interaction with people living nearby, with many more falling at the low end, while the whites are more apt to be medium scorers. The weight of the Protestant proportions falls to the high interactors, while Catholics are at best medium neighborhood socializers. The Germans are the most likely to be high scorers, while the numbers of other nationality members are too scattered to show any tendencies, except that the Irish are evenly distributed, and the Poles are in the middle range. Widows of men who were the same age are likely to engage in frequent and multi-form neighboring. The respondents defining their financial condition as comfortable or above are also more apt than the more restricted ones to be high scorers; they are disproportionately apt to have an operating base of over $7,000 per year. Density of population seems to be an important factor, because high scorers live not so often in private homes, as would be expected by the income distributions, but rather in buildings of seven or more dwelling units.

Care for an ailing husband can be an isolating experience in neighboring or may require moving because of financial problems; it does, however, often increase contact with siblings. The high scorers in neighboring are not likely to have cared for their husband during his final illness at home. The intervening variable may be that husbands who did not require prolonged care were apt to have been younger, and the younger widows are the high interactors.

The woman's own physical condition may decrease her chance of being a high scorer as a neighbor, but it is more likely to place her in the middle position than in the lowest. Although there are only a few cases, the woman who finds no problems in widowhood is likely to be a high scorer. The high interactor wants to remarry and is hopeful of being able to do so; at least, the few women who so answer that set of questions are very apt to be involved in the role of neighbor. They are also apt to report an increase in freedom as a compensation of widowhood.

The profile of the low scorer in the role of neighbor indicates she is apt to be seventy years of age or older and to have been widowed either from seven to nine years or over thirty years. She came to the city from other parts of the United States or from Europe, after reaching the age of forty or even fifty, and she had completed no more than four grades of school or was a college drop-out. Her husband was in the first educational category, and he was disproportionately apt to have been a laborer, a craftsman, or a clerk. The black woman is more apt than her white counterpart to be a low scorer, as is the Scotch or English widow. The women in these nationalities tend to be the oldest in the group, which may account for these figures. The husband of the low scorer is apt to have been older than she. Her current financial situation is most likely to be really restricted or rather short by her own definition, although the category of women living on from $11,000 and $15,999 is also not very neighborly. The low scorer lives in a building of three units and cared for her husband during his last illness at home. Her own physical condition is experienced as limiting. She lists several problems of widowhood, money and raising a family being most often sources of difficulty. Special circumstances of her life at the time of widowhood, besides those coded for other respondents, are also problems to her. She is the most likely of all respondents to limit loneliness to the feeling that other people shun her. This type of woman does not want to remarry, so it is not this desire which keeps her from being involved in relations with her neighbors. She does not know what could be a compensation for widowhood but wishes for more money and peace of mind.

All in all, neighboring seems to require health, money, and sufficient education to have the self-confidence and skills to enter and retain new relations. The pattern is similar to that observed for the other roles. Once engagement in any set of relations is broken, as is neighboring with geographical movement of residency, the person must have the facilities for re-engagement in a different place with new people. As the records of many of the older widows show, the lower-class women have not been socialized into pre-planned and event-centered contact. They are dependent upon spontaneous encounters which are less and less likely to occur, as restrictive forces begin to limit mobility in a territory. Thus, disengagement from neighboring may be a consequence of the withering of facilities for contact and a lack of the skills needed to replace them by a new plan of action. If one does not see neighbors on the way to work or to the store, one must invent new ways of coming into contact with them or become isolated from such patterned interaction. The current study cannot discover whether any of the women were ever involved in neighboring even during the years of their children's youth. All indications are that a sizable number of those who are now low scorers in the role of neighbor were never above this level and that present deficiencies and attitudes operated in the past as well.

Interestingly enough, very few of the relations-restrictive attitudes scale proved significantly associated with scores on the role of neighbor scale. In fact, only two of the thirty-six items proved significant when measured by chi square, and four when measured by gammas (see Table 46). Belief that widows are constantly sexually propositioned, even by the husband of their friends, is inversely associated with neighboring. This means that women who score poorly on the role of neighbor scale

TABLE 46: HIGH, MEDIUM, AND LOW SCORES ON THE ROLE OF NEIGHBOR SCALE BY AGREEMENT WITH SELECTED RELATIONS-RESTRICTIVE ATTITUDES

| | Role of Neighbor | | | | | | | |
| | High | | Medium | | Low | | | |
| Attitude Agreement | % | N | % | N | % | N | Gamma | $x^2$ |
|---|---|---|---|---|---|---|---|---|
| Total sample | 10 | | 26 | | 64 | | | |
| Widows are constantly sexually propositioned | 3 | 2 | 18 | 10 | 79 | 46 | −.45 | 8.43* |
| We pretended not to know how ill husband was | 8 | 6 | 38 | 27 | 54 | 38 | .26 | 6.35** |
| My faith helped me most after widowhood | 9 | 21 | 30 | 70 | 60 | 138 | .27 | 3.69 |
| OK for widows to have sexual relations | 6 | 2 | 22 | 7 | 72 | 23 | −.25 | 1.75 |
| People take advantage of widows | 7 | 8 | 22 | 26 | 71 | 83 | −.25 | 4.51 |
| My husband had his activities, I had mine | 10 | 8 | 38 | 30 | 52 | 41 | .23 | 4.94 |

d.f. $= 2; x^2 = 6.0; p < .001$

are much more likely to hold this attitude than are the medium or high scorers. They believe, too, that it is all right for widows to have sexual relations without marriage. They are also apt to feel that people take advantage of widows. Several of these women are the lower-class blacks who have been widowed many years without remarrying. The low scorers are not apt to feel their faith helped them much or to have realized the seriousness of the husband's illness, or pretended not to know. They agree that the relations with the spouse had been sex-segregated. Thus, they do not hold positive attitudes toward others, but there is not a total package of rejective sentiments since many much stronger statements in the scale were not picked up for special attention by these women. Their attitudes toward males tend, however, to be different from those of the high and medium scorers.

The high scorers are relatively few in number, and the only significant way they differ from the expected distribution is by the strong rejection of the statement that widows are sexually propositioned, even by husbands of friends. The medium scorers vary from the expected by also rejecting this statement and by agreeing to both statements dealing with the late husband. Thus, they define their marriage as sex-segregated and even lacking the trust to share the knowledge of his fatal illness. Medium scorers are not rejective yet tend to lead sex-segregated lives and not to be strongly oriented toward others.

That the degree of involvement in the role of neighbor is not significantly dependent upon attitudes toward the world in general is indicated by the complete lack of association between the neighboring scores and the scores on the relations-restrictive attitude scale. There is, however, a very strong association between the role of neighbor scale and the frequency of contact in all relations scale (see Table 47), as well as a less dramatic, but present, association with the isolation scale.[1a] This means that women who are active in neighboring also go out and see other people. There is an association between the role of neighbor and the role of sibling,[1b] and an even higher one between the role of neighbor and the role of friend.[1c] There is also a connection between neighboring and the rank order given to the various social roles of women. The low scorers in neighboring are prone to find the role of mother the most important one a woman can perform, while the high scorers so designate the role of wife. Thirty-one percent of those highly involved in neighboring, forty-two percent of the medium interactors, and forty-five percent of the low interactors chose the role of mother; fifty-nine percent, forty-nine percent, and forty-two percent of widows in these levels, respectively, gave the first rank to the role of wife. The low scorers are likely to place the role of daughter in one of the first four positions, seventy-two percent listing

TABLE 47: ASSOCIATION BETWEEN THE NEIGHBORING SCALE
AND THE FREQUENCY OF CONTACT SCALE
(BOTH COLLAPSED)

| *Frequency of Contact* | | *Role of Neighbor* | | |
|---|---|---|---|---|
| | *Row Sums* | *High (10–18)* | *Medium (05–09)* | *Low (00–04)* |
| High | 35 | 12 | 16 | 7 |
| (50–80) | | 34.2R | 45.7R | 20.0R |
| | 11.6 | 44.4C | 19.2C | 3.6C |
| Medium | 133 | 12 | 43 | 78 |
| (49–26) | | 9.0R | 32.3R | 58.6R |
| | 44.1 | 44.4C | 51.8C | 40.8C |
| Low | 133 | 3 | 24 | 106 |
| (01–25) | | 2.2R | 18.0R | 79.6R |
| | 44.1 | 11.1C | 28.9C | 55.4C |
| Column | | 27 | 83 | 191 |
| Sums | | 8.9 | 27.5 | 63.4 |

Gamma             .60
Chi-Square        57.62    (d.f. $= 4$); p $< .001$
Percent base $= 301$

it somewhere there, as compared to fifty-four percent of their high scoring counterparts. The difference between the extreme groups in their ranking of the role of housewife and the role of worker is not significant, and the only variation in ranking the community role is that active women in the role of neighbor are more apt to give it a higher rank than that given by the more isolated women. However, the differences are not dramatic, indicating that interaction with people living in the immediate vicinity does not necessarily produce orientation toward the larger community.

## VOLUNTARY ASSOCIATIONS

Numerous studies of the membership and degrees of involvement in voluntary associations among American women have concluded that these commitments depend not only on the type of community, but also on the individual's present socio-economic status and stage of the life cycle. Membership tends to be lower when children are small and higher during the *full-house plateau* stage when the children's activities outside of the home tend to expand the mother's horizons. At this stage voluntary associations become additional sources of meeting potential friends for middle- and upper-class women. Participation in voluntary associations tends to broaden the outlook of people beyond the immediate neighborhood and *vice versa,* except in the cases of block clubs whose function is the development of the immediate vicinity. Even PTA's draw members from more than a few blocks, and churches draw their congregations from a wide region.

Membership in voluntary associations can serve many functions. Chicago area widows aged fifty and over contributed the following list:

1. As a means of "keeping busy" or filling time, often recommended to new widows "to take your mind off of your problems."
2. As a means for carrying on certain activities, such as sewing, skiing, singing, etc. The assumption is usually made that people join voluntary associations primarily for relational reasons, but the task itself may be the main purpose.
3. As a means for continuing association with peers. The activities of a group offer opportunities for patterned and repeated contacts sometimes difficult to maintain in other ways. A widow can continue as a member of the women's bowling league, even if she no longer meets the married members in couple-companionate situations.
4. As a way of meeting potential friends.
5. As a means of meeting potential husbands or men in general. Often the life of the widow becomes barren of male companionship, to which she has become accustomed and which provides a kind of stimulation different from female friendship.
6. As a step toward re-engagement in society, after the limbo stage of grief is passed.
7. As a means of increasing involvement in other social roles, such as employment, community, etc.
8. As a means of developing a multi-dimensional social life space, often after a period during which it had been narrowed down to the family institution.

One respondent, who had grieved for a long time after the suicide of her husband who had been ill for years with cancer, explains how she became re-engaged in associational life with the help of a neighbor:

Q. *How did you join an organization?*

A. *Well, Mrs. Duncan, she said "You just can't sit around, you just can't live in that garden all the time." She was a great gardener too, and she said, "You're too young for that." She was about fifteen years older than I, and she said "You have to get out and you have to meet people," and she said: "You haven't made a contribution to this world," and she said: "It has to be more than just creating beauty for yourself. You have to get out and do it for other people." And so she got me into the Women's Club, and she also belonged to the Garden Club. Of course, I used to have florist shops of my own at one time, and so I got into the flower arranging business. I do the Christmas programs now. I'll do the Garden Club for Christmas, and I'll do the Women's Club for Christmas. Working with evergreens and things —it's always great fun—oh, it's just so much fun. That's how you do it— you just do it. Just get out and do it, hoping that somebody will maybe help you, take you by the hand and lead you a little bit of the way. But you have to take hold, too, because you can be led, and if you don't take hold of it, it doesn't mean anything—you have to want to.*

This respondent thus used voluntary associations to work out of grief, more than for any other reason. However, as her involvement increased, she started gaining other rewards from her participation. When she feels lonely she does "busy work" such as baking cookies and taking them over to a hospital, and she has a very active social life.

*I teach in flower arranging, and I'm conservation chairman of all McHenry County. I was just appointed that last week, and I have a big project next week, taking a busload of ladies into Garfield Park, and my minutes are counted, really. And then in the summertime, you know, trying to take care of this and be a part of all of that. Really, you find yourself coming and going. But it's good.*

*Q. Do you hold offices in any of these groups?*

*A. Yes, I'm Flower, Fruit and Guild Chairman for the Garden Club, Conservation Chairman for the McHenry Women's Club, and Conservation Chairman for the McHenry County Federation of Women's Clubs.*

Widows who move to new neighborhoods, immediately after the death of the husband or with later life changes, find voluntary associations an excellent means of integrating themselves in the area and developing new relations. A pastor's wife explained this process in great detail, beginning with a newcomer's group and the church. Of course, the use of organized social groups to meet such functions depends upon knowledge as to how to find them, how to judge if they will be compatible, how to contact representatives, and so forth. There is a whole ritual of involvement, often unknown to older women who lack a history of such engagement. Furthermore, joining voluntary associations requires self-confidence and trust that one is acceptable and will not be hurt in the encounters. Some widows join social groups, or continue memberships held in the past, because of a strong interest in an activity carried out within them. Others involve themselves as a reaction to lonesome widowhood, with no concern for the specific goals of the association: "Before my husband's death, I did not belong to anything. I was all absorbed with my family, and I'm not sure that's always a good thing. I think you should be involved in some outside activities because, if you're not, it takes a while to become involved and unless you're fortunate enough to have friends that sort of entice you or push you into things, you're inclined to build a wall around yourself. I know I could have closed every door and just stayed here, but that isn't healthy," explains one of the active women. The most frequent advice offered to a hypothetical new widow by the respondents is: "Get out of the house and join groups" or "If you can't get a job, do volunteer work."

Most respondents who do not belong to any voluntary associations simply declare such a lack of involvement, but some feel a need to explain why they never were or are no longer members or active participants. Several complain that the only groups available to widows are sex-segregated, while they are accustomed to couple-companionate activities and interactions. Such statements are usually underscored by hostility or frustration. Very few clubs encourage membership by unmarried men and women, an exception being "Parents without Partners." One respondent, who has since remarried, was complaining during the original interview that she had no chance to meet men:

Q. *And there are no clubs or organizations?*

A. *Well, there's a girl in the office who is divorced. She is quite a bit younger than I am, and she is very anxious to remarry. And so she wanted to go to this "Parents Without Partners." So we went there. One night we went to Crystal Lake; but oh, the type of people were different than we were. And then we went to one at Rolling Meadows and they were a much nicer type of people, but Rolling Meadows is so far and in order to really become a part of a group like that you have to go to many things they do, which meant we would be making the trip several times a week and we didn't think it seemed worth the effort.*

The explanations of non-involvement in voluntary associations reflect the difficulties of life for widows. Old groups must be dropped if membership depended upon being married or the presence of a particular companion. This holds true for women's auxiliaries of male groups. Widows who move from an area have trouble attending meetings, either because they have no convenient transportation or because traveling back and forth costs so much. Many older women are afraid to go out alone at night and do not want to impose on friends to pick them up or drop them off. Some do not even know people well enough to consider making such a request. In fact, the lack of means for getting to meetings appears as the major restraint, and no one reported transportation service as part of the activity of their voluntary associations, in spite of the obvious need. Health and money constraints, lack of interest because of the death of the husband, work role conflicts, the break-up of the group itself as the members age; these are some of the reasons given by older widows why they do not belong to social groups or why they are not active. Participation may be broken off suddenly, or the process may be gradual. The most costly or inconvenient groups are dropped first, and those giving most meaning to members are clung to longer. Some women report being limited to clothing in which they are ashamed to appear in public, others gradually lose self-confidence as to their desirability as members. The stigma of appearing old or disfigured, or of not being able to hear what is going on, to walk fast enough, and do the work involved in being active is enough to wither motivation. Some women never did belong to organized groups. One respondent explained this very bluntly: "That didn't come into my category of class. I just never had the education to join anything."

### Characteristics of Widows Belonging to Voluntary Associations

Almost half (forty-eight percent) of the respondents claim never to have belonged to any voluntary association prior to the husband's death, thirty-three percent identified one or two such groups, and nineteen percent, or a full fifth, belonged to three or more groups (see Table 48). At the time they were being interviewed, however, sixty-three percent were not active in any group and only thirteen percent were involved in three or more associations. Thus, widowhood was accompanied by a drop in participation. An interesting aspect about the changes in memberships and degree of involvement in social organizations is the relative consistency by age. The only age category which suffers a disproportionate loss of active memberships is between sixty-five and sixty-nine. A gradual decrease of both memberships and active involvement was expected with increased age.

Education is the one characteristic which differentiates most strongly the amount of past participation (see Table 49). The significance of the relation between education and the number of memberships prior to the death of the husband is very high. Variations occur in the type of group to which older women belonged by race. The whites more often belong to national, i.e. ethnic, groups or women's lodges in men's organizations; the blacks more often belonged to church groups. The differences in

TABLE 48: THE NUMBER OF ASSOCIATIONS THE RESPONDENTS BELONGED TO PRIOR TO WIDOWHOOD AND THE ONES IN WHICH THEY ARE NOW ACTIVE, BY THEIR AGE IN FIVE YEAR INTERVALS

| | | *Memberships* | | | | | |
| | | *Ever Belonged* | | | *Now Belongs* | | |
| *Age* | *Number* | *None* | *1 or 2* | *3 plus* | *None* | *1 or 2* | *3 plus* |
|---|---|---|---|---|---|---|---|
| TOTAL | | %<br>48 | %<br>33 | %<br>19 | %<br>63 | %<br>24 | %<br>13 |
| 54– | 39 | 56 | 23 | 20 | 69 | 17 | 13 |
| 55–59 | 40 | 48 | 35 | 18 | 60 | 22 | 18 |
| 60–64 | 72 | 43 | 35 | 22 | 58 | 26 | 15 |
| 65–69 | 46 | 44 | 36 | 22 | 70 | 17 | 13 |
| 70–74 | 35 | 43 | 40 | 17 | 51 | 37 | 11 |
| 75–79 | 42 | 52 | 36 | 12 | 69 | 24 | 7 |
| 80–84 | 16 | 50 | 31 | 19 | 69 | 18 | 12 |
| 85 plus | 11 | 54 | 27 | 18 | 73 | 27 | 00 |

TABLE 49: THE NUMBER OF ORGANIZATIONS OF WHICH RESPONDENT WAS A MEMBER BEFORE BECOMING A WIDOW, BY EDUCATION OF RESPONDENT

| | | | *Number of Memberships* | | | | | |
| *Education* | *None* | | *One or Two* | | *3 Plus* | | *Total* * | |
|---|---|---|---|---|---|---|---|---|
| | *No.* | % | *No.* | % | *No.* | % | *No.* | % |
| less than 8 | 43 | 57 | 26 | 34 | 7 | 9 | 76 | 25 |
| 8–12 | 92 | 48 | 67 | 35 | 34 | 18 | 193 | 64 |
| 13 plus | 8 | 25 | 8 | 25 | 16 | 50 | 32 | 10 |
| Total | 143 | 48 | 101 | 34 | 57 | 19 | 301 | 99 |

* $x^2$ with 4 d.f. = 35.8 or p < .001

type of association account for the fact that, contrary to many assumptions, there are no differences by race in the number of groups in which widows were active.

Income is an important factor so far as current memberships are concerned. The least involved income group is that between $1,000 and $2,999. From the peak of seventy-four percent who are now active in no social organization the percentage of inactives falls gradually and steadily to seventeen percent for those with incomes over $16,000. Fifty-four percent of the respondents who refused to answer the question about their current income also do not belong to any group. At either extreme of the membership continuum, seven percent of respondents who live on incomes under $1,000, and fifty percent of those with the highest incomes, belong to three or more voluntary associations. The proportion rises steadily with the exception of the $9,000 to $10,999 category which, for some reason, are involved in no more than two groups. In fact, only one of the nine persons in that income category belongs to more than one group. Thus, there is a direct relationship between highest family income and non-participation. One hundred percent of the wives of farm and other laborers, and eighty percent of the wives of managers, are not active in any group. The lowest proportion for non-participants is found among the widows of professionals; they are also the most likely to be involved in more than two groups (twenty-four percent), followed by the widows of salesmen (twenty-two percent) and of craftsmen (seventeen percent).

The woman's occupation seems to influence her involvement in voluntary associations, in that memberships are held mainly by women in three work groups. Few professionals are completely inactive, and they are also the most to be involved in more than two groups. Twenty-four percent of them have multiple memberships with twenty-two percent of the saleswomen and seventeen percent of the craftswomen being equally active.

The Protestant Chicago area widows are more likely to have multiple groups in which they are active than are Catholics or members of other faiths. On the other end of the scale, the Protestants have the second highest proportion (seventy-one percent) of women who are not active in any organization, the highest being of women who lack any religious affiliation. Since memberships of older widows are so often connected with a church, it is not surprising that the religiously unaffiliated have no group connection. Jewish women are the most apt to belong to one group; proportionately very few of them (thirty-three percent) are total abstainers. The differences between these groups are significant. In terms of national identity, the English, Welsh, and Scotch widows are the most likely to be in many groups, and the least likely of the major nationalities to abstain from membership. Italians, Scandinavians, Russians and Poles are not active, nor are those in the "other" category, which usually refers to blacks.

Multiple memberships in voluntary associations are related to a generally broad social life space in the past and present. These women now have, and always have had, more money than the non-members. They are better educated and had been married to better educated men. They do not have major health constraints, partly, if not mainly, due to the fact that they led a less physically damaging life than their non-active counterparts. The highly involved widow in voluntary associations has some, though not very many, children, some living siblings, and some grandchildren. She tends to be involved in relations with them at a level measured at least as medium, if not high.

A profile of the widow who is most likely not to belong to any organizations would include the following characteristics: an income of between $1,000 and $2,999 (seventy-four percent); born outside of the United States (seventy-four percent, compared to sixty-seven percent for other areas in America, and fifty-six percent for Chicago); worked most of her married life (seventy-five percent); Catholic (seventy-one percent), or lacking religious identification entirely (eighty-six percent); Italian national background (seventy-seven percent); eight children (one hundred percent); no siblings (seventy-four percent); no friends who are also widows (eighty-eight percent) or all friends in that marital situation (seventy-five percent); and length of widowhood, thirty years or over.

The widows who are no longer members of voluntary associations—and all but fifteen percent of them never had been so involved—do not wish to remarry (sixty-six percent); define the compensation of widowhood as less work (seventy-eight percent); yet feel that the main problem of this marital condition is not having anyone around whom work can be focused (one hundred percent with six cases), or not having anyone to care for (eighty-nine percent with nine cases). Again, as with friendship, the women isolated from social groups see no change in themselves as a result of widowhood, unless it be increased worry (sixty-nine percent).

Those who are active in more than one group see changes in themselves, listing freedom (twenty-eight percent) and independence (seventeen percent); twenty-three percent listing being more busy as a second change. Twenty-six of the very active women define the change in their social life upon widowhood: "I do more now." Not surprisingly, the respondents who belong to and actively participate in many voluntary associations are more likely to list the role of community member in a high rank than widows who belong to no group. Few respondents put the community role in the first or second position, usually reserving these places for motherhood and wifehood, but twenty-nine percent of those who rank it third have multiple memberships, and forty-six percent have no affiliation. It must be remembered that the total population includes only thirteen percent of activists and sixty-three percent of non-affiliated women. The contrast is significant and indicates a strong association between attitudes toward the community and involvement in it.

All in all, most widows do not list community participation as the most important obligation of women, with fifty percent placing it last, and thirty-two percent placing it fifth in a rank order of this role in comparison to those of wife, mother, housewife, daughter, and worker. Half never belonged to any voluntary associations. Those who dropped out after reaching widowhood tend to have listed their prior level of involvement as inactive or now restricted because of health and finances.

## THE ROLE OF WORKER

Many sociologists have found that the role of worker lacks real significance in the lives of American women in any but professional occupations and that involvement has been dependent upon the family life cycle. In prior centuries, women worked as unpaid members of the family unit or as servants in the homes of others. The beginning of industrialization brought them piecemeal work in crafts or the needle industries in their homes (Smutz, 1959). Lower-class and caste women have often been forced to work for people other than their families and they have continued out of sheer necessity to seek employment as societies urbanized and industrialized. Traditionally, the middle- and upper-class women have not been involved in occupations away from the home, because of the assumption that their fathers, husbands, and sons would support them. In fact, the male members of the family often objected to females' attempts to find employment, because of the implication that their support was inadequate. Unmarried girls were the first to enter the urbanized and industrialized labor force in great numbers, and most female Americans have worked prior to marriage. The recent trend in paid employment has involved increasingly large proportions of the middle-class married women who are mothers. This trend is statistically significant. At first, only those urbanites whose children were well on their way out of the home or who were left with the first phase of *the shrinking circle stage* ventured into the labor market. In recent years, however, the employment of women outside of the home has been increasingly accepted, if not expected, not only in America but in Europe. The age of workers has gone down with an increasingly large number of women staying at their jobs and simply taking maternity leaves. However, as P. Chombard de Lauwe (1962) concluded, lower-class women work for basic necessities and the economically better situated wives work for luxuries.

Either way, the working woman is not considered, and does not consider herself, as involved in a job for reasons other than the passing of time until marriage or obtaining money to help its life style. Even women who enjoy working or their specific job justify their employment with economic arguments. It is quite possible that the recent women's liberation movement will change this orientation toward the occupations, but as of now this role is considered inferior to those of wife and mother. This attitude holds true not only for women who are actually in the *full-house plateau* of both sets of relations, but even for other females in different stages of the life cycle.

The presence of such attitudes is evident in the orientations toward life and in the work careers of the Chicago area widows. Work histories tend to be very erratic in terms of the average number of years at any particular job and the number of entrances and exits from the labor force. Few of the respondents identify with a particular occupation, partly because very few are, or have been, in prestige-giving and loyalty-producing professions, and partly because few people of either sex develop strong identifications with employing organizations. Like the industrial workers whose social worlds were investigated by Robert Dubin (1956), the older woman in the Chicago area can easily leave a job, even when she enjoys it, if life circumstances change. However, few have actually held jobs which gave them pleasure or a sense of worth and identification.

Seventy-four percent of the widows now fifty years of age or over worked prior to marriage. When asked about their "best" job, fifty percent of the women responded that they left it by 1950. The highest proportion of the respondents did not work during marriage. Only eleven percent worked "all the time," eleven percent were employed "most of the time," thirty-eight percent "some of the time," and forty percent "never." Those who were working "some of the time" often did some baby-sitting or took a job before Christmas. Whatever the working pattern they had established, it was not usually affected by the last illness of the spouse, either because the husband died suddenly, because they did not need to change the pattern, or because they were themselves by then beyond the age of employment. The thirty-seven women whose work patterns were changed by the husband's last illness include eleven who had to go to work, eleven who had to increase the time devoted to this role, and fifteen who had to either quit the job or decrease its number of hours of involvement.

Forty-eight percent of the respondents were employed during widowhood. However, only fifty-two of these 145 women found relevant the question: "Were you able to get the kind of job you had held before, one not as good, or a better one?" The others had either never worked before or were already employed before their husband's death. Forty-four percent of the fifty-two women who returned to work obtained jobs they evaluated as on the same level as their previous jobs, which is not surprising considering the kind of occupations to which they were limited (see Table 11, or Table 50). The initial assumption underlying the design for the interviews was that the majority of women seeking employment after their husband's death would be housewives who would have to take jobs vastly inferior to those held in past years or that they would have to obtain training to make them more competent. The assumption ignored the fact that these older women were unlikely ever to have had highly specialized skills. Most of the widows had been in clerical jobs, in unskilled or semi-skilled operative positions in factories, or in private domestic service, none of which require formal updating and retraining. Only five

TABLE 50: OCCUPATIONAL DISTRIBUTIONS OF RESPONDENT
IN BEST JOB AND IN LAST OR PRESENT JOB

|  | Best Job | | Present or Last Job | |
|---|---|---|---|---|
| Occupation | Percent | Number | Percent | Number |
| Professionals | 9 | 25 | 9 | 20 |
| Farmers | — | 1 | — | — |
| Managers | 4 | 10 | 4 | 10 |
| Clerical | 34 | 91 | 26 | 59 |
| Sales Worker | 3 | 9 | 4 | 10 |
| Craftswomen | 4 | 12 | 5 | 12 |
| Operative | 22 | 58 | 21 | 49 |
| Service Worker | 22 | 59 | 28 | 64 |
| Farm Laborer | 1 | 2 | 1 | 2 |
| Laborers | 1 | 3 | 2 | 4 |
| No Answer | 1 | 3* | 2 | 5 |
| Not appropriate | — | 29 | — | 29 |
| Percent Base | 100 | 270 | 100 | 230 |

* Not counted in percentages.

of the 301 respondents went back to school in widowhood, and three entered special programs preparing them for new jobs. The whole series of questions referring to retraining is simply irrelevant to this population.

When asked why they left their best jobs, a high proportion of the widows replied: "I got married" (thirty-two percent of a base of 226 respondents). Eight percent did so because they had a baby, two percent were influenced by the husband's last illness or death, twelve percent faced a deterioration of their own health, and another twelve percent had to retire. Unusual circumstances, such as geographic mobility, faced thirty-four respondents. Quite a few women quit in response to other emergencies in the family or problems of the work organization, reflecting the marginal position of such workers and their companies. For example, several mentioned that the firm folded or had to lay off workers during the depression; some replied that mothers, children, or other relatives became ill in their homes, so that their care had to supercede job obligations.

Many of the older widows worked on-and-off as emergencies arose, in order to provide finances to carry them on to the next stage of life. A job is not regarded by them as part of "engagement" in a larger community, but merely as "work" for money. This attitude extends not only to day-work with private families, but to factories and other occupational locations which require minimal skills and offer impersonal treatment and easy entrance and exit. The combined history of the involvement of widows in economic roles defies the "career" and other middle-class biases of much of occupational research. The ebb and flow of work is usually assumed to follow a systematic model: work prior to marriage, possibly extending up until the birth of the first child; cessation of employment while children are small, and sometimes during the life of the husband; and a return after some training, when widowhood creates such a necessity. The model is not pure fantasy, since it is applicable to middle-aged women of America; it does not, however, coincide with the experience of the older widow in an urban center.

The comments regarding working history are particularly applicable to the residents of Chicago's black community. The factor of race is significant here as in other aspects of social integration, and the differences in life start early. Almost eighty percent of the whites, compared to only fifty-four percent of the blacks, worked before marriage. There are two main reasons for this variation. In the first place, the blacks married at a much younger age. In the second place most of them grew up in the rural or semi-rural South, where jobs for young girls were rare, if not totally absent. Most of the work they reported before marriage fits the American stereotype of women with such a background: they picked cotton or helped their families in other forms of marginal farming. Some of the European immigrants also mentioned working with their families in agricultural pursuits, but most of the whites listed their first job as one in a secondary organization with a specified amount of pay. Another basic difference between the two races is that twenty-six percent of the blacks, compared to three percent of the whites, do not remember the dates they began and finished their best or their last job. Life circumstances are again a major factor in these differences. Most blacks are or have been domestics, and this kind of service does not have the formal organization's clear-cut beginning and ending. It usually involves, especially in modern times in the urban north, a high turnover of employers. The freedom to change employers or working schedules, to drop out of work for a while and then return, are major advantages to such marginal women who often find it impossible to maintain a regular schedule. "I like day-work, because you get the money right away" is a statement of another advantage to this kind of a job. Such conceptions, however, contain minimal identification with the employer. The work itself is usually performed alone and is sufficiently exhausting, when combined with inadequate diets and work at home, to prevent the job from being a means of social integration. The exceptions to these domestic workers are the respondents who report continued and very satisfactory relations with employers viewed as members of the family, rather than through the "day-work" mentality (see Liebow, 1967).

Only three of the blacks, or six percent, worked before marriage, but never during marriage or in widowhood; thirty-two percent worked only while they were legally married, and before their former husband had died. Eight percent worked both before and during marriage, and fourteen percent during and after, but not before. This leaves thirty percent who "always" worked. However, only twenty percent of the women actually spent all of their married life in full-time employment. Another twenty percent worked most of their marital careers, and thirty-four percent worked some of the time. By contrast, only one percent of the whites worked only during marriage, twenty-two percent worked before and during, but not after, nine percent during and after, and twenty-seven percent "always." The distributions show striking differences. White respondents are not likely to have worked only during marriage; they either have an in-and-out entrance into the market or they work before and some time during marriage. Black women are more likely to work to help support the family or to be vague about the connection between marriage and work. Proportionally more of the blacks (twelve percent) than the whites (seven percent) never worked in a regular job. In addition, black working women are most likely to have worked all during marriage or most of the time.

A higher proportion of whites than blacks specify the best job either as one in the past, followed by a lesser job, or one which is identical to the last (see Table 51). The differences are due mostly to the fact that, while ninety percent of the whites held specifically memorable jobs and were willing to define one as the best, most black respondents have had such complex but periphery work careers in terms of employer and dates, within a simplified range of occupations, that their history is difficult to trace. More whites than blacks are able to state that they had different kinds of jobs in their lives and that one of these stands out in memory as particularly good. The fact that the average number of years of work in a particular job is similar for both groups is due mostly to this tendency of the black women to generalize their employers and to state that their

TABLE 51: AVERAGE NUMBER OF YEARS OF BLACK AND WHITE
WIDOWS IN THEIR BEST AND IN THEIR LATEST
JOB AND THE PERCENTAGES OF WOMEN IN EACH
COMMUNITY WHO HAVE SUCH A WORK HISTORY

| | Black Respondents | | White Respondents | |
|---|---|---|---|---|
| Type of Job | Average No. of Years in Job | % of Persons | Average No. of Years in Job | % of Persons |
| Best job | 9 | 22 | 9 | 36 |
| Years in job, not working now | 6 | 14 | 6 | 23 |
| Years in job, still working there | 7 | 8 | 5 | 13 |
| Last job is best, not working now | 13 | 34 | 10 | 45 |
| Last job is best, still working there | 11 | 10 | 16 | 9 |
| Never worked | | 12 | | 7 |
| Don't know which best; all the same | | 24 | | 3 |
| | N = 52 | 102 | N = 249 | 100 |

work history consisted of 22 or 30 years of continued service, while the
whites who had not been domestics (most have not) are likely to list the
number of years with each employer or in each type of job. The exceptions to these comments are white women who worked in family businesses or ones who held professional or semi-professional positions with
several employers. Thus, a doctor's receptionist did not list each medical
man for whom she worked. Family businesses or assistant's positions
provide work for very few widows at the present time of their lives partly
because they are harder to maintain sporadically than domestic service.
Being a widow of an entrepreneur whose business is retained or a nurse
to her own husband are events not likely to be experienced by the older
black resident of metropolitan Chicago.

The effects of the employment differences between black and white
women show up in the way these women met their expenses immediately
after the death of the husband (see Table 52). It was much harder for
the blacks than for the whites to build a solid foundation for themselves,
because they had not experienced a consistent history of increasing family
income in prior years. Not only did they go in and out of work, but they
were without a husband for longer periods of time and did not have a
steady flow of support coming from the male. Thus, they had less of a
cushion to fall back upon when suddenly faced with the illness or the
death of the husband. Sixty percent of the white women had enough
money on hand or were able to convert holdings into funds to carry them
through this period of time, but only half of that proportion of Negro

TABLE 52: PERCENTAGES OF NEGRO AND WHITE WIDOWS
USING SELECTED MEANS OF OBTAINING FUNDS FOR
SELF-MAINTENANCE AFTER THE HUSBAND'S DEATH

| | Proportion Using This Means | | | | |
| *Means* | *Negro* | *N* | *White* | *N* | $x^2$ |
|---|---|---|---|---|---|
| Continued to work | 41% | 19 | 20% | 45 | 10.04* |
| Went to work | 17 | 8 | 11 | 25 | 1.50 |
| Had enough on hand, cashed bonds,etc. | 33 | 15 | 60 | 138 | 11.87* |
| Family gave help | 9 | 4 | 25 | 58 | 6.06** |
| Had to borrow from family | 2 | 1 | 4 | 9 | .32 |
| Had to borrow from friends | 4 | 2 | 1 | 3 | 1.94 |
| Borrowed from lending institution | 4 | 2 | 1 | 2 | 3.20 |
| Had to go on relief or welfare | 13 | 6 | 5 | 11 | 4.47 |
| Did not spend, did not pay bills, or got in debt | — | — | 4 | 9 | 1.86 |

d.f. $= 2$; $p < .001 = 13.8$
\* $p < .01 = 9.2$
\*\* $p < .05 = 6.0$
Categories not mutually exclusive

widows were able to do this. Fifty-eight percent of the blacks either went to work or continued in jobs already held during marriage.

## The Rank Order Assigned to the Role of Worker

A significant aspect of the interviews of Chicago area widows proved to be their judgment of the relative importance of the role of worker in relation to that of mother, daughter, friend, and community member. Several factors influenced these assignments, including the woman's education, her working experience during marriage and widowhood, income and general financial condition, length of widowhood, and the number of living children and siblings. Of particular significance is the proportion of time the respondent was employed during marriage (see Table 53): Several interesting facts emerge from the relation between working experience and the rank given the role of worker. Only two percent of the respondents rank this role as the most important, but these are the women who have worked all their married lives. At least, this group forms eleven percent of the sample, but fifty percent of those who rank the working role above any other, and thirty-eight percent of those who assign it second place. At the other end of the continuum, thirty-five percent of the respondents consider it as the least important role a woman can perform, and these are the women who have never worked. This

TABLE 53: PERCENTAGES OF WOMEN ASSIGNING THE ROLE
OF WORKER TO ONE OF SIX POSITIONS IN A RANK
ORDER OF IMPORTANCE BY THE PROPORTION OF
TIME THEY WORKED DURING MARRIAGE

| Work Proportion During Marriage | Row Sums | Rank of Importance | | | | | | No Answer |
|---|---|---|---|---|---|---|---|---|
| | | First | Second | Third | Fourth | Fifth | Sixth | |
| All the time | 11 | 50 | 38 | 19 | 16 | 10 | 3 | 10 |
| Most of time | 10 | 17 | 15 | 14 | 8 | 12 | 6 | 17 |
| Some of time | 38 | 17 | 31 | 43 | 48 | 39 | 34 | 40 |
| Never | 40 | 17 | 15 | 24 | 29 | 38 | 56 | 33 |
| Column Sums | 100 | 2 | 5 | 8 | 14 | 36 | 35 | 11* |

* Not included in percentages, which are based on 271 cases. Eleven percent includes
30 cases.

distribution can be explained by the fact that women who have experienced work in conjunction with other familial roles "understand" its
value, that is, its contribution to a total life; those who did not participate
underplay its importance. Also, women who value the role of worker
or career builder are the most likely to have sought and obtained work
even during marriage. It is quite probable that both of these factors are
operating simultaneously, with mutual influence of one upon the other.

Women who have been employed since widowhood are also likely to
rank the role of worker higher than their housewife counterparts. Half
of the total sample had that experience after the death of the husband,
but sixty-seven percent of those who placed the role of worker in first
rank, sixty-nine percent of those who gave it second place, eighty-one
percent of those who rank it third, fifty-eight percent of those assigning
it the fourth slot, forty-eight percent relegating it to fifth place, and
thirty-eight percent of those who see it as the least important role had
worked at that time. Widows who were forced by the death of their
husband to seek employment for either financial or psychological reasons
tend to rank the role of wife and mother first or second and to put the
role of worker immediately following, ahead of the roles of daughter,
friend, and community member. The during-marriage workers sometimes replace either the mother or wife role with the occupational one,
perhaps feeling less of an obligation to declare their identification with
the husband.

In general, women who have lived on limited family budgets, who
came from Europe or maintained black families, and who have not been
highly educated usually find work roles more important than women who

are financially comfortable, who have and have had higher incomes, and who are more established in their life style. The native Chicagoan is most likely to place the role of worker (career woman) in fourth or sixth place; the migrant from other parts of America, in second place; and the immigrant from other parts of the world, in first or second place. College graduates rank it as the least important role of women, while fifth- to seventh-grade finishers find it the most important, and those with less education assign it second rank. Even professionally trained women place this role in third position, behind that of wife and mother. The women who do not know how many years of schooling their husbands achieved are likely to place the role of worker second or third in importance; the wives of first- through fourth-grade finishers are apt to see it as second. The higher the education of the man, the lower the role of worker descends. The occupational location of the late husband has a similar effect: wives of service workers are much more apt to put the employment role of the woman in one of the first three positions than are wives of professional men (thirty-five percent to fifteen percent). A very dramatic difference appears when the factors of current income and self-definition of financial condition are considered. Interestingly enough, the income itself is less significant than the evaluation of its sufficiency. There is a clear negative relation between the judgments of the role of worker and of current financial comfort: the higher the latter, the lower the former. All of the few "fairly wealthy" widows place the worker role in one of the two bottom positions, but half of the women who give it first order importance are located in the "really restricted" category.

The income which the widows now have available to them also influences how they feel about the relative importance of the worker role. Those trying to live on less than $1,000 definitely feel that being employed is the first or second most important role a woman can perform, while those living on $9,000 to $10,999 assign it last place. Interestingly, women in even higher income categories tend to move the worker role into higher positions. This is often due to the professional involvement of the widow, which contributes to both the income and the judgment of the occupational role as the third most important.

The number of children a woman has still living is somewhat related to the number to which she gave birth and her past socio-economic position which facilitated their survival; these factors, too, influence her ranking of the role of worker. Those with no children are disproportionately likely to rank the occupational set of relations in the first four positions, while those with three or more children place it fifth or last. Although women having no children form only eighteen percent of the population, they comprise eighty-three percent of those ranking work as the most important role of their sex, twenty-three percent of those giving it second place, twenty-eight percent of those assigning it third rank and twenty-nine percent of those putting it fourth. Mothers of one surviving child are most apt to give the work role third position, after those of wife and mother. At the other end of the continuum, mothers of two or more children refused to rank the role of worker first, and only three of the twenty-eight respondents who have five or more children place it in one of the top three positions. Having several living siblings also tends to make women less oriented toward the role of worker than having only one brother or sister. Those with none or with only two siblings are the most likely to place it second. With the exception of widows with five siblings, who do not follow the pattern by assigning work to second or third rank, those with more siblings place it further down in comparison to other roles. The general trend seems to be that women coming from large families whose members have managed to survive and to produce several living offspring do not put working roles in the top positions in an order of importance. The less educated and the poorer widows, who have faced many problems of self-maintenance, tend to respect the occupational role above those of community member and daughter, friend and sometimes even above wife and mother.

The respondents most likely to rank the role of worker in the top three positions are likely to have been widowed a long time. Those newly deprived of their husbands never rank it first or second, but place it a step higher than those who have already worked out a method for handling their financial problems.

## SUMMARY AND CONCLUSIONS

Generally speaking, the educational achievement of the widow and of her late husband, as well as the financial and occupational status they were able to achieve separately or jointly, influences heavily the widow's participation in her community, whether through neighboring, voluntary associations, or work. The lower-class woman depends more on chance to determine her residence and her relations with people living nearby than the middle-class woman. Her whole life tends to be minimally involved in the community and sporadic in that contact is easily broken by mobility. Her work career is similar, being one of in and out ventures in jobs chosen haphazardly. She does not determine her residential or employment location by a careful analysis of the environment and her needs. The more middle-class woman leads a more organized life, arranging for event-socializing with neighbors, going to meetings of voluntary associations, and either presently working or having a history of multiple-contact employment.

More widows belonged in the past to voluntary associations than are currently active in such groups. Financial and health constraints, as well as geographical mobility, are the main reasons for a drop in memberships. Those who never belonged are foreign or born outside of Chicago, and worked most of their lives, although usually in marginal occupations.

Regardless of class, most of the older widows who have worked in the past held jobs sporadically, in response to family events. The more desperately they needed the income produced through employment, the more highly they value the role of worker. Women who enjoyed a comfortable life through the efforts of the husband do not consider women's employment to be important. Those who depended on their own income, both in marriage and in widowhood, and who were always on the borderline of poverty respect the worker role. These are very realistic attitudes, if an occupation or "career" is seen as significant for women only because of the money. For these generations of women covered by the study, employment means exactly that—a chance to bring money to the home. Other rewards of work were not sufficient to warrant its placement among the most important roles for women, either because of personal value judgments or because of the cultural rejection of such sets of relations.

The involvement of women in the community, through neighboring, voluntary associations, or jobs emphasizes again the importance of education and other background traits which determine socio-economic status. The urban situation demands voluntaristic involvement which is dependent upon personally developed abilities and attitudes. Without these the less educated, lower-class woman remains at the periphery of the social world, particularly in later life and in widowhood.

## NOTES

1  a. Gamma $-.31$; $x^2 = 15.28$; d.f. $= 4$; p $<.005$
   b. $x^2 = 8.74$; d.f. $= 4$; border between p $<.10$ and p $<.05$ Gamma $= .32$
   c. $x^2 = 19.09$; d.f. $= 4$; p $<.001$; Gamma $.05$
   d. $x^2 = 35.8$; d.f. $= 4$; p $<.001$

# 7

# Summary,
# Conclusions, and Implications

## SUMMARY AND CONCLUSIONS

This book is a result of research focused upon the roles and life styles of
a very specific group of people: American urban widows fifty years of age
or older. These women form only a segment of at most two generations
of one society; they present an historical instance of people born and
brought up under conditions which are not likely to be duplicated in
future generations of human beings. However, exploratory investigations
of family literature and other sources of sociological data indicate the
relevance of this type of study for understanding the broad trends of
world change. Not only the United States, but many other countries as
well, are undergoing dramatic modifications in the degrees and forms of
urbanization, industrialization, and social complexity. Purposely introduced or repercussive changes are affecting the very foundations of the
lives of their members, particularly in their relations to each other and
to the larger social structure. The whole process involves people unsys-
tematically, without any institutionalized steps assisting role and relational shifts. The general facts about life changes accompanying these
social trends are known. This study hopes to clarify the actual effects
of these changes upon the lives of a specific category of societal members,
a category which is deeply affected by, and inadequately prepared for,
them. By holding constant age over fifty years, sex, marital status, and
metropolitan residence, we are able to follow in greater depth the way in
which modern life affects social relations than would be possible if all
categories of societal participants were covered.

The basic conclusion of this study is that the way in which different
types of women re-engage in society following the death of the husband
reflects their location in the modern social system. The overall trends in
social structure are toward increasingly voluntaristic engagement in

achieved, functionally-oriented social roles which are performed in large groups and contain secondary social relations. The cultural background of many societal members, however, is such as to prevent the utilization of most of the resources of the complex urban world, restricting them to a small social life space, with almost automatically ascribed social relations. The societies from which most Americans came purposely taught their members to value only long-lasting social relations, to suspect strangers, large groups, and the broader world outside. People were socialized and educated for established social roles, built into packages around the *status roles* of nobleman, peasant, woman, eldest offspring, etc. (see Lopata, 1964). They were discouraged from experimentation in actions deemed inappropriate to such status roles. The basis of traditional societies, many aspects of whose culture survive in modern life— particularly in the family institution—lay in passive stances from all but the elite, that is, acceptance of established norms, leadership figures, and personality models for given roles. Each person was dependent upon formalized need suppliers. He was socialized only in his own set of roles, without full understanding of the components of complementary roles. In such a society, wives were able to function only if they had husbands or husband substitutes in the form of kin members who received the rights and provided the necessary tools and cooperative actions. The relatively self-sufficient unit of the farm, the village, the small town, or the ethnic community surrounded each individual from birth to death with familiar faces, behaviors, and demands within a constricted social life space.

Urbanization, industrialization, and increasing complexity (Winch and Blumberg, 1968) of the social structures have removed the foundations of traditional roles without introducing relevant re-education or necessary modification in the socialization of existing members. Nor have the societies developed adequate means for preserving the self-identity and dignity of those members who are made obsolete by the changes. People quite capable of living in the society in which they were born and socialized are often unable to function in the society in which they are now located. Extremes of success in matching society and person are clearly visible among urban residents. The modern society is sometimes matched by the "modern" man or woman, who is socialized into a multi-dimensional problem-solving personality. Such an individual is able to examine the social environment, to determine objectively future goals in many levels of involvement, to think out the possible consequences of alternative solutions for reaching these goals, and to put into action complex but flexible plans. Given seventy-plus years, this kind of person is able to change his social relations, to enter and to exit from social roles as he reaches the different stages of life or redefines his situation, and to constrict or expand his social life space by self-initiated action rather than reaction to external events.

In the case of widows, such a self-initiating woman, though experiencing strong life disorganization at her husband's death, is nonetheless able to withdraw from, modify, or enter social relations in terms of her own re-examination of life styles and goals. After the period of temporary passivity experienced in grief, this kind of woman selects certain aspects of the role of wife to be continued after her husband's death and does not try to hang onto aspects impossible to maintain. She relates to adult children in a free flow of interaction, recognizing the self-defined needs of both sides of the relation. She moves away from friendships which were based only on couple-companionate leisure-time activities to ones providing greater or different personal intimacy. She enters or retains roles in the greater community and the society and builds a life style suited to her individual needs and developed potentials. She remains flexible, assuming that solutions found to be satisfactory at one stage of life may not be so at a later date. Realizing that the presence of her late husband resulted in a role and personality specialization which makes widowhood difficult, she develops substitutes for his contributions by taking over certain of his functions, assigning some to others, or dropping a duty or right entirely. The complexity of the change in her life is likely to be great, but her consciousness of the need to make constant behavioral and relational adjustments is much more developed than that of other widows. Thus, she is not apt to state that she and her life have not changed as a result of the death of the husband. Rather, she spends the time following this event in re-examining the resources of the complex society to see how she can match them with her present and future life goals.

A different type of urbanite is able to retain or duplicate the village type of life for which the traditional socialization prepared her (see Herbert Gans', *Urban Villagers*, 1962). Ethnic communities still survive in which the residents have lived for decades and in which life may be limited to a particular group of houses, streets, and shops. The rest of the city or the society simply do not exist in the minds or identities of these residents. In the case of a woman, such a situation may prevent any dramatic change from following the death of her husband. Being immersed in kin relations, a very close peer group, or a network of neighbors, such a woman may continue many of her involvements with little modification after becoming a widow. This is particularly true of the lower-class urbanite. A similar lack of change may apply in the case of a suburbanite who had never developed multi-faceted relations with the husband, but lived in a sex-segregated world.

A third type of urban widow is the social isolate, either because of her lack of ability to engage in modern society, or because of downward mobility. The widow socialized into passive stances *vis-à-vis* the world gradually becomes isolated, as the extended kin group or neighborhood are no longer available for contact. Never highly engaged in the broader society, such a widow is unable to retain prior involvements for a variety of reasons, including mobility, poor finances, or health. Friends die or move away and she can not replace them. She lacks the ability to re-engage in new social roles as old ones fall away or to convert relations of greater social distance into closer ones. Such a widow sees the world as inhabited either by old-time contacts with whom she used to be close, or by privacy-invading strangers. For such societal members each role loss or break in a social relation constricts the social life space long before the time approved by the social disengagement theory.

The downwardly mobile Chicago area widow who becomes isolated, though not yet frequent among the older population, will probably increase in proportion with the years to come. She can no longer maintain a prior active and voluntaristic middle-class pattern of social interaction, primarily because she can not afford to. The loss of her husband and other life changes results in a serious drop in her social status; she can not maintain contact with former friends or engage in the activities she enjoyed in the past and she rejects presently available relations and activities.

The presence of socially isolated widows in the Chicago area sample bears further examination, particularly in view of the social disengagement theory that posits a voluntary withdrawal of people and society from each other as age increases. As the following table demonstrates, however, those who are socially isolated are not happy with the world. At least, they hold many negative attitudes toward people in general and toward their former intimates:

The association between social isolation and scores on the relations-restrictive attitude scale can be examined in greater detail (see Table 55). The widows who are socially isolated believe that people take advantage of women in their position, that old friends cannot be replaced, and that it is all right for widows to move soon after the death of the husband. They also think that women in their marital status are sexually propositioned, even by husbands of friends. They do not want more male companionship; while wishing for more friends, they have trouble being nice to past associates whom they define as unhelpful. They feel that

TABLE 54: HIGH, MEDIUM, AND LOW SCORES ON THE
RELATIONS-RESTRICTIVE ATTITUDE SCALE BY THE
SAME LEVELS OF THE SOCIAL ISOLATION SCALE

| Social Isolation Scale | Relations Restrictive-Attitude Scale | | | | | | | |
|---|---|---|---|---|---|---|---|---|
| | High | | Medium | | Low | | Total | |
| | % | N | % | N | % | N | % | N |
| High | 26 | 10 | 10 | 20 | 12 | 8 | 13 | 38 |
| Medium | 66 | 25 | 73 | 144 | 65 | 42 | 70 | 211 |
| Low | 8 | 3 | 17 | 34 | 23 | 15 | 17 | 52 |
| Total | 13 | 38 | 66 | 198 | 22 | 65 | 100 | 301 |

Gamma .24 $x^2$ 10.40 d.f. 4 p $<$ .05

TABLE 55: SIGNIFICANT RELATIONS AND ASSOCIATIONS
BETWEEN THE SOCIAL ISOLATION SCALE AND
OTHER SCALES AND SPECIFIC ATTITUDES

| Attitudes and Roles | Gamma | $x^2$ | d.f. | p |
|---|---|---|---|---|
| A new widow should not move too soon after death of husband | −.31 | 5.75 | 2 | n.s. |
| Many widows who remarry are unhappy in that marriage | .39 | 9.46 | 2 | .01 |
| Widows are constantly sexually propositioned, even by husbands of their friends | .39 | 9.65 | 2 | .01 |
| People take advantage of you when they find out you are a widow | .41 | 12.38 | 2 | .01 |
| Old friends cannot be replaced no matter how one tries to make new | .61 | 24.03 | 2 | .001 |
| My present income makes it impossible to maintain old friendships | .38 | 6.86 | 2 | .01 |
| I wish people wouldn't try to get me out to do things | .38 | 8.37 | 2 | .05 |
| I wish I had more male companionship | −.37 | 7.44 | 2 | .05 |
| I have trouble being nice to people who did not help in grief | .65 | 13.91 | 2 | .001 |
| I wish I had more friends | .31 | 7.06 | 2 | .05 |
| This time of my life is actually easier than any other time | .23 | 8.84 | | |
| Role of wife | −.31 | 13.84 | 4 | .01 |
| Role of mother | −.36 | 12.30 | 4 | .02 |
| Role of Neighbor | −.35 | 15.28 | 4 | .01 |

their life is easier now than prior to widowhood, in spite of a constriction
of income which makes old contacts impossible to retain. Their rejective
attitude is reflected by their wish to be left alone. This passive and hostile

package of attitudes is reflected by a negative association and significant
relation between the social isolation scale and scores in the roles of wife,
mother, and neighbor. This means that the socially isolated achieves her
lack of interaction from being low in all three of those roles.

At the other end of the social engagement continuum, widows who
have a high frequency of social contact disagree with most of the restrictive statements (see Table 56). There is a significant relation between

TABLE 56: SIGNIFICANT RELATIONS AND ASSOCIATIONS
BETWEEN THE FREQUENCY OF CONTACT SCALE
AND OTHER SCALES AND SPECIFIC ATTITUDES

| *Attitudes and Roles* | *Gamma* | $x^2$ | *d.f.* | *p* |
|---|---|---|---|---|
| One problem with adult children is that they always want favors | −.36 | 12.25 | 2 | 05 |
| Relatives are your only true friends | −.30 | 6.78 | 2 | .05 |
| Other women are jealous of a widow when their husbands are around | −.30 | 7.75 | 2 | .05 |
| Widows are sexually propositioned, even by husbands of friends | −.47 | 12.69 | 2 | .01 |
| People take advantage of you when they know you are a widow | −.46 | 19.55 | 2 | .001 |
| My present income makes it impossible to maintain friendship | −.34 | 10.71 | 2 | .01 |
| My brothers and/or sisters became much more important after widowhood | .36 | 12.54 | 2 | .01 |
| Relations-restrictive attitude scale | −.22 | 9.88 | 4 | .05 |
| Role of mother scale | .50 | 31.98 | 4 | .01 |
| Role of sibling scale | .57 | 35.65 | 4 | .001 |
| Role of friend scale | .30 | 15.94 | 4 | .01 |
| Role of neighbor scale | .60 | 57.62 | 4 | .001 |

the frequency of contact scores and the relations-restrictive attitude
scores. These women reject the belief that children pester them for favors,
that widows are sexually propositioned, that other women are jealous of
them, that relatives are the only people with whom primary relations
are developed, and that people are out to take advantage of them. Their
income is not so restricted as to prevent retention of old relationships, and
even brothers and sisters have become close to them. Their contact score,
added to the positive attitudes, builds up high scores in all the major
social roles. Certainly, these two types of women, the socially isolated
and the very active, are opposites.

A very basic difference between the strongly engaged women and the
social isolates is education (see Table 57). The woman who is passive

TABLE 57: HIGH, MEDIUM, AND LOW SCORES ON THE *SOCIAL ISOLATION SCALE* BY EDUCATION OF RESPONDENT

*Social Isolation Score*

| Education | High (55–80) No. | % | Medium (26–54) No. | % | Low (01–25) No. | % | Total No. | % |
|---|---|---|---|---|---|---|---|---|
| No school | 1 | 9.0 | 10 | 90.9 | —** | .0 | 11 | 3.6 |
| Grades 1–4 | 3 | 12.5 | 21 | 87.5 | —** | .0 | 24 | 7.9 |
| Grades 5–7 | 3 | 31.7 | 27 | 65.8 | 1 | 2.4 | 41 | 13.6 |
| 8th Grade | 12 | 17.1 | 46 | 65.7 | 12 | 17.1 | 70 | 23.2 |
| Some high School | 4 | 6.5 | 49 | 80.3 | 8 | 13.1 | 61 | 20.2 |
| Completed high school | 4 | 6.4 | 41 | 66.1 | 17 | 27.4 | 62 | 20.5 |
| Some college | 1 | 5.5 | 10 | 55.5 | 7 | 38.8 | 18 | 5.9 |
| College graduate | —** | .0 | 4 | 50.0 | 4 | 50.0 | 8 | 2.6 |
| Graduate or professional training | —** | .0 | 3 | 50.0 | 3 | 50.0 | 6 | 1.9 |
| Total | 38 | 12.6 | 211 | 70.0 | 52 | 17.2 | 301 | 99.4 |

$x^2$ with 16 d.f. $= 45.92$ or p $<.001$
\* not counted in percentage base
\*\* in order to compute $x^2$ the number "1" was substituted for "0" in blank cells. The additions are not sufficient to warp results.

and uninvolved is apt to have received little education. Skills in building social relations are learned or encouraged in the formal school system and those women who never become involved in this societal structure or who spend few years within it are not apt to engage strongly in other areas of community life during adult and old age. The same characteristics of social class and consequent personality which keep them from school or that result in their dropping out at an early age are the ones that operate throughout life. They led them to a marriage with a man of the same low level of schooling or with one whose accomplishments the widow does not even know. The family income of such people was minimal when the husband was alive, and the widow is financially very restricted at the present time. After the death of a husband with whom she led a sex-segregated life, the woman may be left alone or with small children. Her isolation is made easy by the fact that she was always marginal to the social system and that she was not socialized into any skills for expanded re-engagement into society. Fearful and lacking self-confidence, her social involvement is dependent upon chance and the action of others. Having had a hard life in the past, she is often willing just to sit out the rest of her years, without the work or irritation produced by sharing a home or maintaining too close contact with anyone, even her offspring. This same difficulty of life makes her apt not to have living siblings or children; friendship or satisfactory relations at work were never part of her social life (see also Rainwater, *et. al.,* 1959; Komarowsky, 1967; Berardo, 1967, 1968; Pihlblad and Rosencranz, 1968; Adams, 1969).

Other societies protect, provide for, and insure the social involvement of the widow. Decreases in the functionality and availability of the extended family, independence of women, social and geographical mobility, and increasing societal voluntarism have made the case of the isolated widow an increasingly frequent phenomonon.

The generations or types of widows who had been socialized into traditional immersion in ascribed social roles, but who are living in a voluntaristic system of secondary relations or achieved primary ones, face social isolation, loneliness, and a restricted social life space. The widow socialized into a voluntaristic engagement in achieved social roles but no longer having the facilities to retain social involvement faces a similar problem. The best position is that of the widow who was socialized into the modern social system and has enough financial and health resources to participate. Her social relations may be changed as a result of widowhood, but they tend to be multi-dimensional in a relatively broad social life space, both in marriage and after recovery from the death of her husband.

## RECOMMENDATIONS FOR MEETING THE NEEDS OF URBAN WIDOWS

The final question to which a study of widowhood in an American city must address itself is how the acquired knowledge can be applied in practice to help widows. The answer obviously depends upon the needs of each particular widow, her relations to her helpers, and her stage of widowhood. The helpers can be classified, in order of decreasing intimacy to the widow, as: relatives, friends, voluntary associations, the community, and the society. The needs depend upon the unique combination of personality and life circumstances.

The short-range needs of widows, regardless of typology or life circumstances, can be summarized as five-fold:

1. "grief work"
2. companionship
3. solution of immediate problems
4. building of competence and self-confidence
5. help in re-engagement

## Grief Work

Psychiatrists working with people who have recently suffered bereavement agree with Eric Lindemann (1944) that the most important need at this stage of widowhood is the process of "grief work." The grieving person must be allowed to express his or her emotions, sorrow, guilt, loneliness, and the whole gamut of sentiments activated by the death of a significant other. The American culture performs a disservice to the grieving person by downplaying emotion and de-institutionalizing mourning rituals (see Gorer, 1965). Social scientists in general recommend that the widow be encouraged to cry if she wishes, to talk of her late husband and of how badly she feels. Family members, friends, and especially trained counselors ought to be available to allow the griever a personal rhythm of working out emotions and of gradually redefining life. All the phases of grief, from shock to final acceptance and willingness to rebuild life, must be worked out, according to Lindemann (1944), Parkes (1964 a and b), Maddison (1968), and the other Harvard Medical School psychiatrists and sociologists dealing with this problem.

## Companionship

Chicago area widows explain the help they most appreciated from people right after the death of their husbands in terms of rather passive companionship, "just being here," or active sharing of activities. The stress upon "just being here" indicates a grief-work need, but it also points up a very realistic problem of widowhood among older people. The death of a wife or husband at an age after children have left home often reduces the household to only one person. The widow must learn to live alone for the first time of her life. Since this process is complicated by grief and all of its manifestations, psychologists and the majority of widows advise companionship during the year following the husband's death. The widow is longing for her husband as a particular individual, for another person in the house, for someone around whom to organize time and work, for a contributor to the maintenance of the home, and for a partner in a variety of activities. Television watching and eating, to say nothing of the activities outside of the house, can be lonely. The widow is not used to going out by herself evenings, feels like a fifth wheel if she accompanies couples, fears taking public transportation and going out at night, and is hesitant about entering public places or functions without a male escort. Anything friends and relatives can do to alleviate these problems is a major help. Any program developed among unmarried or no longer married friends of the new widow to engage her during mealtimes and weekends could make an important contribution to meeting her companionship needs.

The need for companionship which begins with grief but continues into later years is not easily met by former social intimates. Both the widows and their friends complain about each other, holding negative attitudes. The friends complain that the widow makes impossible demands, has a chip on her shoulder, or is not pleased with their attempts to help. The widow lives in fear of being dropped by her friends and ignored by her relatives, partly because the sub-culture contains many tales of such desertions and partly because she does not really feel that she is worth much as an individual. The latter sentiment is reinforced by the low status of a widow in American society and by her prior dependent identity as a wife accompanying a particular husband. There is sometimes an almost paranoic anxiety about social relations, which results in behaviors dysfunctional to continuing satisfactory interaction. Widows refuse invitations which they feel are extended as an act of charity rather than as a result of a desire for their company, yet they are hurt when they hear of a party to which they have not been invited. The set of attitudes which forms the tightest cluster in the relations-restrictive attitude scale reflects the frustration which many widows feel in their interaction with friends, because of the form of help which is or is not offered when they are in grief or even later. Some complain that they are never asked what help they actually desire, but are given only the kind which others wish to offer. They think friends and relatives hold many beliefs and attitudes about widows which are unrealistic and even irrelevant to their needs. "They just don't understand" is their frequently voiced complaint.

Basically, the best recommendation this study can offer to intimates of a widow is to try to understand the emotionally ambivalent nature of her psychological state and consistently give her what *she defines* as her relational needs, without taking offense at slights or even withdrawals. This period is hard for both parties, but it is the widow, not the friend, who has the strongest cause for irrational and highly demanding behavior. The friends can also examine their own motives, making sure that the withdrawal or diminishing of contact is not due to avoidance of problem situations, only rationalized as "good for the widow." There is a very strong possibility that some truth may be behind the widow's assertion that she is being shunned because of distaste for the whole topic of death or because of jealousy. Realization of the relatively short duration of the grief-period should encourage friends and relatives to be really helpful on the widow's own terms.

## Advice: Solution of Problems and Competence-Building

A very important cause of strain in the relations between a widow and her significant others during the period immediately after her husband's death is too much of the wrong kind of advice. Unfortunately, everyone around her is full of advice, and the bits she receives are often contradictory and irrelevant or unbeneficial from her point of view. Psychiatrists and lawyers recommend that the widow avoid making any important decisions during the first year of widowhood, because the possibility of mistakes is great, and because her life and outlook will change after she completes grief-work. She may deeply resent having decided something during this period at the insistence of a well-meaning friend or relative. Experts also recommend that people close to the widow not offer her too much dependency-producing advice. They should simply help her meet the immediate crises and contribute to her own decision-making ability by providing the necessary knowledge and by training her to be an increasingly competent person. No one should make decisions for her, unless absolutely necessary to avoid a serious disaster. There are several reasons for these recommendations. In the first place, relatives are usually ill-informed as to the alternative solutions to many of the widow's problems. If they feel obliged to interfere in her life, they should obtain the professional advice of experts, without assuming that they themselves know what is best for the widow. Secondly, a major problem of widowhood is this very attitude of significant others—that they, not she, know all the answers to her situation. This attitude diminishes her self-confidence in her own abilities. She depended upon a husband in the past, but she now must develop the competence and self-confidence to make her own decisions. The significant others must help her by showing trust in her resources. Advice-giving is dysfunctional, if it robs her of self-confidence. The third disadvantage to advice is that it was worked out from others' vantage points. It was based on what relatives and friends think the widow "should" need, or "should" want, or "should" do, rather than on her own definition of her situation, needs, and goals. It ignores her personality. Finally, advice is often contradictory, since it comes from different sources.

Thus, the most frequent expert recommendation of short-range help for new widows is to provide opportunity for grief-work, to guarantee quiet companionship as well as partnership in activities, to help directly in solving immediate problems, such as funeral arrangements, temporary financial difficulties, etc., and to refrain from giving advice as to major changes in life style. Close associates should make available the services of experts: ministers, doctors, lawyers, bankers, and specialists in mental health. Simultaneously, any action which they can undertake to increase her knowledge and skills in problem-solving is of immense importance.

## Community Help to Widows

The community within which the widow lives can contribute to both her short-range and long-range adjustment. The widow-to-widow program instituted in Boston and New York as a result of research conducted by the Harvard Medical School is an excellent example of societally provided help for such crisis situations. Women who have already gone through the stages of grief contact new widows and offer several different services. In the first place, they make her feel that at least one other person "understands" how she feels. The matching of the caller and the "client" by socio-economic background is important here, because of the class differences in response to widowhood. In addition, the caller, if adequately trained, can provide specific knowledge about relevant sources of help in meeting new problems. She can come equipped with legal information or at least with an approved list of lawyers. The caller can be informed of work, training, voluntary associations, and other resources available to widows who are unfamiliar with them because of past life style. Finally, she can keep in continuous touch and be available for future information or comfort. Organizations such as NAIM, the Catholic group for the widowed, or senior women's clubs can serve as an organizing center for such widow-to-widow personal contact and for subsequent group integration. The point is, of course, that an organized and continuing social group is needed to train the callers, to serve as a clearinghouse of information, and to expand the contact beyond the one-to-one interaction. A group whose whole activity is oriented toward problems of widowhood or one catering to older people would be a natural, not only for carrying out the suggested type of help, but for experimenting with different means of assisting widows.

The widow who has been socially isolated for some time presents a different kind of problem to the community. She is hard to discover, because of her very isolation, and she needs greater understanding and more intensive attention. She lacks skills in social relations, and her complex of problems is barrier-creating. It took years for her to develop her marginal position *vis-à-vis* society, and such barriers cannot be broken down in one contact situation. She is not likely to join NAIM (which is, even at its best, limited to Catholic women), a Newcomer's group, or even a club within a church, where she could be individually approached in social interaction. She is the long-term non-member or drop-out from community life. Welcome Wagons seldom seek her out, because of her poverty, and even when they do, the contact is impersonal.

One of the recommendations of the researchers involved in the study of aging in small towns of Missouri (see Pihlblad and Rosencranz, 1968) was that the local churches involve the older person by insuring transportation and programs designed to meet their interests. All voluntary associations in metropolitan centers should be encouraged to help decrease the social isolation and minimal involvement of residents. The first step would be to find the isolated and break down their attitudinal barriers; then the lonely must be re-engaged. This is a complex task and should not be undertaken haphazardly as in the past. There should be specific groups within each parent organization who would have the primary function of finding the isolated and the lonely, sending "callers" to them, building trust, and gradually increasing involvement. Steps should include:

1. Canvassing social areas and/or past membership lists to locate inactive members and socially isolated persons
2. Gathering sufficient background information on the person to facilitate interaction rituals
3. Selection of a person to initiate the contact who has particular empathy for each type of "client"
4. Training the caller in procedures for initiating contact, developing rapport, and encouraging client-involvement in the community
5. Providing the caller with relevant data about:
   a. the client
   b. resources for the solution of some of the client's problems (medicare, employment, housing, etc.)
   c. steps facilitating entrance into new social roles, especially jobs (how to apply, be interviewed, etc.)
6. Securing facilities for the client's increased participation in the activities of that association or of any other group, for that matter. For instance, transportation, wardrobe expansion (special day for older people at rummage sales), detailed information about events, and particularly company in going to and returning from such events
7. Making sure that the client is worked into the group in such a way that she makes a visible contribution to its functioning

Several members of NAIM with whom the author spoke during the exploratory stage of this research explained that a "hard case" of widowhood was helped by "putting her to work," referring to voluntary tasks which facilitated the actual functioning of the group. Widows who lack self-confidence and the ability to communicate with others are nevertheless given tasks requiring some social interaction, but they are not expected to blossom suddenly into "social butterflies."

The community and the society at large could set up official agencies supplementing the activities of voluntary associations. Financial advice is badly needed by widows, who often do not take full advantage of existing societal resources because they simply do not know of them. They get help only if they become welfare cases, and even in such situations complete information is not guaranteed. To the middle-class urban dweller, the great ignorance of some of the older widows concerning the law, social security, medical care, pensions, etc., is staggering. Many widows are not aware that buses in Chicago have special rates for the elderly, nor have they ever been to the "loop" or the center of the city. In addition, they do not trust their informants, having discovered from past experience that people around them are also ignorant.

Many of the problems of widows could be solved by just a few hours of undivided and expert attention involving pre-contact and voluntaristic follow-up. One of the existing governmental offices could set up a limited number of centers to which the widowed could go for specific advice as to the best methods of re-engagement in society. Such centers could contain a lawyer, a social worker, a physician, an accountant, and related personnel. Consultants might be available for special cases. In addition, the city, state, or federal government could set up series of lectures, perhaps conducted in such centers or in public housing complexes, which would teach people the simple procedures for developing social interaction. The widows need to learn how to get a job, join an organization, build friendship, look well, etc. Beauticians, fashion coordinators and others who train people how to be socially acceptable ought to provide this information to the widows who never learned to be publicly presentable, or who have been out of social circulation so long as to have rusty or out-moded resources. This knowledge is vital in our modern voluntaristic society. It is provided for the young, but the older persons who are very apt to need it do not receive it. There are some programs in "hard core" inner city areas which teach women to cook, sew, etc., but these adult education programs must be expanded to include interactional training of older people.

One of the discoveries of the exploratory period of research on widowhood is the pervasiveness of the "disengagement theory." Many people working with the elderly believe that social isolation is a result of the natural process of withdrawal of the person and the society from each other. This study indicates that factors other than choice are frequently operating to isolate the person. Basically, those who are isolated or lonely are those who lack the skills, money, health, and transportation for engaging or re-engaging in society. Widows are either unhappy over their restricted social life space or "adjusted." Unfortunately, adjustment can refer to the passive decision that life can not be changed but rather must be waited out. Such widows live in a society which assumes the perfect engagement of all those members who wish to be engaged, in the directions and levels which meet their needs. This study of widowhood indicates that the assumption is false for at least some widows and that much can still be done to re-engage people who have for some reason or another suffered breaks in their life patterns or who have always been marginal to the present social system. If such people are to be helped, a fresh view of the relation between the urban, industrial, and complex modern world and its residents is required, and new action programs must be creatively developed.

## APPENDIX A: THE INTERVIEW SCHEDULE

TIME BEGAN: ........ A.M.                              CONFIDENTIAL
                    P.M.                               Survey 4059

NATIONAL OPINION RESEARCH CENTER
University of Chicago

WIDOWHOOD INTERVIEW

1. (Transfer age from Screening form)                 AGE....

2. How long have you been widowed?

                                                      RECORD YEARS....

I have just two short questions about your husband.
3. What did your husband die of? (What was the official cause of death?)

4. How long was he hospitalized?           RECORD MONTHS....

5. Where were you born?        Chicago Metropolitan Area (GO TO Q. 6) .. 1
                               Other United States (ASK B) ............. 2
                               Out of United States (ASK A & B) ........ 3
   A. How old were you when you came to America?        AGE ....
   B. How old were you when you moved to (Chicago/name of suburb?) AGE ....

PROBE FOR OCCUPATION AND INDUSTRY
6. What was your father's main occupation during the years you were growing up?
   Please describe what he did and the kind of company he worked for.

7. What is the highest grade you completed in school?
   No school ............(ASK A).. 1    Completed high school (ASK A).. 6
   1–4 grades ...........(ASK A).. 2    Some college ................... 7
   5–7 grades ...........(ASK A).. 3    Graduated from college ......... 8
   8th grade ............(ASK A).. 4    Graduate or professional training
   Some high school .....(ASK A).. 5      (SPECIFY) .................. 9
   A. *IF HIGH SCHOOL OR LESS:*
      Did you have any further technical or trade or business training?
      Yes .... (SPECIFY) ........ 1    No ........................... 2

8. Did you ever work before you were married?
   Yes ......................... 5    No ............................. 6

9. During your marriage did you work all of the time, most of the time, some of the time, or never?
   All of the time ................. 1    Some of the time ................ 3
   Most of the time ............... 2    Never ......................... 4

*IF APPROPRIATE*
10. Did your husband's illness change your work patterns?
    Yes .................(ASK A).. 5    No ............................. 6
    A. *IF YES:*
       Did you begin working then, quit working then, did you work more, or work less?
       Began to work .............. 1    Worked more .................. 3
       Quit work .................. 2    Worked less .................. 4

11. Have you worked since you became a widow?
    Yes ...............(ASK A–D).. 5    No ............................. 6
    *IF YES:*
    A. How soon after becoming a widow did you go to work?
       RECORD MONTHS ....    IF ALWAYS WORKED GO TO Q. 12
    B. How many years had it been since you worked before that?
       RECORD YEARS ....
    C. *IF WORKED BEFORE:* Were you able to get the kind of job you had held
                           before, one not as good, or a better one?
       Same kind of job .... 1    One not as good ... 2    A better one ...... 3
    D. Did you get more education or training either before, or at the time you went
       back to work?
       Yes ..............(ASK E).. 5    No ..................(ASK F).. 6

       E. *IF YES TO D:* Was that more education in school, a special training
                         program, or on-the-job training?
       More education in school ... 1    Special training program ... 2
       On the job training ... 3
       F. *IF NO TO D:* Was that because you didn't need training, or was none
                        available?
       Did not need training ........ 5    None available ................. 6

*EVERYONE WHO HAS EVER WORKED*

12. What is the best job you ever held?

. . . . . . . . . . . . . . . . . . . . . . . . . . . . . .     . . . . . . . . . . . . . . . . . . . . . . . . . . . . . .

OCCUPATION                           INDUSTRY

A. What year did you begin that job?                          YEAR . . . .
B. What year did you leave this job?                          YEAR . . . .
   IF PRESENTLY ON JOB SKIP TO 13. B.
C. Why did you leave that job? FIELD CODE.
   Got married or remarried . . . . . . . . . . 1     Health got bad . . . . . . . . . . . . 5
   Had a child, children . . . . . . . . . . . . . . 2     Retirement . . . . . . . . . . . . . . . . 6
   Husband's illness or death . . . . . . . . . . 3     Other (SPECIFY) . . . . . . . . 7
   Moved from the locality where job was 4

13. What (is/was) your (present/most recent) job? Please describe what you (do/ did). What kind of company (is/was) that?

. . . . . . . . . . . . . . . . . . . . . . . . . . . . . .     . . . . . . . . . . . . . . . . . . . . . . . . . . . . . .

OCCUPATION                           INDUSTRY

A. What year did you begin this job?                          YEAR. . . .
B. How many hours a week (did you/do you) work?              HOURS. . . .
*ASK UNLESS CURRENTLY WORKING*
C. What year did you leave this job?                          YEAR. . . .

14. How many children do you have? ....
      (IF ANY, ASK 14 A–G FOR EACH. IF NONE, SKIP TO Q. 15.)

| | A. | B. | C. | D. |
|---|---|---|---|---|
| | What is the name of your (oldest) child? And the next oldest? And the next? | Code sex of each person mentioned. (ASK IF NOT OBVIOUS.) | What is (his/her) age? | (IF 16 YEARS OR OLDER) What is (his/her) marital status? |

Person No.

| | M | F | | Married | Separated | Divorced | Widowed | Never Married |
|---|---|---|---|---|---|---|---|---|
| 01 | 1 | 2 | | 1 | 2 | 3 | 4 | 5 |
| 02 | 1 | 2 | | 1 | 2 | 3 | 4 | 5 |
| 03 | 1 | 2 | | 1 | 2 | 3 | 4 | 5 |
| 04 | 1 | 2 | | 1 | 2 | 3 | 4 | 5 |
| 05 | 1 | 2 | | 1 | 2 | 3 | 4 | 5 |
| 06 | 1 | 2 | | 1 | 2 | 3 | 4 | 5 |
| 07 | 1 | 2 | | 1 | 2 | 3 | 4 | 5 |
| 08 | 1 | 2 | | 1 | 2 | 3 | 4 | 5 |

G. How many times altogether, would you say you talk on the telephone to your children within a week? ....

E.

Does (he/she) live in the neighborhood?

IF YES, ASK (1). IF NO, ASK (2) AND (3).

| (1) | (2) | (3) | |
|---|---|---|---|
| Where does (he/she) live—in the same DU, same bldg. but other DU, same block, or somewhere else in the neighborhood? (GO TO F.) | How long does it take to get to (his/her) house —an hour or less, over an hour or over a day? | What is your usual mode of transportation? Do you usually go by car, by local bus or "L," by Greyhound bus or train, or by airplane? | ASK UNLESS SAME DU OR SAME BUILDING. Howe often do you see (*child*)—almost daily, every week or so, about every month, a few times a year or less often than that? |

| Same DU | Same Bldg., Other DU | Same Block | Somewhere Else in the Neighborhood | | An Hour or Less | Over an Hour | Over One Day | | Car | Local Bus or "L" | Greyhound or Train | Airplane | | Almost Daily | Every Week or So | About Every Month | A Few Times a Year | Less Often Than That |
|---|---|---|---|---|---|---|---|---|---|---|---|---|---|---|---|---|---|---|
| 1 | 2 | 3 | 4 | | 5 | 6 | 7 | | 1 | 2 | 3 | 4 | | 5 | 6 | 7 | 8 | 9 |
| 1 | 2 | 3 | 4 | | 5 | 6 | 7 | | 1 | 2 | 3 | 4 | | 5 | 6 | 7 | 8 | 9 |
| 1 | 2 | 3 | 4 | | 5 | 6 | 7 | | 1 | 2 | 3 | 4 | | 5 | 6 | 7 | 8 | 9 |
| 1 | 2 | 3 | 4 | | 5 | 6 | 7 | | 1 | 2 | 3 | 4 | | 5 | 6 | 7 | 8 | 9 |
| 1 | 2 | 3 | 4 | | 5 | 6 | 7 | | 1 | 2 | 3 | 4 | | 5 | 6 | 7 | 8 | 9 |
| 1 | 2 | 3 | 4 | | 5 | 6 | 7 | | 1 | 2 | 3 | 4 | | 5 | 6 | 7 | 8 | 9 |
| 1 | 2 | 3 | 4 | | 5 | 6 | 7 | | 1 | 2 | 3 | 4 | | 5 | 6 | 7 | 8 | 9 |
| 1 | 2 | 3 | 4 | | 5 | 6 | 7 | | 1 | 2 | 3 | 4 | | 5 | 6 | 7 | 8 | 9 |

*ASK EVERYONE:*

15. How many brothers or sisters do you have?      . . . .
    (IF ANY, ASK 15 A–E FOR EACH.  IF NONE, SKIP TO Q. 16.)

| | A. | B. | C. |
|---|---|---|---|
| | What is the name of your oldest brother or sister? And the next oldest? And the next? | Code sex of each person mentioned. (ASK IF NOT OBVIOUS.) | Is (*name*) older, younger, or the same age as you? |

Per-
son
No.

| | M | F | Older | Younger | Same Age |
|---|---|---|---|---|---|
| 01 | 1 | 2 | 3 | 4 | 5 |
| 02 | 1 | 2 | 3 | 4 | 5 |
| 03 | 1 | 2 | 3 | 4 | 5 |
| 04 | 1 | 2 | 3 | 4 | 5 |
| 05 | 1 | 2 | 3 | 4 | 5 |
| 06 | 1 | 2 | 3 | 4 | 5 |
| 07 | 1 | 2 | 3 | 4 | 5 |
| 08 | 1 | 2 | 3 | 4 | 5 |
| 09 | 1 | 2 | 3 | 4 | 5 |

**D.**

Does (*name*) live in this neighborhood?
IF YES, ASK (1). IF NO, ASK (2) AND (3).

| (1) | (2) | (3) |
|-----|-----|-----|
| Where does (he/she) live—in the same DU, same bldg. but other DU, same block, or somewhere else in the neighborhood? (GO TO E.) | How long does it take to get to (his/her) home? An hour or less, more than an hour, or over a day? | What is your usual mode of transportation? Do you usually go by car, by local bus or "L," by Greyhound bus or train, or by airplane? |

**E.**

ASK UNLESS SAME DU OR SAME BUILDING:
How often do you see (*name*)—almost daily, every week or so, about every month, a few times a year, or less than that?

| Same Du | Same Bldg., Other DU | Same Block | Somewhere Else in the Neighborhood | | An Hour or Less | More Than an Hour | Over a Day | | Car | Local Bus or "L" | Greyhound or Train | Airplane | | Almost Daily | Every Week or So | About Every Month | A Few Times a Year | Less Often Than That |
|---|---|---|---|---|---|---|---|---|---|---|---|---|---|---|---|---|---|---|
| 1 | 2 | 3 | 4 | | 5 | 6 | 7 | | 1 | 2 | 3 | 4 | | 5 | 6 | 7 | 8 | 9 |
| 1 | 2 | 3 | 4 | | 5 | 6 | 7 | | 1 | 2 | 3 | 4 | | 5 | 6 | 7 | 8 | 9 |
| 1 | 2 | 3 | 4 | | 5 | 6 | 7 | | 1 | 2 | 3 | 4 | | 5 | 6 | 7 | 8 | 9 |
| 1 | 2 | 3 | 4 | | 5 | 6 | 7 | | 1 | 2 | 3 | 4 | | 5 | 6 | 7 | 8 | 9 |
| 1 | 2 | 3 | 4 | | 5 | 6 | 7 | | 1 | 2 | 3 | 4 | | 5 | 6 | 7 | 8 | 9 |
| 1 | 2 | 3 | 4 | | 5 | 6 | 7 | | 1 | 2 | 3 | 4 | | 5 | 6 | 7 | 8 | 9 |
| 1 | 2 | 3 | 4 | | 5 | 6 | 7 | | 1 | 2 | 3 | 4 | | 5 | 6 | 7 | 8 | 9 |
| 1 | 2 | 3 | 4 | | 5 | 6 | 7 | | 1 | 2 | 3 | 4 | | 5 | 6 | 7 | 8 | 9 |
| 1 | 2 | 3 | 4 | | 5 | 6 | 7 | | 1 | 2 | 3 | 4 | | 5 | 6 | 7 | 8 | 9 |

*IF ANY CHILDREN*

16. How many grandchildren do you have? ....
    (IF NONE, GO TO Q. 17.)
    A. Do you feel particularly close to (one or more of) your grandchildren?
    Yes ................(ASK B).. 1    No ............(SKIP TO C).. 2
    B. *IF YES TO A:* Why do you suppose that's true?
    C. How many great grandchildren do you have? ....
    D. Do you feel particularly close to (one or more of) your great grandchildren?
    Yes ..............(ASK E).. 1    No. .........(GO TO Q. 17).. 2
    E. *IF YES TO D:* Why do you suppose that's true?

*IF ANY BROTHERS OR SISTERS*

17. Are you particularly close to (any of) your (brothers/sisters)?
    Yes (ASK A) 1    Not really, not very close ...(ASK A).. 2    No .... 3
    A. *IF YES, OR UNCERTAIN ASK:* Which brother or sister is closest to you?

18. Did you have any close relatives who passed away after you were widowed?
    Yes ............(ASK A & B).. 1    No ...........(GO TO Q. 19).. 2
    *IF YES:*
    A. Who was that? ...............................    ....................
    B. In what ways was your life changed by (his/her/their) death?
    PROBE FULLY.

ASK Q. 19 IF ANY CHILDREN.
*INTERVIEWER INSTRUCTION: USE THE PERSON NUMBER ASSIGNED TO EACH CHILD IN QUESTION 14.*

19. We realize that individual circumstances alter how much help children can be to their widowed mothers—some are able to do more than others for one reason or another. We'd like to know something about the help received from your (child/ children) in the following areas of your life.
(FOR ONLY CHILD, USE SECTION A—FOR MORE THAN ONE CHILD, USE SECTION B.)

|  | **A.** FOR ONLY CHILD Has your child helped you much or little in the following areas of life? ASK (1)–(9) | | | **B.** IF MORE THAN ONE CHILD Which of your children has helped you the most, and which has helped you the least in the following areas of life? ASK (1)–(9). | | | |
|---|---|---|---|---|---|---|---|
|  | *Much* | *Little* | *Does Not Apply* | *The Most* ENTER PERSON # | *The Least* ENTER PERSON # | *Can't Decide* | *Does Not Apply* |
| (1) During your husband's last illness | 1 | 2 | 3 |  |  | 4 | 5 |
| (2) During the funeral | 1 | 2 | 3 |  |  | 4 | 5 |
| (3) With finances | 1 | 2 | 3 |  |  | 4 | 5 |
| (4) By being close to you | 1 | 2 | 3 |  |  | 4 | 5 |
| (5) Emotionally, when you are blue | 1 | 2 | 3 |  |  | 4 | 5 |
| (6) By giving advice | 1 | 2 | 3 |  |  | 4 | 5 |
| (7) By performing services | 1 | 2 | 3 |  |  | 4 | 5 |
| (8) By inviting you to (his/her) home | 1 | 2 | 3 |  |  | 4 | 5 |
| (9) By coming to see you | 1 | 2 | 3 |  |  | 4 | 5 |

20. A. How have your husband's relatives fitted into your life since your husband's (illness/accident)? (Did/have) they helped you often, seldom, or never. READ (1)–(7).

|  | Often | Seldom | Never | Not Appropriate |
|---|---|---|---|---|
| (1) ... during your husband's last illness .............. | 1 | 2 | 3 | 4 |
| (2) ... with your children and home after your husband's death ................... | 5 | 6 | 7 | 8 |
| (3) ... by coming to visit you or inviting you over ....... | 1 | 2 | 3 | 4 |
| (4) ... by giving you gifts or money ................. | 5 | 6 | 7 | 8 |
| (5) ... by giving your children gifts or money .......... | 1 | 2 | 3 | 4 |
| (6) ... by visiting the children, and inviting them over .... | 5 | 6 | 7 | 8 |
| (7) ... by other contact, help (SPECIFY) ............ | 1 | 2 | 3 | 4 |

B. Did your husband's relatives help you during the funeral?
Yes ....................... 5    No ............................. 6

C. Has there been any change in how often they visit you, or invite you over, since the period just after your husband passed away—do they visit you more often, less often, or about as often?
More often .... 1    Less often ........ 2    About the same .... 3

*ASK EVERYONE*

21. A. Who is living here with you at the present time? (Anyone else?)
LIST IN COLUMN BELOW. IF NO ONE, INDICATE AND GO TO Q. 22.

ASK FOR EACH PERSON LISTED IN *A*
B.    C.
How is (person) related to you?    How old is (person)?

*UNLESS LIVES ALONE*
D. Whose home is this?

22. Have you ever lived with any (other) of your children for longer than a month?
Yes ............(ASK A & B).. 1    No ........................... 2
*IF YES:*
A. How long was the longest time? ...............
B. What factors influenced you to move to another place after living there?

23. Many women say that there are problems in living with children after they are grown up and married, no matter how nice everyone is. What (is/do you think would be/was) the most important problem in the situation? PROBE FULLY. And the next most important?

24. Where did you live just before your husband passed away—here, somewhere else in the neighborhood, somewhere else in (Chicago/suburb) but not nearby, or somewhere else?

Here, same housing unit as now (SKIP TO Q. 25) .............. 1

Somewhere in the same neighborhood (ASK A–F) ............... 2

Somewhere else in (Chicago/suburb) (ASK A–F) .................... 3

Somewhere else (different metropolitan area) (ASK A–F) ........... 4

*UNLESS SAME DU, ASK:*

A. Did you live in a house or an apartment?

House ....... 5     Apartment ........ 6     Other (SPECIFY) . 7

B. Did you rent it, or own it?

Own ......... 1     Rent ............. 2     Other (SPECIFY) . 3

C. When did you move from that (house/apartment)? Was that during your husband's illness, right after the funeral, within six months, in a year, or over a year after your husband's death?

During husband's illness ...... 5     Within a year ................... 8

Right after funeral ........... 6     Over a year .................... 9

Within six months ........... 7

D. Why did you move at that time?

E. Altogether, how many times have you moved since you became a widow?

F. How many years ago did you move to this (apartment/house)?

25. During the past year, have you stayed overnight in anyone's home (aside from people in this household)—someone like children, brothers or sisters, other relatives or friends?

Yes ............. (ASK A & B).. 1     No ............................. 2

*IF YES:*

A. Who was that? CIRCLE ALL THAT APPLY.

Children .................... 5     Friends ........................ 8

Siblings .................... 6     Other .......................... 9

Other relatives ............. 7

B. Altogether, how many nights did you stay?

6. And during the past year, did anyone come to visit *you* for overnight, or longer?
Yes .............(ASK A & B).. 1     No ............................ 2
IF YES:
A. Who was that? (CIRCLE ALL THAT APPLY)
   Children .................. 5     Friends ....................... 8
   Siblings .................. 6     Other ......................... 9
   Other relatives ............. 7

B. Altogether, how many nights did (he/she/they) stay?

7. (Excluding these visits) How many overnight trips have you taken during the past year?
A. IF ANY: How long were you away altogether?

8. Have you ever been out of the United States since becoming a widow?
Yes .......................... 1     No ............................ 2

9. What is the total number of relatives who live in the neighborhood?
A. Who is that/are they? CIRCLE ALL THAT APPLY.
Children ...... 1     Siblings .......... 2     Others (SPECIFY) . 3

10. How many widows would you say live in this neighborhood? Would it be many, some, a few, or none?
Many ...............(ASK A).. 5     A few ..............(ASK A).. 7
Some ...............(ASK A).. 6     None ...............(ASK A).. 8
A. Why is that?

. Do you know your neighbors?
Yes .................(ASK A).. 1     No .......... (GO TO Q. 32).. 2
A. *IF YES:* How often do you and your neighbors . . . (read each item below) frequently, occasionally, seldom, or never?

|  | *Frequently* | *Occasionally* | *Seldom* | *Never* |
|---|---|---|---|---|
| (1) Casually talk outside | 1 | 2 | 3 | 4 |
| (2) Borrow or lend—sugar or things like that | 1 | 2 | 3 | 4 |
| (3) Drop into each other's home | 1 | 2 | 3 | 4 |
| (4) Visit by invitation to each other's homes | 1 | 2 | 3 | 4 |
| (5) Go to club meetings together | 1 | 2 | 3 | 4 |
| (6) Go out together (for lunch, dinner, bowling) | 1 | 2 | 3 | 4 |
| (7) Other (SPECIFY) | 1 | 2 | 3 | 4 |

32. We'd like to know something about the organizations you've been involved with at various times during your life. Have you ever belonged to any groups, clubs or organizations of any kind? HAND RESPONDENT CARD A.

Yes ................(ASK A).. 1

No .........(GO TO Q. 33).. 2

| *Type of Organization* | A. Thinking back to *before* your widowhood which of the kinds of groups listed on this card did you belong to at that time? MEMBER THEN. | B. How many (*type*) organizations did you belong to? ENTER NUMBER. | C. At that time were you a very active member of (that/any of those) organization(s)? | |
|---|---|---|---|---|
| | | | Yes | No |
| Family | x | #............... | 1 | 2 |
| National | x | #............... | 1 | 2 |
| Religious | x | #............... | 1 | 2 |
| Recreational | x | #............... | 1 | 2 |
| Educational | x | #............... | 1 | 2 |
| Community | x | #............... | 1 | 2 |
| Union | x | #............... | 1 | 2 |
| Charity | x | #............... | 1 | 2 |
| Older | x | #............... | 1 | 2 |

ASK B AND C FOR EACH MEMBERSHIP IN A:

| D.<br>And which of these kinds of groups are you a member of now?<br>MEMBER NOW. | ASK E & F FOR EACH<br>MEMBERSHIP IN D:<br>E.<br>How many (*type*) organizations do you belong to?<br>ENTER NUMBER | | F.<br>Are you a very active member of (that/any of those) organization(s)? | G.<br>ASK FOR EACH TYPE OF GROUP IN WHICH MEMBERSHIP OR ACTIVITY LEVEL HAS CHANGED.<br>What would you say accounts for the change in your (membership/activity) in (*type*) group? |
|---|---|---|---|---|
| | | *Yes* | *No* | |
| 1 | #············ | 1 | 2 | |
| 1 | #············ | 1 | 2 | |
| 1 | #············ | 1 | 2 | |
| 1 | #············ | 1 | 2 | |
| 1 | #············ | 1 | 2 | |
| 1 | #············ | 1 | 2 | |
| 1 | #············ | 1 | 2 | |
| 1 | #············ | 1 | 2 | |
| 1 | #············ | 1 | 2 | |

33. Do you drive a car now?
Yes .......................... 5    No .................(ASK A).. 6
A. *IF NO:* How do you usually get places—by public transportation, do people drive you places, or do you go by taxi? CODE ONE.
Public transportation ... 1    People drive .... 2    Taxi .......... 3

34. Do you have any hobbies?
Yes .................(ASK A).. 5    No .......................... 6
A. *IF YES:* What are your hobbies?
Gardening ..................... 1    Cards ...................... 4
Sewing, knitting, crocheting ...... 2    TV, radio ................... 5
Reading ...................... 3    Other (SPECIFY) ........... 6

35. Have you taken any course or training programs since becoming a widow?
CIRCLE ALL THAT APPLY.
Yes .................(ASK A).. 5    No .......................... 6
A. *IF YES:* What kinds of courses?
Cards, (bridge, etc.) .......... 1    Work, job, upgrading, professional 6
Sports, games ................ 2    Academic, general interest,
Sewing, millinery and related        extension, adult classes ........ 7
fields ...................... 3    Financial, business, knowledge
Cooking, baking ............. 4    and skills ..................... 8
Decorating, flower arranging,        Other (SPECIFY) ............. 9
other house and garden ........ 5

36. (Other than on your job,) how many times a day do you usually talk to people on the telephone?

37. (Other than on your job,) how many letters do you usually write within an average week?

38. How many of your friends are widows? All, most, half and half, a few, one or two, none.

All ........................... 1     One or two ..................... 5
Most .......................... 2     None .......................... 6
Half and half ................. 3     I have no friends ............. 7
A few ......................... 4

*IF AT LEAST ONE:*
39. Did you become friends before you were widowed, after you were widowed, or what?

Before ........... 7     After ............. 8     Other (SPECIFY) . 9

*ASK EVERYONE*
40. What is your religion?

Protestant ....... (ASK A & B).. 1     Jewish (SPECIFY, Orthodox, Con-
Roman Catholic ...... (ASK B).. 2      servative, Reform) ..(ASK B) .. 4
Greek Orthodox ...... (ASK B).. 3      Other (SPECIFY) .............. 5
                                       None ....... (SKIP TO Q. 42).. 6

A. *IF PROTESTANT:* What denomination?

Baptist .................... 1     Congregational (United Church
Methodist ................. 2      of Christ) ..................... 6
Episcopalian .............. 3      Disciples of Christ ............. 7
Presbyterian .............. 4      Other (SPECIFY) .............. 8
Lutheran .................. 5      No denomination ............... 9

B. How important is your religion to you personally—extremely important, fairly important, not very important, or not at all important?

Extremely important ........... 1     Not very important ............ 3
Fairly important .............. 2     Not at all important .......... 4

41. How many of your friends are (ANSWER TO Q. 40 OR 40-A)—all, most, about half, a few, only one or two, or none?

All .......................... 3     One or two ..................... 7
Most ......................... 4     None .......................... 8
Half and half ................ 5     I don't have friends .......... 9
A few ........................ 6

42. What is your nationality?
PROBE FOR ANSWERS OTHER THAN "AMERICAN" OR "MIXED."
IF ABSOLUTELY CANNOT ANSWER, SKIP TO Q. 45.

| | | | |
|---|---|---|---|
| English, Scotch | 1 | Italian | 6 |
| French | 2 | Norwegian, Swedish, Danish | 7 |
| German | 3 | Polish | 8 |
| Greek | 4 | Russian | 9 |
| Irish | 5 | Other (SPECIFY) | 0 |

*IF SPECIFIC NATIONALITY:*

43. Do you consider yourself: (ANSWER TO Q. 42), an (ANSWER TO Q. 42) -American, an American of (ANSWER TO Q. 42) descent, or an American?

| | | | |
|---|---|---|---|
| Answer to Q. 42 | 1 | An American | 4 |
| Answer to Q. 42 -American | 2 | Other (SPECIFY) | 5 |
| An American of Q. 42 descent | 3 | | |

44. How many of your friends are the same nationality as you—all, most, half and half, a few, one or two, or none?

| | | | |
|---|---|---|---|
| All | 3 | One or two | 7 |
| Most | 4 | None | 8 |
| Half and half | 5 | I don't have friends | 9 |
| A few | 6 | | |

45. Have you been married more than once?

| | | | |
|---|---|---|---|
| | | No (ASK A & B, AND THEN | |
| Yes | (ASK A–E).. 1 | SKIP TO Q. 48) | 2 |

*ASK EVERYONE:*
A. What year were you married (for the first time)?
B. How many years were you married (for the first time)?

*IF YES TO Q. 45:*
C. How did (your/that) marriage end—in divorce, in widowhood, or in divorce first, and then widowhood?

| | | | |
|---|---|---|---|
| Divorce | (ASK E).. 1 | Widowhood | (ASK D).. 2 |
| | | Divorce first, then widowhood | (ASK E).. 3 |

D. *IF ENDED IN WIDOWHOOD:* Were you living with your husband just before his death or were you separated?

| | | | |
|---|---|---|---|
| Living with husband just before | | | |
| his death | (GO TO Q. 46).. 5 | Separated | (ASK E).. 6 |

E. *IF DIVORCED OR SEPARATED:* How many years had you been (divorced/separated) before your husband's death?

*ASK Q. 46 AND 47 IF MORE THAN ONE MARRIAGE.*

46. How many years was it before you remarried after your first marriage ended?
    A. How many years were you married the second time?
    B. How did that marriage end—in divorce, in widowhood or in divorce first and then widowhood?

    Divorce .......... (ASK D) .. 1    Widowhood .......... (ASK C) .. 2
    Divorced, then widowed ................................. (ASK D) .. 3
    C. *IF ENDED IN WIDOWHOOD:* Were you living with your husband just
    before his death or were you separated?

    Living with husband just before his death .. 5    Separated .......... 6
    D. *IF DIVORCED OR SEPARATED:* How many years had you been
    (divorced/separated) before your
    husband's death?

47. Did you marry the third time?
    Yes ............. (ASK A & B) .. 1    No ........... (GO TO Q. 48) .. 2
    *IF YES:*
    A. How many years was it before you remarried after your second marriage ended?
    B. How many years were you married that time?

*ASK EVERYONE:*

48. How old was your (last) husband when he died?

49. Was he older than you, younger than you, or the same age?
    Older .. (ASK A) .. 1    Younger (ASK A) .. 2    Same age (GO TO Q. 50) 3
    A. *IF OLDER OR YOUNGER:* How many years (older/younger) than you
    was your husband?

50. What was the last year of schooling of your husband?
    No schooling ......... (ASK A) .. 1    Completed high school (ASK A) .. 6
    1–4 grades ........... (ASK A) .. 2    Some college ................... 7
    5–7 grades ........... (ASK A) .. 3    Graduated from college .......... 8
    8th grade ............ (ASK A) .. 4    Graduate or professional training .. 9
    Some high school ..... (ASK A) .. 5    Don't know ..................... 0
    A. *IF HIGH SCHOOL OR LESS:* Did he have any further technical or trade
    or business training?

    Yes (SPECIFY) ... 1    No ............... 2    Don't know ....... 3
51. When your husband was growing up, what was his father's occupation?

52. What was your husband's religion?
    Protestant ... (ASK A & B) ....... 1    Jewish (SPECIFY, Orthodox,
    Roman Catholic ...... (ASK B) .. 2    Conservative, Reform) . (ASK B) .. 4
    Greek Orthodox ...... (ASK B) .. 3    Other (SPECIFY) .............. 5
    None .......... (GO TO Q. 53) .. 6

A. *IF PROTESTANT:* What denomination?

| | |
|---|---|
| Baptist ........................ 1 | Congregational (United Church |
| Methodist ..................... 2 | of Christ) ...................... 6 |
| Episcopalian ................... 3 | Disciples of Christ .............. 7 |
| Presbyterian ................... 4 | Other (SPECIFY) .............. 8 |
| Lutheran ...................... 5 | No denomination ................ 9 |

B. How important was your husband's religion to him personally—extremely important, fairly important, not very important, or not at all important?

| | |
|---|---|
| Extremely important ......... 1 | Not very important .............. 3 |
| Fairly important ............. 2 | Not at all important ............. 4 |

53. What was his nationality?
PROBE FOR SPECIFIC ETHNIC ORIGIN, NOT GENERAL "AMERICAN" OR "MIXED."

| | |
|---|---|
| English, Scotch ................. 1 | Italian .......................... 6 |
| French ......................... 2 | Norwegian, Swedish, Danish ...... 7 |
| German ........................ 3 | Polish .......................... 8 |
| Greek ......................... 4 | Russian ......................... 9 |
| Irish ........................... 5 | Other (SPECIFY) .............. 0 |

54. What was your husband's work status up to the time of his last illness?
Was he working at his usual job, was he retired or what?

Working at usual job 1      Retired ........... 2      Other (SPECIFY) . 3

55. What was his usual occupation?
ASK Q's 56 AND 57 IF APPROPRIATE.

56. How long did your husband's illness keep him from being able to work full time (including any time he was in the hospital, or sick at home)?

57. Did you care for your husband at home after he became ill?
Yes .................(ASK A).. 1      No ........................... 2
A. *IF YES:* How long did you care for him at home?

*ASK EVERYONE:*
58. After the period of initial grief was over, which single individual helped you the most in establishing yourself in a new life?
GET SPECIFIC RELATIONSHIP, E.G., WHICH CHILD, WHICH SIBLING, FRIEND, OTHER RELATIVE, MINISTER, ETC.
A. In what ways did (he/she) help?

59. · Was there an estate?
Yes .............(ASK A & B).. 1      No ........................... 2
IF YES:
A. How long did it take for the estate to be settled?
B. Who were the main beneficiaries?

*ASK EVERYONE:*

60. HAND RESPONDENT CARD B. Listed on this card are ways in which women have told us they got funds to maintain themselves before financial matters were settled after their husband's death. Which of these would you say apply to you—tell me as many as apply.

    CIRCLE ALL THAT RESPONDENT MENTIONS.

    Continued to work .............. 1      Borrowed from lending institution . 6
    Had enough on hand, cashed              Went to work .................. 7
    securities, bonds, etc. ............. 2      Had to go on relief, welfare ...... 8
    Family gave help ............... 3      Did not pay bills, lived without
    Had to borrow from family ....... 4      spending much, got in debt ....... 9
    Had to borrow from friends ...... 5

    A. Are there any other ways not mentioned on the card? What are they?

61. What is your financial condition? Would you say that you are fairly wealthy, comfortable, rather short, or really restricted in your activities?

    Fairly wealthy ................. 1      Rather short ................... 3
    Comfortable ................... 2      Really restricted .............. 4

62. HAND RESPONDENT CARD C.

| Yearly Amount | Letter | A. Which of the groups on this card includes the income you *now* have? Tell me the letter. CIRCLE APPROPRIATE CODE. | B. What was the highest *family* income you ever had? Just tell me the letter. | C. In what year did you have the highest family income? |
|---|---|---|---|---|
| Under $1,000 | A | 1 | 1 | |
| $1,000–2,999 | B | 2 | 2 | _____ (Year) |
| $3,000–4,999 | C | 3 | 3 | |
| $5,000–6,999 | D | 4 | 4 | |
| $7,000–8,999 | E | 5 | 5 | |
| $9,000–10,999 | F | 6 | 6 | |
| $11,000–15,999 | G | 7 | 7 | |
| Over $16,000 | H | 8 | 8 | |

IF A REFUSED,
ENTER CODE FOR
YOUR ESTIMATE
HERE.                                        _____
                                            A. Est.

63. Do you have any long standing physical condition which limits your activity in any way?

Yes ................(ASK A).. 1    No .......................... 2

A. *IF YES:* How does this limit your activities?

64. In thinking over all your experiences since you have become widowed, what do you think is the most important problem of widowhood?

65. What is the next most important problem of widowhood?

66. Would you like to remarry?

Yes .......................... 1    No ........................... 2

A. Do you think you ever will?

Yes ..............(ASK B).. 1    No .................(ASK B).. 2

B. Why is that? PROBE FULLY.

67. How long a time does grief take, (how long before you feel "yourself" again)? TRANSLATE INTO MONTHS.

68. What advice would you give to a new widow? FIELD CODE, AND RECORD VERBATIM FOR ANY "OTHER" RESPONSE.

Keep busy ..................... 1    Don't try to make decisions too soon 3

Go out to work ................ 2    Other (SPECIFY) .............. 4

69. Many women tell us that they change after becoming widows. How do you think you have changed?

70. In spite of the problems of widowhood, several women have told us that there are some compensations. Which advantages or compensations does a widow have which a married woman does not have?

71. What do you and your friends do together? For example, what do you usually do during the day, in the evening, on the weekend?

During the day ........    The evenings ........    On the weekend ........

72. How did your social life change after you became a widow?

73. If you are not with friends, what do you usually do on Saturday night?

*INTERVIEWER*—NOTICE QUESTION 74

SELF-ADMINISTERED.

(Hand Quex to respondent, and record any side comment at the bottom of the page when she returns it to you.)

74. We have been talking about the many roles or jobs a woman has. Here is a list of roles (responsibilities) most often performed by women. Please rank these roles in order of their importance—place a "1" after the role you consider most important, "2" after the role you consider the second most important, "3" after the third most important, etc., until you have rated all six roles.

| *Role* | *How Important* | *Role* | *How Important* |
|---|---|---|---|
| Daughter ................ | _____ | Housewife ................ | _____ |
| Worker, career ............ | _____ | Mother ................ | _____ |
| Wife ................ | _____ | Member of community ..... | _____ |

And now in closing, we'd appreciate your filling out this short booklet. It contains two sets of statements—*for each statement in the first set,* we'd like you to circle the number which indicates whether you agree strongly, agree, disagree, or disagree strongly.

For each statement in the second set, please circle the number for either "True" or "False."

This is the way it works—read the statement and then circle the number which most closely reflects your feeling.

Thank you very much for taking time to talk to me and for contributing your experience to our knowledge of life-changes in widowhood.

May I have your telephone number in case my office wants to verify this interview. Not your name—only the phone number.

Telephone number: ..........................................................

*INTERVIEWER:* If situation warrants, end the interview by asking her to elaborate a bit on one of the happy situations she has mentioned.

TIME ENDED ..........................A.M.

P.M.

### NATIONAL OPINION RESEARCH CENTER
University of Chicago
4059

Please circle the number that represents your opinion. These are general statements—skip any that do not apply to you.

| | Agree Strongly | Agree | Disagree | Disagree Strongly |
|---|---|---|---|---|
| 1. One problem with adult children is that they always want you to do favors for them—baby-sit, or sew, or things like that. | 1 | 2 | 3 | 4 |
| 2. Sons are more help to a widow than daughters. | 1 | 2 | 3 | 4 |
| 3. Relatives are your only true friends. | 1 | 2 | 3 | 4 |
| 4. A widow has to make her own life and not depend on others. | 1 | 2 | 3 | 4 |
| 5. A new widow should not move too soon from the place in which she was living before her husband died. | 1 | 2 | 3 | 4 |
| 6. Other women are jealous of a widow when their husbands are around. | 1 | 2 | 3 | 4 |
| 7. Many widows who remarry are very unhappy in that marriage. | 1 | 2 | 3 | 4 |
| 8. Widows are constantly sexually propositioned even by the husbands of their friends. | 1 | 2 | 3 | 4 |
| 9. One problem of being a widow is feeling like a "fifth wheel." | 1 | 2 | 3 | 4 |
| 10. People take advantage of you when they know you are a widow. | 1 | 2 | 3 | 4 |
| 11. Sharing one's home with anyone causes nothing but trouble for a widow. | 1 | 2 | 3 | 4 |
| 12. Most widows prefer living near other widows. | 1 | 2 | 3 | 4 |
| 13. It is all right for a widow to have sexual relations with a man without planning on marriage. | 1 | 2 | 3 | 4 |
| 14. The hardest thing for a widow to learn is how to make decisions. | 1 | 2 | 3 | 4 |
| 15. Women lose status when they become widows—they lose respect and consideration. | 1 | 2 | 3 | 4 |
| 16. Old friends cannot be replaced no matter how one tries to make new friends. | 1 | 2 | 3 | 4 |

In this next set of statements, please circle the number which shows whether each statement is true or false for you.

|  |  | True | False |
|---|---|---|---|
| 1. | My husband was an unusually good man. | 1 | 2 |
| 2. | My husband and I did not do too many things together; he had his activities, and I had mine. | 1 | 2 |
| 3. | I did not know anything about our finances when my husband died. | 1 | 2 |
| (IF APPLICABLE) | | | |
| 4. | My husband and I pretended we did not know how sick he really was. | 1 | 2 |
| 5. | My sexual relations with my husband were very good until his last illness. | 1 | 2 |
| 6. | I would do more things outside of the house if someone would come and pick me up. | 1 | 2 |
| 7. | I felt angry at the doctor and the hospital for not doing enough for my husband when he was ill. | 1 | 2 |
| 8. | My married friends have not been much help to me. | 1 | 2 |
| 9. | My present income makes it impossible for me to maintain old friendships. | 1 | 2 |
| 10. | My marriage was above average and no second marriage could match it. | 1 | 2 |
| 11. | I wish people wouldn't try to get me to go out and do things all the time. | 1 | 2 |
| 12. | My brothers and/or sisters became much more important to me after I became a widow. | 1 | 2 |
| 13. | I wish I had more male companionship. | 1 | 2 |
| 14. | I have trouble being nice to people who did not help during my period of grief. | 1 | 2 |
| 15. | I like living alone. | 1 | 2 |
| 16. | I wish I had more friends. | 1 | 2 |
| 17. | My faith helped me more than anything else after my husband's death. | 1 | 2 |
| 18. | Of the men I have dated, I have most in common with widowers. | 1 | 2 |
| 19. | I feel sorry for some of my married friends who have little freedom to do as they please. | 1 | 2 |
| 20. | This time of my life is actually easier than any other time. | 1 | 2 |
| 21. | I feel more independent and free now than before I became a widow. | 1 | 2 |

*INTERVIEWER: FILL IN ITEMS BELOW IMMEDIATELY AFTER LEAVING RESPONDENT.*

A. Total length of interview: .........minutes

B. Total length of editing: ..........minutes

C. Race of respondent:
Negro ............ 1    White ............ 2    Other (SPECIFY) . 3

D. Were there any adults present during the interview?
Yes ............(ASK E & F) .. 1    No ............................. 2

*IF YES:*
E. How many?    Number................

F. Did any of the others present take part in the interview or did Respondent seek advice or opinion from any of them?
Yes ........................... 1    No ............................ 2

G. Is there anything unusual about this Respondent, for example, physical defects or handicaps or serious emotional disorders? Please indicate this below.

H. Respondent's Dwelling:
CHECK BOX IF PUBLIC HOUSING PROJECT AND CIRCLE
APPROPRIATE NUMBER BELOW. ☐

Single family, detached .......... 1    Four to six units ................ 5
Single family, attached (including    Seven to nine units ............. 6
row or town houses) ............. 2    Ten or more units .............. 7
Two family .................... 3    Other (SPECIFY) ............. 8
Three units ................... 4

I. Is Respondent's dwelling better kept, the same, or not as well kept as surrounding dwellings on the block? (This means the outside appearance of the dwelling and the yard.)
Better kept ........ 1    Same ............ 2    Not as well kept ... 3

PLEASE USE THE WORD-PAIR TECHNIQUE TO GIVE THE FOLLOWING
RATINGS ON THE BASIS OF YOUR OBSERVATION OF THE RESPONDENT
AND HER HOME AND NEIGHBORHOOD. CIRCLE ONE NUMBER ON
EACH LINE.

J. *Respondent in Interview Situation:*

| | | | | | | |
|---|---|---|---|---|---|---|
| Not smart | 1 | 2 | 3 | 4 | 5 | 6 | Smart |
| Friendly | 1 | 2 | 3 | 4 | 5 | 6 | Hostile |
| Slow | 1 | 2 | 3 | 4 | 5 | 6 | Quick |
| Silent | 1 | 2 | 3 | 4 | 5 | 6 | Talkative |

**K.** *Respondent's Speech:*

| | | | | | | | |
|---|---|---|---|---|---|---|---|
| Correct Grammar | 1 | 2 | 3 | 4 | 5 | 6 | Incorrect Grammar |
| Heavy Southern or Foreign Accent | 1 | 2 | 3 | 4 | 5 | 6 | No Southern or Foreign Accent |
| Difficult to Understand | 1 | 2 | 3 | 4 | 5 | 6 | Easy to Understand |

**L.** *Respondent's Appearance:*

| | | | | | | | |
|---|---|---|---|---|---|---|---|
| Well Dressed | 1 | 2 | 3 | 4 | 5 | 6 | Poorly Dressed |
| Neat | 1 | 2 | 3 | 4 | 5 | 6 | Sloppy |
| Young Looking (Well preserved) | 1 | 2 | 3 | 4 | 5 | 6 | Old Looking (Wrinkled, bad posture) |
| Healthy Looking | 1 | 2 | 3 | 4 | 5 | 6 | Sick Looking |

**M.** *Respondent's home:*

| | | | | | | | |
|---|---|---|---|---|---|---|---|
| Neat | 1 | 2 | 3 | 4 | 5 | 6 | Disorderly |
| Dirty | 1 | 2 | 3 | 4 | 5 | 6 | Clean |
| Rich | 1 | 2 | 3 | 4 | 5 | 6 | Poor |
| Relaxed | 1 | 2 | 3 | 4 | 5 | 6 | Tense |

**N.** *Respondent's Block* (surrounding dwellings):

| | | | | | | | |
|---|---|---|---|---|---|---|---|
| Well-kept Dwellings | 1 | 2 | 3 | 4 | 5 | 6 | Poorly-kept Dwellings |
| Littered Streets (refuse, glass etc.) | 1 | 2 | 3 | 4 | 5 | 6 | Clean Streets (no refuse, glass, etc.) |
| Very Poor Neighborhood | 1 | 2 | 3 | 4 | 5 | 6 | Very Well-to-do Neighborhood |
| Mainly Apartments | 1 | 2 | 3 | 4 | 5 | 6 | Mainly Single Dwellings |
| Open Spaces (lawns, yards, space between buildings) | 1 | 2 | 3 | 4 | 5 | 6 | Crowded (no lawns, yards, space between buildings) |
| Mainly Commercial and/or Industrial Buildings | 1 | 2 | 3 | 4 | 5 | 6 | No Commercial or Industrial Buildings |

**O.** Interviewer's Signature: ..............................................................

**P.** Date of Interview: ..............................................................

## LIST OF TABLES IN APPENDIX B

A. Living Arrangements in the Past

B. Proportion of Women Living with their Husbands in Houses and owning them Prior to his Death, by Age at Widowhood

C. Working Experience of Respondents

D. Religious Identification and Importance of Religion to Respondent and her Husband

E. Nationality Identifications of the Respondent and of her Husband

F. Husband's Working Status Prior to Death

G. Causes of Husband's Death

H. Degree of Help Given the Respondent by an Only Child

I. Background Information on Living Siblings

J. Feelings of Closeness to Siblings

K. Other Residents in Respondent's Home

L. Ownership of Home in Which Respondent is Living

M. Problems of a Widow Living with Married Children

N. Types of Voluntary Association Memberships Before Widowhood and Currently

O. Current Hobbies of Respondents

P. Number of Times a Day the Respondent Talks on the Telephone (other than on the job)

Q. Number of Letters the Respondent Writes in a Week

R. Characteristics of Friends of Older Widows

S. Marital Histories of Respondents

T. Expectations of Remarriage

U. Compensations of Widowhood

V. Changes in Social Life Upon Widowhood

W. Persons who Helped the Respondent Most in Developing a New Life after Widowhood

## APPENDIX B:  BACKGROUND CHARACTERISTICS OF
## CHICAGO AREA OLDER WIDOWS

### TABLE SET A:  LIVING ARRANGEMENTS IN THE PAST

TABLE A1: RESIDENCE JUST BEFORE WIDOWHOOD

| Residence | Number | Percent |
|---|---|---|
| Same dwelling as now | 152 | 50.7 |
| Elsewhere in same neighborhood | 36 | 12.0 |
| Elsewhere in Chicago or suburb | 64 | 21.3 |
| Other metropolitan area | 48 | 16.0 |
| No Answer | 1* | — |
| Percent Base | | 300 |

* Not included in percent base

TABLE A2: TYPE OF RESIDENCE PRIOR TO WIDOWHOOD

| Type of Residence | Number | Percent |
|---|---|---|
| House | 78 | 52.7 |
| Apartment | 66 | 44.6 |
| Other | 4 | 2.7 |
| No Answer | None | — |
| Not Appropriate | 153* | — |
| Percent Base | | 148 |

* Not included in percent base

TABLE A3: OWNERSHIP STATUS OF RESIDENCE PRIOR TO
WIDOWHOOD

| Ownership Status | Number | Percent |
|---|---|---|
| Own | 59 | 39.9 |
| Rent | 83 | 56.1 |
| Other | 6 | 4.1 |
| No Answer | None | — |
| Not Appropriate | 153* | — |
| Percent Base | | 148 |

* Not included in percent base

TABLE A4: TIME OF RESIDENTIAL CHANGE AFTER
WIDOWHOOD

| Time | Number | Percent |
|---|---|---|
| During husband's illness | 6 | 4.2 |
| Right after funeral | 21 | 14.7 |
| Within six months | 29 | 20.3 |
| Within one year | 10 | 7.0 |
| Over one year | 77 | 53.8 |
| No Answer | 5* | — |
| Not Appropriate | 153* | — |
| Percent Base | | 143 |

* Not included in percent base

TABLE B: PROPORTION OF WOMEN LIVING WITH THEIR
HUSBANDS IN HOUSES AND OWNING THEM PRIOR
TO HIS DEATH, BY AGE AT WIDOWHOOD*

| | Living in Houses | | Owning Houses | | Age Category | |
|---|---|---|---|---|---|---|
| | % | N | % | N | % | N |
| 34 and under | 46 | 6 | 15 | 2 | 9 | 13 |
| 36–39 | 60 | 6 | 10 | 1 | 7 | 10 |
| 40–44 | 73 | 8 | 45 | 5 | 7 | 11 |
| 45–49 | 56 | 15 | 48 | 13 | 18 | 27 |
| 50–54 | 60 | 15 | 40 | 10 | 17 | 25 |
| 55–59 | 43 | 9 | 43 | 9 | 14 | 21 |
| 60–64 | 52 | 11 | 57 | 12 | 14 | 21 |
| 65–69 | 38 | 3 | 25 | 2 | 5 | 8 |
| 70–74 | 44 | 4 | 44 | 4 | 6 | 9 |
| 75 and over | 33 | 1 | 33 | 1 | 2 | 3 |

* Percent base is 148, since remaining widows did not move.

# TABLE SET C: WORKING EXPERIENCE OF RESPONDENTS

TABLE C1: WORKING EXPERIENCE BEFORE MARRIAGE

| Answer | Number | Percent |
|---|---|---|
| Yes | 222 | 73.8 |
| None | 79 | 26.2 |
| No Answer | None | |
| Percent Base | | 301 |

TABLE C2: PROPORTION OF TIME RESPONDENT WORKED
DURING MARRIAGE

| Proportion | Number | Percent |
|---|---|---|
| All of the time | 34 | 11.3 |
| Most of the time | 32 | 10.6 |
| Some of the time | 115 | 38.2 |
| Never | 120 | 39.9 |
| No Answer | None | |
| Percent Base | | 301 |

TABLE C3: WORKING EXPERIENCE SINCE WIDOWHOOD

| Answer | Number | Percent |
|---|---|---|
| Yes | 145 | 48.2 |
| No | 156 | 51.8 |
| No Answer | None | — |
| Percent Base | | 301 |

TABLE C4: WAS RESPONDENT ABLE TO GET THE KIND OF
JOB HELD BEFORE, IF SHE WENT TO WORK
AFTER WIDOWHOOD

| Answer | Number | Percent |
|---|---|---|
| Same kind of job | 23 | 44.2 |
| One not as good | 13 | 25.0 |
| A better one | 16 | 30.8 |
| No Answer | 6* | — |
| Not Appropriate | 243* | — |
| Percent Base | | 52 |

* Not included in percent base

TABLE C5: REASONS WHY THE RESPONDENT LEFT HER
          BEST JOB

| Reason | Number | Percent |
|---|---|---|
| Got married or remarried | 72 | 31.9 |
| Had a child, children | 17 | 7.5 |
| Husband's illness or death | 4 | 1.8 |
| Moved from the locality where job was | 5 | 2.2 |
| Health got bad | 26 | 11.5 |
| Retirement | 26 | 11.5 |
| Other | 76 | 33.6 |
| No Answer | 9* | — |
| Not Appropriate | 66* | — |
| Percent Base | | 226 |

* Not included in percent base

# TABLE SET D:  RELIGIOUS IDENTIFICATION AND IMPORTANCE OF RELIGION TO RESPONDENT AND TO HER HUSBAND

TABLE D1: RELIGIOUS IDENTIFICATION OF SELF AND
          HUSBAND

| Religion | Self | | Husband | |
|---|---|---|---|---|
| | Number | Percent | Number | Percent |
| Protestant | 155 | 51.5 | 162 | 53.8 |
| Roman Catholic | 114 | 37.9 | 105 | 34.9 |
| Greek Orthodox | 3 | 1.0 | 6 | 2.0 |
| Jewish | 15 | 5.0 | 13 | 4.3 |
| Other | 7 | 2.3 | None | — |
| None | 7 | 2.3 | 15 | 5.0 |
| No Answer | None | — | None | — |
| Percent Base | | 301 | | 301 |

* Not included in percent base

TABLE D2: DETAILS OF PROTESTANT DENOMINATIONAL
IDENTIFICATION OF RESPONDENT AND OF HER
HUSBAND

| | Self | | Husband | |
|---|---|---|---|---|
| Denomination | Number | Percent | Number | Percent |
| Baptist | 43 | 27.7 | 41 | 25.3 |
| Methodist | 25 | 16.1 | 28 | 17.3 |
| Episcopalian | 8 | 5.2 | 9 | 5.6 |
| Presbyterian | 17 | 11.0 | 10 | 6.2 |
| Lutheran | 38 | 24.5 | 43 | 26.5 |
| Congregational | 4 | 2.6 | 6 | 3.7 |
| Disciples of Christ | 2 | 1.3 | 2 | 1.2 |
| Other | 15 | 9.7 | 17 | 10.5 |
| No Denomination | 3 | 1.9 | 6 | 3.7 |
| No Answer | None | — | None | — |
| Not Appropriate | 146* | — | 139* | — |
| Percent Base | | 155 | | 162 |

\* Not included in percent base


TABLE D3: IMPORTANCE OF RELIGION TO RESPONDENT
AND TO HER HUSBAND

| | Self | | Husband | |
|---|---|---|---|---|
| Importance | Number | Percent | Number | Percent |
| Extremely important | 180 | 61.2 | 106 | 37.2 |
| Fairly important | 82 | 27.9 | 85 | 29.8 |
| Not very important | 26 | 8.8 | 67 | 23.5 |
| Not at all important | 6 | 2.0 | 27 | 9.5 |
| No Answer | None | — | 1* | — |
| Not Appropriate | 7* | — | 15* | — |
| Percent Base | | 301 | | 301 |

\* Not included in percent base

TABLE E: NATIONALITY IDENTIFICATIONS OF THE
RESPONDENT AND OF HER HUSBAND

| | Self | | | | Husband | | | |
| | First Answer | | Second Answer | | First Answer | | Second Answer | |
| Nationality | Number | Percent | Number | Percent | Number | Percent | Number | Percent |
|---|---|---|---|---|---|---|---|---|
| English, Scotch | 32 | 10.8 | — | — | 40 | 13.6 | — | — |
| French | 3 | 1.0 | 3 | 13.0 | 5 | 1.7 | — | — |
| German | 66 | 22.2 | 3 | 13.0 | 63 | 21.4 | 4 | 22.2 |
| Greek | 3 | 1.0 | — | — | 4 | 1.4 | — | — |
| Irish | 32 | 10.8 | 12 | 52.2 | 30 | 10.2 | 9 | 50.0 |
| Italian | 13 | 4.4 | — | — | 8 | 2.7 | — | — |
| Norwegian, Swedish, Danish | 12 | 4.0 | — | — | 16 | 5.4 | — | — |
| Polish | 34 | 11.4 | 2 | 8.7 | 29 | 9.8 | 2 | 11.1 |
| Russian | 10 | 3.4 | 2 | 8.7 | 6 | 2.0 | — | — |
| Negro, Other | 92 | 31.0 | 1 | 4.3 | 94 | 31.9 | 3 | 16.7 |
| No Answer | 4* | — | 4* | — | 6* | — | 6* | — |
| Not Appropriate | — | — | 274* | — | — | — | 277* | — |
| Percent Base | | 297 | | 23 | | 295 | | 18 |

\* Not included in percent base

# TABLE SET F: HUSBAND'S WORKING STATUS PRIOR TO DEATH

TABLE F1: HUSBAND'S WORK STATUS UP TO HIS LAST ILLNESS

| Work Status | Number | Percent |
|---|---|---|
| Working at usual job | 181 | 62.0 |
| Retired | 81 | 27.7 |
| Other | 30 | 10.3 |
| No Answer | 9* | — |
| Percent Base | 292 | |

\* Not included in percent base

TABLE F2: LENGTH OF TIME HUSBAND DID NOT WORK
FULL-TIME  BECAUSE OF LAST ILLNESS

| Length of Time | Number | Percent |
|---|---|---|
| Not at all | 38 | 19.8 |
| 1 to 13 days | 35 | 18.2 |
| 14 to 27 days | 3 | 1.6 |
| 4 to 8 weeks | 15 | 7.8 |
| 3 to 5 months | 26 | 13.5 |
| 6 to 11 months | 19 | 9.9 |
| 1 year or more | 56 | 29.2 |
| No Answer | 8* | — |
| Not Appropriate | 101* | — |
| Percent Base | | 192 |

* Not included in percent base

TABLE G: CAUSE OF HUSBAND'S DEATH

| | Number | Percent |
|---|---|---|
| Accident | 19 | 3.4 |
| Heart Disease | 137 | 47.1 |
| Cancer | 50 | 17.2 |
| Stroke | 18 | 6.2 |
| Pneumonia | 11 | 3.8 |
| Diabetes | 6 | 2.1 |
| Combined | 8 | 2.7 |
| Other | 51 | 17.5 |
| No Answer | 10* | |
| Percent Base | | 291 |

* Not included in percent base

TABLE H: DEGREE OF HELP GIVEN THE RESPONDENT BY AN
ONLY CHILD

| | Degree of Help | | Not | Percent |
|---|---|---|---|---|
| Type of Help | Much | Little | Appropriate | Base |
| During husband's last illness | 51.7 | 17.2 | 31.0 | 58 |
| During the funeral | 64.4 | 8.5 | 27.1 | 59 |
| With finances | 15.8 | 26.3 | 57.9 | 57 |
| By being close | 79.3 | 13.8 | 6.9 | 58 |
| Emotionally, when she is blue | 62.7 | 18.6 | 18.6 | 59 |
| By giving advice | 51.7 | 29.3 | 19.0 | 58 |
| By performing services | 61.7 | 21.7 | 16.7 | 60 |
| By inviting her to their home | 55.9 | 5.1 | 39.0 | 59 |
| By coming to see her | 45.8 | 15.3 | 39.0 | 59 |

TABLE I: BACKGROUND INFORMATION ON LIVING SIBLINGS

| | Number of Sibling | | | | | | | | |
|---|---|---|---|---|---|---|---|---|---|
| *Sex* | 1 | 2 | 3 | 4 | 5 | 6 | 7 | 8 | 9 |
| Male | 42.3 | 39.7 | 42.7 | 44.9 | 47.5 | 55.6 | 50.0 | 50.0 | 25.0 |
| Female | 57.7 | 60.3 | 57.3 | 55.1 | 52.5 | 44.4 | 50.0 | 50.0 | 75.0 |
| Percent | 241 | 174 | 117 | 69 | 40 | 18 | 10 | 4 | 4 |
| | | | | | | | | | |
| *Older, Younger, or Same Age* | | | | | | | | | |
| Older | 39.6 | 37.0 | 25.0 | 16.2 | 7.5 | 5.6 | — | — | — |
| Younger | 40.0 | 62.4 | 74.1 | 83.8 | 92.5 | 94.4 | 100.0 | 100.0 | 100.0 |
| Same age | — | 0.6 | 0.9 | — | — | — | — | — | — |
| Percent Base | 240 | 173 | 116 | 68 | 40 | 18 | 10 | — | 4 |
| | | | | | | | | | |
| *Neighborhood Residence* | | | | | | | | | |
| Same dwelling | 17.7 | 14.3 | 10.5 | 33.3 | — | — | — | 100.0 | — |
| Same building, other dwelling | 17.7 | 4.8 | 10.5 | — | — | — | — | — | — |
| Same block | 14.7 | 4.8 | 10.5 | — | — | — | — | — | — |
| Somewhere else in the neighborhood | 50.0 | 76.2 | 68.4 | 66.7 | 100.0 | 100.0 | 100.0 | — | 100.0 |
| Percent Base | 34 | 21 | 19 | 12 | 4 | 1 | 1 | 1 | 1 |
| | | | | | | | | | |
| *Non-Neighborhood Residence* | | | | | | | | | |
| One hour or less | 34.8 | 33.6 | 39.1 | 45.6 | 33.3 | 52.9 | 50.0 | 66.7 | 66.7 |
| Over an hour | 35.3 | 33.6 | 32.6 | 21.1 | 36.1 | 23.5 | 20.0 | — | — |
| Over one day | 29.9 | 32.9 | 28.3 | 33.3 | 30.6 | 23.5 | 30.0 | 33.3 | 33.3 |
| Percent Base | 201 | 146 | 92 | 57 | 36 | 17 | 10 | 3 | 3 |
| | | | | | | | | | |
| *Method of Transportation* | | | | | | | | | |
| Car | 49.2 | 51.8 | 50.5 | 51.9 | 52.9 | 62.5 | 66.7 | 66.7 | 66.7 |
| Local bus or "L" | 12.3 | 12.1 | 14.3 | 16.7 | 5.9 | 6.3 | 11.1 | — | — |
| Greyhound or train | 17.6 | 16.3 | 13.2 | 18.5 | 26.5 | 12.5 | 11.1 | 33.3 | 33.3 |
| Airplane | 20.9 | 19.9 | 22.0 | 13.0 | 14.7 | 18.8 | 11.1 | — | — |
| Percent Base | 187 | 141 | 91 | 54 | 34 | 16 | 9 | 3 | 3 |
| | | | | | | | | | |
| *Frequency of Contact* | | | | | | | | | |
| Almost daily | 5.0 | 5.0 | 7.4 | 1.6 | 2.5 | — | — | — | — |
| Every week or so | 13.1 | 13.0 | 17.6 | 15.9 | 20.0 | 11.1 | — | — | — |
| About every month | 17.1 | 14.9 | 20.4 | 22.2 | 12.5 | 27.8 | 40.0 | — | 33.3 |
| A few times a year | 23.9 | 25.5 | 17.6 | 19.0 | 25.0 | 11.1 | 30.0 | 100.0 | 66.7 |
| Less often than that | 41.0 | 41.6 | 37.0 | 41.3 | 40.0 | 50.0 | 30.0 | — | — |
| Percent Base | 222 | 161 | 108 | 63 | 40 | 18 | 10 | 3 | 3 |

## TABLE SET J: FEELINGS OF CLOSENESS TO SIBLINGS

### TABLE J1: DOES RESPONDENT HAVE A FEELING OF CLOSENESS TO SOME SIBLINGS

| Answer | Number | Percent |
|---|---|---|
| Yes | 160 | 66.4 |
| Not very | 10 | 4.1 |
| No | 71 | 29.5 |
| No Answer | 1* | — |
| Not Appropriate | 59* | — |
| Percent Base | | 241 |

\* Not included in percent base

### TABLE J2: SIBLING TO WHOM RESPONDENT FEELS CLOSEST

| Answer | Number | Percent |
|---|---|---|
| Only sibling | 41 | 24.4 |
| Older sister | 27 | 16.1 |
| Older brother | 8 | 4.8 |
| Younger sister | 48 | 28.6 |
| Younger brother | 15 | 8.9 |
| Equally | 29 | 17.3 |
| Other | None | — |
| No Answer | 2* | — |
| Not Appropriate | 131* | — |
| Percent Base | | 168 |

\* Not included in percent base

### TABLE K: OTHER RESIDENTS IN RESPONDENT'S HOME

| Relationship | 1 | 2 | 3 | 4 | 5 | 6 | 7 | 8 |
|---|---|---|---|---|---|---|---|---|
| Son | 12.0 | 21.5 | 3.3 | 5.3 | 12.5 | — | — | — |
| Daughter | 18.9 | 26.2 | 20.0 | 10.5 | — | — | — | — |
| Mother | 0.7 | 3.1 | — | — | — | — | — | — |
| Father | 0.7 | — | — | — | — | — | — | — |
| Sister | 3.0 | 1.5 | — | 5.3 | 12.5 | — | — | — |
| Brother | 1.0 | — | — | — | — | — | — | — |
| Other relative | 7.0 | 21.5 | 66.7 | 73.7 | 75.0 | 100.0 | 100.0 | 100.0 |
| Daughter-in-law | — | 1.5 | — | — | — | — | — | — |
| Son-in-law | 1.3 | 10.8 | — | — | — | — | — | — |
| Non-relative | 6.3 | 13.8 | 10.0 | 5.3 | — | — | — | — |
| Lives alone | 49.2 | — | — | — | — | — | — | — |
| No Answer | — | — | — | — | — | — | — | — |
| Percent Base | 301 | 65 | 30 | 19 | 8 | 5 | 3 | 1 |

TABLE L: OWNERSHIP OF HOME IN WHICH RESPONDENT
IS LIVING

| Ownership | Number | Percent |
|---|---|---|
| Own home | 105 | 69.1 |
| Child's home | 32 | 21.1 |
| Parent's home | 3 | 2.0 |
| Sibling's home | 4 | 2.6 |
| Other relative's home | 6 | 3.9 |
| Non-relative's home | 2 | 1.3 |
| No Answer | 1* | — |
| Lives alone | 148* | — |
| Percent Base | | 152 |

* Not included in percent base

# TABLE SET M: PROBLEMS OF LIVING WITH MARRIED CHILDREN

TABLE M1: SOURCES OF PROBLEMS OF A WIDOW LIVING
WITH MARRIED CHILDREN

| Source | Number | Percent |
|---|---|---|
| Self | 30 | 10.1 |
| Son-in-law | 32 | 10.8 |
| Own child | 6 | 2.0 |
| Grandchild | 4 | 1.3 |
| Household member | None | — |
| Other | 1 | 0.3 |
| No one person | 175 | 58.9 |
| Not specified | 2 | 0.7 |
| No problem | 47 | 15.8 |
| No Answer | 4* | — |
| Percent Base | | 297 |

* Not included in percent base

TABLE M2: TYPES OF PROBLEMS OF LIVING WITH MARRIED CHILDREN

| Problem | Number | Percent |
|---|---|---|
| Generation gap | 65 | 26.0 |
| Two women | 44 | 17.6 |
| Respondent wants independence | 34 | 13.6 |
| Argument | 10 | 4.0 |
| Behavior | 73 | 29.2 |
| Commotion and noise | 9 | 3.6 |
| Other | 15 | 6.0 |
| No problem | 47* | — |
| No Answer | 4* | — |
| Percent Base | | 250 |

* Not included in percent base

## TABLE SET N: TYPES OF VOLUNTARY ASSOCIATION MEMBERSHIPS BEFORE WIDOWHOOD AND CURRENTLY

TABLE N1: TYPES OF VOLUNTARY ASSOCIATION MEMBERSHIPS BEFORE WIDOWHOOD

| Type of Group | Belong Yes | No | N | Active Yes | No | No Answer | Not Appropriate | Percent Base |
|---|---|---|---|---|---|---|---|---|
| Family | 4.0 | 96.0 | 301 | 81.8 | 18.2 | 1* | 289* | 11 |
| National | 21.3 | 78.7 | | 66.7 | 33.3 | 1* | 237* | 63 |
| Religious | 45.2 | 54.8 | | 85.1 | 14.9 | 2* | 165* | 134 |
| Recreational | 24.9 | 75.1 | | 87.8 | 12.2 | 1* | 226* | 74 |
| Educational | 15.3 | 84.7 | | 79.5 | 20.5 | 2* | 255* | 44 |
| Community | 13.0 | 87.0 | | 89.2 | 10.8 | 2* | 262* | 37 |
| Union | 5.6 | 94.4 | | 43.8 | 56.3 | 1* | 284* | 16 |
| Charity | 11.0 | 89.0 | | 81.3 | 18.8 | 1* | 268* | 32 |
| Older | 2.3 | 97.7 | | 83.3 | 16.7 | 1* | 294* | 6 |

* Not included in percent base

TABLE N2: TYPES OF CURRENT VOLUNTARY ASSOCIATION
MEMBERSHIPS

| | Belong | | | Active | | No | Not Appro- | Percent |
|---|---|---|---|---|---|---|---|---|
| Type of Group | Yes | No | N | Yes | No | Answer | priate | Base |
| Family | 2.0 | 98.0 | 301 | 60.0 | 40.0 | 1* | 295* | 5 |
| National | 12.6 | 87.4 | | 44.7 | 55.3 | None | 263* | 38 |
| Religious | 33.2 | 66.8 | | 64.0 | 36.0 | None | 201* | 100 |
| Recreational | 19.3 | 80.7 | | 80.7 | 19.3 | 1* | 243* | 57 |
| Educational | 6.6 | 93.4 | | 68.4 | 31.6 | 1* | 281* | 19 |
| Community | 7.6 | 92.4 | | 73.9 | 26.1 | None | 278* | 23 |
| Union | 2.3 | 97.7 | | 14.3 | 85.7 | None | 294* | 7 |
| Charity | 7.6 | 92.4 | | 77.3 | 22.7 | 1* | 278* | 22 |
| Older | 2.7 | 97.3 | | 75.0 | 25.0 | None | 293* | 8 |

\* Not included in percent base

TABLE O: CURRENT HOBBIES OF RESPONDENT

| | Yes | | No + Not Appropriate | |
|---|---|---|---|---|
| Hobby | Number | Percent | Number | Percent |
| No hobbies | 79 | 26.2 | — | — |
| Gardening | 39 | 13.0 | 262 | 87.0 |
| Sewing, knitting, crotcheting | 120 | 39.9 | 181 | 60.1 |
| Reading | 63 | 20.9 | 238 | 79.1 |
| Cards | 42 | 14.0 | 259 | 86.0 |
| TV, radio | 68 | 22.6 | 233 | 77.4 |
| Other hobby | 73 | 24.3 | 228 | 75.7 |

Percent base = 301

TABLE P: NUMBER OF TIMES A DAY THE RESPONDENT TALKS
ON THE TELEPHONE (OTHER THAN ON THE JOB)

| Number of Calls | Number | Percent |
|---|---|---|
| None | 49 | 16.7 |
| One | 69 | 23.5 |
| Two | 73 | 24.8 |
| Three | 43 | 14.6 |
| Four | 19 | 6.5 |
| Five | 15 | 5.1 |
| Six | 11 | 3.7 |
| Seven | 2 | 0.7 |
| Eight | 1 | 0.3 |
| Nine | 8 | 2.7 |
| Ten or over | 4 | 1.4 |
| No Answer | 7* | — |
| Percent Base | | 294 |

* Not included in percent base


TABLE Q: NUMBER OF LETTERS THE RESPONDENT WRITES
IN A WEEK

| Number of Letters | Number | Percent |
|---|---|---|
| None | 154 | 51.3 |
| One | 47 | 15.7 |
| Two | 33 | 11.0 |
| Three | 17 | 5.7 |
| Four | 18 | 6.0 |
| Five | 9 | 3.0 |
| Six | 8 | 2.7 |
| Seven | 1 | 0.3 |
| Eight | 4 | 1.3 |
| Nine | 6 | 2.0 |
| Ten or over | 3 | 1.0 |
| No Answer | 1* | — |
| Percent Base | | 300 |

* Not included in percent base

# TABLE SET R: CHARACTERISTICS OF FRIENDS OF OLDER WIDOWS

## TABLE R1: PROPORTION OF FRIENDS WHO ARE WIDOWS

| Proportion | Number | Percent |
|---|---|---|
| All | 12 | 4.0 |
| Most | 57 | 18.9 |
| Half and half | 63 | 20.9 |
| A few | 83 | 27.6 |
| One or two | 46 | 15.3 |
| None | 33 | 11.0 |
| Have no friends | 7 | 2.3 |
| No Answer | None | — |
| Percent Base | | 301 |

* Not included in percent base

## TABLE R2: LENGTH OF FRIENDSHIP OF WIDOWS

| Length of Friendship | Number | Percent |
|---|---|---|
| Before she was widowed | 172 | 69.1 |
| After she was widowed | 57 | 22.9 |
| Both | 5 | 2.0 |
| Other | 15 | 6.0 |
| No Answer | 12* | — |
| Not Appropriate | 40* | — |
| Percent Base | | 249 |

* Not included in percent base

## TABLE R3: PROPORTION OF FRIENDS OF RESPONDENT WHO ARE OF THE SAME RELIGION OR NATIONALITY AS THE RESPONDENT

| Proportion | Same Religion | | Same Nationality | |
|---|---|---|---|---|
| | Number | Percent | Number | Percent |
| All | 51 | 17.5 | 56 | 21.5 |
| Most | 112 | 38.5 | 55 | 21.1 |
| Half and half | 53 | 18.2 | 42 | 16.1 |
| A few | 46 | 15.8 | 55 | 21.1 |
| One or two | 16 | 5.5 | 13 | 5.0 |
| None | 7 | 2.4 | 34 | 13.0 |
| Don't have friends | 6 | 2.1 | 6 | 2.3 |
| No Answer | 3* | — | 13* | — |
| Not Appropriate | 7* | — | 27* | — |
| Percent Base | 291 | | 261 | |

* Not included in percent base

# TABLE SET S: MARITAL HISTORIES OF RESPONDENTS

TABLE S1: NUMBER OF TIMES RESPONDENT MARRIED

| Times | Number | Percent | Percent Base |
|---|---|---|---|
| Once | 239 | 79.4 | 301 |
| More than once | 62 | 20.6 | 301 |
| Twice | 52 | 83.9 | 62 |
| Three times or more | 10 | 16.1 | 62 |

TABLE S2: MEANS BY WHICH FIRST AND SECOND MARRIAGES
ENDED FOR THOSE WHO MARRIED MORE
THAN ONCE

| Means | First Marriage | | Second Marriage | |
|---|---|---|---|---|
| | Number | Percent | Number | Percent |
| Divorce | 34 | 54.8 | 6 | 9.7 |
| Widowhood | 27 | 43.5 | 56 | 90.3 |
| Divorced, then widowed | 1 | 1.6 | — | — |
| No Answer | — | — | — | — |
| Not Appropriate | 239* | — | 239* | — |
| Percent Base | | 62 | | 62 |

* Not included in percent base

TABLE S3: AGE OF THE LAST OR ONLY HUSBAND IN
COMPARISON TO AGE OF WIFE

| Answer | Number | Percent |
|---|---|---|
| Older | 238 | 79.3 |
| Younger | 29 | 9.7 |
| Same age | 33 | 11.0 |
| No Answer | 1* | — |
| Percent Base | | 300 |

* Not included in percent base

## TABLE SET T: EXPECTATIONS OF REMARRIAGE

### TABLE T1: LEVEL OF EXPECTATION OF REMARRIAGE

| Level | Number | Percent |
|---|---|---|
| No | 37 | 13.0 |
| No one wants me | 7 | 2.5 |
| Don't want to | 120 | 42.1 |
| Too old | 53 | 18.6 |
| Don't know yet | 25 | 8.8 |
| No chance to meet men | 12 | 4.2 |
| Maybe | 9 | 3.2 |
| Yes, I hope so | 20 | 7.0 |
| I am going to | 2 | 0.7 |
| Don't know | 6* | — |
| No Answer | 10* | — |
| Percent Base | | 285 |

* Not included in percent base

### TABLE T2: REASON FOR REJECTION OF REMARRIAGE

| Reason | Number | Percent |
|---|---|---|
| I'm free, independent | 67 | 26.7 |
| No man as good | 54 | 21.5 |
| Stepfather not good | 9 | 3.6 |
| Can't trust men | 16 | 6.4 |
| Care for illness | 21 | 8.4 |
| Wouldn't be happy | 12 | 4.8 |
| Had enough | 10 | 4.0 |
| Remarriage not good | 9 | 3.6 |
| Other | 53 | 21.1 |
| No Answer | 10* | — |
| Not Appropriate | 40* | — |
| Percent Base | | 251 |

* Not included in percent base

TABLE U: COMPENSATIONS OF WIDOWHOOD

| Compensation | First Listed Number | First Listed Percent | Second Listed Number | Second Listed Percent | Third Listed Number | Third Listed Percent |
|---|---|---|---|---|---|---|
| Free time | 104 | 35.6 | — | — | — | — |
| Less work | 9 | 3.1 | 78 | 67.2 | — | — |
| Independence, own boss | 25 | 8.6 | 31 | 26.7 | 70 | 79.5 |
| Peace of mind | 3 | 1.0 | 5 | 4.3 | 16 | 18.2 |
| More money | 2 | 0.7 | 1 | 0.9 | 2 | 2.3 |
| Other | 3 | 1.0 | 1 | 0.9 | — | — |
| None | 146 | 50.0 | — | — | — | — |
| Don't know | 5* | — | — | — | — | — |
| No Answer | 4* | — | 4* | — | 4* | — |
| Not Appropriate | — | — | 181* | — | 209* | — |
| Percent Base | | 292 | | 116 | | 88 |

* Not included in percent base

## TABLE SET V:  CHANGES IN SOCIAL LIFE UPON WIDOWHOOD

TABLE V1: CHANGES IN QUALITY AND QUANTITY OF SOCIAL LIFE WITH WIDOWHOOD

| Changes | Number | Percent |
|---|---|---|
| None now | 8 | 2.7 |
| Less | 113 | 38.3 |
| More | 34 | 11.5 |
| Different activity | 4 | ˙ |
| Different people | 10 | 3.4 |
| Changed | — | . |
| Same | 126 | 42.7 |
| No Answer | 6* | — |
| Percent Base | | 295 |

* Not included in percent base

TABLE V2: TYPE OF ACTIVITY CHANGED SINCE WIDOWHOOD

| Activity | Number | Percent |
|---|---|---|
| Stay home | 12 | 7.1 |
| Watch TV | 1 | 0.6 |
| Usually alone | 3 | 1.8 |
| Visit or have company | 45 | 26.6 |
| Play cards in homes | 6 | 3.6 |
| Go to public places | 98 | 58.0 |
| Club meetings | 4 | 2.4 |
| No Answer | 6* | — |
| Not Appropriate | 126* | — |
| Percent Base | | 169 |

* Not included in percent base


TABLE V3: REASONS FOR CHANGES IN SOCIAL LIFE SINCE WIDOWHOOD

| Reasons | Number | Percent |
|---|---|---|
| No longer invited | 18 | 10.7 |
| Couples, do not want to go | 59 | 34.9 |
| Old, less healthy | 13 | 7.7 |
| Restricted, child, others | 12 | 7.1 |
| Afraid to go out alone | 11 | 6.5 |
| "Can't" go places | 17 | 10.1 |
| Homebody | 4 | 2.4 |
| Husband did not go out | 10 | 5.9 |
| Freer, busy | 24 | 14.2 |
| Other | 1 | 0.6 |
| No Answer | 6* | — |
| Not Appropriate | 126* | — |
| Percent Base | | 169 |

* Not included in percent base

TABLE W: PERSONS WHO HELPED THE RESPONDENT MOST
IN DEVELOPING A NEW LIFE AFTER WIDOWHOOD

| | First Reference | | Second Reference | |
|---|---|---|---|---|
| *Person* | *Number* | *Percent* | *Number* | *Percent* |
| Son | 37 | 12.5 | 1 | 3.6 |
| Mother | 10 | 3.4 | — | — |
| Father | 2 | 0.7 | — | — |
| Sister | 27 | 9.1 | 3 | 10.7 |
| Brother | 7 | 2.4 | 2 | 7.1 |
| Other relative | 16 | 5.4 | — | — |
| Children—Family | 29 | 9.8 | 1 | 3.6 |
| Non-relative | 19 | 6.4 | 2 | 7.6 |
| No one | 43 | 14.5 | — | — |
| Other, faith, etc. | 61 | 20.5 | 15 | 53.6 |
| No Answer | 4* | — | 4* | — |
| Not Appropriate | — | — | 269* | — |
| | | | | |
| Percent Base | | 297 | | 28 |

* Not included in percent base

## APPENDIX C: SIGNIFICANT RELATIONS BETWEEN BACKGROUND CHARACTERISTICS AND ROLE INVOLVEMENTS OR ATTITUDES OF CHICAGO AREA OLDER WIDOWS

### LIST OF TABLES IN APPENDIX C

Table I. Significant associations between the statement "My husband was an unusually good man," and other statements in the relations-restrictive attitude scale.

Table II. Significant associations between the statement "My marriage was above average and no second marriage could match it," and other statements in the relations-restrictive attitude scale.

Table III. Age at widowhood and agreement with the statement: "My marriage was above average and no second marriage could match it."

Table IV. Tests of association and relational significance between the role of wife scale and relations-restrictive attitudes and scores.

Table V. Characteristics of widows who score at the extreme levels of high or low (not medium) in the role of wife.

Table VI. Percentages of widows agreeing and disagreeing with selected attitudes toward husbands and other men, by race.

Table VII. Significant associations between the statement "Sons are more help to a widow than daughters," and relational scores or other statements of the relations-restrictive attitude scale.

Table VIII. Significant associations between the statement: "One problem with adult children is that they always want you to do favors for them—baby-sit, or sew, or things like that," and relational scores or other statements of the relations-restrictive attitude scale.

Table IX. Number of children in each birth order by their marital status.

Table X. Agreement with the statement: "I like living alone," by age at widowhood in five-year intervals.

Table XI. Significant associations between the statement: "I like living alone," and other statements of the relations restrictive attitude scale.

Table XII.    Collapsed scores in the role of mother scale by the top three ranks assigned to the major roles of women.

Table XIII.   Selected characteristics of widows scoring high on the role of mother scale.

Table XIV.    Selected characteristics of widows scoring low on the role of mother scale.

Table XV.     Collapsed scores in the role of sibling scale by the role of mother scale.

Table XVI.    Significant associations between the statement: "My married friends have not been much help to me," and other statements of the relations-restrictive attitude scale, with percentages.

Table XVII.   Significant associations between the statement: "One problem of being a widow is feeling like a 'fifth wheel'," and other statements of the relations-restrictive attitude scale, with percentages.

Table XVIII.  Significant associations between the statement: "Other women are jealous of a widow when their husbands are around," and other statements of the relations-restrictive attitude scale, with percentages.

Table XIX.    Significant associations between the statement: "Relatives are your only true friends," and other statements of the relations-restrictive attitude scale, with percentages.

Table XX.     Significant associations between agreement with the statement: "Old friends cannot be replaced, no matter how one tries to make new ones," and other statements of the relations-restrictive attitude scale, with percentages.

Table XXI.    Significant associations between the statement "I wish I had more friends," and other statements of the relations-restrictive attitude scale, with percentages.

Table XXII.   Significant associations between agreement with the statement: "I feel sorry for some of my married friends who have little freedom to do as they please," with selected statements of the relations-restrictive attitude scale, with percentages.

Table XXIII.  Percentages of widows expressing different extremes and types of agreement with the statements in the relations-restrictive attitude scale.

TABLE I: SIGNIFICANT ASSOCIATIONS BETWEEN AGREEMENT
WITH THE STATEMENT "MY HUSBAND WAS AN
UNUSUALLY GOOD MAN," AND OTHER STATEMENTS
OF THE RELATIONS-RESTRICTIVE ATTITUDE SCALE

| *Statement* | *Gamma* |
|---|---|
| My husband and I did not do too many things together; he had his activities, and I had mine. | −.87 |
| I did not know anything about our finances when my husband died. | −.41 |
| Other women are jealous of a widow when their husbands are around. | −.25 |
| Widows are constantly sexually propositioned, even by the husbands of their friends. | −.35 |
| It is all right for a widow to have sexual relations with a man without planning on marriage. | −.51 |
| I like living alone. | −.64 |
| I feel sorry for some of my married friends who have little freedom to do as they please. | −.68 |
| This time of my life is actually easier than any other time. | −.49 |
| I feel more independent and free now than before I became a widow. | −.71 |
| One problem with adult children is that they always want you to do favors for them—baby-sit, or sew, or things like that. | −.30 |
| Of the men I have dated, I have most in common with widowers. | .50 |
| A new widow should not move too soon from the place in which she was living before her husband died. | .57 |
| The hardest thing for a widow to learn is how to make decisions. | .49 |
| My faith helped me more than anything else after my husband's death. | .38 |
| I have trouble being nice to people who did not help during my period of grief. | 1.00 |
| A widow has to make her own life and not depend on others. | .29 |
| One problem of being a widow is feeling like a "fifth wheel." | .36 |
| My marriage was above average and no second marriage could match it. | .98 |
| My sexual relations with my husband were very good until his last illness. | .75 |
| My husband and I pretended we did not know how sick he really was. | .53 |

TABLE II: SIGNIFICANT ASSOCIATIONS BETWEEN AGREEMENT
WITH THE STATEMENT: "MY MARRIAGE WAS
ABOVE AVERAGE AND NO SECOND MARRIAGE
COULD MATCH IT," AND OTHER STATEMENTS IN
THE RELATIONS-RESTRICTIVE ATTITUDE SCALE

| *Statement* | *Gamma* |
|---|---|
| I felt angry at the doctor and the hospital for not doing enough for my husband when he was ill. | .56 |
| I have trouble being nice to people who did not help during my period of grief. | .46 |
| My present income makes it impossible for me to maintain old friendships. | .27 |
| Women lose status when they become widows—they lose respect and consideration. | .34 |
| The hardest thing for a widow to learn is how to make decisions. | .44 |
| A widow has to make her own life and not depend on others. | .25 |
| Widows are constantly sexually propositioned, even by the husbands of their friends. | -.34 |
| Other women are jealous of a widow when their husbands are around. | -.31 |
| I wish I had more male companionship. | .51 |
| Many widows who remarry are very unhappy in that marriage. | .35 |
| My sexual relations with my husband were very good until his last illness. | .40 |

TABLE III: AGE AT WIDOWHOOD AND AGREEMENT WITH THE STATEMENT: "MY MARRIAGE WAS ABOVE AVERAGE, AND NO SECOND MARRIAGE COULD MATCH IT"

| | Row Sums | 34 and Under | 35–39 | 40–44 | 45–49 | 50–54 | 55–59 | 60–64 | 65–69 | 70–74 | 75 and Over |
|---|---|---|---|---|---|---|---|---|---|---|---|
| True | 72.3 | 35.7C | 75.0C | 55.5C | 73.1C | 78.7C | 78.2C | 75.0C | 68.0C | 78.9C | 77.7C |
| False | 27.6 | 64.2C | 25.0C | 44.4C | 26.8C | 21.2C | 21.7C | 25.0C | 32.0C | 21.0C | 22.2C |
| No Answer | 11.0 | 7.1C* | 16.6C* | 11.1C* | 17.0C* | 10.6C* | 13.0C* | 12.5C* | .0C* | 5.2C* | 11.1C* |
| Column | | 14 | 12 | 18 | 41 | 47 | 46 | 40 | 25 | 19 | 9 |
| Sums | | 5.1 | 4.4 | 6.6 | 15.1 | 17.3 | 16.9 | 14.7 | 9.2 | 7.0 | 3.3 |

* Not included in percent base

TABLE IV: TESTS OF ASSOCIATION AND RELATIONAL
SIGNIFICANCE BETWEEN THE ROLE OF WIFE SCALE
AND RELATIONS-RESTRICTIVE ATTITUDE

| Scales and Attitudes | Measures of Association | | | |
|---|---|---|---|---|
| | Gamma | $x^2$ | d.f. | p |
| Isolation Scale | −.31 | 13.84 | 4 | .01 |
| Relations-Restrictive Attitude Scale | .19 | 9.30 | | .05 |
| My husband was an unusually good man | .94 | 73.91 | 2 | .001 |
| Our sexual relations were very good until his last illness | .80 | 53.50 | | .001 |
| My husband had his activities, I had mine | −.76 | 61.10 | | .001 |
| My marriage was above average and no other marriage could match it | .69 | 64.79 | | .001 |
| I feel more independent now | −.46 | 22.97 | | .001 |
| This time of my life is easier | −.35 | 11.66 | | .01 |
| A new widow should not move too soon | .33 | 8.36 | | .025 |
| Widows have to make own life | .31 | 3.61 | | n.s. |
| My husband and I pretended we did not know how sick he was | .31 | 10.30 | | .01 |
| I feel sorry for some of my married friends who have little freedom | −.31 | 14.26 | | .001 |
| It is hard for widows to learn to make decisions | .25 | 6.79 | | .05 |

TABLE V: CHARACTERISTICS OF WIDOWS WHO SCORE AT THE EXTREME LEVELS OF HIGH OR LOW (NOT MEDIUM) IN THE ROLE OF WIFE

| Characteristic and Category | Level in Scale of Wife | | |
|---|---|---|---|
| | High % | Medium % | Low % |
| Percentage of total group in these levels = expected percentage | 31 | 43 | 26 |
| Age Decade: H = 40–49* | 38 | 46 | 16 |
| L = 80 plus** | 26 | 37 | 37 |
| Age came to Chicago: H = 50–59 | 67 | 33 | — |
| L = 30–39 | 28 | 34 | 38 |
| Education: H = college grade | 62 | 38 | — |
| L = none | 36 | 27 | 36 |
| Religion: H = Jewish | 73 | 27 | — |
| L = Protestant | 30 | 47 | 23 |
| Ethnic: H = Russian | 80 | 20 | — |
| L = Other (Negro mostly) | 24 | 42 | 34 |
| Married more than once: H = No | 33 | 48 | 18 |
| L = Yes | 27 | 44 | 29 |
| Husband's schooling: H = professional | 67 | 33 | — |
| L = none | 33 | 17 | 50 |
| Husband's occupation: H = managers | 48 | 45 | 6 |
| L = farm laborers | 8 | 46 | 46 |
| Financial condition: H = fairly wealthy | 67 | 33 | — |
| L = really restricted | 26 | 48 | 26 |
| Income: H = $11,000–15,999 | 57 | 43 | — |
| L = $1,000–2,999 | 27 | 44 | 29 |
| Problems of widowhood: H = loneliness | 46 | 45 | 8 |
| L = other (not covered) | 6 | 44 | 50 |
| Would you like to remarry: H = Yes | 42 | 47 | 11 |
| L = No | 30 | 48 | 22 |
| Race: H = White | 36 | 48 | 16 |
| L = Negro | 15 | 40 | 44 |
| R's Dwelling: H = 10 or more units | 44 | 41 | 15 |
| L = 4–6 | 24 | 37 | 39 |
| Length of Widowhood: H = 7–9 | 42 | 48 | 10 |
| L = 30+ | 13 | 43 | 43 |

\* H stands for high, or the highest percentage of respondents having a high score.
\*\* L stands for low, or the highest percentage of respondents having a low score.

TABLE VI: PERCENTAGES OF WIDOWS AGREEING AND DISAGREEING WITH SELECTED ATTITUDES TOWARD HUSBANDS AND OTHER MEN, BY RACE

| Attitudes Toward Husband and Other Men | Agree | | | | Disagree | | | | No Answer | | Total | $x^2$ |
|---|---|---|---|---|---|---|---|---|---|---|---|---|
| | Black % | N | White % | N | Black % | N | White % | N | Black N | White N | N | |
| The hardest thing for a widow to learn is how to make decisions. | 37 | 18 | 61 | 145 | 62 | 30 | 39 | 94 | 4 | 5 | 287 | 8.76 |
| It is all right for a widow to have sexual relations with a man without planning on marriage. | 41 | 17 | 6 | 14 | 58 | 24 | 94 | 208 | 11 | 22 | 263 | 187.84 |
| Widows are constantly sexually propositioned, even by the husbands of their friends. | 45 | 20 | 18 | 38 | 54 | 24 | 82 | 168 | 8 | 38 | 250 | 14.84 |
| Other women are jealous of a widow when their husbands are around. | 59 | 29 | 39 | 87 | 40 | 20 | 61 | 135 | 3 | 27 | 271 | 6.56 |
| Many widows who remarry are very unhappy. | 72 | 36 | 49 | 98 | 28 | 14 | 51 | 101 | 2 | 50 | 249 | 42.67 |
| My husband was an unusually good man. | 76 | 36 | 94 | 221 | 23 | 11 | 6 | 13 | 5 | 10 | 281 | 15.98 |
| My marriage was above average, no other could match it. | 62 | 30 | 76 | 172 | 38 | 19 | 24 | 54 | 3 | 23 | 275 | 4.58 |
| My sexual relations with my husband were very good until his last illness. | 57 | 24 | 80 | 153 | 43 | 18 | 19 | 37 | 10 | 54 | 232 | 10.41 |
| My husband and I did not do too many things together; he had his activities, I had mine. | 48 | 24 | 24 | 58 | 52 | 25 | 76 | 184 | 3 | 7 | 291 | 12.6 |
| I did not know anything about our finances when my husband died. | 29 | 14 | 25 | 58 | 71 | 34 | 74 | 170 | 4 | 16 | 276 | .28 |
| I felt angry at the doctor and the hospital for not doing enough for my husband when he was ill. | 10 | 4 | 17 | 33 | 90 | 38 | 83 | 164 | 10 | 47 | 239 | 1.38 |
| I wish I had more male companionship. | 26 | 13 | 20 | 45 | 73 | 36 | 80 | 180 | 3 | 19 | 274 | 1.03 |
| Of the men I have dated, I have most in common with widowers. | 26 | 10 | 34 | 32 | 74 | 29 | 66 | 62 | 13 | 150 | 133 | .82 |
| I feel sorry for some of my married friends who have little freedom to do as they please. | 50 | 23 | 28 | 60 | 50 | 23 | 72 | 155 | 6 | 29 | 261 | 8.54 |

N: Black 52 + White 249 = 301

TABLE VII: SIGNIFICANT ASSOCIATIONS BETWEEN AGREEMENT
WITH THE STATEMENT: "SONS ARE MORE HELP
TO A WIDOW THAN DAUGHTERS," AND
RELATIONAL SCORES OR OTHER STATEMENTS
OF THE RELATIONS-RESTRICTIVE ATTITUDE SCALE

| *Attitude* | *Sons Are More Help Than Daughters* | | | |
|---|---|---|---|---|
| | *Gamma** | $x^2$ | *d.f.* | *p<* |
| Relations-Restrictive Attitude Scale | .34 | 6.55 | 2 | .05 |
| Role of Sibling Scale | −.50 | 7.37 | 2 | .025 |
| Relatives are your only true friends. | .36* | | | |
| Sharing one's home causes nothing but trouble for widows. | .51 | | | |
| Widows prefer living near other widows. | .31 | | | |
| Women lose status when they become widows. | .37 | | | |
| I would do more outside if I were picked up. | .26 | | | |
| Married friends have not been much help to me. | .45 | | | |
| I wish people wouldn't try to get me to go out. | .41 | | | |
| I wish I had more male companionship. | −.25 | | | |
| I wish I had more friends. | .24 | | | |
| Of men I have dated, I have most in common with widowers. | −.36 | | | |
| My husband had his activities, I had mine. | .30 | | | |
| I did not know anything about our finances. | .63 | | | |
| We pretended not to know how sick he was. | .31 | | | |
| Our sexual relations were very good until his last illness. | −.24 | | | |
| I feel sorry for some married friends with little freedom to do as they please. | .26 | | | |

* Only gamma associations were obtained for attitudes because of an emphasis on clustering.

TABLE VIII: SIGNIFICANT ASSOCIATIONS BETWEEN AGREEMENT WITH THE STATEMENT: "ONE PROBLEM WITH ADULT CHILDREN IS THAT THEY ALWAYS WANT YOU TO DO FAVORS FOR THEM—BABY-SIT, OR SEW, OR THINGS LIKE THAT," AND RELATIONAL SCORES OR OTHER STATEMENTS ON THE RELATIONS-RESTRICTIVE ATTITUDE SCALE

| Score or Attitude | Adult Children Want Favors Measures of Association | | | |
|---|---|---|---|---|
| | Gamma | $x^2$ | d.f. | $p<$ |
| Isolation Scale | .30 | 5.75 | 2 | .05 |
| Relations-Restrictive Attitude Scale | .59 | 25.48 | 2 | .001 |
| Frequency of Contact Scale | −.36 | 12.25 | 2 | .005 |
| Role of Mother Scale | −.28 | 11.81 | 2 | .005 |
| Average frequency of contact with children. | −.25 | 11.17 | 5 | .05 |
| Sons are more help to widows than daughters. | .34 | | | |
| Relatives are your only true friends. | .28 | | | |
| People take advantage of you when they know you are a widow. | .33 | | | |
| Sharing one's home cause trouble for widows. | .31 | | | |
| Women lose status when they become widows. | .42 | | | |
| I felt angry at the doctor and hospital. | .45 | | | |
| My married friends have not been much help to me. | .25 | | | |
| My present income makes it impossible to maintain old friendships. | .26 | | | |
| I wish people would try to get me out of the house. | .34 | | | |
| I have trouble being nice to people who did not help during my period of grief. | .37 | | | |
| I with I had more friends. | .36 | | | |
| My husband was an unusually good man. | −.30 | | | |
| I did not know anything about finances. | .33 | | | |

TABLE IX: NUMBER OF CHILDREN IN EACH BIRTH ORDER
BY THEIR MARITAL STATUS

| Marital Status | | | | Birth Order | | | | | |
|---|---|---|---|---|---|---|---|---|---|
| | 1 | 2 | 3 | 4 | 5 | 6 | 7 | 8+ | Total |
| Married | 177 | 133 | 74 | 41 | 27 | 13 | 8 | 3 | 476 |
| Separated | 6 | 7 | 7 | 3 | 1 | — | 1 | — | 25 |
| Divorced | 9 | 2 | 1 | 1 | 1 | — | — | — | 14 |
| Widowed | 9 | 5 | 2 | — | — | — | — | — | 16 |
| Never married | 39 | 31 | 17 | 10 | 3 | 4 | 7 | 1 | 108 |
| Total | 240 | 178 | 101 | 55 | 32 | 17 | 12 | 4 | 639 |
| Not appropriate (Does not have that many) | 61 | 123 | 200 | 246 | 269 | 284 | 289 | 297 | |

TABLE X: AGREEMENT WITH THE STATEMENT: "I LIKE
LIVING ALONE" BY AGE AT WIDOWHOOD IN
FIVE-YEAR INTERVALS

| Age at Widowhood | Total | | I Like Living Alone | | |
|---|---|---|---|---|---|
| | No. | % | True | False | No Answer* |
| 34 and under | 14 | 6 | 78 | 21 | 1 |
| 35–39 | 11 | 4 | 64 | 36 | 3 |
| 40–44 | 15 | 6 | 60 | 40 | 5 |
| 45–49 | 42 | 17 | 55 | 45 | 6 |
| 50–54 | 41 | 17 | 58 | 41 | 11 |
| 55–59 | 42 | 17 | 52 | 48 | 10 |
| 60–64 | 37 | 15 | 54 | 46 | 8 |
| 65–69 | 22 | 9 | 50 | 50 | 3 |
| 70–74 | 14 | 6 | 50 | 50 | 4 |
| 75 and over | 8 | 3 | 38 | 62 | 2 |
| Total | 246 | 100 | | | 55 |

* Not included in percent base.

TABLE XI: SIGNIFICANT ASSOCIATIONS BETWEEN THE
STATEMENT: "I LIKE LIVING ALONE" AND OTHER
STATEMENTS OF THE RELATIONS-RESTRICTIVE
ATTITUDE SCALE

| *Attitudes* | *Gamma* |
|---|---|
| My husband was an unusually good man. | −.64 |
| I did not know anything about our finances when my husband died. | .32 |
| My faith helped me more than anything else after my husband's death. | .22 |
| I have trouble being nice to people who did not help during my period of grief. | .49 |
| Sharing one's home with anyone causes nothing but trouble for the widow. | .47 |
| I wish I had more male companionship. | −.22 |
| Widows are constantly sexually propositioned, even by husbands of their friends. | .25 |
| It is all right for a widow to have sexual relations with a man without planning on marriage. | .46 |
| Other women are jealous of a widow when their husbands are around. | .33 |
| I feel sorry for some of my married friends who have little freedom to do as they please. | .32 |
| This time of my life is actually easier than any other time. | .54 |
| I feel more independent and free now than before I became a widow. | 52 |

TABLE XII: COLLAPSED SCORES IN THE ROLE OF MOTHER
SCALE BY THE TOP THREE RANKS ASSIGNED
TO THE MAJOR ROLES OF WOMEN

| Role and Rank Order | | Total | | Role of Mother Score | | | No Children |
| | | | | Actual | | | |
| | | N | % | High % | Medium % | Low % | N |
|---|---|---|---|---|---|---|---|
| Mother | first | 107 | 46 | 56 | 53 | 31 | 28 |
| | second | 101 | 43 | 43 | 39 | 49 | 35 |
| | third | 24 | 10 | — | 8 | 17 | 22 |
| Wife | first | 103 | 46 | 41 | 41 | 54 | 47 |
| | second | 73 | 32 | 41 | 36 | 24 | 26 |
| | third | 24 | 11* | 9 | 10 | 11 | 16 |
| Daughter | first | 6 | 3 | — | 2 | 4 | 6 |
| | second | 7 | 3 | — | 4 | 2 | 6 |
| | third | 51 | 23 | 23 | 24 | 22 | 12 |
| Housewife | first | 20 | 9 | 4 | 6 | 14 | 17 |
| | second | 39 | 17 | 9 | 17 | 20 | 34 |
| | third | 97 | 42 | 59 | 45 | 34 | 26 |
| Worker | first | 1 | — | — | — | 1 | 10 |
| | second | 10 | 4 | 4 | 4 | 5 | 6 |
| | third | 15 | 7 | 9 | 4 | 10 | 12 |
| Community member | first | — | — | — | — | — | 1 |
| | second | 6 | 3 | 4 | 3 | 1 | 4 |
| | third | 18 | 8 | — | 11 | 12 | 15 |

* These are column totals but they do not add up to 100% in most cases because all
six ranks are not given.

TABLE XIII: SELECTED CHARACTERISTICS OF WIDOWS
SCORING HIGH ON THE ROLE OF MOTHER SCALE

| Characteristic | Total N | % | Role of Mother High % | Medium % | Low % | No Children % |
|---|---|---|---|---|---|---|
| Age 60 to 69 | | 39 | 54 | 35 | 42 | 39 |
| Came to Chicago age 20 to 29 | 25 | 19 | 31 | 18 | 17 | 25 |
| White racial identity | | 84 | 92 | 86 | 79 | 74 |
| Catholic religion | 93 | 38 | 54 | 40 | 30 | 39 |
| Irish ethnic group | 28 | 11 | 29 | 10 | 8 | 8 |
| Highest education—none | 11 | 4 | 12 | 2 | 6 | — |
| Husband's schooling—none | 5 | 2 | 14 | — | 3 | 2 |
| Husband's occupation operative | 40 | 16 | 29 | 15 | 15 | 15 |
| Husband older | | 81 | 88 | 81 | 79 | 72 |
| Yearly income $3,000 to $4,999 | 40 | 18 | 33 | 15 | 17 | 24 |
| Rather short finances | 63 | 26 | 29 | 25 | 25 | 22 |
| Physical limitations | 110 | 62 | 67 | 57 | 68 | 66 |
| Widowed 10 to 14 years | 54 | 22 | 38 | 25 | 13 | 18 |
| Raise family problem | 28 | 11 | 26 | 13 | 6 | — |
| Second money | 51 | 7 | 20 | 6 | 6 | 3 |
| Loneliness "others shun" | 25 | 14 | 28 | 17 | 4 | 10 |
| Change in self—none | 109 | 44 | 58 | 43 | 43 | 54 |
| Second change—more worry | 17 | 20 | 50 | 14 | 22 | 28 |
| Free time compensation | 84 | 9 | 17 | 7 | 9 | 8 |
| Would not like to remarry | 192 | 81 | 95 | 81 | 77 | 81 |
| Do not expect to remarry | 194 | 91 | 95 | 91 | 89 | 96 |
| Been married only once | 197 | 80 | 88 | 81 | 75 | 78 |
| General problems living with children | 144 | 58 | 71 | 57 | 57 | 61 |

TABLE XIV: SELECTED CHARACTERISTICS OF WIDOWS
SCORING LOW ON THE ROLE OF MOTHER SCALE

| Characteristic | N | % | Role of Mother High % | Medium % | Low % | No Children % |
|---|---|---|---|---|---|---|
| Age: 70 to79 | 61 | 25 | 17 | 26 | 25 | 30 |
| Came to Chicago 10 to 19 | 21 | 16 | 8 | 14 | 20 | 31 |
| Race: Negro | 39 | 16 | 8 | 14 | 21 | 26 |
| Religion: Protestant | 129 | 52 | 42 | 48 | 62 | 48 |
| German ethnic group | 55 | 22 | 8 | 23 | 25 | 22 |
| Education: high school | 49 | 20 | 12 | 22 | 18 | 24 |
| Don't know husband's schooling | 46 | 23 | 14 | 20 | 31 | 23 |
| Husband's occupation— | | | | | | |
| Laborer | 5 | 2 | — | 1 | 4 | — |
| Husband is the same age | 24 | 10 | 4 | 11 | 9 | 17 |
| Income $1,000 to $2,999 | 104 | 46 | 33 | 47 | 48 | 41 |
| Finances restricted | 49 | 20 | 12 | 16 | 28 | 22 |
| Physical limitations | 110 | 44 | 38 | 44 | 47 | 50 |
| Widowed 15 to 19 years | 27 | 11 | 4 | 11 | 12 | 9 |
| Loneliness problem | 115 | 47 | 30 | 45 | 54 | 54 |
| Second money | 51 | 31 | 13 | 29 | 37 | 27 |
| Miss partner | 53 | 29 | 17 | 28 | 33 | 26 |
| Miss second, someone around | 18 | 18 | — | 17 | 24 | 17 |
| Change self, independent | 86 | 35 | 29 | 35 | 36 | 30 |
| Change second, freedom | 22 | 26 | — | 31 | 22 | 43 |
| Free time compensation | 84 | 35 | 30 | 38 | 32 | 38 |
| Would like to remarry | 45 | 19 | 5 | 19 | 23 | 19 |
| Think will remarry | 19 | 9 | 5 | 8 | 11 | 4 |
| Married more than once | 50 | 20 | 12 | 19 | 25 | 22 |
| In-law problem—living with | 29 | 12 | 4 | 9 | 18 | 6 |

TABLE XV: COLLAPSED SCORES IN THE ROLE OF SIBLING
SCALE BY THE ROLE OF MOTHER SCALE

| | Row Sums | Role of Sibling | | | No Siblings |
| | | High (16–24) | Medium (08–15) | Low (00–07) | |
|---|---|---|---|---|---|
| High (30–50) | 18 | 4 | 4 | 10 | 6 |
| | | 22.2R | 22.2R | 55.5R | 33.3R* |
| | 8.9 | 50.0C | 9.3C | 6.6C | 13.0C |
| Medium (17–29) | 107 | 2 | 26 | 79 | 27 |
| | | 1.8R | 24.2R | 73.8R | 25.2R* |
| | 53.2 | 25.0C | 60.4C | 52.6C | 58.6C |
| Low (01–16) | 76 | 2 | 13 | 61 | 13 |
| | | 2.6R | 17.1R | 80.2R | 17.1R* |
| | 37.8 | 25.0C | 30.2C | 40.6C | 28.2C |
| No Children | 41 | 4 | 19 | 18 | 13 |
| | | 9.7R | 46.3R | 43.9R | 31.7R* |
| | 20.3 | 50.0C* | 44.1C* | 12.0C* | 28.2C* |
| Column Sums | | 8 | 43 | 150 | 46 |
| | | 3.9 | 21.3 | 74.6 | 22.8* |

Total Sum = 201
Gamma = .28
Chi-Square = 18.75; (d.f. = 4); p < .001
* Not used in computing percentages.

TABLE XVI: SIGNIFICANT ASSOCIATIONS BETWEEN THE STATEMENT, "MY MARRIED FRIENDS HAVE NOT BEEN MUCH HELP TO ME," AND OTHER STATEMENTS OF THE RELATIONS-RESTRICTIVE ATTITUDE SCALE, AND PERCENTAGES

| *Attitude* | Q | Married Friends No Help | | | |
|---|---|---|---|---|---|
| | | *True-True* | *False-True* | *True-False* | *False-False* |
| | | % N | % N | % N | % N |
| A widow must make her own life and not depend on others | .80 | 99(78) | 90(165) | 1(1) | 10(19) |
| My present income makes it impossible to maintain old friendships | .66 | 57(32) | 43(24) | 22(43) | 78(155) |
| Sons are more help to a widow than daughters | .45 | 43(26) | 22(33) | 57(34) | 78(114) |
| My husband had his activities, and I had mine | .30 | 35(28) | 23(41) | 64(51) | 77(139) |
| I did not know anything about our finances when my husband died | .38 | 35(27) | 20(35) | 65(50) | 80(143) |
| My husband and I pretended we did not know how sick he really was | .36 | 46(26) | 29(40) | 54(30) | 71(99) |
| I felt angry at doctor, hospital for not doing enough for my husband | .39 | 23(16) | 11(18) | 77(54) | 87(139) |
| I would do more if someone would pick me up | .36 | 47(36) | 30(53) | 53(40) | 70(125) |
| When they become widows, women lose status, respect, and consideration | .36 | 29(22) | 16(29) | 71(54) | 84(150) |
| I have trouble being nice to those who did not help me in grief | .32 | 16(12) | 9(15) | 84(65) | 91(159) |
| People take advantage of you when they know you are a widow | .36 | 53(40) | 34(62) | 47(36) | 66(119) |
| One problem of being a widow is feeling like a "fifth wheel" | .37 | 74(55) | 57(100) | 26(19) | 43(75) |
| Adult children problem cause want favors always | .25 | 47(32) | 35(58) | 53(36) | 65(108) |
| Relatives are your only true friends | .33 | 35(26) | 21(37) | 65(49) | 79(139) |
| Other women are jealous of a widow when husband around | .25 | 52(38) | 39(64) | 48(35) | 61(99) |
| Widows are sexually propositioned, even by husbands of friends | .25 | 28(19) | 19(31) | 72(49) | 81(133) |
| I feel more independent and free now | .45 | 59(44) | 36(64) | 40(30) | 64(114) |
| I feel sorry for my married friends who have little freedom | .28 | 37(28) | 25(44) | 63(47) | 75(130) |
| I wish I had more friends | .26 | 45(34) | 32(57) | 55(42) | 68(120) |
| My faith helped me more than anything else after my husband's death | .30 | 73(57) | 83(150) | 27(21) | 17(30) |

= Does not feel that married friends have been no help but agrees with independent statement.

TABLE XVII: SIGNIFICANT ASSOCIATIONS BETWEEN THE
STATEMENT: "ONE PROBLEM OF BEING A WIDOW
IS FEELING LIKE A 'FIFTH WHEEL',", AND OTHER
STATEMENTS OF THE RELATIONS-RESTRICTIVE
ATTITUDE SCALE, AND PERCENTAGES

| *Attitude* | *Q* | *True—* *True* | *False=* *—True* | *—True* *False* | *False—* *False* |
|---|---|---|---|---|---|
| | | % N | % N | % N | % N |
| Of the men I have dated, I have most in common with widowers | .54 | 44(31) | 19(11) | 56(39) | 81(46) |
| The hardest thing for a widow is to make decisions | .45 | 66(111) | 42(43) | 34(58) | 58(59) |
| Sharing one's home with anyone causes nothing but trouble | .39 | 63(99) | 43(40) | 36(57) | 56(52) |
| Most widows prefer living near other widows | .39 | 44(71) | 26(25) | 56(89) | 74(72) |
| A widow has to make her own life and not depend on others | .38 | 95(164) | 90(93) | 5(8) | 10(10) |
| My married friends have not been much help to me | .37 | 35(55) | 20(19) | 64(100) | 80(75) |
| When they become widows, women lose status, respect, and consideration | .34 | 26(43) | 15(15) | 74(122) | 85(86) |
| I wish I had more male companionship | .33 | 26(42) | 15(15) | 74(119) | 85(85) |
| My present income makes it impossible to maintain old friendships | .32 | 27(43) | 16(16) | 72(115) | 84(83) |
| Widows are sexually propositioned, even by husbands of friends | .30 | 27(42) | 17(15) | 73(112) | 83(74) |
| OK for widows to have sexual relations without marriage | .26 | 10(16) | 16(15) | 90(144) | 84(79) |
| People take advantage of you when they find out you are a widow | .28 | 46(77) | 32(33) | 54(90) | 68(69) |

= Does not feel like a "fifth wheel," but agrees with independent variable

TABLE XVIII: SIGNIFICANT ASSOCIATIONS BETWEEN THE
STATEMENT: "OTHER WOMEN ARE JEALOUS OF
A WIDOW WHEN THEIR HUSBANDS ARE
AROUND," WITH SELECTED STATEMENTS OF
THE RELATIONS-RESTRICTIVE ATTITUDE
SCALE, AND PERCENTAGES

| *Attitude* | *Q* | *Other Women Jealous* | | | |
|---|---|---|---|---|---|
| | | *True— True* | *False = —True* | *True— False* | *False— False* |
| | | % N | % N | % N | % N |
| Widows are sexually propositioned, even by the husbands of friends | .86 | 46(47) | 6(8) | 54(56) | 94(126) |
| People take advantage of you when they know you are a widow | .64 | 60(66) | 26(37) | 39(43) | 74(108) |
| When they become widows, women lose status, respect, and consideration | .50 | 33(36) | 14(20) | 67(73) | 86(121) |
| I have trouble being nice to people who did not help during grief | .50 | 17(18) | 6(9) | 83(86) | 93(129) |
| Many widows who remarry are very unhappy in that marriage | .49 | 67(67) | 41(50) | 33(33) | 59(72) |
| OK for widows to have sexual relations without marriage | .40 | 17(18) | 8(11) | 83(87) | 92(124) |
| Most widows prefer living near other widows | .31 | 47(51) | 32(44) | 53(57) | 68(94) |
| My marriage was above average and no second marriage could match it | .31 | 63(67) | 77(102) | 37(39) | 23(31) |
| I wish I had more male companionship | .32 | 30(32) | 18(25) | 70(76) | 82(115) |
| I like living alone | .33 | 64(59) | 47(58) | 36(33) | 53(65) |
| My married friends have not been much help to me | .25 | 37(38) | 26(35) | 63(64) | 74(99) |

= Does not feel that other women are jealous, but agrees with independent variables.

TABLE XIX: SIGNIFICANT ASSOCIATIONS BETWEEN
AGREEMENT WITH THE STATEMENT "RELATIVES
ARE YOUR ONLY TRUE FRIENDS," WITH
SELECTED STATEMENTS OF THE RELATIONS-
RESTRICTIVE ATTITUDE SCALE, WITH
PERCENTAGES

| *Attitude* | *Q* | *Relatives True Friends* | | | |
| --- | --- | --- | --- | --- | --- |
| | | *True— False* | *False= —True* | *True— False* | *False— False* |
| | | % N | % N | % N | % N |
| When they become widows, women lose status, respect, and consideration | .52 | 39(26) | 17(33) | 61(41) | 83(163) |
| My present income makes it impossible to maintain old friendships | .47 | 38(26) | 18(34) | 62(43) | 82(156) |
| I wish I had more friends | .41 | 52(35) | 31(60) | 48(32) | 68(131) |
| People take advantage of you when they know you are a widow | .34 | 53(36) | 36(70) | 47(32) | 64(126) |
| Widows are sexually propositioned, even by husbands of friends | .32 | 31(19) | 19(34) | 69(42) | 81(146) |
| Of the men I have dated, I have most in common with widowers | .33 | 22(8) | 36(32) | 78(29) | 64(58) |
| My married friends have not been much help to me | .33 | 41(26) | 26(49) | 59(37) | 74(139) |
| I wish people wouldn't try to get me to go out | .32 | 33(23) | 20(39) | 67(46) | 79(151) |
| A widow has to make her own life and not depend on others | .29 | 89(64) | 94(188) | 11(8) | 6(13) |
| Problem with adult children always wanting favors | .28 | 49(31) | 35(62) | 51(32) | 65(115) |
| Many widows who remarry are very unhappy in that marriage | .27 | 62(39) | 48(79) | 38(24) | 52(85) |
| I would do more if someone would pick me up | .27 | 44(30) | 31(60) | 56(38) | 69(133) |
| I have trouble being nice to people who did not help in grief | .25 | 15(10) | 10(18) | 85(57) | 90(171) |

= Does not feel that "Relatives are your only friends," but agrees with independent
variables.

TABLE XX: SIGNIFICANT ASSOCIATIONS BETWEEN AGREEMENT
WITH THE STATEMENT: "OLD FRIENDS CANNOT
BE REPLACED, NO MATTER HOW ONE TRIES TO
MAKE NEW ONES," WITH SELECTED STATEMENTS
OF THE RELATIONS-RESTRICTIVE ATTITUDE
SCALE, WITH PERCENTAGES

| Attitude | Q | Old Friends Not Replaced | | | |
| --- | --- | --- | --- | --- | --- |
| | | True—<br>True | False—<br>True | True—<br>False | False—<br>False |
| | | % N | % N | % N | % N |
| When they become widows, women lose status, respect, and consideration | .55 | 25(52) | 9(6) | 75(155) | 91(61) |
| I wish people would try to get me to go out | .48 | 28(58) | 12(8) | 72(146) | 88(58) |
| I felt angry at doctor and hospital for not helping husband more | .46 | 16(28) | 7(4) | 84(146) | 93(56) |
| Many widows who remarry are very unhappy in that marriage | .45 | 59(105) | 36(20) | 41(72) | 64(36) |
| My faith helped me most after widowhood | .37 | 84(174) | 71(46) | 16(33) | 29(19) |
| The hardest thing for a widow to learn is decisions | .35 | 61(128) | 43(30) | 39(82) | 57(40) |
| Widows are sexually propositioned, even by husbands of friends | .27 | 25(46) | 16(10) | 75(138) | 84(52) |
| A widow has to make her own life and not depend on others | .26 | 93(197) | 88(62) | 7(15) | 11(8) |
| People take advantage of you when they know you are a widow | .27 | 44(91) | 31(21) | 56(116) | 69(47) |

= Does not feel that "Old friends cannot be replaced," but agrees with independent
variables.

TABLE XXI: SIGNIFICANT ASSOCIATIONS BETWEEN
AGREEMENT WITH THE STATEMENT "I WISH I
HAD MORE FRIENDS" WITH SELECTED
STATEMENTS OF THE RELATIONS-RESTRICTIVE
ATTITUDE SCALE, WITH PERCENTAGES

| *Attitude* | Q | *I Wish I Had More Friends* | | | |
| --- | --- | --- | --- | --- | --- |
| | | *True— True* | *False— True* | *True— False* | *False— False* |
| | | % N | % N | % N | % N |
| I would do more things if people picked me up | .58 | 57(53) | 26(45) | 43(40) | 74(129) |
| I have trouble being nice to people who didn't help | .56 | 62(18) | 32(72) | 38(11) | 68(156) |
| My present income makes it impossible to maintain old friendships | .52 | 57(35) | 30(60) | 43(26) | 70(140) |
| Relatives are your only true friends | .41 | 52(35) | 31(60) | 48(32) | 68(131) |
| Adult children always wanting favors | .36 | 48(45) | 30(44) | 52(49) | 70(102) |
| The hardest thing for a widow to learn is how to make decisions | .37 | 44(67) | 26(30) | 56(87) | 74(84) |
| Husband had his activities, I had mine | .38 | 36(36) | 20(35) | 64(63) | 80(136) |
| I did not know anything about finances when husband died | .32 | 34(33) | 21(35) | 66(64) | 79(132) |
| Many widows who remarry are very unhappy in that marriage | .37 | 45(55) | 28(29) | 55(67) | 72(76) |
| Widows are sexually propositioned, even by husbands of friends | .28 | 47(26) | 34(62) | 53(29) | 66(122) |
| OK for widows to have sexual relations without marriage | .27 | 48(15) | 35(77) | 52(16) | 65(143) |
| My married friends have not helped much | .26 | 45(34) | 32(57) | 55(42) | 68(120) |

= Does not wish more friends, but agrees with independent statement.

TABLE XXII: SIGNIFICANT ASSOCIATIONS BETWEEN
AGREEMENT WITH THE STATEMENT: "I FEEL
SORRY FOR SOME OF MY MARRIED FRIENDS
WHO HAVE LITTLE FREEDOM TO DO AS THEY
PLEASE," WITH SELECTED STATEMENTS OF THE
RELATIONS-RESTRICTIVE ATTITUDE SCALE,
WITH PERCENTAGES

| Attitude | Q | Feel Sorry for Married Friends | | | |
|---|---|---|---|---|---|
| | | True—True | False—True | True—False | False—False |
| | | % N | % N | % N | % N |
| I feel more independent and free now than before I became a widow | .68 | 72(59) | 33(57) | 28(23) | 67(115) |
| This time of my life is actually easier than any other time | .53 | 61(48) | 32(56) | 39(31) | 68(119) |
| My husband was an unusually good man | .68 | 82(65) | 96(172) | 18(14) | 4(7) |
| I wish people wouldn't try to get me out doing things all the time | .52 | 40(32) | 17(30) | 60(49) | 83(147) |
| OK for a widow to have sexual relations without marriage | .57 | 23(18) | 8(13) | 77(59) | 92(154) |
| My present income makes it impossible to maintain old relationships | .49 | 36(30) | 16(29) | 63(52) | 83(146) |
| Other women are jealous of a widow when their husbands are around | .43 | 58(45) | 36(59) | 42(32) | 64(106) |
| Widows are sexually propositioned, even by friends husbands | .40 | 33(26) | 18(28) | 67(52) | 82(132) |
| Many widows who remarry are very unhappy in that marriage | .38 | 66(49) | 47(68) | 34(25) | 53(77) |
| I have trouble being nice to people who did not help in grief | .41 | 16(13) | 8(13) | 84(67) | 92(160) |
| Women lose status when they become widows | .36 | 30(24) | 16(29) | 70(57) | 83(146) |
| Husband had his activities, I had mine | .39 | 38(31) | 21(38) | 62(50) | 79(141) |
| I did not know about our finances when my husband died | .32 | 35(28) | 22(38) | 65(52) | 78(138) |
| People take advantage of you when they know you are a widow | .29 | 51(42) | 37(64) | 49(40) | 63(110) |
| I feel angry at doctor and hospital for not doing more for husband | .26 | 19(13) | 12(19) | 81(56) | 88(138) |
| My married friends have not been much help to me | .28 | 38(28) | 26(47) | 61(44) | 72(130) |
| I like living alone | .32 | 65(47) | 49(75) | 35(25) | 51(78) |
| My faith helped me more than anything else | .30 | 86(70) | 78(138) | 14(11) | 22(40) |
| Sons are more help than daughters | .26 | 35(24) | 24(33) | 65(45) | 76(106) |
| We pretended we did not know how sick he was | .28 | 25(14) | 38(53) | 53(29) | 28(40) |

TABLE XXIII: PERCENTAGES OF WIDOWS EXPRESSING
DIFFERENT EXTREMES AND TYPES OF
AGREEMENT WITH THE STATEMENTS IN THE
RELATIONS-RESTRICTIVE ATTITUDE SCALE

| *Statements of Attitude* | *Level of Agreement* | | | | |
|---|---|---|---|---|---|
| | *Agree Strongly* | *Agree* | *Disagree* | *Disagree Strongly* | *No Answer* |
| One problem with adult children is that they always want you to do favors for them—baby-sit, or sew, or things like that. | 8 | 24 | 38 | 15 | 14 |
| Sons are more help to a widow than daughters. | 7 | 14 | 42 | 13 | 24 |
| Relatives are your only true friends. | 6 | 18 | 51 | 16 | 9 |
| A widow has to make her own life and not depend on others. | 50 | 40 | 6 | 2 | 2 |
| A new widow should not move too soon from the place in which she was living before her husband died. | 36 | 40 | 15 | 4 | 4 |
| Other women are jealous of a widow when their husbands are around. | 9 | 28 | 40 | 9 | 13 |
| Many widows who remarry are very unhappy in that marriage. | 7 | 36 | 32 | 5 | 20 |
| Widows are constantly sexually propositioned, even by the husbands of their friends. | 4 | 16 | 47 | 18 | 16 |
| One problem of being a widow is feeling like a "fifth wheel." | 18 | 40 | 27 | 7 | 8 |
| People take advantage of you when they know you are a widow. | 11 | 28 | 46 | 9 | 6 |
| Sharing one's home with anyone causes nothing but trouble for a widow. | 20 | 29 | 30 | 8 | 13 |
| Most widows prefer living near other widows. | 6 | 28 | 46 | 8 | 11 |
| It is all right for a widow to have sexual relations with a man without planning on marriage. | 2 | 9 | 31 | 48 | 11 |
| The hardest thing for a widow to learn is how to make decisions. | 13 | 42 | 34 | 8 | 3 |
| Women lose status when they become widows—they lose respect and consideration. | 4 | 12 | 53 | 20 | 7 |
| Old friends cannot be replaced no matter how one tries to make new friends. | 24 | 47 | 20 | 3 | 6 |

# REFERENCES

Adams, Bert.
1968 "The middle-class adult and his widowed or still-married mother." *Social Problems* 16 (Summer): 50–59.

Adams, David.
1969 "Adjustment to widowhood." Columbia, Missouri: University of Missouri. (mimeographed)

Babchuk, Nicholas and Alan Bates.
1963 "Primary relations of middle-class couples: a study of male dominance." *American Sociological Review* 28 (June): 374–384.

Barsky, Stephen F.
1971 "The fragmentation and consolidation of local communities in Chicago." Ph.D. dissertation proposal, University of Chicago, Department of Sociology (November).

Becker, Howard S.
1953 "Becoming a marihuana user." *American Journal of Sociology* 59 (November): 235–242.

Bell, Wendell.
1956 "Social structure and participation in different types of formal associations." *Social Forces* 34 (May): 345–350.

Bennis, Warren G., *et al.*
1968 Interpersonal Dynamics. Homewood, Illinois: The Dorsey Press.

Berardo, Felix.
1967 "Social adaptation to widowhood among a rural-urban aged population." Agricultural Experiment Station Bulletin 689 (December). Washington State University.
1968 "Widowhood status in the United States: perspective on a neglected aspect of the family life-cycle." *The Family Coordinator* 17 (July): 191–203.
"Survivorship and social isolation: the case of the aged widower." (mimeographed)

Berger, Bennett M.
1960 Working Class Suburb. Berkeley: University of California Press.

Berger, Peter, and Hansfried Kellner.
1970 "Marriage and the construction of reality." in Hans Dreitzel (ed.), *Recent Sociology #2.* London: Collier-Macmillan: 50–73.

Bernard, Jessie.
1956 *Remarriage.* New York: Dryden Press.

Bettleheim, Bruno.
1962 "Does communal education work? The case of the Kibbutz." *Commentary* (February).

Blau, Peter.
1957 "Social mobility and interpersonal relations." *American Sociological Review* 21:290–295.

Blood, Robert O.
1969 Marriage. New York: The Free Press of Macmillan.

Blood, Robert O., and Donald M. Wolfe.
    1960    Husbands and Wives. New York: The Free Press of Macmillan.
Bohannan, Paul J.
    1963    Social Anthropology. New York: Holt, Rinehart and Winston.
Bott, Elizabeth J.
    1957◀ Family and Social Network. London: Tavistock Publications, Ltd.
Broom, Leonard, and Philip Selznick.
    1968    Sociology. New York: Harper and Row, Publishers.
Brotman, Herman.
    1968    "Year-end statistical round-up." *Useful Facts* 16 (January). Administration on Aging, Health, Education and Welfare. "A profile of the older American." Administration on Aging, Health, Education, and Welfare. (mimeographed)
Buck, Pearl.
    1934    The Mother. New York: John Day Company.
    1964    Pavillion of Women. New York: John Day Company.
Bultena, Gordon, and D. Marshall.
    1969    "Family patterns of migrant and non-migrant retirees." Department of Rural Sociology, University of Wisconsin. (mimeographed)
Bultena, Gordon, and V. Wood.
    1969    "The American retirement community: bane or blessing?" *Journal of Gerontology* 24 (April): 209–217.
Burchinal, Lee.
    1962    "Parental aid to married children: some implications for family functioning." *Marriage and Family Living* 24 (November): 320–332.
Burgess, Ernest, et al.
    1963    Marriage and Family. New York: American Book Company. (3rd edition).
Campbell, John K.
    1964    Honour, Family and Patronage. Oxford: Clarendon Press.
Carnegie, Dale
    1936    How to Win Friends and Influence People. New York: Simon and Schuster.
Chicago Housing Authority
    1967    "Annual statistical report." (December 31): Table 5.
Coleman, James, et al.
    1961    Adolescent Society: The Social Life of the Teenager and Its Impact on Education. New York: The Free Press of Macmillan.
Cooley, Charles H.
    1915    Social Organization. New York: Charles Scribner's Sons.
    1922    Human Nature and the Social Order. New York: Charles Scribner's Sons. Revised edition.
Cumming, Elaine, and William E. Henry.
    1961    Growing Old: The Process of Disengagement. New York: Basic Books.

de Beauvoir, Simone
1953   The Second Sex. New York: Alfred Knopf.
De Hoyos, Arturo, and G. De Hoyos.
1966   "The amigo system and alienation of the wife in the conjugal Mexican family." Pp. 102–115 in Bernard Farber (ed.), Kinship and Family Organization. New York: Wiley.
de Lauwe, P. Chombard.
1962   "Images of women in society." *International Social Science Journal*. Paris: NESCO, Organization for Economic Cooperation and Development.
Department of Administration on Aging.
1968   "The American family in poverty." *Useful Facts* (November).
Deutsch, Morton.
1954   "Field    ⌐ory in social psychology," in Gardner Lindsey (ed.), Handbook oι Social Psychology. Volume One. Mass.: Addison-Wesley Publishing Co., Inc.
Dubin, Robert.
1956   "Industrial workers' world: study of the central life interests of industrial workers." *Social Problems* 3: 131–142.
Durkheim, Emile
1947   The Division of Labor in Society. Translated by George Simpson. New York: The Free Press of Glencoe of Macmillan.
Duvall, Evelyn.
1967   Family Development. New York: J. B. Lippincott Co. Third edition.
Egleston, Jim, and Janet Egleston.
1961   Parents without Partners. New York: Ace Books.
Farber, Bernard.
1964   Family: Organization and Interaction. San Francisco: Chandler Publishing Co.
Felton, Monica.
1966   A Child Widow's Story. New York: Harcourt, Brace and World.
Fischel, Walter.
1967   Ibn Khaldun in Egypt; his public functions and his historical research. Berkeley: University of California Press.
Flacks, Richard.
1967   "The liberated generation: an exploration of the roots of student protest." *Journal of Social Issues* 23 (July): 52–75.
1970   "Social and cultural meanings of student revolt: some informal comparative observations." *Social Problems* 17 (Winter): 340–357.
Foote, Nelson, and Leonard Cottrell, Jr.
1955   Identity and Interpersonal Competence. Chicago: University of Chicago Press.
Force, Marianne, and Wendell Bell.
1956   "Urban neighborhood types and participation in formal associations." *American Sociological Review* 21 (February): 25–34.

Freedman, Maurice.
   1965   Lineage Organization in Southeastern China. New York: The Humanities Press, Inc.

Fromm, Erich.
   1947   Escape from Freedom. New York: Rinehart and Co.
           Man for Himself. New York: Rinehart and Co.

Fulton, Robert L.
   1961   "The clergyman and the funeral director: a study in role conflict."
           *Social Forces* 39:317–323.

Gans, Herbert.
   1967   Levittowners. New York: Pantheon.
   1962   Urban Villagers. New York: The Free Press of Macmillan.

Gibson, Geoffrey.
           "Kin family networks: overheralded structure in past conceptualization
           of family functioning." (Undated).

Ginzberg, Eli, et al.
   1966   Life Styles of Educated Women. New York: Columbia University Press.

Gist, Noel P., and Sylvia F. Fava.
   1964   Urban Society. New York: Thomas Y. Crowell Co.

Glaser, Barney G., and Strauss, Anselm L.
   1968   *Time for Dying.* Chicago: Aldine.

Goffman, Erving.
   1956   "The nature of deference and demeanor." *American Anthropologist* 58
           (June): 473–502.
   1961   "Role distance." in Erving Goffman (ed.), Encounters. Indianapolis,
           Ind.: The Bobbs-Merrill Co.

Goode, William.
   1956   "Community with a community: the professions." *American Sociological Review* 22: 194–200.
   1963   World Revolution and Family Patterns. New York: The Free Press of
           Macmillan.

Gorer, Geoffrey.
   1965   Death, Grief and Mourning. New York: Doubleday and Co.

Gouldner, Alvin W.
   1957   "Cosmopolitans and locals." *Administrative Science Quarterly* (December): 281–306.

Gumplowicz, Ludwig.
   1899   The Outlines of Sociology. Translated by F. W. Moore. New York:
           American Academy of Political and Social Science.

Habenstein, Robert.
   1962   "Sociology of occupations: the case of the American funeral director."
           in Arnold Rose (ed.), Human Behavior and Social Process. Boston:
           Houghton Mifflin Co.

Hartley, Ruth E.
   1961   "Current patterns in sex roles: children's perspectives." *Journal of the
           National Association of Women Deans and Counselors* 25 (October):
           3–13.

1964 "Sex-role identification: a symposium." Merrill-Palmer Quarterly of Behavior and Development 10.

Hertzler, Joyce.
1961 Social Institutions. Boston: Allyn and Bacon, Inc.

Hill, Rubin C., and D. G. Marshall.
1968 Department of Rural Sociology, College of Agriculture and Life Sciences, University of Wisconsin, Madison. Population Series 15 (August).

Honnen, James S., *et al.*
1969 Department of Rural Sociology, College of Agriculture and Life Sciences, University of Wisconsin, Madison. *Population Series* 19( July).

Housing and Urban Renewal Progress Report.
1964 "The elderly in Chicago." Chicago: Community Renewal Program (June 30).

Hume, David.
1911 A Treatise of Human Nature, IV and V. London: J. M. Dent and Souss Ltd.

Kenniston, Kenneth.
1965 Young Radicals. New York: Harcourt, Brace and World.

Kitagawa, Evelyn H., and Karl E. Taeuber.
1963 Local Community Factbook: Chicago Metropolitan Area, 1960. Chicago: Chicago Community Inventory, University of Chicago.

Komarovsky, Mirra.
1946 "The voluntary associations of urban dwellers." *American Sociological Review* 11:686–698.
1953 Women in the Modern World. Boston: Little, Brown and Co.
1967 Blue-Collar Marriage. New York: Random House.

Kosa, J., *et al.*
1960 "Sharing the home with relatives." *Marriage and Family Living* 22 (May): 129–131.

Kuhn, Mumford.
1962 "The interview and the professional relationship." Pp. 193–206 in Arnold Rose (ed.), Human Behavior and Social Processes. Boston: Houghton Mifflin Co.

Lenski, Gerhard E.
1954 "Status crystallization." *American Sociological Review* 19:405–413.

Leslie, Gerald.
1967 The Family in Social Context. New York: Oxford University Press.

Liebow, Elliot.
1967 Tally's Corner. Boston: Little, Brown, and Co.

Lindemann, Eric.
1944 "Symptomology and management of acute grief." *American Journal of Psychiatry* 101 (July): 141–148.

Litwak, Eugene.
1960 "Occupational mobility and extended family cohesion." *American Sociological Review* 25:9–21.

1963 "Use of extended family groups in the achievement of social goals." Pp. 477–484 in Marvin Sussman (ed.), Sourcebook in Marriage and the Family. Boston: Houghton-Mifflin Co.

Litwak, Eugene, and M. Sussman.
1960 "Geographical mobility and extended family cohesion." *American Sociological Review* 25:385–394.

Lopata, Helena Znaniecki.
1964 "A restatement of the relation between role and status." *Sociology and Social Research* 49 (October): 58–68.

1965 "The secondary features of a primary relationship." *Human Organization* 24 (Summer): 116–123.

1966 "The life cycle of the social role of housewife." *Sociology and Social Research* 51:5–22. (Also Pp. 110–124 in Marcello Truzzi (ed.), Sociology and Everyday Life. New Jersey: Prentice-Hall, Inc., 1968.)

1967 Noel, Joseph, co-author. "The dance studio: style without sex." *Transaction* (January–February).

1969a "Social psychological aspects of role involvement." *Sociology and Social Research* 53 (April): 285–298.

1969b "Loneliness: forms and components." *Social Problems* 17 (Fall) · 248–262.

1970a "Social relations of widows in urbanizing societies." Paper given at the International Sociological meetings in Varna, Bulgaria (September). (Also accepted for publication in *Sociological Quarterly,* Spring, 1972).

1970b "The social involvement of American widows." *American Behavioral Scientist* 14 (September–October): 41–58.

1970c "Widows as a minority group." *Gerontologist* 11 (Spring, Part 2): 67–77.

1971a Occupation: Housewife. New York: Oxford University Press.

1971b "Self-identity in marriage and widowhood." Paper given at the American Sociological Association meetings in Denver, Colorado (August).

1971c "Work histories of American urban women." *Gerontologist* 11 (Winter).

1971d "Role changes in widowhood: a world perspective," in Donald Cowgill and Lowell Holmes (eds.), Aging and Modernization. New York: Appleton-Century-Crofts.

1972a "The association between educational achievement and social isolation of urban women." Accepted for publication, *American Journal of Sociology.*

1972b "Living arrangements of American urban widows." Paper given at Gerontological Society meetings, Toronto, 1970; *Sociological Focus* 5 (Autumn).

Mack, Raymond W.
1956 "Occupational determinateness: a problem and hypothesis in role theory." *Social Forces* 35 (October): 20–24.

Maddison, David.
  1968  "The relevance of conjugal bereavement for preventive psychiatry."
        *British Journal of Psychology* 41:223–233.
Maddison, David and W. L. Walker.
  1967  "Factors affecting the outcome of conjugal bereavement." *British Journal of Psychiatry* 113 (October): 1057–1067.
Marris, Peter.
  1958  Widows and Their Families. London: Routledge and Kegan Paul, Ltd.
Merton, Robert.
  1957  "The role set." *British Journal of Sociology* 8:106–120.
Metropolitan Life Insurance Co.
  1945  "The chances of remarriage for the widowed and divorced." *Statistical Bulletin* 26 (May): 1–3.
  1962  "The American widow." *Statistical Bulletin* 43 (November): 1–4.
  1969  "Chances of dependency." *Statistical Bulletin* 50 (January): 10–11.
Mitford, Jessica.
  1963  The American Way of Death. New York: Simon and Schuster.
Monahan, W., and D. Marshall.
  1968  "Retirement and migration in the north central states." *Population Series* 14 (June).
National Center for Health Statistics.
  1965  "Changes in mortality trends: England and Wales, 1931–1961." *Vital and Health Statistics* 3 (November): 35.
Nelson, Joel J.
  1966  "Clique contacts and family orientation in the nuclear family." *American Sociological Review* 31 (October): 663–672.
Neugarten, Bernice.
  1968  "Adaptation and the life cycle." Paper given at the FFRP Conference, Puerto Rico (June): 10.
Neugarten, Bernice, and K. Weinstein.
  1964  "The changing American grandparent." *Journal of Marriage and the Family* 26 (May): 199–204.
Nimkoff, M. F., and R. Middleton.
  1960  "Types of family and types of economy." *American Journal of Sociology* 60:215–225.
Parkes, C. Murray.
  1964a  "Grief as an illness." *New Society* (April).
  1964b  "Effects of bereavement on physical and mental health, a study of the medical records of widows." *British Medical Journal* 2 (August): 274–279.
  1965  "Bereavement and mental illness: a clinical study." *British Journal of Medical Psychology* 38:1–26.
Parkes, C. Murray, and B. Benjamin.
  1967  "Bereavement." *British Medical Journal* 3 (July-September): 232–233.

Parsons, Talcott.
    1943    "The kinship system of the contemporary United States." *American Anthropologist* 34 (January-March): 22–38.
Parsons, Talcott, and R. Bales.
    1955    The Family and Socialization.
Pihlblad, Terence, and Howard Rosencranz.
    1968    Old People in the Small Town. Columbia, Missouri: University of Missouri.
Ploski, Harry A., and Roscoe C. Brown, Jr. (eds.).
    1963    The Negro Almanac. New York: Bellwether Publishing Co., Inc.
Practical Builder.
    1966    "What makes Ross W. Cortese the world's largest home builder?" *Practical Builder* (May): 82–92.
Rainwater, Lee, *et al.*
    1959    Workingman's Wife. New York: Oceana Publications, Inc.
Rainwater, Lee, and Wm. C. Yancey.
    1967    The Moynihan Report and the Politics of Controversy. Cambridge, Mass.: M.I.T. Press.
Riesman, David.
    1954    The Lonely Crowd. New York: Doubleday-Anchor Books.
Rose, Arnold.
    1961    "The inadequacy of women's expectations for adult roles." *Social Forces* 30 (October): 69–77.
Rosenmayr, Leopold, and E. Kockeis.
    1963    "Propositions for a sociological theory of aging and the family." *International Social Science Journal* 15: 410–426.
Rosow, Irving.
    1967    The Social Integration of the Aged. New York: The Free Press of Macmillan.
Ross, Arlene.
    1961    The Hindu Family in its Urban Setting. Toronto: The University of Toronto Press.
Rossi, Alice.
    1965    "Barriers to the career choice of engineering, medicine or science among American women." Pp. 51–127 in Jacquelyn A. Mattfelt and Carol G. VanAken (eds.), Women and the Scientific Professions. Cambridge, Mass.: The M.I.T. Press.
Rossi, Peter.
    1955    Why Families Move. New York: The Free Press of Macmillan.
Ruark, Robert.
    1955    Something of Value. New York: Doubleday and Co., Inc.
Sarasvati, Pundita R.
    1888    The High-Caste Hindu Woman. Philadelphia: The James B. Rodgers Printing Co.

Schapera, Isaac.
  1941  Married Life in an African Tribe. New York: Sheridan House.
Shanas, Ethel.
  1962  The Health of Older People. Cambridge, Mass.: Harvard University Press.
  ᵕ968  Old People in Three Industrial Societies. New York: Atherton Press.
Shanas, Ethel, and Gordon R. Streib (eds.).
  1965  Social Structure and the Family: Generational Relations. Englewood Cliffs, N. J.: Prentice-Hall, Inc.
Simmons, Leo W.
  1945  The Role of the Aged in Primitive Society. London: Oxford University Press.
Smuts, Robert W.
  1959  Women and Work in America. New York: Columbia University Press.
Social Security Administration.
  1955  "Recipients of old age assistance in early 1953." *Public Assistance Report* 26 (June): Table 52.
Stouffer, Samuel, *et al.*
  1949  The American Soldier. Princeton, N. J.: Princeton University Press.
Stehouwer, Jan.
  1968  "The household and family relations of old people." in Ethel Shanas (ed.), Old People in Three Industrial Societies. New York: Atherton Press.
Stein, Maurice.
  1960  The Eclipse of Community. Princeton, N. J.: Princeton University Press.
Sussman, Marvin.
  1962  "The isolated nuclear family: fact or fiction." Pp. 49–57 in Robert Winch et al. (eds.), Selected Studies in Marriage and the Family. New York: Holt, Rinehart, and Winston.
Sussman, Marvin, and Lee Burchinal.
  1966  "Kin family network: Unheralded structure in current conceptualization of family functioning." Pp. 123–133 in Bernard Farber (ed.), Kinship and Family Organization. New York: John Wiley and Sons, Inc.
Thomas, P.
  1964  Indian Women Through the Ages. New York: Asia Publishing House.
Thomas, W. I., and Florian Znaniecki.
  1958  The Polish Peasant in Europe and America. New York: Dover.
Tonnies, Ferdinand.
  1957  Community and Society. Translated and edited by Charles P. Loomis. East Lansing, Michigan: The Michigan State University Press.
Townsend, Peter.
  1957  The Family Life of Old People. London: Routledge, and Kegan Paul.
  1968  "Isolation, desolation and loneliness." in Ethel Shanas, et al., Old People in Three Industrial Societies. New York: Atherton Press.

Tunstall, Jeremy.
1966   Old and Alone. London: Routledge and Kegan Paul.
United Nations.
1947   The Demographic Yearbook. Lake Success, New York.
United States Bureau of the Census.
1971   *Current Population Reports*. Series P-23, No. 37, "Social and economic characteristics of the population in metropolitan and nonmetropolitan areas: 1970 and 1960." U. S. Government Printing Office, Washington, D. C.
United States Department of Commerce.
1968   Statistical Abstracts of the United States, 89th ed.
United States Department of Labor.
1966   "Why women work." WB 67–6 (August): 1.
Ward, Barbara (ed.).
1963   Women of New Asia. Paris: UNESCO.
Weber, Max.
1930   The Protestant Ethic and the Spirit of Capitalism. London: George Allen and Unwin.
1964   The Theory of Social and Economic Organization. Translated by A.M. Henderson and Talcott Parsons. New York: The Free Press of Macmillan.
Weiss, Robert.
1969   "The fund of sociability." *Trans-action* (Summer): 43–63.
Whyte, William H. Jr.
1955   The Organization Man. New York: The Free Press of Macmillan.
Williams, Richard H., and Martin Loeb.
1960   "Changing status, roles and relationships." in Clark Tibbitts (ed.), Handbook of Social Gerontology. Chicago: University of Chicago Press.
Wilmott, Peter, and Michael Young.
1960   Family and Class in a London Suburb. London: Routledge and Kegan Paul, Ltd.
Winch, Robert.
1962   Identification and Its Familial Determinants. Indianapolis: The Bobbs-Merrill Co.
1963   The Modern Family. New York: Holt, Rinehart and Winston.
Winch, Robert, and Ray Blumberg.
1968   "Social complexity and family organization," in Robert F. Winch and Louis W. Goodman, (eds.), Selected Studies in Marriage and the Family. New York: Holt, Rinehart, and Winston.
Young, Michael, and Peter Wilmott.
1957   Family and Kinship in East London. New York: The Free Press of Macmillan.
Znaniecki, Florian.
1965   Social Relations and Social Roles. San Francisco: Chandler Publishing Co.

# Subject Index

Achieved friendship, 180, 183, 203–4
Adult children, 151–2
  attitude toward, 105–109, 152–3, 198
  conflicts with, 115, 120–22
  contact with, 124, 127–35, 147–48
  distance from, 123–127
  help from, 48–9, 54–5, 60–61, 101–9, 198
  and isolation, 265, 268, 270
  living with, 112, 114–23, 125–26 (*see also* Living with adult children)
  and widow's friends, 198, 206
Advice, 101, 121, 273–374
Age, 20–25, 32–33, 45, 89, 152, 172
  and attitudes about women's roles, 62–63, 78–79
  and community involvement, 19, 222–3, 248–49
  and contact with adult children, 102–03, 123
  and extended-family relations, 142, 160–61, 164–65, 172, 174
  and household composition, 25–27, 110–13
  of husband, 79, 81, 210, 240–41
  and life style, 19, 40
  and mother role, 137, 142
  and neighbor role, 228–29, 234–35, 239–41
  and problems with widowhood, 71–72, 75
  and social relations, 181, 183–86, 208–09
  and work experience, 27, 255, 262
Age at migration to Chicago, 82, 142–43
Age at widowhood, 100, 174
  and attitudes, 45, 65
  in Chicago area, 17, 20–21, 33
  and friendship, 184–85, 188, 201–02
  and grandmother role, 171–72, 175
American society, 139, 215, 219
  attitudes in, about social life, 184, 191, 208
Anomic non-interaction, 233
Apartments, 212
  *See also* Housing
Appearance of widows, 34
Ascribed friendship, 180, 183, 215
Attitudes, 38, 60, 126–27, 229–32
  about dead husband, 60–63, 78, 84, 113, 163
  about former marriage, 63–66, 85
  about friendship, 163, 214–15
  about men, 87, 89, 163
  about sex without marriage, 60–61, 85
  about siblings, 159, 163
  about the world, 77, 197, 214–15
  *See also* Adult children, attitude toward; Living alone, attitude toward
Attitudes about remarriage, 62–66, 77, 84–85, 90–91, 201–04
  and community roles, 241, 251
  and friendship, 190, 207, 210, 212–13
  and loneliness, 71, 74
  and sibling role, 158–59, 166–67
Auburn-Gresham, 30
Austria, 18, 114

Babysitting, 106–09, 129, 148, 170, 175, 234
Baptists, 35
Bathroom, 118
Becoming, 39
Becoming a widowed mother, 97–109
Becoming a wife, 41–42
Being, 39
Being a mother, 95–97
Being a widow, 56–66
Being a wife, 42–44
Bereavement, 17, 51
  *See also* Grief
Bilateral family, 18

Birth order, 102–3
Blacks, 35, 80–87
  *See also* Race
Block clubs, 245
Borrowing, 233–35, 238
Bride price, 10–11, 13n6
British Islanders (in Chicago), 210
  *See also* English women (in
    Chicago); Scotch women; Irish
    women
Brothers, 165
  *See also* Siblings

Career, 255, 262
  *See also* Work; Worker role;
    Working women
Catholics, 35, 112
  and family roles, 137, 143, 158, 166
  and social life, 209, 240, 250–51
Chicago Housing Authority (CHA),
  31, 226, 230–31
Childhood memories, 156–57
Childless women, 44
  *See also* Children, number of
Child-orientation, 139–46
Child rearing, 67, 72–3, 98–99
  and grandmother role, 121, 153–54,
    172
Children, 99–100, 151–52, 162, 192–93
  and community roles, 173–74,
    234–35, 251
  number of, 34, 97
  number of, and mother role, 125–26,
    129, 131, 138, 141–42, 144
  number of, and social relations, 110,
    237, 258, 260–61
  *See also* Adult children
China, 119–20
Church, 186, 245, 250
  *See also* Voluntary associations
City life, 219–22, 230–32
Cliques, 181–82
Clubs, 190, 232–35, 248, 274–76
  *See also* Voluntary associations
Community, 16–17, 219–262, 274–77
  types, 219–20, 244

  *See also* Neighborhood
Community-member role, 79, 167,
  169, 244, 251–52
Companionate relations, 11, 44, 67, 89
  *See also* Couple-companionate
    relations
Companionship, problems of, 271–72,
  274
  *See also* Loneliness
Compensations of widowhood, 74–77,
  91, 123, 207
  and social relations, 167, 188–89,
    205, 212, 251, 267
Counselors, 271, 274
Couple-companionate relations, 17, 70,
  127, 182, 216, 232–33
  in friendship, 182–84, 188–89,
    191–92, 194, 202, 208–09
  after widowhood, 265
  *See also* Companionate relations;
    Fifth-wheel feeling; Sex-
    segregated relations
Couple interaction, 43–44
Couples, 190, 195
Crystallization, 3
  *See also* Status decrystallization
Cultural change, 139, 152, 172
  *See also* Social change

Data sources, 4–5, 13n4
  *See also* Methodology; Sample
Dating, 18, 100, 189, 200, 202, 237
  *See also* Escorts
Daughter-in-law of widow, 118–20
Daughter-in-law, role of, 57
Daughter role, 142, 153–56, 167,
  174–75, 243–44
Daughters, 120, 124, 147
  *See also* Adult children
Dead husband, 59–60, 67, 92n1
  evaluation of, 107, 168, 207
  *See also* Attitudes, about dead
    husband
Dead persons, 51–54
Death, 53–54, 73, 158
  of husband, 47–50, 196, 198, 265,

270
  of husband and effects on friendship,
    187–93, 201, 215, 273
  of husband and worker role, 253,
    257–59
  in widow's family, 155–56, 159
  *See also* Funeral
Decision-making problems, 72, 197,
    237, 273–74
Definition of the situation, 5, 40
Denmark, 18, 114
Disengagement, 8, 17, 196, 209, 242
  from roles, 39
  in widowhood, 67, 92
Disengagement theory, 113, 216, 266,
    276–77
Divorce and desertion, 80–83
  *See also* Marital status
Doctors, anger at, 50, 107, 199
Dropping over. *See* Visiting
Duties, of widow, 56–60, 90
  *See also* Roles, social

Eating, 76, 79, 226–271
Education, 27–29, 35–36, 239
  and community roles, 222, 228, 234,
    238–41, 248–50, 258–61
  and extended-family, 156, 158,
    160–61, 165–66
  and friendship, 183, 186, 191, 203,
    209–10
  and marriage roles, 42–44, 79, 87
  and mother role, 100, 132, 134,
    137–38, 143–44
  and perception of roles, 76, 79
  and problems of widowhood, 71–75,
    268–69
  and re-engagement, 230
Education of husband, 35–36, 158
  and social roles, 42, 144, 209,
    240–41, 250, 260–61
Egalitarian family, 18, 57
Emotional problems, 101–102, 147,
    196, 271–73
Empty-nest stage, 89
  *See also* Housewife role

England, 153
English women (in Chicago), 35, 158
  and social roles, 137, 143, 241, 250
English women (in England), 18, 114
Entertaining, 129, 144, 188
Escorts, 68–69, 188–91, 272
  *See also* Dating
Ethnic groups, 16, 35, 110, 186
  and neighbor role, 43, 221–22,
    227–28, 231–32
  and social roles, 79, 143, 209,
    259–60
  *See also* British Islanders; English
    women; German women; Greek
    women; Irish women; Italian
    women; Mexican women;
    Norwegian women; Polish women;
    Russian women; Scandinavian
    women; Scotch women; Welsh
    women
Expanding circle state, 44, 98, 106
  *See also* Housewife role
Exploitation, fear of, 203–04, 207,
    213, 242–43, 266–70
Expressive help, 102–03
Extended family, 8, 11, 16–17, 156

Faith, religious, 162, 167–68, 198,
    207, 242–43
Family, 114, 127, 151, 258, 261,
    271–73
  and social relations, 32, 177
  of husband, 19 (*see also* In-Laws)
  of orientation, 8, 56, 153, 155–56,
    165 (*see also* Siblings)
  of procreation, 56, 152 (*see also*
    Adult children)
Family structure, 96, 159
  *See also* Bilateral family; Extended
    family; Neolocal family; Nuclear
    family; Matriarchal family;
    Patriarchal family.
Family orientation, 74, 105
Father of widow, 154, 156
Father role, 97–100
Favoritism, 104–05

Fears, 70, 188–89, 231–32, 247, 272

Fifth-wheel feeling, 198–99, 213, 237, 272

Financial help, 56–60, 101–04, 108–09, 156, 276

Financial problems, 59, 64, 67, 72, 91, 262

Financial resources, 86–87, 91, 194–95, 236, 257–58
  *See also* Income; Money

Foreign-born respondents, 251, 255, 262

Foreign stock, 30

Fraternal relations, 177

Frequency of contact score, 140, 164, 243–44, 268
  *See also* Interaction

Friend-orientation, 212

Friend role, 208–15, 243

Friends, 74, 109, 199–208
  help from, 175, 258, 271–3
  and voluntary associations, 247, 251

Friendship, 43, 179–81, 215–17
  and family roles, 106–7, 137, 164, 168
  and isolation, 265–70
  *See also* Achieved friendship;
    Ascribed friendship; Couple-
    companionate relations; Fifth-
    wheel feeling

Full-house plateau, 44, 73, 95, 106, 146, 244
  and paid work, 78, 253

Functional roles, 17–18, 39, 179

Funeral, 52–56, 101–02, 198

Future-orientation, 207, 212

Ganda widows, 92n1

Generation gap, 115, 127, 147, 170, 175
  *See also* Adult children, conflicts
    with

German women, 35, 110, 209, 240
  and mother role, 137, 143
  and sibling role, 158, 161, 166

Grandchildren, 123, 142, 148, 169–71, 175

Grandmother role, 169–173
  changes in, 106–08, 122, 153–54

Great-grandchildren, 170, 172, 175

Greek women, 110, 137

Grief, 17, 51–54, 77, 92, 196, 265
  and friendship, 195–98, 205, 208, 245–47
  stages of, 55, 75, 202, 207

Grief work, 271, 273

Guilt feelings, 159, 195–96

Happiness, 216–17

Health, 211, 254
  and mother role, 132–33, 145
  and sibling role, 159, 162, 165
  and social life, 188–89, 211, 241
  and voluntary associations, 248, 250, 262

Home-orientation, 192, 196

Home ownership, 31–32, 46
  *See also* Household composition;
    Housing

Hospital, 47–48, 50, 107, 199

Hostility, 45, 198–99, 203, 210, 215, 247, 267–68
  toward family, 57, 156
  toward opposite sex, 5, 42, 60, 73, 83, 138

Household composition, 20, 31, 33–34, 39, 147, 171
  *See also* Living alone; Living
    arrangements; Living with adult
    children

Household repairs, 69

Housewife role, 41–42, 73, 115–19
  and family roles, 42–43, 136, 141–42, 167
  and neighbor role, 234, 244
  rank of, 44, 76, 78–79
  *See also* Empty-nest stage; Expand-
    ing circle stage; Full-house
    plateau; Shrinking circle stage

Housework, 69, 72, 76, 117–19

Housing, 29–31, 34, 46, 56, 222–26, 236–7

and social roles, 160–62, 241
Husband, 86
  age of, at death, 33
  and friendship, 181–84, 200, 218n2
    (*see also* Couple-companionate
    relations)
  death of, 33, 49–50, 271–72 (*see
    also* Death, of husband)
Husband's illness, 47–50, 77, 240–43
  help during, 101–2, 157, 166
  and social roles, 210, 253–54
Human Relations Area Files (HRAF),
  4, 13n4

Illinois Old Age Assistance, 32
Immigrants, 228, 230
  *See also* Foreign-born respondents;
    Migration to Chicago
Income, 27, 31, 37, 47, 58, 87
  attitude toward, 72, 161, 210–11
  and contacts with adult children,
    111–12, 132
  and contact with siblings, 157, 159,
    161–62, 166
  and family roles, 80, 145, 156
  and friend role, 191, 194–5, 198,
    204–5, 210–11, 213
  and social life, 188, 191, 226, 241,
    249–51, 269–70
  and work roles, 257, 259–62
  *See also* Financial resources; Money
Independence, 168
  as a compensation, 61, 71, 75–77,
    123, 207
  and household composition, 110–14,
    122–23, 147, 158
  and mother role, 73, 141
  and problems of widowhood, 108–09,
    188–89, 204
  and race, 83, 87
  and sibling role, 159, 162, 168
  wish for, 56–57, 200
India, 119–20
*In-genetricem* rights, 9, 19, 56
Inheritance, 11, 18–19, 58
In-laws, 54–58, 91, 104, 118–20, 148

Instrumental help, 102–03
Interaction
  and community roles, 220, 225–29,
    232–33, 242, 245
  and family roles, 139–40, 169
  and friendship, 186, 196–97, 214,
    216
  *See also* Frequency of contact
Interviewer, rating scale of, 223
Interviews, 4–5
Intimacy at a distance, 18, 100, 114,
  146, 147
Irish women, 143, 210, 240
Isolation, 8, 15–16, 189, 237, 266–70
  and friendship, 188–89, 192, 197
  and mother role, 132–33, 139–40
  and neighbor role, 217, 240, 243
  and sibling role, 163–4, 168–9
Italian women, 110, 143, 250–51

Jealousy, 60–61, 65, 85
  and friendship, 198–200, 201, 207,
    213
  and isolation, 266–68, 273
Jews, 35
  and money problems, 72, 75
  and mother role, 137, 143
  and role ranking, 79–80
  and sibling role, 158, 166
  and social life, 209–10, 250

Kansas City, 45
Kinship, 9, 88
  *See also* Family structure

Leisure, 17, 19, 88, 106
  with neighbors, 232–35, 238
Lending, 233–35, 238
Length of widowhood, 33
  and community involvement, 240–41,
    251
  and friend role, 145, 165, 209
  and sibling role, 158, 160, 165
  and worker role, 258, 261
Letter writing, 135, 157
Levirate, 7–10, 13n6, 19

Life cycle, 2, 129, 177, 183
  and social roles, 211, 220, 244
  *See also* Housewife role
Life expectancy, 17, 21
Life style, 19, 40, 75
Living alone, 69, 91, 109–115, 271
  attitude toward, 60–61, 75, 112–114,
    201, 207
  and other social roles, 105, 162,
    167–68
Living arrangements, 25–27, 156, 200
  and friend role, 205–06, 213–14
Living with adult children, 114–123,
  129, 146–48, 171, 228
Linearly-oriented societies, 10
London, friendship in, 182
Loneliness, 5, 80, 91–2, 92n1, 201, 232
  description of, 67–72, 74
  help with, 101, 246–47, 271–72
  and independence, 147, 200
  and satisfaction in widowhood,
    207–08
  and social roles, 138, 159, 167,
    211–12, 241
  *See also* Isolation
Loop, 29–30
Love, 18, 89
Lovers, 179
Lutherans, 35

Male guardianship, 9
Malnutrition, 79
Marital status, 18, 20–24, 26, 45
  and friendship, 184–85, 190, 193–5,
    197–200, 205
Marriage, 41–42, 75, 88
  and social relations, 49, 69, 78, 178,
    181–83, 254
  *See also* Attitudes, about former
    marriage; Companionate relations;
    Couple-companionate relations
Marriage contract, 18–19
Matriarchal family, 10, 183
Mayor's Commission on Senior
  Citizens, 31, 76
Meals on Wheels, 76

Men
  attitude toward, 106, 114 (*see also*
    Hostility; Sex; Propositioning)
  companionship with, 85–86, 199,
    201, 245, 247, 266–68 (*see also*
    Escorts)
Methodists, 35
Methodology, 4–7, 32–38
  for role of friend, 208
  for role of mother, 139
  for role of neighbor, 239
  for role ranking, 44, 78
  for role of worker, 253–54
  *See also* Scales
Mexican women, 157
Middle age, 89
Middle generation, 171–72, 175
  *See also* Adult children
Migration to Chicago, 82, 84, 173–74,
  222–23, 231
  and community participation, 220,
    228, 230, 240–41
  and social roles, 79, 110, 157, 165,
    180–81, 215, 259–60
  *See also* Moving
Migratory communities, 226
Missouri, 114, 133, 184, 275
Modern society, 122, 219–20, 263 64
  and family roles, 91, 125, 151
  and friendship, 178, 180–181
  and women's roles, 87–90, 97, 140
  *See also* Urban society
Money, 57, 64, 72–75, 248
  and work, 255, 262
  *See also* Financial resources; Income
Motherhood, 95–96, 100, 139
  and work, 252, 254
Mother, of widow, 152–155, 175
  *See also* Daughter role
Mother role, 41–43, 78, 145, 199
  and adult children, 107, 141, 167
    (*see also* Adult children)
  importance of, 121–23, 135–39,
    148, 152–53
  rank of, 79, 136–39
  and sibling role, 164, 169

and social life, 136, 208, 243, 267–68
and social relations, 111, 121, 140–42
in widowhood, 8–10, 92, 98
*See also* Becoming a widowed
mother; Being a mother; Scales
Mothers, in suburbs, 170, 235, 239
Mourning, 17, 51, 54, 271
*See also* Grief
Moving, effects of, 236–37, 266–67
Moynihan's report, 80, 143
Multi-dimensional personality, 264–65
Multi-dimensional relations, 41, 106,
201, 220–21
definition of, 3, 89
in marriage, 67, 86, 88, 207
as problems in widowhood, 71,
89–90, 189
Multi-dimensional social life space,
166, 245
definition of, 15, 12n2

NAIM, 4, 274–76
Nationality, 185–86
*See also* Ethnic groups
Neighborhood, 30–33, 125, 173–4, 176,
265
and social life, 19, 182, 191, 225–32,
246
Neighboring, 43, 164, 227, 229, 232–44,
261
Neighbor role, 169, 208, 222, 239–44,
267–68
Neighbors, 29–31, 72
Neolocal family, 11, 18
National Opinion Research Center
(NORC), 4, 32, 223–24
North Laundale, 30–31
Norwegian Women, 209
Nuclear family, 57–58, 176n1

Occupation, 36–37, 253–54
and problems in widowhood, 70, 73,
75
and role ranking, 79, 137–38, 260
and social life, 182, 250, 261
*See also* Work

Occupational mobility, 125
*See also* Social mobility; Status
decrystallization
Occupation of husband, 36, 47, 78–79
and community roles, 210, 240–41,
250, 260–61
and family roles, 42–43, 84, 79–80,
89, 144–45

Parent-Teacher Association (PTA),
245
Parents without Partners (PWP), 99,
247
Passive acceptance of widowhood, 75
Passive dependence and loneliness,
69–70
Passiveness, 16, 163, 193, 196, 206, 230
Past life, feeling about, 61, 204, 207,
210–11
*See also* Attitudes, about dead
husband; Attitudes, about former
marriage
Patriarchal families, 8, 10–11, 55, 183
Patriarchal society
and family life, 136, 139, 147, 151
and friendship, 182, 192
Patrilineal society, 15, 124, 147, 182
Patrilocal residence, 11, 124, 151, 182
Parenthood, 181–83
*See also* Motherhood
Polish community, 221–22
Polish women, 35, 110, 210, 250
and neighboring, 221–22, 240
and role ranking, 137, 143
and sibling role, 161, 166
Poverty, 32, 37–38, 262
*See also* Income
Presbyterians, 35
Primary relations, 15
definition of, 178–9, 217n1, 218
in social relations, 127–29, 181, 203,
216–17, 221
Privacy, 206, 212, 226
Problems of widowhood, 271–76
and age, 19, 66–75
and social roles, 138, 196–98, 211,

241
solutions for, 270
*See also* Decision-making problems;
Emotional problems; Entertaining;
Exploitation, fear of; Fears;
Financial problems; Loneliness;
Transportation
Propositioning, 60–61, 65, 85
and social roles, 142–43, 168,
198–204, 213, 266–68
Protestants, 35, 72, 240, 250
and role ranking, 137, 143
and sibling role, 158, 166
Public places, 188, 191
*See also* Escorts
Public housing, 19
Purification of marriage. *See* Attitudes,
about former marriage
Purification of husband. *See* Attitudes,
about dead husband

Race, 21–25, 31–32, 71–72, 78–80
and contact with sibling, 157,
160–61, 166
and family roles, 80, 137–39, 143,
171
and friendship, 202, 210
and household composition, 109–10,
116, 148, 152
and migration, 158, 222–23
and neighbor role, 227, 234, 237–38,
240
and problems in widowhood, 71–73,
257–58
and voluntary associations, 248–50
and work experience, 255–60
*See also* Blacks
Reality construction, definition of, 43
Re-engagement, 8, 190, 276
in modern society, 263–64, 270
process of, 229–30, 241, 245
Rejection, feelings of, 123
Relations, social, 2
Relations-restrictive attitudes, 199
and attitudes toward husband, 60,
107, 242

and family roles, 105, 107, 164,
167–68
and friendship, 197, 202, 204, 210,
213–14
and social isolation, 266–68
Relation-verses-task approach, 89
Relatives, 151–176, 199, 203
and friendship, 181, 189, 203–05,
217
help from, 49, 56–60, 96, 99, 106
living with, 33, 109
and loneliness, 71, 74
as neighbors, 173–74, 176, 227
and social isolation, 268, 271–73
and voluntary associations, 251
*See also* specific types of relatives,
e.g. Siblings
Religion, 17–18, 35, 72
and death, 53–54, 61
and social roles, 162, 186–87
*See also* Church; Faith
Remarriage, 17, 45, 64, 81–82, 91
*See also* Attitudes, about remarriage
Rent, 31–32
Roles, social, 6–9, 42–43
action in, 41, 220–21, 241
definition of, 2–3, 12n3
ranking of, 44, 78, 251
and relations with others, 132, 136,
235, 243, 245
and social change, 263–64
*See also* Becoming; Being; and
specific roles, e.g. Mother role
Role conflict, 3
and family roles, 104, 116–19, 129,
132
Role distance, 39–40
Role scale, 6
Role strain, 69
Rural residence, 24–25, 28–29
Russian women, 210, 250

Sample, 29–38, 45–47, 263
Sanctification of husband. *See*
Attitudes, about dead husband
Sanctification of marriage. *See*

Attitudes, about former marriage
Safety, 227
Scales, 6–7
  interviewer rating, 223
  role of friend, 208
  role of mother, 139
  role of sibling, 163–64
  role of wife, 79
Scandinavian women, 161, 250
Scottish women, 35, 241, 250
Secondary relations, 15, 221
  definition of, 128, 178, 217n1
  and friendship, 181, 206
Self-confidence, 239, 248
Self-identity, 41, 50, 212, 253
Service-exchange, 232, 234–36
Sex, 76, 200–02
  *See also* Jealousy; Propositioning
Sex in previous marriage, 60–61
Sex-ratio, of widows and widowers,
  17, 20–21
Sex-segregated relations, 43, 60, 86, 89
  and friendship, 181–84, 189–90,
  192–94, 206–07, 209
  and problems in widowhood, 73, 106
  and social roles, 112, 168, 233,
  242–43, 247
Sex without marriage, 76–77, 91
  and social relations, 114, 141, 168
Shopping, 227, 234
Shrinking circle stage, 39, 78, 95,
  152–3, 252
Sibling role, 141, 156–69, 175, 208
  and community roles, 173–74, 243,
  251, 258, 261
  and friendship, 192–93, 208
  and isolation, 268, 270
  and mother role, 141
Siblings, relations with, 148, 153, 156,
  175, 199
Single-dimensional life space, definition
  of, 12n2
Sisters, 165
  *See also* Sibling role
Sisters-in-law, 57
Social change, 149n1, 263–64

Social circle, 1–2, 39
Social class
  and attitude about life situations,
  64, 206, 212
  and attitude toward men, 5, 60, 89,
  144
  and community participation,
  244–45, 261–62
  and friendship, 180–84, 186, 191,
  208, 215
  and mother role, 131, 134, 144, 148
  and neighbor role, 43, 228–29,
  233–35, 239
  and problems of widowhood, 67,
  70–71, 73–74, 90, 236–37, 265–66
  and role ranking, 78–79, 139
  and sibling role, 158, 160, 169
  and social integration, 226–27,
  229–30, 242, 269
  and wife role, 18–19, 42–44, 80, 84
  and working, 252, 262
  *See also* Education; Education of
  husband; Occupation; Occupation
  of husband; Status
Social distance, 210
Socialization, 73, 120, 220
Social life space, 15, 37–38, 89,
  187–89, 264
  definition of, 12n2
  *See also* Multi-dimensional relations
Social mobility, 36, 120, 153, 172, 266
Social person, 1–2, 40–41
Social relations, 1, 42, 178–79
  *See also* Primary relations; Role;
  Secondary relations
Society of widows, 45, 184, 188,
  190–191
Society types
  *See* Traditional society; Urban
  society
Sons, 103
Sons-in-law, 119
Status, 17, 43–46
  drop in widowhood, 7–9, 69–70, 90,
  191, 200, 202
  effects of, loss, 111, 198, 201, 203,

213, 266
Status crystallization, 3
Status decrystallization
definition of, 4, 72
and family roles, 124–25, 143, 151,
156, 165
Status role, 3, 8, 12n3, 264
Strangers, 180–81
Suburban women, 136
Suburbs, 233, 235, 239
Suttee, definition of, 7

Task-orientation, 42, 72, 178, 212
*See also* Secondary relations
Telephoning, 74, 134–35
Television, 193, 271
Time-distance, 125, 133
from adult children, 125–26, 130–31
and contact with siblings, 157, 160
Traditional attitudes, 16, 122
Traditional community, 220
Traditional society, 264
and contacts with children, 96, 116,
124
and friendship, 177, 179–81
roles in, 3, 73, 188, 252
widowhood in, 7–12, 15–20
Transportation, 194, 227, 247–48, 272

Unescorted women, 188–91
Urban families, 57
Urban residence, 24–25
Urban society, 3, 7–12, 15–20, 67
community involvement in, 220–22,
262
social relations in, 96, 178, 182–83,
216–17
working women in, 252, 255

*See also* Modern society
Visiting, 101–04, 128–29, 133–34,
188, 232–35, 238
Voluntary associations, 222, 244–52,
261–62, 274–76
and friendship, 189, 191

Wake, 53
Welfare Council of Metropolitan
Chicago, 32
Welsh women, in Chicago, 250
Widow, 10, 37, 52–54, 56–60, 118
*See also* Becoming a widowed
mother; Being a widow
Widower, 17, 20–21, 200, 237
Widowhood, 7–12, 15–29, 61, 265–77
among blacks, 80–81, 83
role of, 8, 10–11, 41, 75, 87–91
trends in, 23–24, 98
*See also* Compensations of widow-
hood; Problems of widowhood.
Widow inheritance, 7–10, 19
Wife role, 9–10, 20, 39–93, 136, 267
and friendship, 181–84, 208
rank of, 78–80, 141–42, 152–53, 243
*See also* Scales
Work, 27–28, 181, 222, 247
and friendship, 184, 186, 189–90,
193, 202, 212
meaning of, 17, 106, 137–38, 167
Working women, 72, 129, 136, 234,
251
Worker role, 41–42, 79, 167, 244,
252–61
Women's Liberation, 252, 264

Young Men's Christian Association
(YMCA), 4

# Name Index

Adams, Bert, 347
Adams, David, 4, 17, 33, 114, 133, 270, 347

Babchuk, Nicholas, 183, 218, 347
Bales, Robert, 103, 354
Barsky, Stephen F., 219, 347
Bates, Alan, 218, 347
Becker, Howard S., 39, 347
Bell, Wendell, 347, 349
Benjamin, Bernard, 353
Bennis, Warren G., 92n2, 347
Berardo, Felix, 4, 17, 270, 347
Berger, Bennett, 347
Berger, Peter, 43, 347
Bernard, Jessie, 45, 347
Berringer, Herbert, 176
Bettleheim, Bruno, 97, 153, 347
Blau, Peter, 347
Blood, Robert O., 42, 44, 59, 347, 348
Blumberg, Ray, 1, 114, 256, 356
Bohannan, Paul J., 7, 9, 56, 348
Bott, Elizabeth, 44, 88, 153, 181, 182, 348
Broom, Leonard, 348
Brotman, Herman, 27, 28, 348
Brown, Roscoe C., 354
Buck, Pearl, 348
Bultena, Gordon, 19, 348
Burchinal, Lee, 176, 348
Burgess, Ernest, 44, 178, 219, 348

Campbell, John K., 137, 348
Carnegie, Dale, 348
Chicago Community Renewal Program, 31, 32
Chicago Housing Authority, 31, 348
Coleman, James, 41, 348
Cooley, Charles H., 128, 177, 178, 217, 348
Cottrell, Leonard, 349
Cowgill, Donald, 352
Cumming, Elaine, 8, 45, 68, 78, 184, 190, 348

de Beauvoir, Simone, 349
de Hoyos, Arturo, 181, 349
de Hoyos, Genevieve, 181, 349
de Lauwe, P. Chombart, 252, 349
Department of the Administration on Aging, 27, 349
Deutsch, Morton, 12n2, 349
Dubin, Robert, 181, 253, 349
Durkheim, Emile, 53, 178, 349
Duvall, Evelyn, 95, 98, 349

Egleston, Janet, 349
Egleston, Jim, 349

Farber, Bernard, 176, 349
Fava, Sylvia F., 350
Felton, Monica, 8, 349
Fischel, Walter, 349
Flacks, Richard, 349
Foote, Nelson, 349
Force, Marianne, 349
Freedman, Maurice, 11, 116, 350
Fromm, Erich, 195, 350
Fromm-Reichmann, Frieda, 92n2, 350
Fulton, Robert L., 54, 350

Gans, Herbert, 228, 265, 350
Gibson, Goeffrey, 176, 350
Ginsberg, Eli, 41, 350
Gist, Noel P., 350
Glaser, Barney G., 47
Goffman, Erving, 40, 122, 350
Goode, William, 1, 11, 120, 220, 350
Goodman, Louis, 350
Gorer, Geoffrey, 17, 52, 54, 271, 350
Gouldner, Alvin, 350
Gumplowicz, Ludwig, 177, 350

Habenstein, Robert, 54, 350
Hartley, Ruth, 41, 350
Henry, William E., 8, 45, 68, 78, 113,

184, 190, 348
Hertzler, Joyce, 12n1, 351
Hill, Rubin, 351
Holmes, Lowell, 352
Honnen, James S., 351
Housing and Urban Renewal Progress
  Report, 351
Hume, David, 176, 351
Hunt, Morton, 86

Ibn-Khaldun, 177, 349

Kellner, Hansfried, 43, 347
Kenniston, Kenneth, 351
Kitagawa, Evelyn H., 29, 30, 31, 219,
  351
Kockesis, Eva, 18, 100, 114, 208, 354
Komarovsky, Mirra, 42, 43, 44, 86,
  270, 351
Kosa, John, 114, 351
Kuhn, Mumford, 351

Lenski, Gerhard, 351
Leslie, Gerald, 17, 81, 95, 148, 351
Lewin, Kurt N., 12n2
Liebow, Elliot, 256, 351
Lindemann, Eric, 4, 51, 196, 271, 351
Lindsey, Gardner, 12n2, 349
Litwak, Eugene, 18, 128, 152, 156, 176,
  351, 352
Loeb, Martin, 12n2, 356
Lopata, Helena Z., 2, 4, 7, 12n3, 39,
  41, 42, 43, 44, 78, 92n2, 96, 136,
  149n1, 152, 179, 182, 183, 186, 264,
  352

McGinnis, Robert, 176
Mack, Raymond, 2, 352
Maddison, David, 4, 51, 70, 198, 271,
  353
Marris, Peter, 4, 50, 56, 57, 70, 123,
  152, 353
Marshall, Douglas, 19, 348, 351, 353
Mattfelt, Jacquelyn, 354
Merton, Robert, 2, 353
Metropolitan Life Insurance Company,

17, 20, 21, 25, 353
Middleton, Russell, 1, 353
Mitford, Jessica, 54, 353
Monahan, William, 353
Moynahan, Daniel, 80

National Center for Health Statistics,
  21, 353
Nelson, Joel J., 44, 182, 353
Nimkoff, M. F., 1, 353
Noel, Joseph R., 179, 352

Orbach, Harold, 178, 217

Parkes, C. Murray, 4, 51, 52, 70, 271,
  353
Parsons, Talcott, 103, 176, 354
Philblad, Terence, 4, 17, 19, 114, 133,
  184, 270, 275, 354
Ploski, Harry A., 354
Practical Builder, 19, 181, 354

Rainwater, Lee, 80, 81, 137, 270, 354
Reisman, David, 172, 234, 354
Rose, Arnold, 41, 350, 351, 354
Rosencranz, Howard, 4, 17, 19, 114,
  133, 184, 270, 275, 354
Rosenmyer, Leopold, 18, 100, 114, 208,
  354
Rosow, Irving, 18, 19, 45, 78, 173, 186,
  190, 212, 226, 354
Ross, Arlene, 8, 116, 354
Rossi, Alice, 41, 354
Rossi, Peter, 231, 354
Ruark, Robert, 354

Sarasvati, Pundita-Ramatai, 8, 13n5,
  354
Schapera, Issac, 7, 9, 13n6, 355
Selznick, Philip, 348
Shanas, Ethel, 18, 58, 88, 92n2, 96,
  114, 128, 141, 149n1, 152, 156, 355
Simmons, Leo W., 11, 355
Smutz, Robert W., 252, 355
Social Security Administration, 32, 355
Stehauwer, Jan, 26, 27, 355

Stein, Maurice, 219, 355
Stouffer, Samuel, 180, 355
Strauss, Anselm L., 47
Street, David, 12
Streib, Gordon, 18, 58, 96, 128, 152, 355
Sussman, Marvin, 18, 128, 152, 176, 352, 355

Taeuber, Karl E., 29, 30, 31, 219, 351
Thomas, Peter, 7, 355
Thomas, William I., 221, 230, 355
Tibbits, Clark, 12n2, 356
Tonnies, Ferdinand, 178, 355
Townsend, Peter, 70, 92n2, 125, 155, 355
Tunstall, Jeremy, 92n2, 356

United Nations, 356
United States Bureau of the Census, 20, 22, 23, 24, 25, 31, 356
United States Department of Commerce, 36, 356
United States Department of Labor, 28, 356

Van Aken, Carol G., 354

Walker, William L., 51, 70, 198, 353
Ward, Barbara, 7, 11, 356
Weber, Max, 178, 356
Weinstein, K., 173, 353
Weiss, Robert, 4, 51, 127, 182, 198, 356
Whyte, William H., 172, 181, 234, 356
Williams, Richard, 12n2, 356
Wilmott, Peter, 88, 181, 356
Winch, Robert, 1, 41, 114, 120, 127, 152, 176, 264, 355, 356
Wolfe, Donald, 42, 44, 59, 348
Wood, Vivian, 19, 348

Yancey, William C., 80, 81, 354
Young, Michael, 88, 181, 356

Znaniecki, Florian, 1, 12n3, 177, 179, 221, 230, 355, 356
Zorbaugh, Harvey, 219